The Sharp End of War

L Battery's Heroic Stand.

The Sharp End of War

42 Accounts of the Early Battles of the First World War by Allied Soldiers & Sailors

Walter Wood

The Sharp End of War
42 Accounts of the Early Battles of the First World War by Allied Soldiers & Sailors
by Walter Wood

FIRST EDITION

First published under the titles
Soldier's Stories of the War
and
In the Line of Battle

Leonaur is an imprint of Oakpast Ltd

Copyright in this form © 2013 Oakpast Ltd

ISBN: 978-1-78282-279-0 (hardcover)
ISBN: 978-1-78282-280-6 (softcover)

http://www.leonaur.com

Publisher's Notes

The views expressed in this book are not necessarily those of the publisher.

Contents

Mons and the Great Retreat	7
With the Field Artillery	20
"Greenjackets" in the Firing Line	28
The Struggle on the Aisne	37
"The Most Critical Day of All"	47
British Fighters in French Forts	59
A Brother's Revenge	68
Life in the Trenches	76
Sapping and Mining	86
Royal Horse Artillery's Stand	94
Sixteen Weeks of Fighting	106
A Daisy-Chain of Bandoliers	114
Despatch-Riding	122
The Three Torpedoed Cruisers	131
The Runaway Raiders	141
Campaigning With the Highlanders	148
Transport Driving	157
British Gunners as Cave-Dwellers	164
With the "Fighting Fifth"	173

The Victory of the Marne	181
An Armoured Car in Ambush	196
Exploits of the London Scottish	202
The Rout of the Prussian Guard at Ypres	211
The British Army at Neuve Chapelle	222
How Trooper Potts Won the V.C. on Burnt Hill	234
A Prisoner of War in Germany	246
Gassed Near Hill 60	259
A Linesman in Gallipoli	266
An Anzac's Adventures	278
"Imperishable Glory" for the Kensingtons	292
Ten Months in the Fighting-Line	303
A Gunner at the Dardanelles	317
The "Flood"	329
The Belgians' Fight With German Hosts	332
A Blinded Prisoner of the Turks	343
How the "Formidable" was Lost	352
A Trooper's Tale	360
A Diarist Under Fire	367
A Stretcher-Bearer at Loos	379
A Fusilier in France	386
The Daily Round	395
Saving the Soldier	405

CHAPTER 1

Mons and the Great Retreat

History does not give a better account of courage and endurance than that which is afforded by the Battle of Mons and the subsequent retreat. The British Expeditionary Force, straight from home, without time for preparation, and only two days after a concentration by rail, was confronted by at least four times its number of the finest troops of Germany, and, after a four days' furious battle, remained unconquered and undismayed. What might have been annihilation of the British forces had become a throwing off of the weight of the enemy's pursuit, allowing a preparation for the driving back of the German Army. At Mons the 1st Battalion Gordon Highlanders lost most of their officers, non-commissioned officers and men in killed, wounded and missing. This story is told by Private J. Parkinson, of the Gordons, who was invalided home at the finish of the Great Retreat.

To be rushed from the routine of a soldier's life at home in time of peace into the thick of a fearful fight on the Continent is a strange and wonderful experience; yet it happened to me, and it was only one of many amazing experiences I went through between leaving Southampton in a transport and coming to a London hospital.

We landed at Boulogne, and went a long journey by train. At the end of it we found ourselves, on Saturday, August 22nd, billeted in a gentleman's big house and we looked forward to a comfortable night, little dreaming that so soon after leaving England we should be in the thick of a tremendous fight.

It was strange to be in a foreign country, but there was no time to dwell on that, and the British soldier soon makes himself at home, wherever he is. Those of us who were not on duty went to sleep; but we had not been resting very long when we were called to arms. That was about half-past three o'clock on the Sunday morning, August 23rd.

There was no bugle sound, no fuss, no noise; we were just quietly roused up by the pickets, and as quietly we marched out of the *château* and went along a big, sunken road—the main road to Paris, I think. We started at once to make trenches alongside the road, using the entrenching-tool which every soldier carries; and we went on steadily with that work for several hours on that August Sunday morning—a perfect Sabbath, with a wonderful air of peace about it. The country looked beautiful and prosperous—how soon it was to be turned into a blazing, ruined landscape, with thousands of dead and wounded men lying on it!

It would be about nine o'clock when we heard heavy firing in a wood near us—there is plenty of wooded country about Mons—and we were told that the engineers were blowing up obstacles; so we went on entrenching, for although we knew that the Germans were not far away, we had no idea they were as close as they soon proved to be.

I am a first-class scout, and, with a corporal and three men, I was sent on picket some time before noon.

Just on the right of us was a farm, and the people who came out gave us some beer and eggs. We drank the beer and sucked the eggs, and uncommonly good they were, too, on that blazing hot August Sunday, when everything looked so pleasant and peaceful. You had it hot at home, I know; but I dare say we had it hotter, and we were in khaki, with a heavy kit to carry.

There was a big tree near us, and I made for it and climbed up, so that I could see better over the countryside. I was hanging on to a branch, and looking around, when all at once a bullet or two came, and we knew that the Germans had spotted us. I got down from that tree a vast deal quicker than I had got up into it, and we made ready to rush back to the trenches; but before scuttling we told the civilians to clear out at once, and they began to do so. The poor souls were taken aback, naturally, but they lost no time in obeying the warning, leaving all their worldly treasures—belongings which they were never to see again, for the Germans were soon to destroy them, and, worse than that, were to take the lives of innocent and inoffensive people who had not done them the slightest wrong in any way.

As soon as we had raised the alarm a whole section of Germans opened fire on the four of us, and as we could not do anything against

"We were helped by the Germans throwing Searchlights on us."

them, being heavily outnumbered, we ran for it back to the trenches. Yes, we did run indeed, there is no mistake about that. Luckily for us we knew the way back; but if the Germans had been able to shoot for nuts with their rifles, not one of us would have been spared. We laughed as we ran, and one of the scouts, named Anderson, laughed so much that he could scarcely run, though there was nothing special to laugh at; but, as you know, there are some odd chaps amongst Highlanders. They don't care a rap for anything.

It was soon reported that there were in front of us about 15,000 Germans, including some of the finest of the *Kaiser's* troops, amongst them the Imperial Guard, who have worked military miracles—at peace manoeuvres. And to oppose that great body of men we had only the 8th Brigade, consisting of the Royal Scots, the Royal Irish, the Middlesex—the old "Die-Hards"—and the Gordon Highlanders, of which I was in B Company.

The Royal Scots were on our right, and the Royal Irish and the Middlesex on our left. We had Royal Field Artillery, too, and never did British gunners do more splendid work and cover themselves with greater glory than in the Battle of Mons.

The Royal Irish were getting their dinners when the Germans opened fire on them with their machine-guns, doing some dreadful damage straight off, for they seemed to have the range, and there was no time for the Royal Irish to get under cover.

That, I think, was really the beginning of the battle; but I had better try and give you an idea of the battlefield, so that you can understand what actually took place.

Mons itself is a fair-sized manufacturing town, with plenty of coal-mines about, and we were in a pleasant village near it, the main road to Paris cutting through the village. From our trenches we could see across the country, towards the mines and other villages, and we had a clear rifle-range of well over a mile, because a lot of obstruction in the shape of hedges, foliage and corn had been cut away.

To our rear, on each side of us, was a forest, and between the two forests were our gunners, who were to do such awful mischief in the German hosts. The "Die-Hards" were in a sort of garden, and I saw only too clearly what happened to them when the fight was in full swing.

It was just before noon when the most fearful part of the battle started, and that was the artillery duel. Our own guns were making a terrible commotion near us; but the din was a very comforting sound, because it meant something very bad for the German gunners, who were making havoc in our brigade.

I saw the awful effects of the German shrapnel amongst the men of the Middlesex in that fair Belgian garden on what should have been a peaceful Sunday afternoon. The Middlesex were practically blown to pieces, and the fearful way in which they suffered was shown later, when the casualty lists were published, and it was seen that most of them were either killed, wounded or missing.

Then the Gordons' turn came. The Germans had got our position, and they opened fire on us; but we were lucky—perhaps the German batteries were too far away to be really effective. At any rate, they did not harm us much.

The battle had opened swiftly, and it continued with amazing speed and fury, for both sides soon settled into their stride—and you know, of course, that the Germans were on the promenade to Paris and were going to mop the British Army up. It took a lot of mopping!

Our own field-gunners were doing magnificently, and the Germans were first-rate hands at the deadly game. If they had been anything like as accurate with the rifle as they were with the artillery I think that very few British soldiers would have been left to tell the tale of Mons. But with the rifle they were no good.

The Germans came out of their trenches in big heaps in close formation, because their game was to rush us by sheer weight of numbers; but we just shot them down. Yet as soon as we shot them down others came out, literally like bees. No wonder the poor chaps are called by their officers "cannon-fodder"! British officers don't talk of their men in that brutal way; and the British officer always leads—shows the way; but the German officer seems to follow his men, and to shove and shoot them along.

It was marvellous to watch the Germans come on in their legions, and melt away under our artillery and rifle fire. We simply took deliberate aim at the masses of figures, grey clad, with their helmets covered with grey cloth; but it seemed as if not even our absolutely destructive fire would stop them. On they came, still on, the living actually sheltering behind the dead. But it was no use. We kept them off, and they kept themselves off, too, for it was perfectly clear that they had a horror of the bayonet, and would not come near it.

The nearest the Germans got to us, as far as I can tell—that is, to the Gordons—was about 300 yards; but that was near enough, seeing that they outnumbered us by four to one, and were amongst the finest troops of Germany. Some of the enemy's cavalry—I suppose the much-talked-of *Uhlans* came into the sunken road in front of us, hoping to do business; but our machine-guns got on them, and we had a go at them with our rifles, with the result that the *Uhlans* made a cut for it and most of them got away. Even so, there were plenty of riderless horses galloping madly about.

Our officers had told us to carry on and carry on—we did, then and later.

What was I feeling like? Well, of course, at the start I was in a bit of a funk and it wasn't pleasant; but I can honestly say that the feeling soon vanished, as I'm certain it did from all of us, and we settled down to good hard pounding, all the time seeing who could pound the hardest and last longest. And I can assure you that, in spite of everything, men kept laughing, and they kept their spirits up.

You see, we had such splendid officers, and there is always such a fine feeling between officers and men in Highland regiments. Our colonel, a Gordon by name and commanding the Gordons, was a real gallant Gordon, who won his Victoria Cross in the South African War—a regular warrior and a veteran; amongst other things he was in at the storming of Dargai, and he had more experience of actual fighting, I should think, than all the Germans in front of us put together.

Another brave officer was Major Simpson, my company officer, a Companion of the Distinguished Service Order, which is the next best thing to the V.C. Major Simpson and a private went to fetch some ammunition. To do that they had to leave shelter and rush along in a literal hail of fire—shrapnel and bullets. It seemed as if no living thing could exist, and they were watched with intense anxiety. Shells were bursting all around us—some in the air and others on the ground, though there were German shells that did not burst at all.

Suddenly, with a fearful shattering sound, a shell burst just beside the major and the private, and for the moment it looked as if they had been destroyed. Some Gordons rushed towards them, and picked them up and put them on a horse. It was seen that they were badly hurt, but even so, and at a time like that, the major actually laughed, and I am sure he did it to keep our spirits up. He was taken away to hospital, and was laughing still when he said

"It's all right, lads! There's nothing much the matter with me! Carry on!"

Oh, yes! There were some fine cool things done on that great Sunday when the Germans were like bees in front of us in the turnip-fields at Mons, and we were settling down into our stride.

And the N.C.O.'s were splendid, too.

Our section sergeant, Spence, when the firing was fiercest, popped up to take a shot, which is always a risky thing to do, because a bullet is so much swifter than a man's movements. The sergeant fired, and the instant he had done so he fell back into the trench, saying, "I believe they've got me now!" But they hadn't. He was taken to hospital, and it was found that a bullet had come and so cleanly grazed his head— on the left side, like this—that the hair was cut away in a little path, just like a big parting, as if it had been shaved. It was touch and go with death, the closest thing you could possibly see; but, luckily, the sergeant was all right, and he made no commotion about his narrow shave.

There was a gallant young officer and brave gentleman of the Gordons—Lieutenant Richmond who had been doing his duty throughout that Sunday afternoon.

Dusk was falling, and Lieutenant Richmond made his way out of the trench and over the open ground, crawling, to try and learn something about the Germans. He was crawling back—that is the only way in such a merciless fire—and was only about three yards from the trench when he rose up and was going to make a final dash for it. Just as he rose, a bullet struck him in the back and came out through his heart—and killed him straight away. He was in my trench, and I saw this happen quite clearly. It was such sights as that which made the Gordons all the more resolved to carry on and mow the Germans down as hard as they could—the Germans who seemed to be for ever rushing at us from the turnip-fields in front and never getting any nearer than their own barriers of dead.

I never thought it possible that such a hell of fire could be known as that which we endured and made at Mons. There was the ceaseless crackle of the rifles on both sides, with the everlasting explosions of the guns and the frightful bursting of the shells. They were particularly horrible when they burst on the cobbled road close by—as hundreds did—so near to us that it seemed as if we were certain to be shattered to pieces by the fragments of shrapnel which did so much mischief and killed so many men and horses, to say nothing of the gaping wounds they inflicted on the troops and the poor dumb beasts.

But you can best understand what the German artillery fire was like when I tell you that all the telegraph-poles were shattered, the very wires were torn away, and trees were smashed and blown to pieces. It seemed miraculous that any human being could live in such a storm of metal fragments and bullets.

From before noon until dusk, and that was a good eight hours, the Battle of Mons had been truly awful; but we had held our own, and as the evening came I realised what a fearful thing a modern battle is—especially such a fight as this, brought on in a peaceful and beautiful country whose people had done no wrong.

All the villages in front of us were burning, either set on fire deliberately by the Germans, or by shells; but there was no halting in the fight, and when we could no longer see the enemy because it was dark we blazed away at the flashes of their rifles—thousands of spurts of flame; and the field-gunners crashed at the straight lines of fire which could be seen when the German artillerymen discharged their guns. We were helped, too, in a way that many of us never expected to be, and that was by the Germans throwing searchlights on us. These long, ghastly beams shone on us and gave a weird and terrible appearance to the fighters in the trenches, and more so to the outstretched forms of soldiers who had fought for the last time.

It was a dreadful yet fascinating sight, and one which I shall never forget; nor shall I ever forget the extraordinary fact that, in spite of the annihilating hail of missiles and the deafening din of battle, some of our fellows in the trenches went to sleep, and seemed to sleep as peacefully and soundly as if they were in feather beds. They went to sleep quite cheerfully, too. I should say that half our chaps were having a doze in this way and taking no notice of the fight and the screech and roar of shells and guns.

Sunday night—and such a night! The sky red with burning villages, the air rent with awful noises of guns and rifles, men and horses—a terrible commotion from the devilish fight that was going on. The villagers had left; they had fled on getting our warning, but they were not too far away to see the utter ruin of their homes.

I do not want to say too much about the villagers—it is too sad and makes one too savage; but I will tell of one incident I saw. An old man was running away, to try and get out of danger, when he was hit in the stomach. I saw him fall, and I know that he bled to death. Think of that—an absolutely innocent and inoffensive old man who had done nothing whatever to harm the brigands who were over-running Belgium!

Just about midnight we got the order to retire. We joined the survivors of the 8th Brigade and began a march which lasted nearly all night. We were weary and worn, but as right in spirit as ever, and didn't want to retire. There was no help for it, however, and the Great Retreat began. Everything that the Red Cross men could do had been done for the wounded; but there were some who had to be left, as well as the dead.

It was fearfully hot, and we were thankful indeed when we were able to lie down in a field and get about two hours' sleep—the sleep that you might suppose a log has.

When we awoke it was not to music of birds, but of shrapnel; for the Germans were following us and began to fire on us as soon as we started to retire again. Hour after hour we went on, feeling pretty bad at having to retreat; but a bit cheered when, at about two o'clock on the Monday afternoon, we began to dig trenches again. We had the field-gunners behind us once more, and joyous music it was to hear their shells screaming over our heads.

It was about dinner-time on the Monday when we had one of the most thrilling experiences of the whole fight—one of the extraordinary incidents that have become part and parcel of a modern battle, although only a very few years ago they were looked upon as mad fancies or wild dreams. We were marching along a road when we sighted a German aeroplane—a birdlike-looking thing in the sky. It was keeping watch on us, and signalling our position to the main German body. It gave the position, and the Germans promptly gave us some shells. The thing was most dangerous and unpleasant; but the German airman was not to have it all his own way.

Two of our own aeroplanes spotted him and went for him, just like immense birds—the whole business might have been carried out by living creatures of the air and there was as fine a fight in the air as you could hope to see on land—firing and swift manoeuvring with the object of killing and destroying, and both sides showing amazing pluck and skill. It was an uncommonly exciting spectacle, and it became all the more thrilling when we opened fire with our rifles.

I blazed away as hard as I could, but an aeroplane on the wing is not an easy thing to hit. Whether I struck the machine or not I can't say, but it came down in the road just where my company was. As far as I know the aeroplane was not struck—the chap that was in it planed down. He was determined not to be caught cheaply, for as soon as he landed he fired his petrol tank to destroy his machine, and then ran for it. He went off at a hard lick, but some of our cavalry rushed after him and caught him, and it was found that he was not hurt.

Just on our right was a railway, with a big cutting, and we were ordered to retire down into it; so into the cutting we got and along the line we went, retreating all that day by the railway and the roads, our gunners giving the Germans socks throughout that hard rearguard action.

On the Tuesday we were still retreating, and a miserable day it was, with a deluge of rain that soaked us to the skin. We reached a village and slept in barns, and a good sleep we got, without the trouble of undressing or drying our clothes or taking our boots off.

Early on the Wednesday morning the pickets quietly roused and warned us again, and we went out in front of the village and entrenched.

There was a big lot of coal-mines in front of us, about a mile away, with the refuse-heaps that are common to mines. Behind one of these great mounds a battery of German artillery had got into position, and one of the finest things you could have seen was the way in which our own grand gunners got on the Germans. They seemed to have found the range of the enemy exactly, and that was a good job for us, because the German shells were dropping just between us and our own artillery, and we expected to have them bang on us. But our guns silenced our opponents, and, what was more, scattered a lot of German infantry, about 1,500 yards away, who were making for us.

We got straight into our trenches, and in this respect we were lucky, because we went into one that the Engineers had made, while most of the other companies had to dig their own.

Our trench was in a cornfield. The corn had been cut down, and we spread it and other stuff in front of the trenches, on top of the earth, to make us invisible. From that queer hiding-place we resumed our blazing away at the pursuing Germans.

When Wednesday came we were at Cambrai, where hell itself seemed to be let loose again; for first thing in the morning we heard heavy artillery fire on all sides of us, and it was clear that a fearful battle was going on. We were utterly worn and weary, but were cheered by looking forward to a good dinner. We knew that the food was in the field cookers, in preparation for serving out to the men. But the dinner never came, and it was not until next day that we heard the reason why—then we learned that a German shell had blown the field cookers to smithereens.

Now all this time, from the moment the battle opened at Mons till we were blazing away again at the Germans at Cambrai we were waiting for the French to come—waiting and longing, for we were utterly outnumbered and completely exhausted; but we never had a glimpse of a Frenchman, and we know now, of course, that the French themselves were so hard pressed that they could not spare any help at all for the British.

At about half-past four in the afternoon we resumed the retreat, for a major of artillery had galloped up and shouted "Retire!" B Company retired across the level ground behind us. This was a good bit off a sunken road that we wanted to get back to, because it would give us comparative safety. Eventually we reached it, and were thankful to find that we were pretty secure, though shells were still bursting all around and over us.

From that time we never saw any more of the rest of the regiment, and I lost sight of our gallant colonel. He became numbered with the missing.[1] There were only about 175 of my own company and parts of other companies who had got away and joined us.

A terrible time it was at Cambrai, and one that I shan't forget in a hurry. The last I clearly remember of the place is that several men were killed near me; but by that time killing had become a matter of course. The Red Cross men did noble work, but they could not cover all the cases. I am sorry to say it, but it is true that the Germans deliberately fired on the hospitals at Mons and also at Cambrai. It sounds incredible, but there were many things done in Belgium by the Germans that you could not have believed unless you had seen them.

Well, from that dreadful carnage at Cambrai we went on retreating, and we never really rested until the Sunday, seven days after the battle started, when we reached Senlis, about forty miles from Paris. We had then marched between 130 and 140 miles, and had made one of the longest, hardest, swiftest and most successful retreats in history—I say successful, because Sir John French and his generals had got us out of what looked like a death-trap. We were cursing all the time we were retreating—cursing because we had to retire, though we knew that there was no help for it.

A wonderful change came with the Wednesday, because we did no more fighting. We forged ahead, blowing up bridges and doing all we could to stop the Germans.

We had a splendid time going through France, as we had had in going through Belgium, and when we reached Paris there was noth-

---

1. Colonel Gordon was twice reported killed; but it was definitely ascertained, later, that he was a prisoner of war.

ing the French people thought too good for us. We were taken across Paris in *char-a-bancs*, and flowers, cigarettes and five-*franc* pieces were thrown at us. A lot of Americans spoke to us, and were very kind. They were particularly anxious to know how we were getting on, and what we had gone through. It was very pleasant to hear our own language, as most of us did not understand a word of French.

We trained to Rouen, but had not the slightest idea that we were going to England—we thought we were being sent to hospital at Havre; but at that port we were put into motors and driven down to the quay and shoved on board a transport and brought at last to London.

I am not wounded. I was struck on the leg by a bullet, but it did not really hurt me. I was utterly worn out and exhausted, however, and rheumatism set in and crippled me, so I was sent to hospital; and here I am. But I'm almost fit and well now, and all I want to do is to fall in again before the fighting's done.

"SOME OF OUR CAVALRY CAUGHT HIM".

Chapter 2

With the Field Artillery

The war was begun by Germany in a spirit of ruthlessness which was to spare neither man, woman nor child, and was to leave innocent people "only their eyes to weep with." The neutrality of Belgium was outraged and German hosts poured into that country. In repelling them an immortal part was played by the British Expeditionary Force, which fought against enormous odds. This story of the earlier days of the war is told from the narrative of Driver George William Blow, Royal Field Artillery, who was invalided home after having two of his ribs broken and five horses killed under him.

It was a blazing hot Sunday, and the place was Mons. We had got into camp about one on the Saturday afternoon, and had billeted till four on the Sunday morning, when we were ordered to harness up and prepare for action, but we did not receive actual fighting orders until noon; then we had to march into a place in the neighbourhood, and as soon as we reached it German shells burst over us.

That was the beginning of a long and terrible battle. We went straight into it, without any warning; but the Germans were ready, and knew what to expect, because they had been waiting for us for forty-eight hours.

It was field artillery we were up against. The Germans at that time had not got the big siege guns, which we called Black Marias, Jack Johnsons and Coal Boxes. I will tell you about them later.

We, the drivers, took the guns up into action, then we retired under cover with the horses. While we were retiring the bullets from the German shells were dropping all around us, and farther away our men at the guns and the other troops were carrying on that desperate fight against immense odds which will be always known as the battle of Mons. From start to finish we were heavily outnumbered, but we knocked them out.

We were soon hard at it, pounding away, while our infantry were simply mowing the Germans down. We had some terrible fire to put up with, and at the end of about four hours we were forced to retire from the position. At that time we were the only battery left in action out of the whole of our brigade.

An officer was sent to reconnoitre, to see where we could retire to, and he picked out a little valley, a sort of rain-wash, and the battery thundered into it. This was a hard place to tackle, and all our attention was needed to keep the horses from falling down, because the ground was so rough and steep.

So far we had not seen any of the German infantry at close quarters, but as soon as we had got into the level of the valley we ran into a lot of them, and saw that we were ambushed. In this ambush I had one of the experiences that were so common in the retreat, but I was lucky enough to come out of it safely. Many brave deeds were done there which will never be officially known—for instance, when we were going through the valley and were being heavily fired on, and it seemed as if there was no chance for us, Corporal Holiday ran the gauntlet twice to warn us that the enemy had us in ambush.

We made a desperate effort to get out of the valley, but before we could get clear many horses were shot down, amongst them being the one I was riding. I did the only thing I could do—I lay there amongst the dead horses. I had had a narrow shave, for my cap had been shot off by a piece of shell.

The first gun and two waggons had got through, and our corporal could have got safely out, but he wasn't built that way, and wasn't thinking about himself.

He shouted, "Well, boys, your horses are down, and the best thing you can do is to run for it."

I scrambled up and dashed through some brambles—they nearly scratched me to pieces. Just as I and one or two more men got out five Germans potted at us. I had no weapon—nothing except my whip—if we had had arms we could have settled a lot of Germans that day—so I had to make a dash for cover. But the corporal, with his rifle, did well, for he picked off three of the Germans, and the other two bolted.

If it had not been for the corporal I should not have been here to tell the tale; I should either have been killed or made a prisoner.

Had it not been for him, in fact, they would have wiped the lot of us completely out.

We were in that deadly ambush for about five hours—from five till ten—no gunners with us, only drivers. It was night and dark, but the darkness was made terrible by the glare of the villages which the Germans had set fire to.

There we were, ambushed and imprisoned in the valley, unable to move either backward or forward, because the roadway was choked up with dead horses.

At last our major went away some distance, and inquired of a woman in a house which would be the best way for us to get out of the valley. While he was talking with her the house was surrounded by Germans, and it seemed certain that he would be discovered; but in the darkness they could not make him clearly out, and he was clever enough to shout to them in their own language. It was a critical and dangerous time, but the major scored. He baffled the Germans, and got himself out of the house, and us out of the ambush in the valley. It was a grand performance and I believe the major was recommended for the D.S.O. on account of it.

We were thankful when we were clear of the valley, but about two miles farther on we ran into some more Germans; there were Germans everywhere, they swarmed over the whole countryside, day and night, and, as I have told you, they heavily outnumbered us all the time and at every turn. But by this time we were better able to meet them, for we had plenty of infantry with us—Gordons, and Wiltshire and Sussex men—who were joining in the retreat.

That retirement was a terrible business. Our infantry had been fighting in the trenches and in the open, and they were fighting all the time they were retiring. The Germans gave them no rest, and, some showed no mercy to our wounded, as we discovered when we got back to Mons again, as we did in time. We saw lots of our wounded who had been killed by the butts of the Prussian rifles. They had the finest troops of Prussia at Mons, and I suppose some wanted to get some of their own back for having been so badly mauled by Sir John French's "contemptible little army."

In the earlier hours of the battle, during that awful Sunday at Mons and in the neighbourhood, the British had suffered heavily. Twelve men of my own battery and a dozen of the horses had been killed, and a waggon limber had been blown to pieces. Mind you, I am talking only of our own battery and our own brigade, and dealing with only a very small part of the battle. No man who shared in it can do more. Our brigade consisted of three batteries of six guns each.

It had been a day of ceaseless fighting and terrific strain on men and horses, and we were utterly done up when we got into camp at about one on the Monday morning. We hoped we might rest a bit, but we had to harness up at two, and shift off at three, because the Germans were preparing to shell the village we were in.

There was a hospital in the village, and by that time a good many of our wounded were in it. The Germans could see plainly enough that it was a hospital, and knew that it must be filled with wounded, but they deliberately shelled it and set fire to it. Our captain and my sergeant were in the hospital when the Germans fired it, but I don't know whether they got away or were left in the burning building.

By the time we were on the move again it was full daylight. We dropped into action again three or four times, but were forced to resume our retirement, harassed all the time by the Germans.

During the retirement we had several shots at German aeroplanes, which were flying about spying out our positions and signalling them to their own people; but field-guns are not much use against aircraft, because the muzzles cannot be elevated sufficiently high. You need howitzers for the work, because they are specially made for high-angle fire and can throw their shots right over aeroplanes.

We were retiring from the Monday till the Wednesday; then we got the order to drop into action again. That was at eight o'clock in the morning, and by that time we were at Cambrai, a good distance from Mons, as you can see from the map.

Mons was bad, but Cambrai was far worse. We had been retreating all the time, day and night, fighting a heavy rearguard action, so that men and horses were utterly worn out. Again the artillery did hard work, and had to pay for it. The 6th Battery had lost two guns and a waggon at Mons, because the horses were killed, and they also had another gun put out of action. They lost a further gun at Cambrai, and the battery was almost completely cut up, but for their loss we in the 23rd Battery were able to make up in a way.

Our own guns were concealed so cleverly that the Germans could not find them anyhow. The nearest they could get to us was about fifty yards in front or fifty yards behind, and in dropping shells fifty yards make a lot of difference, as the Germans found to their cost. Our concealed battery did heavy execution amongst them, and they deserved all they got.

When I was clear of the valley I got two fresh horses; but at Cambrai, on the Wednesday, they were both killed. A shell burst and took off the head of the riding horse, and bullets killed the off horse, so I was dismounted again; and not a few of my chums were in the same unfortunate position.

Cambrai was the last battle we had before we turned the tables on the Germans, and began to drive them back at the Marne, where a tremendous fight went on for many days. Altogether we had been retiring pretty well a week, and we rejoiced when the advance began.

The advance made new men of us, especially when we saw what the Germans had done. There were plenty of wrecks of our convoys on the roads, where the enemy had got at them. That sort of thing was all right, of course, and came in fairly enough in warfare; but it made our blood boil to see the wanton damage that these so-called civilised soldiers had committed on a people who had done no greater crime than defend their hearths and families.

You ask about German cruelties and barbarities. Well, I will tell you something about what I saw myself, and people can form their own opinion as to what generally happened.

When the British troops retired from Mons the villages and the country were untouched. No words can tell how kind the Belgians and the French were to us, and I am glad to say that they were no worse for our passage through their towns and villages and farms. They gave us food and wine, and helped our sick and wounded, and wherever they were they did all they could for us.

Villages and towns and farms were peaceful and prosperous when we passed through them first; but they were terribly changed when we returned and went through them a second time, after the Germans had been at their foul work. Sword, rifle, artillery and fire had done their dreadful mischief, and deeds had been committed which filled us with horror. I will mention two or three things by way of illustration, and these are only instances of hosts of cases.

On the first day of the advance we were passing through a small village. I saw a little child which seemed to be propped up against a window. There were some infantry passing at the same time as ourselves—Gordons, I think they were—and one of the officers went into the cottage and took the little creature from the window. He found that it was dead. The Germans had killed it.

The officer had a look over the house, and in the next room he found the mother. She was dead also, and mutilated in a most ferocious way.

The interior of the cottage was in a state of absolute wreckage. The barbarians had not spared anything. They had destroyed the furniture, thrown everything about, and done their best to ruin inoffensive people whose country they had laid waste, and who had not done them the slightest wrong. When our men saw that, they went almost mad.

I will give you another instance. We passed through a village about two hours after some of the *Uhlans* had visited it, and we saw how courageous they can be when they have only old men and women and children to deal with. They sing a different song when the British cavalry are after them. There was a farmhouse which had been the home of two old people, a farmer and his wife. I believe the poor old couple looked after the farm themselves.

We found the old lady at the farm all alone, and I saw her. A pitiful spectacle she was, and well she might be, for the *Uhlans* had come and taken her poor old husband out into a field and shot him, and left his dead body there. They had robbed the house of everything—all the money and every bit of food—and had left the old lady almost demented.

When our own troops came up she was sitting outside the house, crying, they gave the poor old soul the bully beef and biscuits which had been served out to them that very morning, and which they themselves needed badly.

We heard of several cases like that from the people of the country as we returned through it, and cases of these German bullies holding revolvers to women's heads and forcing the frightened creatures to give them their rings and jewellery and everything they could lay their hands on. This was the sort of thing we saw, or heard at first hand, and it made us all the more thankful that we were driving the Germans back and getting level with them.

We fell into action that morning about seven o'clock. We had to make our way straight across country, regardless of fields or roads; and all the time the Germans shelled us. It didn't matter where we were, the shells fell beyond us; but the enemy weren't clever enough to find our twelve batteries, which were in action, and which properly "gave them socks."

We held that village till about eight o'clock, then we started on the advance again, driving the Germans back; and when once they start going they travel very quickly—when the enemy is after them.

That was the last battle we had before we got to the River Marne.

So far, we had had a lot to do with the German field-guns; now we were to make the acquaintance of the bigger chaps I have referred to—Black Marias, Coal Boxes and Jack Johnsons, as I have said we called them, because they fired a big shell, a 90-pounder, which burst and made a thick cloud of filthy, greasy smoke which was enough to poison you if it got at you. I believe that the fumes of some of the German shells will actually kill you if you get them properly into your system.

The Battle of the Marne was a long and big affair, lasting about three weeks, and the Black Marias did a good deal of mischief. On the Sunday, as our ambulance waggons retired, the Germans shelled them with these siege guns, and blew them to pieces. At the finish there was not an ambulance waggon available. Yes, that is what they did, and it was done deliberately, because any soldier can tell an ambulance waggon when he sees it.

The Germans stuck at nothing to gain their ends; no trick is too dirty for them to play. One particularly vile one was the using of ambulance waggons for the purpose of carrying machine-guns. Our troops did not dream of firing at ambulance waggons; but when we saw that this wicked use was being made of them—and we did see it, for they came quite close to us—we gave the Germans in them what for.

The Germans tried three or four times to break through our lines, but our Tommies were too good for them, and sent them back a great deal faster than they had come on. They swept them away with rifle fire, and the Germans never had a chance when our men could get fairly in with the bayonet.

During that long month of fighting we were in a good many places in France and Belgium. At one time we were actually on the field of Waterloo, and could see in the distance the monument put up in memory of the battle. I dare say the Germans fancied they were going to do a lot with us at Waterloo; but it all ended in fancy, and we kept on the driving game with them till they were altogether forced back.

When we could get at them we could beat them, though they were sometimes about ten to one, and in one little affair I saw twenty of our "Jocks"—Gordons, I think they were—scatter something like two hundred Germans. The Jocks badly wanted to get at the Germans with the steel, but the Germans just as badly didn't want to be bayoneted, and those who weren't shot scuttled.

The fighting was not the only hard part of the Battle of the Marne.

For nearly three weeks we never had a dry shirt on owing to the wet weather, and we never had our boots off; we hadn't time for it, and we were kept too well at it. The poor horses were fearfully knocked up. They were like us—never had a chance to rest—and were three or four days without food.

Once, during the retirement, we had only two hours' rest in four days; but we daren't stop. Sometimes we were on foot, sometimes in the saddle, and the Germans were after us in motor-lorries, full of troops.

But however badly they handled us, I think it was nothing to the way in which we mangled them when our artillery got really to work, and especially when it came to "gun fire"—that is, rapid firing, each gun firing as soon as it is loaded. This means that you take no time between rounds; you simply blaze away, and the guns become quite hot. In one particular position every sub-section fired 150 rounds, so that, taking a whole battery, I should think they pretty well fired a thousand rounds in a day.

It was on the Marne that my fifth horse was killed under me. A shell struck him, and before I could clear myself I fell over into a ditch, the horse on top of me, shot and shell flying all around as I went over. Two of my ribs were broken, and I was put out of action. I was picked up and carried down to the camp. I was in hospital there for three days before I was sent to London.

I had a complete *Uhlan's* uniform with me, and wanted to bring it home, but this bit of the saddle is all I have left. The *Uhlan's* saddle is a wonderful thing, weighing 78 lb., compared with 12 lb. for the British saddle. Here is the piece; you can see that it is filled in with lead—why, I don't know. And here is the torn khaki jacket I was wearing when my fifth horse was killed under me at the Marne—and this part is sodden with his blood.

I had a round month of fighting, retreating, advancing, and fighting again, and apart from the broken ribs I was utterly done up; but I am pretty well again now. I am just off to see the doctor; the day after tomorrow I am to get married, the next day I rejoin, and after that—well, who can tell?

Chapter 3

"Greenjackets" in the Firing Line

The King's Royal Rifle Corps, the famous old 60th Rifles, the "Greenjackets," have had a large share in the war and have added to their glorious distinctions. Many of the officers of this regiment have given their lives for their country, amongst them being Prince Maurice of Battenberg. Some details of the prince's service in the war before he was killed in action are given in this story by Rifleman Brice, of the 60th, who was wounded at the Battle of the Aisne and invalided home.

When we first landed in France we were welcomed and cheered by crowds of French people who decked us with flowers and couldn't do too much for us, and they kept that kindness up all the time I was over there until I was sent home with a lot more wounded. Throwing flowers at us was a great deal pleasanter than the shells and bullets which were shot at us a few days later, when we were in the thick of trench-digging and fighting. It's astonishing how soon you settle down to a state of things that you've never been used to and how extraordinarily war alters life and people.

The Greenjackets are very proud of themselves, especially in time of peace, and have many little ways of their own; but a war like this makes all soldiers chums and equals and even the officers are practically just like the men. Our own colonel did his share in the trench-digging, and a royal officer like Prince Maurice of Battenberg, who is now resting in a soldier's grave, was living the same life as the rest of us. Many an act of kindness did the prince show to his riflemen, and many a fierce fight he shared in before he was killed in battle; many a word of cheer did he utter to men who were almost exhausted and nearly dying of thirst, and I have seen him go and buy fresh bread, when it could be got, and give it to us as a treat—and a glorious treat it was!

One of the first things we had to do after the retirement from Mons was to bury German dead, and you will get some idea of the awful losses they suffered, even at the beginning of the war, when I tell you that in one place alone we were about eight hours in doing this unpleasant task.

We got used to digging ourselves in and being shelled out, and to guarding towns and villages while the panic-stricken inhabitants escaped to safety. It was a pitiful sight to see people turned out of their houses, taking their belongings, when they could, in carts, perambulators, wheelbarrows and every available conveyance. They always kept as close to us as they could keep, and our fellows used to collect money amongst themselves for the poor souls and give them all the food they could spare—and they were very grateful if we gave them only a biscuit.

It was terrible work on our way to the Aisne; but the hardships were lightened for us in many little ways that counted a lot. Some of our officers would carry two rifles, when men became too weary to carry their own; the colonel would jump off his horse and give an exhausted man a lift in the saddle, and he would take apples from his pockets and pass them along the ranks to the men. These acts of kindness helped us all enormously. And we were helped on the way by smoking—what a joy it was to get a fag, especially when cigarettes ran so short that one would go round a dozen times, passed from man to man, and a chap was sorely tempted to take a pull that was almost enough to fill him with smoke. When we hadn't a scrap of tobacco of any sort we would roll a fag of dried tea-leaves which had been used for making tea—and that was better than nothing.

It was fighting all the way to the Aisne, heavy rearguard actions most of the time, though in a lesser war many of these affairs would have been reckoned proper battles. One night, at about ten o'clock, after a hard march, we had reached a town, and had thankfully gone into our billets—houses, barns, any sort of place that came handy, and we were expecting a peaceful time; but we were no sooner settling down than we got the alarm to dress and fall in. Getting dressed was the work of seconds only, because undressing was merely a case of putting the pack and equipment and rifle down and resting on the flags or earth, or, if we were lucky, hay or straw; and so, when the alarm was given, we very soon fell in, and with fixed bayonets we rushed for a bridge across the river that we had been ordered to take.

At the point of the bayonet the bridge was carried with a rush, then we had to hold it while our transport and ammunition column got out of the town, and there we were till seven o'clock next morning. The main body of the troops retired and left us as a rearguard; but they had not gone from the town more than ten minutes when we saw the Germans coming towards the bridge in swarms. There was no help for it—we had to get away from the bridge which we had held throughout the night.

We began to retire in good order, fighting desperately, and our men falling killed and wounded. Yard by yard we fell back from the bridge, firing as furiously as we could at the German masses, and for half a mile we kept up an unequal rearguard struggle. It seemed that we should be hopelessly outnumbered and that there was little hope; then we saw two divisions of the French advancing, and knew that we should pull through. The French came on and gave us help, and, covering our retirement, enabled us to get away from the bridge.

It was in one of the charges on a bridge which was held by the Germans, just before we got to the Aisne, that Prince Maurice distinguished himself. He was very daring and was always one of the first in the fighting, no matter where or what it was. I was not actually in the charge, being in the supports behind; but I saw the charge made, and a grand sight it was to watch our fellows rush forward with the steel and take the bridge. At another time the prince was in action with a German rearguard and narrowly escaped death. I was in this affair, and saw a German shell burst about a yard away. It plugged into the ground and made a fine commotion and scattered earth and fragments around us; but a chum and myself laughed as we dodged it, and that was the way we got into of taking these explosions when we became used to the war. You could not help laughing, even if you were a bit nervous. During this fight Prince Maurice was shot through the cap, so that he had a shave for his life, but he made light of his escape, and was very proud of the hole in the cap, which he showed to us when he talked with us, as he often did, before he fell.

There were so many incidents of coolness and disregard of wounds that it is not easy to recollect them all; but I call to mind that our adjutant, Lieutenant Woods, was shot in a little affair with the Germans. A sergeant had taken a maxim gun to put in position at a certain spot; but he had gone the wrong way and the adjutant went after him to put things right. He was too late, however, for the sergeant was spotted by the Germans and was killed. The adjutant himself was struck, but managed to get away, and he came back laughing and saying, "Oh! damn those Germans! They've shot me in the leg!" But in spite of the wound he would not lie up or let anybody do anything for him—he bound up the wound himself and carried on.

I saw another case, later, which illustrates the coolness of the British officer and his determination not to leave the fight till he is forced to do so. I was by that time wounded and in a temporary hospital, and the artillery were keeping up one of the endless duels. The officer had been struck, and he came into the hospital, and I saw that his hand had been partially blown off; but instead of caving in, as he might well have done, [he had the hand bound up and put it in a sling, then he went back to his battery just outside the windows and kept on pounding away at the Germans.

We had plenty of excitement with the German aeroplanes, and often potted at them, but I did not see any of the machines brought down. I remember one day when an aeroplane was trying to locate our position—we were retiring through a French village—and a brigade started firing at it. Just when the aeroplane appeared, the little boys and girls of the village were giving us delicious plums, which they were getting from the trees. We were thoroughly enjoying ourselves, and the youngsters liked it too, when the aeroplane swooped along and we instantly started firing at it. So many rifles going made a tremendous rattle, and the poor little boys and girls were terrified and ran off screaming, and scattered in all directions. We shouted to them and tried to bring them back, but they didn't come, and disappeared in all sorts of hiding-places.

The aeroplane got away, I believe, but at any rate it did no mischief at that particular spot. The French civilian folk got used to running off and hiding. In another village we passed through we came to a large house and found that three young ladies and their parents had been forced into the cellar and locked there by the Germans. When we entered the house, the prisoners were starving, and were thankful for anything that we gave them; but they would not take any money from us. The young ladies spoke English quite nicely.

We got quite used to aeroplanes—our own, the Germans, and the French, and saw several thrilling fights in the air. Once we saw a French aeroplane furiously fired on by the Germans—a regular cannonade it was; but the shells and bullets never got at it, and the aeroplane escaped. It was wonderful to see the way the machine shot down, as if nothing could prevent it from smashing on the ground, then to watch it suddenly turn upward and soar away as safely and swiftly as a bird. The airman's idea seemed to be to dodge the fire, and he darted about in such a bewildering fashion that no gunner or rifleman could hope to do anything with him. We were all greatly excited by this thrilling performance in the air, and glad when we knew that the plucky Frenchman had been swift enough to dodge the shells and bullets.

We had had some very trying work to do, and now we were going to get our reward for it. Some of the hardest of the work was that about which people hear nothing, and perhaps never even think—on sentry at night, for instance, about the most nerve-racking job you can imagine. We were always double sentry, and stood for two hours about five yards from each other, like statues, never moving. I always felt funky at this sort of work at the start—you can imagine such a lot in the dark and the strain is so heavy. At the slightest sound the rifle would be presented, and the word "Halt!" ring out—just that word and nothing more, and if there wasn't an instant satisfactory reply it was a bad look-out for the other party. The Germans were very cunning at getting up to some of the British outposts and sentries, and as so many of them speak English very well, they were dangerous customers to tackle, and this added to the heavy strain of sentry work at night.

Now I come to the Battle of the Aisne. I had three days and nights of it before I was bowled out.

A strange thing happened on the first day of the battle, and that was the appearance of a little black dog. I don't know where he came from, or why he joined us, but he followed the battalion all the rest of the time I was with it, and not only that, but he went into action, so he became quite one of us.

Once, in the darkness, we walked into a German outpost. We found it pretty hard going just about there, for the German dead were so thick that we had to walk over them. That march in the night was a wonderful and solemn thing. Three columns of us were going in different directions, yet moving so quietly that you could scarcely hear a sound. All around us, in that Valley of the Aisne, were burning buildings and haystacks, making a terrible illumination, and showing too well what war means when it is carried on by a nation like the Germans, for this burning and destroying was their doing.

Silently, without any talking, we went on, and then we fell into the outpost. I heard the stillness of the night broken by the sharp sound of voices, a sound which was instantly followed by shots, and the furious barking of our little dog, which up to that point had been perfectly quiet. The shots were fired by Captain Woollen, who killed two of the Germans, and one of our men shot a third. We left them where they fell and retired as quickly as we could; but we had done what we started out to do, and that was to find the position of the enemy.

While advancing again we caught a column of Germans. Our brigade-major saw them and came tearing back and told us that they were about fourteen hundred yards to the left of us. Within ten minutes we had a firing line made and our artillery was in position as well. It was a grand sight to see our fellows running into the firing line smoking cigarettes, as cool as if they were doing a bit of skirmishing on training.

We gave the Germans about three hours' hot firing, then a company went round to take the prisoners. The white flag had been shown, but we had not been allowed to take any notice of that until we were sure of our men, because the Germans had so often made a wrong use of the signal of surrender. When the company got round to the Germans it was found that they had already thrown down their rifles. Our brigade took about 500 prisoners, and the rest we handed over to the 1st Division. The Germans had about a mile and a half of convoy, which got away; but the French captured it in the evening, and so made a very nice little complete victory of the affair.

At that time, early in the war, the Germans thought they were going to have it all their own way, and they considered that any trick, white flag or otherwise, was good enough. So certain were they about victory that in one village we passed through we saw written on a wall, in English, evidently by a German, "We will do the tango in Paris on the 13th." We laughed a good deal when we read that boast, and well we might, for it was on the 13th that we saw the writing on the wall, and the Germans by that time were getting driven a long way back from the French capital.

On the Monday morning we went out as flank guard on the Aisne, and were going along behind some hills when our captain spotted swarms of Germans coming up over a ridge about twelve hundred yards away. He ordered two platoons to go out and line the ridge, and for the ridge we went. When we reached it, our captain told us that not a man was to show his head over the ridge until he gave the word to fire.

The Germans came on, getting nearer and nearer, in dense masses, and it was the hardest thing in the world not to let fly at them. They advanced till they were about seven hundred yards away, then we showed them what British rifles could do. We simply went for them, and our rifles got so hot that we could scarcely hold them. Despite that awful hail of bullets the Germans came on, and hurled themselves against us till they were not more than a hundred yards away; then we wanted to charge them, and begged to be let loose with the bayonet, but our captain told us that there were not enough of us to do it. So we retired to our own battalion, the whole of which had the joy of going for them. But the Germans didn't wait for us. They don't like the British steel, and when we had pushed them right back, without actually getting at them, they cleared off.

This was the kind of thing that went on in the Valley of the Aisne. It was work in the open and work in the trenches, on top of the incessant fighting we had had. On the third day, at night, we had just come out of the trenches, having been relieved by another company. We were in good spirits, for we had been sent to a barn, where we were to spend the night. That was a splendid bit of luck, because it meant that we were to get a nice rest and have a good time. The barn had hay in it, and we simply packed the place. It was on a farm, and during the day we had seen the farmer and his wife. There was a village near, with a church and houses, and it had proved a fine target for the Germans, who constantly shelled the place. We had got quite into the way of watching the shells burst about fifty yards in front of us, and it really was a grand sight to sit and gaze at them. We sometimes did this when we were so heavily bombarded that we could do nothing with the rifle or bayonet. Little did we know what was in store for us at the barn from shells.

The night passed and the morning came. We breakfasted and made ready to march; but were ordered to hold back a bit, and so we put aside our packs and rifles and had a sing-song to pass the time. It was one of the most surprising concerts ever held, I daresay, because all the time about three German batteries were shelling us, and occasionally a shell burst very near us and made an awful commotion. We were still packed in the barn, quite cheerful, when the sergeant who was in charge of us, and was acting as sergeant-major, told us to fall in.

He had hardly spoken the words when the very building seemed to collapse, the wall was blown in, the roof fell, timbers crashed down and the barn was filled with a horrible smoke and dust, and there were deafening and awful cries—screams and groans where a few moments earlier there had been the sound of merriment, for a German shell had

"The Germans came on and hurled themselves against us."

crashed through the wall and exploded in the very thick of us.

I was lying down in the barn, with my pack on, when this thing happened. I sprang to my feet and dashed to the door and rushed into the open air, but as soon as I had left the building a second shell came and burst and I was knocked down. I tried to rise, but my leg was numb, and so I had to wait till the stretcher-bearers came and took me to a big white house about three hundred yards away, which had been turned into a hospital, and there I was put with the rest of the wounded. For about ten minutes I had to wait outside, and there I was struck by a piece of spent shell, but not much hurt. When we were carried off in the stretchers we were kept near the bank of the road, to avoid as much as possible the German fire.

At the hospital it was found that I had been wounded in the leg; but I did not care so much about myself, I wanted to know what had happened in the barn. I soon learned the dreadful truth—the shells had killed eleven of the men and wounded thirty-two, some of whom died afterwards.

Prince Maurice was close at hand when this happened, and at night he attended the burial of the poor fellows near the barn. About an hour after the men were killed he came into the house to see us. "How are you getting on?" he asked me. "I am so sorry such a dreadful thing has happened." And he looked it, too.

I was in the hospital three days before being sent home. All that time there were villagers in the cellars of the hospital, terrified people who were hiding from the German fire, and were fed from our transport.

A lot was crowded into that retirement from Mons and the advance to the Aisne. We had kept our spirits up and had not been downhearted, and when the great day came which brought the order to advance and fight the enemy, we positively shouted and sang. And this was not just swank; it was a real expression of our feelings, for we wanted to do our bit for the Empire.

CHAPTER 4

The Struggle on the Aisne

The Battle of the Aisne began on Sunday, September 13th, 1914, when the Allies crossed the river. The Germans made furious efforts to hack their way through to Paris, but after a struggle lasting three weeks they were driven back with enormous losses. The British losses were: 561 officers and 12,980 men in killed, wounded and missing. The beginning of this tremendous conflict is told by Private Herbert Page, of the Coldstream Guards, who was wounded and had a wonderful escape from instant death on the battlefield.

There was fierce fighting all day on Sunday, September 13th, when the Battle of the Aisne began; but the Coldstreamers were not in it till the Monday. We had had a lot of heavy fighting, though, since the beginning of the business at Mons, and we had had a tough fight at Landrecies—a fight which has been specially mentioned in despatches. At the end of it all the men in my company—Number 2—had their names taken, but I don't know why. Anyway, it was a grand affair, and no doubt some day the real full story of it will be told and everybody will know what the Coldstreamers did there. Landrecies is particularly an affair of the 3rd Coldstreamers.

We had had a very hard time, fighting and marching and sleeping in the open during the cold nights and in thick mud or in trenches that were deep in water; but with it all we kept very cheerful, especially when we knew that we had brought the Germans up with a jerk and were beginning to roll them back.

The Coldstreamers were in the open all day on the Sunday, right on the side of the artillery, behind a big hill, and were very comfortable. The artillery on both sides were hard at it, but the Germans could not get our range and no shells came near us. It was harvest time, and we were lying down on sheaves of wheat, and making ourselves as cosy as we could. That was not altogether easy to do, because it was raining during the best part of the day and everything was rather depressing and very wet. But we put our oil-sheets on the ground, our greatcoats over the oil-sheets, and straw on the top of ourselves, so that we were really pretty snug, taken altogether. The straw, I fancy, was put there not so much to give us comfort as to hide us from the view of the chaps who were always flying about in the German aeroplanes, trying to spot us and make our positions known to their own gunners.

Our own aeroplanes and the Germans' were very busy during that Sunday, and shells were flying about them on both sides, but I don't think they were doing much mischief. We ourselves were doing very nicely indeed. Our transport came up and issued new biscuits, and we got a pot of jam each—and delicious they were, too. We enjoyed them, and didn't care a rap about the German shells. Our transport worked well, and we always had something to go on with. There was no fixed time for any meal, there couldn't be, for we used to march about fifty minutes and take ten minutes' halt.

If we were on a long day's march we would get an hour or two at dinner-time, usually from one o'clock. It was a funny country we were in, hot in the daytime and cold at night; but we soon got used to that. We were helped by the kindness of the French, and we got on very well with the people and had not much difficulty in making ourselves understood, especially as we picked up a few words of the language—and we could always make signs. When we wanted a drink we would hold out our water-bottles and say "*loo*," and they laughed and rushed off and filled our bottles with water.

On the way to the Valley of the Aisne we passed through towns and villages where the Germans had been and we saw what outrages they had committed on both people and property. They had destroyed everything. They had thrown poor people's property out of the windows into the streets and pulled their bedding into the roads to lie on themselves. The Germans acted like barbarians wherever they went—I saw one poor child who was riddled with bullets. We ourselves had strict orders against looting of any sort, but we did not dream of touching other people's property. Whenever we came to a town or village we warned the people to get away, as the Germans were coming, and they went. It was always pleasant to hear them say—as they did to our officers, who spoke to them in French—that they felt safe when the English were there.

The River Aisne runs through lovely country, which looks a bit of a wreck now, because we had to rush across the open and trample down the wheat to get at the Germans. The country's crops were spoiled, but the damage we did was trifling compared with the devastation that the Germans caused.

Throughout that Sunday when the Battle of the Aisne opened we had no casualties, and the day passed pretty well. At night we slept in a barn, which was better than the wet fields. There were no rats, but plenty of rabbits, for the people of the farm seemed to breed them and to have left the hutches open. That night in the barn gave me the best rest I had had since Mons, as I was not even on guard. We had a good breakfast in the barn, tea, bully beef and biscuits, and marched off soon after six in the morning, which was very wet and cold. We marched about four miles, until we came to the Aisne, to a bridge that had been blown up and so shattered that there was only a broken girder left. The rest of the bridge was in the river, which was very deep in the middle, after the heavy rains.

We were now properly in the thick of the battle and a fierce business it was, because the Germans had the range of us and were dropping shells as fast as they could fire. Some of the Guards were got across by boats, but we had to wait our turn to cross over a pontoon bridge which the Engineers had put up, in spite of the heavy fire.

We felt the German artillery fire at this place, near the village of Vendresse, but we could not see them. We watched the Loyal North Lancashires cross the pontoon bridge and saw them march away on the other side of the river, which was well wooded, then we heard them firing hard and knew that they were in action with the Germans. We were not long in following the North Lancashires and over the pontoon bridge we went, going very quietly, as we had been told to make as little noise as possible. In about an hour we were properly in the business ourselves.

After crossing the river we began to feel that at last we were really at the Germans. We made the best of the shelter that the wood gave us, and from behind trees and from the sodden ground we kept up a destructive fire on the enemy, getting nearer to him all the time. Things were growing very hot and the whole countryside rang with the crashing of the guns and the everlasting rattle of the rifles and machine-guns. We were expecting more of our men to cross the river and reinforce us, but the German guns had got the range of the pontoons and no more of our men could cross, so that for the time being we were cut off and had to do as best we could with one of the very strong rearguards of the enemy.

When we had put some good firing in from the wood we left the shelter of the trees and got into the open country, and then we were met by a shell fire which did a great deal of mischief amongst us. These shells were the big chaps that we called Jack Johnsons, and one came and struck an officer of the North Lancashires who was standing on the right of his line. I was not far from him, being on the left of our own line. The shell shattered both his legs and he fell to the ground. I hurried up, and the first thing the officer asked for was a smoke. We propped him up against a haycock and a chap who had some French tobacco made a fag and gave it to the officer—nobody had a cigarette ready made. He smoked half of it and died. By that time the stretcher-bearers had come up and were taking him away. Before he left for the rear I gently pulled his cap over his face. This affair filled the men around with grief, but it put more heart into us to go on fighting the Germans.

Our artillery now began to fire rapidly and the Germans started to retire. There was a big bunch of them, and they made for the hill as fast as they could go, meaning to scuttle down the other side and get away. But our gunners were too sharp for them, and they were properly roused up by that time. They came up in splendid style—the 117th Field Battery, I think they were—and just as the Germans reached the top of the hill in a solid body our gunners dropped three shells straight into them, and three parts of the flying Germans stopped on the top of the hill—dead.

I could not say how many Germans there were against us at this place, but I know that they came on in swarms, and they went down as fast as we could fire. But their going down seemed to make no difference to their numbers. They were only a few hundred yards away, and we could see them quite plainly. They were running all over the place, like a lot of mad sheep, they were so excited. And they were blowing trumpets, like our cavalry trumpets, and beating drums and shouting "*Hoch! Hoch!*" as hard as they could shout.

They kept blowing their charge and banging their drums till they were about 300 yards away, and shouting their "*Hochs!*" They shouted other words as well, but I don't know what they were.

When our chaps heard the trumpets and drums going and the German cheers they answered with a good old British "Hooray!" and a lot of them laughed and shouted, "Here comes the *Kaiser's* rag-time band! We'll give you '*Hoch!*' when you get a bit nearer!" And I think we did. At any rate we kept on firing at them all the time they were advancing; but they swept ahead in such big numbers that we were forced to retire into the wood.

As soon as we got into the wood we came under very heavy machine-gun fire from the Germans, and the bullets rained about us, driving into the earth and into the trees and whizzing all around us everywhere. The German shells were smashing after us, too, but were not doing much damage at that point.

It was now that I lost a very old chum of mine, a fine chap from Newcastle named Layden, a private. He was in the thick of the machine-gun fire, a few paces from me, when he suddenly cried out and I knew that he was hit. The first thing he said was, "Give me a cigarette. I know I shan't go on much longer." When we asked him what the matter was he said he was hurt. "Are you wounded?" he was asked. "Yes, I'm hit in the stomach," he answered—and he was, by about seventeen bullets.

The call went round for a cigarette, but nobody had one—lots of cigarettes were sent out to the soldiers that never reached them—but poor Layden was soon beyond the need of fags. He was delirious when our stretcher-bearers came and took him to a barn which had been turned into a temporary hospital. He lingered there for some time; but the last I saw of him was on the field. I missed him badly, because we had been good chums, and whatever we got we used to give each other half of it.

For about five hours, until two o'clock in the afternoon, that part of the battle went on, and all the time we were holding the Germans back; then we were reinforced by the remainder of our troops, who came across the pontoon bridge to our assistance.

The Germans now seemed to think that they had had enough of it and they held up white flags, and we left the shelter of the wood and went out to capture them. I should think that there were about three hundred of the Germans at that point who pretended to surrender by holding up the white flag; but as soon as we were up with them their people behind fired at us—a treacherous trick they practised very often. In spite of it all we managed to get the best part of the prisoners safe and drove them in before us to our own lines. When they really surrendered, and did not play the white flag game, we used to go up and take all their rifles, bayonets and ammunition, and throw them away out of their reach, so that they could not make a sudden dash for them and turn on us. When we had chased a few prisoners and had seen what the Germans meant by the white flag signal, we were told to take no notice of it, but to keep on shooting till they put their hands up.

A lot of the prisoners spoke English and said how glad they were to be captured and have no more fighting to do. Some said they loved England too much to want to fight against us, and a German said, "Long live King George, and blow the *Kaiser!*" But I don't know how many of them meant what they said.

We had plenty of talks with the German prisoners who could speak English. Some of them who had lived in England spoke our language quite well, and it was very interesting to hear what they had to say about us and the French and the Belgians. They couldn't stand the British cavalry, and one man said, "We don't like those Englishmen on the grey horses at all," meaning the Scots Greys. Several of the prisoners said they didn't mind so much fighting the French, because the French infantry fired too high, nor the Russians, because they fired too low; "but," they said, "every time the Englishman pulls the trigger he means death." That was a very nice compliment to us, and there was a great deal of truth in what was said about the British rifle fire. I can assure you that when we settled down to the work we often enough plugged into the Germans just as if we were on manoeuvres.

At the very first—and I'm not ashamed to say it—I shook like a leaf and fired anyhow and pretty well anywhere; but when that first awful nervousness had passed—not to return—we went at it ding-dong all the time and fired as steadily as if we were on the ranges. The men were amazingly cool at the business—and as for the officers, well, they didn't seem to care a rap for bullets or shells or anything else, and walked about and gave orders as if there were no such things in the world as German soldiers.

Most of the poor beggars we took were ravenous for want of food, and those who could speak English said they had been practically without food for days, and we saw that they had had to make shift with the oats that the horses were fed with. This starvation arose from the fact that a few days earlier we had captured the German transport and left them pretty short of food.

That rush after the Germans and bagging them was exciting work. It was successful and everything seemed to be going very well. But there was a nasty surprise in store for me and one which very nearly ended my career as a fighting man. I had really a miraculous escape.

I had charge of about four prisoners, and kept them well in front of me, so that they could not rush me. I kept them covered with my rifle all the time, and as I had ten rounds in my magazine I knew that they wouldn't have a ghost of a chance if they tried any German tricks on me—I could easily have finished the lot before they could have got at me.

As I was driving the prisoners I felt as if someone had come up and punched me on the ear. I did not know whether I had been actually hit by somebody or shot, but I turned my head and at once fell to the ground. I was swiftly up again on my feet and scrambled about. I knew that I was hurt, but the thing I mostly cared about just then was my bag of prisoners, so I handed them over to another man, and he took them in. I then found that I had been shot in the neck by a bullet. It had gone in at the collar of the jacket, at the back of the neck—here's the hole it made—and through the neck and out here, where the scar is, just under the jaw. A narrow shave? Yes, that's what the doctor said—it had just missed the jugular vein. The shot bowled me out, but it was a poor performance by the German who fired, because he could not have been more than three hundred yards away, and being six foot one I made a big target at that short distance.

Anyway, he missed me and I was told to go to a barn not far away which had been turned into a hospital, bed mattresses having been placed on the floor. Here my kit was taken off me and I was looked after at once, my kit being given to a North Lancashire man who had lost his own and had been without one for three days. He had been in a small battle and had had to take his choice between dropping his kit and being caught; so he got rid of his kit and was able to escape. When he left the barn he went into the firing line, but he only lasted about ten minutes there. I had seen him leave and I saw him brought back by the stretcher-bearers. As soon as he was inside the barn he asked where I was, and he was told and was laid down close to me. "Look here, old chap," he said pleasantly, "if you'd only been ten minutes later I shouldn't have been here, because I shouldn't have got your kit and gone into the firing line and got hit."

Perhaps he was right. He might have escaped; but as it was he had been shot through both legs.

I didn't like being in the barn and out of the fighting. It was better to be in the firing line, with all its excitement and the knowledge that you were doing your bit to help things along and drive the Germans back to the best place for them, and that's Germany; but our officers,

"From behind trees we kept up a destructive fire on the enemy"

who never lost a chance of cheering and helping us, came in when they could to see how we were getting on. During the afternoon my company officer, Captain Brocklehurst, and the adjutant, came in to see how things were going. Captain Brocklehurst saw me and said, "There are not many of the company left; but we're doing wonderfully well. We've killed a good many of the Germans and taken about five hundred prisoners." That was good news, very good, but it was even better when the captain added, "And we're pushing them back all the time."

The guns were booming and the rifles were crackling all around us while we were lying in the barn, and wounded men were being constantly brought in, keeping the doctors and the ambulance men terribly busy and you can imagine what it must have meant for the Germans if it was like that for us; because we fought in open order, so that we were not easy to hit, whereas the Germans were in their solid formation, which meant that they could not advance against the British fire without being mown down.

I was in the barn, which was crowded with wounded, till about one o'clock in the morning, then we were taken in Red Cross vans to another hospital about three miles away, and as we left the French people showed us all the kindness they could, giving us water, milk and food, in fact all they had. We crossed the pontoon bridge and were put into another barn which had been turned into a hospital, and we stayed there for the night. We left that place in the morning for La Fère, about twenty miles away. There were a great many motor waggons being used as ambulances, and they were all needed, because of the crowds of wounded. All of us who could walk had to do so, as all the vans and lorries were wanted for the bad cases. I could manage to walk for about a mile at a stretch, but I could not use my arms. When I had done a mile, I rested, then went on again, and so I got to the end of the journey, with a lot more who were just about able to do the same.

We didn't grumble, because we were thankful to be able to walk at all and not to be so badly wounded that we could not shift for ourselves. When we got to La Fère the hospital was so full that we were put straight into a hospital train, and I was in it for two days and nights, stopping at stations for brief halts. Again the French people were kindness itself and pressed food and drink on us. We got to Nantes, where my wound was dressed and we had supper, and then I had what seemed like a taste of heaven, for I was put into a proper bed. Yes, after sleeping for so many nights on the ground, anyhow and anywhere, often enough in mud and water, it was like getting into heaven itself to get into a bed. On the Saturday they put us on board a ship and took us round to Liverpool, a four days' journey on the sea. First we went to Fazackerley, and then I was lucky enough to be sent on to Knowsley Hall, where Lady Derby, who has a son in France with the Grenadiers, had turned the state dining-room into a hospital ward. There were sixteen Guardsmen in the ward, with four trained nurses to look after us. Wasn't that a contrast to the barns and flooded trenches! Now I'm back in London, feeling almost fit again, and soon I shall have to report myself.

    I have only told you about the little bit I saw myself of the tremendous Battle of the Aisne. Considering the length of it and the fearful nature of the firing, it sometimes strikes me as a very strange thing that I should be alive at all; but stranger still that some men went through it all, right away from the beginning at Mons, and escaped without a scratch.

CHAPTER 5

"The Most Critical Day of All"

In the first four months of the war nineteen Victoria Crosses were gazetted for valour in the field, and of these no fewer than five were awarded for the sanguinary fighting at Le Cateau on August 26th, 1914. In his despatch dealing with the retreat from Mons Sir John French described the 26th as "the most critical day of all." It was during this crisis of the battle that Corporal Frederick William Holmes, of the 2nd Battalion The King's Own (Yorkshire Light Infantry), "carried a wounded man out of the trenches under heavy fire and later assisted to drive a gun out of action by taking the place of a driver who had been wounded." Corporal Holmes has not only won the Victoria Cross, but he has been also awarded the Médaille Militaire of the Legion of Honour of France. His story gives further proof of the courage and endurance of the gallant British Army in Belgium and in France.

For seven years I was with the colours in the old 51st, which is now the Yorkshire Light Infantry, then I was drafted to the Reserve; but I was called back only a fortnight later, when the war broke out.

The regimental depot is at Pontefract, in South Yorkshire, which some unkind people say is the last place that God started and never finished, and in August, having become a soldier again, after marrying and settling down to civil life in Dublin, I found myself in a region which was almost like the South Yorkshire coalfields. There were the same pit-heads and shale-heaps, so that you could almost think you were in England again—but how different from England's calmness and security! It was around these pit-heads and shale-heaps that some of the fiercest fighting of the earlier days of the war took place.

We had left Dublin and reached Havre at midnight; we had been to the fortified town of Landrecies, where the Coldstreamers were to do such marvellous things, and had got to Maroilles, where Sir Douglas Haig and the 1st Division became heavily engaged. We were at Maroilles, in billets, from the 18th to the 21st. Billets meant almost anything, and we lived and slept in all sorts of places as well as the trenches—but being in the open in summer was no hardship. The fields had been harvested and we often slept on the stacks of corn.

The people were really kind; they gave us every mortal thing as we marched, beer, wine, cigarettes and anything else there was.

At five o'clock on the Saturday afternoon we were billeted in a brewery, where we stayed till Sunday noon, when, as we were having dinner, shells were bursting and beginning things for us. We were ordered to take up a position about two miles from Mons, and on that famous Sunday we went into action near a railway embankment.

People by this time know all about Mons, so I will only say that after that hard business we retired towards Le Cateau, after fighting all day on the 24th and all the following night. After that we took up a position on outpost and stayed on outpost all night, then, at about two in the morning, we dropped into some trenches that we had previously occupied.

I know what Mons was and I went through the battles of the Marne and the Aisne; but nothing I had seen could be compared for fury and horror with the stand of the 5th Division on the 26th. It was essentially a fight by the 5th, because that was the only division employed at Le Cateau. The division was composed of three brigades, the 12th, 13th and 14th. My battalion, the 2nd Yorkshire Light Infantry, was in the 13th, the other battalions with us being the West Riding, the King's Own Scottish Borderers and the West Kent.

There were some coal-pit hills in front of us and the Germans advanced over them in thousands. That was about eleven o'clock in the morning, and the firing began in real earnest again.

The Germans by this time were full of furious hope and reckless courage, because they believed that they had got us on the run and that it was merely a question of hours before we were wiped out of their way. Their blood was properly up, and so was ours, and I think we were a great deal hotter than they were, though we were heavily outnumbered. We hadn't the same opinion of German soldiers that the Germans had, and as they rushed on towards us we opened a fire from the trenches that simply destroyed them.

Some brave deeds were done and some awful sights were seen on the top of the coal-pits. A company of Germans were on one of the tops and an officer and about a dozen men of the "Koylis" went round one side of the pit and tried to get at them. Just as they reached the back of the pit the German artillery opened fire on the lot, Germans and all—that was one of their tricks. They would rather sacrifice some of their own men themselves than let any of ours escape—and they lost many in settling their account with the handful of Englishmen who had rushed behind the pit at a whole company of Germans.

Hereabouts, at the pits, the machine-gun fire on both sides was particularly deadly. Lieutenant Pepys, who was in charge of the machine-gun of our section, was killed by shots from German machine-guns, and when we went away we picked him up and carried him with us on the machine-gun limber until we buried him outside a little village in a colliery district.

He was a very nice gentleman and the first officer to go down. When he fell Lieutenant N. B. Dennison, the brigade machine-gun officer, took charge. He volunteered to take over the gun, and was either killed or wounded. Then Lieutenant Unett, the well-known gentleman jockey, crawled on his stomach to the first line of the trenches, with some men, dragging a machine-gun behind them. They got this gun into the very front of the line of the trenches, then opened fire on the Germans with disastrous effect. Lieutenant Unett was wounded and lay in the open all the time.

This gallant deed was done between twelve noon and one o'clock, and I was one of the few men who saw it. I am glad to be able to pay my humble tribute to it.

There was a battery of the Royal Field Artillery on our left rear, about 800 yards behind the front line of trenches. Our gunners had such excellent range on the Germans that the German gunners were finding them with high explosive shell. It was mostly those shells that were dropping on them till they got the range and killed the gunners. There were only about five who were not either killed or wounded. The officer was wounded; but in spite of that he carried a wounded man round the bottom of the hill, then went back and fetched another man and repeated the journey until he had taken every one of the five away. After that he returned, picked up a spade and smashed the sights of the gun and made it useless. We heard some time afterwards that he had been killed.

This brave deed was witnessed by most of us who were in the front line of trenches.

When the German guns were got into position in front of us and the Germans tried their hardest to blow us out of our trenches, they searched for our artillery and, failing to discover it, they grew more determined than ever to rout us out of the place from which we were doing deadly damage.

In spite of the heavy losses around us we held on, and all the more stubbornly because we expected every moment that the French would come up and reinforce us. The French were due about four o'clock, but owing to some accident they did not arrive, and it seemed as if nothing could save us.

There was a falling off in our artillery fire, and it was clear that one of our batteries had been put out of action. And no wonder, for the German guns were simply raining shells upon us. The Germans at that time were sticking to the dense formations which had been their practice since the war began—and they hurled themselves forward in clouds towards the 37th Field Battery.

So furiously did they rush, so vast were their numbers, and so certain were they that they had the guns as good as captured, that they actually got within a hundred yards of the battery.

It was at this terrible crisis that Captain Douglas Reynolds and volunteers rushed up with two teams and limbered up two guns, and in spite of all the German batteries and rifles did one gun was saved. This was a wonderful escape, in view of the nearness of the German infantry and their numbers, and for their share in the desperate affair the captain and two of the drivers—Drane and Luke—who had volunteered, got the Victoria Cross.

In a way we had got used to retiring, and we were not at the end of it even now, by a good deal, for on our left the Borderers were withdrawing and on our right the Manchesters were being forced right back; fighting magnificently and leaving the ground littered with their dead and wounded.

The Yorkshire Light Infantry were left in the centre of the very front line of the trenches, where we were heavily pressed. We made every mortal effort to hold our ground, and 'C' Company was ordered up from the second line to reinforce us in the first.

Imagine what it meant for a company of infantry to get from one trench to another at a time like that, to leave shelter, to rush across a space of open ground that was literally riddled with shrapnel and rifle bullets, and in the daytime, too, with the Germans in overwhelming force at point-blank range.

But the order had been given, and 'C' Company obeyed. The men sprang from their trench, they rushed across a fire-swept zone—and the handful of them who were not shot down made a final dash and simply tumbled into our trench and strengthened us. They had just about lost their first wind, but were soon hard at it again with the rifle and did murderous work, if only to get something back on account of the comrades who had fallen.

It was a help, a big help, to have 'C' Company with us in the front trench; but even with this reinforcement we could do nothing, and after we had made a hot stand the order came to retire. That was about half-past four in the afternoon.

Things had been bad before; they were almost hopeless now, for to retire meant to show ourselves in the open and become targets for the German infantry; but our sole chance of salvation was to hurry away—there was no thought of surrender.

When the order was given there was only one thing to do—jump out of the trenches and make a rush, and we did both; but as soon as we were seen a storm of bullets struck down most of the men.

At such a time it is every man for himself, and it is hardly possible to think of anything except your own skin. All I wanted to do was to obey orders and get out of the trench and away from it.

I had rushed about half-a-dozen yards when I felt a curious tug at my boot. I looked to see what was the matter and found that my foot had been clutched by a poor chap who was wounded and was lying on the ground unable to move.

"For God's sake, save me!" he cried, and before I knew what was happening I had got hold of him and slung him across my back. I can't pretend to tell you details of how it was all done, because I don't clearly remember. There was no time to think of much besides the bullets and the fastest way of getting out of their reach. Rain was falling, not heavily, but it was drizzling, and this made the ground greasy and pretty hard going.

I had not gone far before the poor chap complained that my equipment hurt him and begged me to get it out of his way. The only thing to be done was to drop the equipment altogether, so I halted and somehow got the pack and the rest of it off, and I let my rifle go, too, for the weight of the lot, with the weight of a man, was more than I could tackle.

I picked my man up again, and had struggled on for twenty or thirty yards when I had to stop for a rest.

Just then I saw the major of the company, who said, "What's the matter with him?"

I could not speak, so I pointed to the man's knees, which were shot with shrapnel; then the major answered, "All right! Take him as far as you can, and I hope you'll get him safely out of it."

I picked him up again and off I went, making straight over the hill at the back of the position we had taken, so that he should be safe from the German fire. The point I wanted to reach was about a mile away, and it was a dreadful journey; but I managed to do it, and when I had got there, after many rests, I started to carry my man to the nearest village, which was some distance off.

I got to the village, but the German heavy shells were dropping so fast that I could not stay there, and they told me to carry him into the next village. I was pretty well worn out by this time, but I started again, and at last with a thankful heart I reached the village and got the man into a house where wounded men were being put.

How far did I carry him?

Well, it was calculated that the distance was three miles; but I never felt the weight. Yes, he was quite conscious and kept on moaning and saying, "Oh!" and telling me that if ever he got out of it he would remember me; but I said that he mustn't talk such nonsense—for I wanted him to stop thanking me and to keep his spirits up.

I don't know how long I was in getting him over the ground, for I had no idea of time.

Having put my man in safety I left the house and began to go back to the position, expecting to find some of the regiments to rejoin, but when I reached the firing line there were no regiments left. They had been forced to retire, and the ground was covered with the dead and wounded, as it was impossible to bring all the wounded away.

There was a road at this particular point, and on reaching the top of it I saw the Germans advancing, about 500 yards away. Between them and myself there was a field-gun, with the horses hooked in, ready to move off; but I saw that there was only a wounded trumpeter with it.

I rushed up to him and shouted, "What's wrong?"

"I'm hurt," he said. "The gun has to be got away; but there's nobody left to take it."

I looked all around, and saw that there were no English gunners left—there were only the Germans swarming up, 500 yards away and badly wanting to get at the gun.

There was not a second to lose. "Come on," I said, and with that

"I HOISTED THE TRUMPETER INTO THE SADDLE."

I hoisted the trumpeter into the saddle of the near wheel horse, and clambering myself into the saddle of the lead horse we got the gun going and made a dash up the hill.

There was only the one road, and this was so littered up and fenced about with wire entanglements that we could not hope to escape by it. Our only chance was by dashing at the hill, and this we did—and a terrible business it was, because we were forced to gallop the gun over the dead bodies of our own men—mostly artillerymen, they were. Many of the poor chaps had crawled away from their battery and had died on the hillside or on the road.

We carried on over the hill, and when the Germans saw what we were doing they rained shells and bullets on us. One or two of the horses were hit, and a bullet knocked my cap off and took a piece of skin from my head—just here. But that didn't hurt me much, nor did another bullet which went through my coat. We carried on, and got over the hill, just driving straight ahead, for we couldn't steer, not even to avoid the dead.

I daresay the bullet that carried off my cap stunned me a bit, at any rate I didn't remember very much after that, for the time being; all I know is that we galloped madly along, and dashed through two or three villages. There was no one in the first village; but in the second I saw an old lady sitting outside a house, with two buckets of water, from which soldiers were drinking. She was rocking to and fro, with her head between her hands, a pitiful sight. Shells were dropping all around and the place was a wreck.

I carried on at full stretch for about ten miles, tearing along to get to the rear of the column. I don't remember that I ever looked back; but I took it that the trumpeter was still in the saddle of the wheel horse.

At last I caught up with the column; then I looked round for the trumpeter, but he was not there, and I did not know what had become of him. That was the first I knew of the fact that I had been driving the gun by myself.

Willy-nilly I had become a sort of artilleryman, and from that time until the 28th I attached myself to the guns; but on that day I rejoined what was left of my old regiment.

I had been in charge of twelve men, but when I inquired about them I found that only three were left—nine had been either killed or wounded, and the rest of the battalion had suffered in proportion. That gives some idea of the desperate nature of the fighting and the way in which the little British Army suffered during the first three days after Mons.

The officer who had seen me carrying the man off did not see me go back, but a sergeant who knew me noticed me passing through the village with the gun and he was the first man of my battalion that I saw. This was Sergeant Marchant, who, for his gallantry in helping another sergeant, who was wounded, was awarded the Distinguished Conduct Medal. In that fine affair he was helped by Company-Sergeant-Major Bolton, and both of them were mentioned in despatches.

Of course I never thought of saying anything about what I had done; but I was sent for and asked if it was true, and I said I had got the man away and helped to take the gun off, and this was confirmed by the major who had seen me carrying the man.

For the day's work at Le Cateau two Victoria Crosses were given to my regiment—one to Major C. A. L. Yate, "Cal," he was called, because of his initials, and one to myself.

Major Yate was a very fine officer. He joined us and took command of B Company just before we went out to the war. On this day he was in the trenches, on our left rear, not very far from where I was. When we went into action he had 220 men, but they caught so much of the hot fire which was meant for the battery behind that he lost all his men except nineteen when he was surrounded and captured. The day before this happened the major declared that if it came to a pinch and they were surrounded he would not surrender—and he did not surrender now. Reckless of the odds against him he headed his nineteen men in a charge against the Germans—and when that charge was over only three of the company could be formed up.

All the rest of B Company were either killed or wounded or taken prisoners, though very few prisoners were taken. The major was one of them; but he was so badly wounded that he lived only a very short time, and died as a prisoner of war. His is one of the cases in which the Cross is given although the winner of it is dead. Major Yate was an absolute gentleman and a great favourite with us all. He had had a lot of experience in the Far East and at home, and I am sure that if he had lived he would have become a general. He was always in front, and his constant cry was "Follow me!"

From Le Cateau we got to the Valley of the Aisne and were in trenches for ten days. At midnight on September 24th we advanced two miles beyond the river, which we had crossed by pontoons because all the other bridges had been blown up.

We reached a little village and stayed there in shelters underneath the houses, where all the inhabitants slept. We stayed in one of these cellars and went on outpost at four in the morning and came off at four next morning, then went on again at four a.m.

We were only 250 yards from the Germans, who were in a small wood outside the village, opposite the houses. They had snipers out and were sniping at us all the time. We barricaded the windows of the houses and knocked bricks out of the walls to make loopholes, and through these loopholes we sniped the Germans, and they did their level best to pick us off too. Every time your head was shown a dozen bullets came, and you could not see where they came from. Two or three of our men were killed by snipers; but there was no real chance of getting to grips, for there was barbed wire everywhere, and nothing could be done till this was cut. Night was the only time when the wire could be cut—and night work was both eerie and nerve-racking.

We had "listeners" to listen for any movement by the enemy. A sentry in peace times means a man who walks up and down, smartly dressed, but in war time, at night, he is a listener, and in the daytime he is a "watcher"—he can see in the daytime and hear at night. That is one of the little things which show how greatly war changes the customs of peace.

It was outside Béthune, when we were in reserve to the rest of the brigade, that I was wounded. We had got well into October and we were behind trenches, with French infantry on our right. At night we advanced, on a level with the firing line, and in the darkness we dug trenches. We were then next to the King's Own Scottish Borderers. We finished the trenches before the early hours of the morning and stuck in them till five in the afternoon, when we heard some shouts, and on looking over we saw that the Germans were making a charge.

We opened rapid fire and the Germans answered very smartly, having dropped down. But they were not down long, for up they sprang and with further shouts on they came and got within three hundred yards of us. Then we were ordered to fix bayonets and be ready to charge at any moment; but before we started charging we rushed into another line of trenches in front of us, and there we mixed with the Borderers.

This fight in the night was a thrilling affair, the chief guide on each side being the flashes of the rifles, and these were incessant. The Germans were firing rapidly at anything they could see; but there was little to see except the tiny forks of flame. They must have heard us, however, and that, of course, would help them. One strange thing happened when we reached the trench, and that was that we had to wake up some of the men. In spite of the fighting they were sleeping—but war turns everything upside down, and the British soldier reaches a point when it takes a lot to disturb him.

Suddenly, at this crisis, I felt as if my leg had been struck by something that vibrated, like a springboard, and I dropped down. I was dizzy, but did not think I was hit, and I supposed that if I stayed down for a few minutes I should be all right and able to go on. So I sat down, but quickly found that I could not move, and on feeling my leg I discovered that it was wet and warm, and I knew what that meant, so I took off my equipment and put it down and began to crawl back to the trench I had left when we charged.

I crawled across a mangel-wurzel field to a house of some sort, then I must have become unconscious, for the next thing I knew was that I was being carried along on a stretcher.

It was only yesterday that a friend in my battalion wrote to tell me that we were crawling pretty close together through the mangel-wurzel field. He was shot in the arm and stopped two of the Borderers' stretcher-bearers just in time to have me put on a stretcher.

I had a natural walking-stick which I had cut from a vine, and of which I was very fond. I had fastened it to my rifle and was so proud of it that I said I would carry it through the war, if I could. My friend must have known how I prized the vinestick, for when he was sent home he brought it with him, and it's waiting for me when I leave hospital.

I also had a letter from my company officer a few days ago. He says he missed me that night, but he could not make out what had happened. He heard that a complete set of equipment had been found, and on learning that I was wounded he assumed that it was mine, and that I had been carried away and left it. He told me that on the very night I was wounded they were relieved by the French infantry, and that he himself was hit ten days afterwards. It was the day before I was wounded that I heard that I was recommended for the French Military Medal, and that was as big a surprise to me as the news that I had been given the Victoria Cross.

That equipment of mine had a tragic history. During the first day of the Aisne I was without equipment and set to work to get some. A bugler of my battalion had been killed by shrapnel and I was told by my officer to go and get his equipment. "Treat him gently, poor chap," said the officer, and you may be sure I did. I helped myself, and thinking that the poor lad's mother might like a memento I brought away his "iron-rations" tin. This is riddled with bullet-holes, just as the bugler was.

There is one thing more that I would like to say, and it is about my birthday, which falls on September 7th. As I had left the colours and gone into the Reserve I thought I could look forward to a fine celebration of the anniversary. And there *was* a fine celebration, too, for on September 7th our retiring before the Germans ended and we started to advance and drive them back.

CHAPTER 6

British Fighters in French Forts

Through this story by Private J. Boyers, of the Durham Light Infantry—the old 68th Foot, long known by reason of its devotion on many a bloody field like Salamanca and Inkerman as the "Faithful Durhams"—we get to know something of the British and French fighting side by side in the forts at Lille, one of the strongest of the famous fortresses of France. Lille is a great manufacturing town, the Manchester of France, and early in October 1914, and later, it was the scene of much desperate fighting between the Allied Armies and the Germans.

I went from England with the first party in the Expeditionary Force, and after landing on the other side of the Channel, we had a march of fifty miles to Mons, where I had my first battle.

I was in the great retirement—but I suppose you have heard enough about that and Mons already, so I will leave it. After that beginning, I took part in the Battle of the Marne and the Battle of the Aisne, and later on I was shot in the thigh and bowled out.

I am only a young soldier—I am a native of Sunderland, and was born in 1891—and I have only been in the army a few months in the old 68th, the "Faithful Durhams," so I think I have seen a fair lot of the big war and have got to know what it means.

The Durhams have done great things and suffered terribly, and many a chum of mine is sleeping with thousands more British soldiers on the battlefields of France and Belgium. A great many have been wounded, and of course there are a number of missing, mostly men, I dare say, who are prisoners of war.

I had been at sea before joining the army, and thought I knew something about roughing it; but even the North Sea in bad weather was nothing compared with the hardships of the retirement from Mons, and the living and sleeping in the trenches when the ground was sodden and deep in water.

Sometimes we were very short of food, and once for several days on end we were almost starving, because the supplies could not get up to us, and we had been forced to throw away a lot of our packs and things.

A good many of us had to carry a seven-pound tin of bully beef in addition to our heavy packs and a great many rounds of ammunition. In the fearfully hot weather we could not carry all this weight, and the tins of beef had to go. We should have been thankful for them later on, when we ran short and some of the beef we had with us had gone bad through the tins getting punctured, which happened in all sorts of strange ways, including bullet-holes and bayonet pricks. But these were things that couldn't be helped, and in spite of them all we kept very cheerful, and often enough, both on the march and in the trenches and French forts, when we got to them, we sang and joked and whistled as if there was no such thing going on as war.

Our officers shared everything with us, and suffered just as we did, though often worse, so that whenever we got a bit downhearted, their example cheered us up and put us right. I don't think there's a man who's fought in this great war who won't say the same thing about his officers.

We had so much fierce fighting when the work really began, and saw so many strange and dreadful things, that it is not easy to say what stands out most clearly in our minds in such a business, but one of the things I do remember, and shall never forget, is the week or so we spent in one of the big French forts at Lille, fighting side by side with French soldiers. I will tell you about that later, but we did a lot before we got to Lille.

When we were on the march we had a great deal of exciting work to do in hunting Germans. Small bodies of them were everywhere, apart from the immense numbers of spies who were in the Lille district and elsewhere.

The French bagged a lot of spies and gave them short shrift. They hid in all sorts of queer places—some of them got into the tall mill chimneys—but they were routed out and shot.

We found a fair lot of Germans in houses and farms when we were on the march. We examined these places thoroughly. When we arrived at farmhouses and suchlike places, a non-commissioned officer, with a small party of men would make inquiries, often with the help of French cavalrymen who were with us and could speak English, and we always found that threats of fearful punishment to the womenfolk had been made by the Germans if they told us that any Germans had been seen about. But the women told us readily enough, especially when there happened to be any Germans in hiding—those who were too drunk to get away and had been left behind. It didn't take long to make these fellows prisoners, and they rubbed their eyes a lot when they got sober and found that the British had bagged them—though I fancy that most of them were glad to be caught and out of the fighting.

We saw some dreadful sights in these farms and houses that we entered, and it was no uncommon thing for us to bury the women who had been done to death by these invaders. We had to carry out this sad work at night, to escape the German fire, for no matter what we were doing they went for us with rifles and machine-guns and anything else that came handy.

Time after time on the march we saw proof of the terrible way in which the French and Germans fought, and saw how bravely the French had defended their country and how freely they had given their lives to get something like even with the enemy.

The Frenchmen were naturally even more upset than the British soldiers were at many of the sights that met us, and in the streets along which we marched we often saw dead bodies of Frenchmen and Germans lying close together, where they had fallen after a desperate fight on the pavements or in the roadway. They had met and fought to the death, and it looked as if no quarter had been given. And with all this there had been a perfectly savage destruction of everything that the Germans could lay their hands on.

The Germans had thieved and killed wherever they had gone, led on in the work by their officers, and little supposing, I fancy, that the day of reckoning had come for them. There is no doubt that they had been taught that they were going to have a walk over in France and were going to have a good time in Paris; but some of them were poor enough specimens when we caught them or they surrendered.

After the terrific battles of the Marne and the Aisne we were transferred rather quickly to La Bassée, which is not far from Lille, and then we had to take a share in defending Lille, in one of the big forts just outside the town.

The Germans had got up into that part of the country in very strong force, and they were making furious efforts to smash the forts and get hold of Lille, which had become a most important place for them.

Lille is a large manufacturing town and was very strongly defended by forts and in other ways. These big forts, about half-a-dozen in number, form a ring round the town and command all the countryside, or rather did, for they have been pretty badly hammered by this time; while the town itself is protected in other ways. Lille was also one of the big centres for French troops, but owing to the heavy drain caused by the immense numbers of Germans that had to be dealt with at the Aisne there were not a great many first-rate troops left, and a good deal of the defence had to fall on the territorials.

The particular fort where I had my strangest experiences was about a mile from Lille, and from the outside it looked like a low hill-top, so much so that when we were getting near it the fort seemed like a little round hill rising from the plain.

The fort was built of immense blocks of stone, and, as far as one could tell, great quantities of steel, so that its strength must have been enormous.

It was a romantic sort of business to get into the fort, because, first of all, we had to pass the sentries, then some huge stone sliding doors were opened, by a lever, I suppose, in the same way as the midway doors of a District Railway carriage open and shut. They were very big and heavy doors, yet they opened and shut quite easily, and when they were closed you could hardly see a crack between them.

Past this gloomy entrance was a narrow walled slope which led into darkness . We went down the slope into what looked like an archway and then we got into proper blackness. It was some time before you could get used to such darkness, but at last I saw that we had reached a large vault; but I can't pretend to give details, because I never had a chance of properly making them out, and we were more concerned about the Germans than we were about the fort.

Of course it can be easily understood that owing to the presence of great quantities of ammunition and inflammable stores, only the dimmest lighting was possible—in fact, there was practically no lighting at all except by little portable electric lamps, and as for smoking, that was absolutely off.

The instant we reached the fort we were told that smoking was most strictly forbidden, and that disobedience was punishable by death. The French soldier is as fond as the British Tommy of his smoke, but it is a remarkable thing that in the darkness of the fort we didn't feel the want of smoking, which isn't much of a catch in the pitch darkness. As a matter of fact I had no wish to smoke when we were in the fort, so I was never tempted to run the risk of being shot.

Cooking, like smoking, was out of the question, for you can no more smoke with safety in a magazine like that than you can in a coal-mine—a spark is enough to do tremendous mischief, let alone a fire; so our rations had to be brought to us by the Army Service Corps, though they, with their carts, were a long way off.

The A.S.C. chaps were excellent all through, and the men in the fighting line owe a lot to them.

In this black dungeon, a sentry's challenge was a good deal more than a formality; but it nearly became one when the welcome commissariat man arrived. But for his coming we should have had to fall back on our emergency rations. These were good, of their kind, but they can't compare with the best efforts of the A.S.C.

But I'm getting off the track a bit. In the side of the vault, or cavern, there was a low, shallow dugout which was meant to hold a rifleman lying at full stretch. This was something like a small cubicle in size and shape, and to enter it in the darkness was a proper problem. After a try or two, however, you got into the way of stumbling comfortably into it. By crouching and creeping, and using your hands and knees, you could secure a position from which it was fairly easy to draw yourself up into the dugout. I dwell on this because I think it is important, seeing that four of us took two-hour watches throughout the twenty-four hours, so that getting to and from such a dugout becomes an event in your daily life.

At one end of the dugout was a loophole for a rifle or a maxim-gun, and here we patiently waited for those pests, the snipers. These German potters gave us no rest; but many a German who thought he was well hidden got the finishing touch from one of our loopholes.

This was thrilling fighting, especially when things became hot, and we manned all the loopholes in the fort, to the number of four, and at a pinch we could use two maxims at each. There were fourteen of us in the fort altogether, four officers and ten men. The orders, being in French, sounded very strange at first, but to my surprise, I soon fell into the way of understanding what was said around me, certainly so far as ordinary little things were concerned. I shall never forget the French for water so long as I remember the thirst I had in the black depths of the fort.

The life in the fort was one of the strangest parts of the whole of the fighting. It was queer enough to be in France, fighting with the French, but a good deal queerer to be living in one of the big famous French forts which the Germans were trying to pound to bits with their enormous siege guns. But we soon settled down and got fairly well used to the sound of the fort's guns and the row of the German artillery and the crashing of the shells around us.

We were told off into parties in the fort, each party being commanded by a non-commissioned officer, who used to light the way for us with an electric lamp that he carried in front of him, hung round his neck.

We ate and drank and slept with the French gunners, and taken altogether we were very comfortable, and were spared something of the awful noise of the firing, for when the guns of the forts were fired the noise was worse than thunderbolts, and everything about was shaken in the most extraordinary manner.

The Germans were mad to get at us and they shot tons and tons of shells at us, and time after time made efforts to storm the forts and Lille itself. In these attempts they lost immense numbers of men, and when we got outside of the fort we saw the dead bodies of the Germans lying about in thousands—so thick on the ground were they that we had to clamber over them as best we could.

Our own fort was pretty lucky, but the next one to us was very badly damaged, huge holes being made where the monster shells got home, and most of the defenders of the fort being wiped out. The German big guns certainly did a vast amount of mischief against forts—so the Germans will know what to expect when our own big guns get to work on forts in Germany.

It was soon clear that it would not be possible to hold on at Lille for long, because we were so hopelessly outnumbered. The fight went on, day and night, for a full week, and the Germans bombarded everything.

On Sunday, October 4th, there was some desperate fighting in the streets of the town and the outskirts. German troops were rushed up in armoured trains and motors, but when it came to hand-to-hand fighting they were not much good, and on the Monday they were driven away with heavy loss.

We had a few goes at them with the bayonet, and that charging was very hard work. It had to be done in short rushes of about a hundred yards, but we could not get near enough to them to give the bayonet a fair chance. In that respect it was the same old story—the Germans

would not face the steel. In anything like equal numbers they can't stand up against a charge. They would mostly run for it, firing at us over their shoulders as they bolted, but not doing a great deal of mischief that way. When they could run no more and saw that the game was up, they would throw away their rifles and surrender, and we then brought them in.

Before the fighting began, and while it was going on, a good many of the inhabitants got into a panic and fled to Boulogne and Calais; but the French troops held out gamely, and on the Tuesday a fearful lot of execution was done amongst the masses of Germans by the French artillery fire. Neither the German guns nor the infantry could make a stand against this onslaught, and at this time the German losses were particularly heavy, hundreds of men falling together At the end of that part of the battle the Germans for the time being were completely routed, and they were driven back a good dozen miles.

The Durhams suffered greatly in the fighting, and the good old West Yorkshires, who had seen a lot of hard work with us, had been badly cut up too. Some help was given by the little Gurkhas, who had joined the British; but unfortunately I was not able to see much of what they did, because soon after they appeared with their famous knives I got my wound.

Some of the most dangerous work was done at night, when we tried to get at the Germans with the bayonet and rout them out of their trenches and positions. We had to do everything so quietly—creep out of the forts, creep along the ground, and creep up to the enemy as near as we could get, and sometimes that was not very close, because of such things as barbed wire entanglements.

These entanglements were particularly horrible, because they were so hard to overcome and tore the flesh and clothing. At first we had a pretty good way of destroying them, and that was by putting the muzzles of our rifles on the wire and blowing it away; but there were two serious drawbacks to that trick—one was that it was a waste of ammunition, and the other was that the noise of the firing gave us away, and let the Germans loose on us with guns and rifles.

We soon got too canny to go on with that practice, and just before I was wounded and sent home a very ingenious arrangement had been fixed to the muzzle of the rifle for wire-cutting—a pair of shears which you could work with a swivel from near the trigger, so that instead of putting the muzzle of the rifle against the wire, you could cut it by using the pliers.

It was in one of these night affairs that I was nearly finished as a soldier. I was ordered to join a reconnoitring party. We got clear of the fort, and made our way over the country for about a mile. We were then in a field which had been harvested and harrowed, so that it was pretty hard ground to go over. In spite of it all we were getting on very nicely when the Germans got wind of our movements and opened a terrible fire with rifles and maxims.

We lost a lot of men, and where a man fell there he had to lie, dead or living.

Suddenly I fell plump on the ground, and found that I could not get up again, though I did my best to keep up with my chums. Then I felt an awful pain in my thigh and knew that I was hurt, but I must have been struck five minutes before I fell, by a bullet from a German rifle. It had gone clean through my right thigh. They told me afterwards that I had had a very narrow shave indeed; but a miss is as good as a mile.

I knew there was nothing for it but pluck and patience, so I made the best of things, and waited till the day broke and brought the battalion stretcher-bearers, who always came out just about dawn to collect the wounded.

I was lying on the ground, in a sort of ditch, for six hours before I was picked up by the stretcher-bearers and carried to a stable which was being used as a temporary hospital.

The Germans fired on the wounded as they were being carried off in the grey light, but they didn't hit me again.

I lay in the stable for about eight hours, waiting for the ambulance, which took me to the railhead, and then I was put in a train and taken to Rouen—and that travelling was simply awful, because the French trains jolt like traction-engines.

All the same, I had a pleasant voyage to Southampton, and hoped that I might be sent to a hospital near home, but I was too ill to go a long journey to the north, so I was taken to Woolwich, and afterwards sent here, to the Royal Hospital at Richmond, where everybody is kindness itself, and can't do enough for you, it seems.

I've had a month in bed, so far, but I'm hoping to be out of it soon and hobbling about.

"We found a fair lot of Germans in houses and farms"

CHAPTER 7

A Brother's Revenge

"Die hard, my men, die hard!" shouted the heroic Colonel Inglis, when, at Albuhera, in the Peninsular War, his regiment, the 57th Foot, were furiously engaged with the enemy. And the regiment obeyed, for when the bloody fight was ended twenty-two out of twenty-five officers had been killed or wounded, 425 of 570 rank and file had fallen and thirty bullets had riddled the King's Colour. The 57th is now the 1st Battalion Middlesex Regiment, but the regiment is still best known by its gallant nickname of the "Die-Hards." It has suffered exceptional losses in this war, and the story of some of its doings is told by Corporal W. Bratby, who relates a tale which he has described as a brother's revenge.

The old "Die-Hards" went into action at Mons nearly a thousand strong; but when, after Mons had been left behind, a roaring furnace, the roll was called, not more than 270 of us were left. D Company came out a shattered remnant—only thirty-six men, and no officers. When what was left of us marched away, other regiments were shouting, "Three cheers for the Die-Hards!" And three rousing cheers they gave; but I had no heart for them, because I had left my younger brother Jack, a "Die-Hard" like myself. They told me that he had been killed by a bursting shell while doing his duty with the machine-gun section.

I did not say much. I asked the adjutant if any of the machine-gun section had returned, and he answered sadly, "No, they've all gone."

Jack and I were brothers and had been good old chums all our lives—I had taught him a bit of boxing and he was most promising with the gloves, and we had a widowed mother to keep; so I really felt as if something had gone snap in my head and that all I cared for was to get my revenge from the Germans. The last words I heard him say were, "Well, Bill, I'm going right into the firing line," and I remember laughing and saying, "Yes, Jack, but you're not the only one who's going to do that."

Jack laughed too and said, "All right, Bill, I'll see you in the firing line," and with that he went and I saw no more of him.

I had been in the regiment five years and nine months when the war broke out and Jack had served more than two years. I had become a corporal and he was a lance-corporal.

The days in the beginning were swelteringly hot; but the "Die-Hards," being typical Cockneys, made the best of them. Our Brigade consisted of ourselves (the 4th Middlesex), the 2nd Royal Scots, the 1st Gordon Highlanders and the 2nd Royal Irish Rifles. We began operations with trench digging, one particular trench, the machine-gun trench, being allotted to B Company. I helped to superintend the construction of the trenches, and I was proud of the work when I saw what was done from them when the Germans showed themselves.

Our machine-gun caused enormous havoc amongst the German ranks, and I am sure that my brother did his part in settling a lot of them, for he was keen on his work and full of go. The Royal Irish at this stage were fighting hard—they were not more than 350 yards from the enemy, separated from them by a railway—and they were lucky enough to fetch one gun out of action again, but the enormously superior numbers of the Germans told and the famous retreat began. The machine-gunners had suffered very heavily and it was hard to learn anything definite about the position in the trenches.

Officers and men were falling everywhere on both sides, and I saw a reconnoitring patrol of *Uhlans* bowled over in trying to avoid some of the 4th Royal Fusiliers. An officer and seven men of the *Uhlans* were killed in that little affair without getting in a shot in return. It was not much, but it was something cheering after what we had gone through at Mons. We looked upon it as a bit of sport, and after that we went into *châteaux*, *cafés* and other places, and discussed affairs in a proper Tommy -like spirit. It is very strange, but if it had not been for the language I could have thought at times that I was back in Kilburn or in London, on strike duty again, as I was at the time of the railway trouble three years ago.

We were fighting a rearguard action for three days right off the reel, and doing that wonderful march to which "Kitchener's test" or anything like it was a mere nothing. Owing to the heat, we discarded overcoats, kits and in some cases rifles and equipment. Our transport was blown to pieces three days after Mons, which to the 8th Brigade is known as *the* Wednesday.

But lost kit and shattered transport mattered little to most of us, and certainly had slight significance for me, because the only thing I had in mind was this determination to get revenge. I am not exaggerating in the least, I am merely putting down on record the state of my feelings and wishing to make you understand how remarkable a change had come over me, an alteration such as is brought about, I take it, by war, and war alone. Perhaps, too, the excessive stress and strain of those early days of the war had something to do with my condition; but whatever the cause, there it was. Danger itself meant nothing, and I, like the rest of us, took the ordinary fighting and the incessant and truly horrible shell fire as a matter of course, a part of the day's work. I bided my time, and it came.

We had crossed the Aisne, a dangerous unit still, in spite of our losses, for we had received reinforcements from the base; but just before crossing the river we sat down on the road, waiting for a favourable opportunity to cross by a pontoon bridge which the Engineers were building. That pontoon replaced a bridge which had been blown up.

On the word "Rise" we fell in, and in doing so a man had the misfortune to shoot himself through the hand.

The colonel came up at once and ordered the injured man to go back to the hospital in a village about a mile and a half up the road, in rear of the bridge. I was told off to take him, and we went to a house that had been turned into a hospital, the people in it being typically French. There were some sad cases there, amongst them one of our own fellows who had been severely wounded and a trooper of the 4th Hussars who was the only survivor of a reconnoitring party. He had been shot while going through the village that morning. Just at that time we had had many losses of small bodies—in one case a sergeant and five men had been blown to pieces.

After I had got the wounded man into the hospital I asked the "*monsieur*" in charge of the house for some tea, which he very willingly produced—it had no milk in it, of course, but by that time I had almost forgotten that milk existed.

At this time the village was being shelled, but that did not affect the enjoyment of my tea-drinking, and after that refreshing draught and a chunk of "bully" and some biscuit crumbs which I found in the corner of a none-too-clean haversack, I "packed down" for the night.

At about four o'clock next morning I awoke and went back to the bridge, which my battalion had crossed on the previous day, the "Die-hards" being the first to cross. By this time we had got past the sweltering stage of things and had become accustomed to soaking weather, and on this particular morning I was thoroughly cold and wet and generally "fed up" with things; but I still glowed with the longing to get level with the Germans.

You must bear in mind that regiments had been broken up and scattered in the most astonishing manner and had become mixed up with other regiments, and I had lost my own and had to set to work to find it.

I got over the bridge and reached some artillery.

"Have you seen anything of the Middlesex?" I asked.

"Yes," the gunners answered, "they've just gone into action on the brow of the hill."

I made my way towards the top of a neighbouring hill and found that my battalion had taken up a position there, but I had to wander about aimlessly, and I did so till I came across one or two men who were separated from the battalion. They directed me to the actual position, which was on the ridge of the hill, and to the ridge I went and found that it was lined with remnants of the brigade.

I tried to find my own company, but could not do so, as it had been surprised in the night; so I attached myself to another and lay down with the corporal on the sodden ground.

Wet through, cold, hungry and physically miserable, but still tough in spirit, we lay there, wishing that all sorts of impossible things would happen.

The corporal showed me where he had hit a German scout. We watched the poor devil rolling about—then we finished him off.

In addition to the wet there was a fog, and under cover of this the Germans crept up and were on us almost before we knew of their presence.

The alarm was first given by a man near us who was suffering from ague or some such ailment and had been moaning and groaning a good deal.

Suddenly he cried, "Here they are, corporal! Fire at 'em!"

My loaded rifle was lying just in front of me. I snatched it up, and as I did so the Germans jumped out of the mist on to us, with loud shouts. I brought the first German down and my chum dropped one;

and we managed to fetch the officer down. He was carrying a revolver and a stick, like most German officers, so that you had no difficulty in distinguishing them.

When the alarm was given I gave a quick look over a small hump in the ground and then we were rushed; but I hated the idea of retiring, and kept on shouting, "Crawl back! Crawl back!"

Machine-guns and rifles were rattling and men were shouting and cursing. In the midst of it all I was sane enough to hang on to my fire till I got a good chance—and I did not wait for nothing.

Up came two Germans with a stretcher. They advanced till they were not more than twenty-five yards away, for I could see their faces quite clearly; then I took aim, and down went one of the pair and *"bang"* off the stretcher fell a maxim. The second German seemed to hesitate, but before he could pull himself together he had gone down too. I began to feel satisfied.

By this time the order to retire had been given and I kept on shouting, "Keep down! Crawl back!" and the lads crawled and jumped with curious laughs and curses.

In that excited retirement the man who was with me was shot in the chest. I halted for a little while to see what had really happened to him, and finding that he was killed I took his waterproof sheet and left him. I hurried on until I was in a valley, well away from the ridge; then an officer managed to get us together and lead us into a wood.

As we got into the wood I spotted a quarry. I said to the officer, "Is it best to go down here, sir?"

"I'll have a look—yes," he answered.

We went into the quarry, where there were Royal Scots, Middlesex, Gordons and Royal Irish.

The officer was afraid that we might be rushed, in which case we should be cut up, so he put a man out on scout. We were not rushed, however, and when the firing ceased we filed out and lined the ridge again, and there we lay, expecting the Germans to come back, but for the time being we saw no more of them.

By some means one of the Irishmen had got drunk and wanted to fight the Germans "on his own." He was shouting for them to come on and was wandering about. Soon afterwards he was found lying on the top of the hill, having been shot in the thigh. He was carried out of action and I have never heard of him since.

After that affair of the hill-crest we had a lot of trench work, and very harassing it was. For five days we stayed in trenches, so near to the enemy that it was death to show your head.

Trench fighting is one of the most terrible features of the war, for not only is there the constant peril of instant death, which, of course, every soldier gets accustomed to, but there is also the extreme discomfort and danger of illness arising from insanitary surroundings. Often enough, too, when a new trench was being dug we would find that we were working on ground that had been previously occupied, and the spades brought up many a ghastly reminder of an earlier fight.

Sometimes in this warfare we were so very close to the Germans that when we sang hymns—and many a hymn that a soldier has sung at his mother's knee has gone up from the trenches from many a brave lad who has given his life for his country—the Germans would harmonise with them. It was strange to hear these men singing like that and to bear in mind that they were the soldiers who had done such monstrous things as we saw during the retreat, when they thought that certain victory was theirs. Time after time, with my own eyes, I saw evidence of the brutal outrages of the German troops, especially on women and children, yet it seems hard to convince some of the people at home that these things have been done.

At one time in the trenches, for a whole week, we were so situated that we dare not even speak for fear of revealing our position—we were subjected to an enfilade fire and did not dare to speak or light a fire, which meant that we had no hot food for a week, and we could not even smoke, which was the biggest hardship of all for a lot of the lads. We were thankful when we were relieved; but were sorry indeed to find how dearly the newcomers paid for their experience. We had been cramped and uncomfortable, but pretty safe, and the Germans had not been able to get at us to do us any real mischief, but our reliefs walked about as unconcernedly as if they were on furlough, with the result that on the very first night they went into action they lost a hundred men.

The system of trenches grew into a sort of enormous gridiron, and if you walked about—which you could only attempt to do at night—you were almost certain to drop into a trench or a hole of some sort. This made getting about a very exciting job, and it added enormously to the intense strain of fighting in the trenches, a strain which was hardest to bear in the night-time, when we were constantly expecting attacks and when the Germans adopted all kinds of devices to get at us.

I remember going into one church after the Germans had occupied it and being shocked at their conduct. In this particular place they had been able to lay hands on a good deal of champagne and they had drunk to excess, turning the church into a drinking-place, so that when we reached it there was an indescribable scene—filthy straw on the floor, empty champagne bottles littered everywhere, and the whole building degraded and desecrated.

The Germans had got a French uniform and stuffed it with straw and propped it up to resemble a man, and on the uniform they had stuck a piece of paper with some writing on it in German. I do not know what the writing was, but I took it to be some insult to the brave men who were defending their country and preventing the Germans from getting anywhere near Paris.

But that dirty fighting does not mean that the Germans do not fight bravely—far from it; they are hard cases, especially when they are in overwhelming numbers, which is the form of fighting that they like best of all. They are great believers in weight and hurling masses of men at a given point, and they are absolutely mad at times when their opponents are the English.

I will tell you of a case which illustrates this particular hatred. One night we were attacked by the Germans, though there was but little hope of them doing anything serious, in view of the fact that we were in trenches and that there were the barbed wire entanglements everywhere. There had been no sign of an attack, but in the middle of the night a furious assault was made upon us and a young German by some extraordinary means managed to get through the entanglements. An officer of the Buffs was near us, and in some way which I cannot explain the German managed to reach him. With a fierce cry he sprang directly at the officer, put an arm round his neck, and with the revolver which he held in the other hand shot him.

It was the work of a moment; but it succeeded—so did our bayonet attack on the German, for almost as soon as his shot had rung out in the night a dozen bayonets had pierced him. He died very quickly, but not before he had managed to show how intensely he hated all the English. He was a fine young fellow, not more than seventeen or eighteen years old, and it was impossible not to admire the courage and cleverness he had shown in getting through the awful barbed wire entanglements and hurling himself upon us in the trenches in the middle of the night. The point that puzzles me even now, when I recall the incident, is how the young German managed to make such a clean jump for the officer. I daresay there was something more than luck in it.

At this time we were with the Buffs, who told us that they were being badly troubled by snipers. I was in a trench with Lieutenant Cole, who was afterwards killed, and he said to me, "Corporal, the snipers are worrying our people, but it's very difficult to locate them. Try and see what you can make out of it."

It was very difficult, but I set to work to try and make something out. Before long, with the help of the glasses, I concluded that the sniping came from a wood not far-away, and I told the officer that I thought they were in a tree there. The consequence was that a platoon loaded up, went round, concentrated their fire on this particular spot and brought down two German roosters from a tree. We were glad to be rid of the pests, and they ought to have been satisfied, for they had had a very good innings.

I have been telling about the determination I had to be revenged for my brother's death. That was my great object, and I kept it in mind before anything else—and I think I carried it out. Apart from any motive, it is the British soldier's duty to do everything he can to settle the enemy, especially the Germans, and I am glad that I did my bit in this respect.

Now listen to what has really happened. After all that fighting and suffering with the grand old "Die-Hards" I got my own turn, after many wonderful escapes. A shell burst near me and the fragments peppered me on the, right hand here and about this side of the body, and bowled me out for the time being. I was sent home, and here I am in London again, getting well and expecting the call to come at any time to go back to the front.

Look at this postcard. It is written, as you see, by a British soldier who is a prisoner of war in Germany, and it tells the glad news that my brother, who, I was told, was killed months ago by a bursting shell, is not dead, but is alive and well, although he is a prisoner of war.

CHAPTER 8

Life in the Trenches

The first winter of the war was marked by an abnormal rainfall and storms of uncommon severity: also by the extraordinary development of trench warfare. The rain and storms, the frost and snow, made it impossible to carry out the greater operations of campaigning, with the result that both sides dug themselves in and fought from rival trenches which in many cases were separated by only a few yards. This story deals with life in the trenches, at La Bassée, and it gives an understanding of the privations that have been borne by British soldiers. The teller is Private G. Townsend, 2nd Battalion East Lancashire Regiment, who has had more than six years' service with the colours. These long-service men have compelled the attention of even the Germans who despised the "contemptible little army."

When the rebellion broke out in South Africa we—the old "Lily Whites"—were the only imperial regiment kept in that country. We were sitting still and stiff for twenty days, till General Botha got his own troops ready. During that time we were guarding Cape Town, and it took us all we knew to hold in, because the big war was on, and we were about seven thousand miles away from the seat of it. We had to wait till General Botha was ready, and that was not for more than a month after the British and the Germans met in Belgium.

We were eager to get away from South Africa, and at last we sailed—but what a slow voyage it was! Almost a record, I should think. We were thirty-two days getting to Southampton; but that was because we had halts on the way and were convoyed by some of the British warship. We had with us a cruiser which on a later day, though we thought her slow, knocked more speed out of herself than the builders ever dreamed of, and that was when she helped to sink the

German warships off the Falkland Islands.

By the time we reached the south of England some big things had happened, and we were keener than ever to get to the front. We had not long to wait. We landed, and in less than a week we left England and crossed over to France, where we went into billets for four days, to settle down. From the billets we marched nearly seven miles and went into trenches. For three full months, in the worst time of a very bad year, I ate and drank, and slept and fought, in trenches, with intervals in billets, sometimes up to the hips in water and often enough sleeping on a thick couch of mud. I cannot go into too much detail, but I can say that our officers always tried to go one better than the Germans, for the sake of the men—and for the most part they succeeded. We have picked up a lot from the Germans in this trench game. They have a main trench and about four trenches behind that, the first of the four being about twenty yards away; so that if you knock them out of one you knock them into another.

That march to the trenches was a thing that can never be forgotten. It was very dark and raining heavily, so that we were thoroughly soaked; but we had no time to think of that, for we were bound for the firing line, we were going to fight for the first time, and we wondered who amongst us would be absent when the next roll was called. The trench to which we were bound was in its little way famous. It had been the scene of some terrible fighting. The Indian troops were holding it, but they had been driven out by the Germans, who took possession and thought they were going to hold it; but the Connaught Rangers made a desperate charge, routed the Germans with the bayonet and retook the trenches. The Connaughts won, but at a very heavy cost, and about 150 of the brave fellows fell and were buried near the little bit of sodden, muddy ground on which they had fought. It was to relieve the Connaughts that we went into the trenches on La Bassée Road that stormy night.

It was not a very cheerful beginning, and as much unlike going into action as anything you can imagine. But we felt queer, this being our first taste of fighting, as we slipped into the trenches with our rifles loaded and prepared to fire in the wild night at an enemy we could not see. As soon as we went into the trenches we were ankle-deep in mud, and we were in mud, day and night, for seventy-two hours without a break. That was the beginning of three solid months of a sort of animal life in trenches and dug-outs, with occasional breaks for the change and rest in billets without which it would not be possible to live.

In a storm-swept trench—a barricade trench we called it—pointing my rifle at an enemy I could not see, I fired my first shot in battle. My section of thirteen men was in the trench which was nearest to the Germans, and that meant that we were separated from them by only a very few dozen yards. An officer of the Connaughts had given a descriptive object to fire at, and this was a small white outhouse which could be dimly made out in the darkness. The outhouse had the German trenches just in front of it, and we made a target of the building in the hope of potting the men in the trenches.

The order came, one man up and one man down, which meant that a man who was firing was standing for two hours and the man who was down was sitting or otherwise resting, or observing, as we call it.

Throughout that long night we kept up fire from the trenches, all anxious for the day to break, so that we could see what sort of a place we were in and what we were doing; but when the melancholy morning broke there was nothing to see in front of us except the portholes of the German trenches.

We had got through the first night of battle safely and had given the Germans good-morning with what we came to call the "awaking fire," though it sent many a man to sleep for the last time—and we were settling down to make some tea. That was shortly after midday of our first day in the trenches. I was working "partners" with my left-hand man, Private Smith, who said, "I'll just have a look to see what's going on."

He popped his head over the top of the trench 'and almost instantly he fell into my arms, for he had been shot—there must have been a sniper waiting for him—and had received what proved to be a most extraordinary wound. A bullet had struck him on the side of the head, just below the ear, and gone clean through and out at the other side, leaving a hole on each side.

"I'm hit!" said Smith, as he fell—that was all.

I was badly upset, as this was the first man I had seen shot, and being my special chum it came home to me; but I didn't let that prevent me from doing my best for him. Smith was quite conscious, and a plucky chap, and he knew that there was nothing for it but to see it through till night came. We bandaged him up as best we could and he had to lie there, in the mud and water and misery, till it was dark, then he was able to walk away from the trench to the nearest first-aid station, where the doctor complimented him on his courage and told him what an extraordinary case it was and what a miraculous escape he had had. Later on Smith was invalided home.

During the whole of that first spell in trenches we had no water to drink except what we fetched from a natural trench half-a-mile away. Men volunteered for this duty, which was very dangerous, as it meant hurrying over open ground, and the man who was fetching the water was under fire all the time, both going and coming, if the Germans saw him. This job was usually carried out a little before daybreak, when there was just light enough for the man to see, and not enough for the Germans to spot him; and a chap was always thankful when he was safely back in the trench and under cover.

At the end of the seventy-two hours we left the trenches. We came out at ten o'clock at night, expecting to be out for three days. We marched to an old barn which had been pretty well blown to pieces by shells, and into it we went; but it was no better than the trenches. The rain poured on to us through the shattered roof and it was bitterly cold, so that I could not sleep. We had everything on, so as to be ready for a call instantly, and without so much as a blanket I was thoroughly miserable. Instead of having three days off we were ordered to go into a fresh lot of trenches, and next afternoon we marched into them and there we stayed for six weeks, coming out seven or eight times. In these trenches we were in dug-outs, so that we got a change from standing sometimes hip-deep in mud and water by getting into the dugout and resting there. A dugout was simply a hole made in the side of the trench, high enough to be fairly dry and comfortable.

During the whole of these six weeks it meant practically death to show yourself, and so merciless was the fire that for the whole of the time a dead German soldier was lying on the ground about a hundred yards away from us. He was there when we went and was still there when we left. We could not send out a party to bury him and the Germans themselves never troubled about the poor beggar. One day a chum of mine, named Tobin, was on the look-out when his rifle suddenly cracked, and he turned round and said, "I've hit one." And so he had, for he had knocked a German over not far away and no doubt killed him.

What with the weather and the mud and the constant firing we had a very bad time. Each night we had four hours' digging, which was excessively hard work, and if we were not digging we were fetching rations in for the company. These rations had to be fetched at night from carts three-quarters of a mile away, which was the nearest the drivers dare bring them. These expeditions were always interesting, because we never knew what we were going to get—sometimes it would be a fifty-pound tin of biscuits and sometimes a bag of letters or a lot of cigarettes, but whatever it was we took it to our dug-outs, just as animals take food to their holes, and the things were issued next morning.

One way and another we had between fifty and sixty men wounded in our own particular trenches, mostly by rifle fire, though occasionally a shell would burst near us and do a lot of mischief; and what was happening in our own trenches was taking place all around La Bassée. We should have suffered much more heavily if we had not been provided with periscopes, which have saved many a precious life and limb.

We paid very little attention to the German shell fire, and as for the "Jack Johnsons" we took them as much as a matter of course as we took our breakfast. Some of the German artillery fire actually amused us, and this was when they got their mortars to work. We could see the shot coming and often enough could dodge it, though frequently the great fat thing would drive into the ground and smother us with mud. For some of the German artillery fire we were really very thankful, because in their rage they were smashing up some farm buildings not far away from us. The cause of our gratitude was that this shelling saved us the trouble of cutting down and chopping firewood for warmth and cooking in the trenches. When night came we simply went to the farmhouse, and the firewood, in the shape of shattered doors and beams and furniture, was waiting for us. The farm people had left, so we were able to help ourselves to chickens, which we did, and a glorious change they were on the everlasting bully beef. A chicken doesn't go very far with hungry soldiers, and on one occasion we had a chicken apiece, and remarkably .good they were too, roasted in the trenches. Another great time was when we caught a little pig at the farm and killed it and took it to the trenches, where we cooked it.

When we had finished with the second lot of trenches we went into a third set, and I was there till I was wounded and sent home. These trenches were only about a hundred and twenty yards from the second lot, so that the whole of the three months I spent in .trenches was passed in a very little area of ground, an experience which is so totally different from that of so many of our soldiers who were out at the war at the very beginning, and covered such great distances in marching from place to place and battle to battle. These chaps were lucky, because they got the change of scene and the excitement of big fighting, but the only change we had was in going out of one trench into another.

It was now the middle of December and bitter weather, but we were cheered up by the thought of Christmas, and found that things were getting much more lively than they had been. One night a splendid act was performed by Lieutenant Seckham, one of our platoon officers, and two of our privates, Cunningham and Harris.

An officer of the Royal Engineers had gone out to fix up some barbed wire entanglements in front of our trenches. The Germans were firing heavily at the time, and they must have either seen or heard the officer at work. They went for him and struck him down and there he lay in the open. To leave the trenches was a most perilous thing to do, but Mr. Seckham and the two men got out and on to the open ground, and bit by bit they made their way to the Engineer officer, got hold of him, and under a furious fire brought him right along and into our trench, and we gave a cheer which rang out in the night above the firing and told the Germans that their frantic efforts had failed. Mr. Seckham was a splendid officer in every way and we were greatly grieved when, not long afterwards, he was killed. Another of our fine young platoon officers, Lieutenant Townsend, has been killed since I came home.

We were so near the Germans at times that we could throw things at them and they could hurl things at us, and we both did, the things being little bombs, after the style of the old hand-grenade. We got up a bomb-throwing class and hurled our bombs; but it was not possible to throw them very far only twenty-five yards or so. The West Yorkshires, who were near us, got a great many of these missiles thrown at them, but they did not all explode. One day a sergeant of ours—Jarvis—was out getting wood when he saw one of them lying on the ground. He picked it up and looked at it, then threw it down and instantly it exploded, and he had no fewer than forty-three wounds, mostly cuts, caused by the flying fragments, so that the bomb made a proper mess of him.

Our own bombs were made of ordinary pound jam tins, filled with explosive and so on, like a little shell, which, as the case of the sergeant showed, was not anything like as sweet a thing to get as jam. The Germans were very fond of flinging these hand-bombs and seemed to

"We were so near the Germans that they could hurl bombs at us."

have a great idea of their value in attacks and defence.

Christmas Eve was with us, Christmas Day was soon to dawn—and what a strange and terrible Christmas it was to be!

On Christmas Eve itself we plainly heard the Germans shouting.

"A merry Christmas to you!" they said, and there was no mistaking the German voices that came to us in our trenches out of the darkness.

"A merry Christmas to you!"

Again the Germans greeted us, though we could not see them, and there was something pathetic in the words, which were shouted in a lull in the fighting. Some of our men answered the wish, but I did not—I had no heart to do so, when I knew that the message meant so little.

It may have been a matter of sentiment, because this was the time of peace on earth and goodwill towards men, or it may not; but at any rate the order came that if the Germans did not fire we were not to fire. But Christmas or no Christmas, and in spite of their greetings, the Germans went on firing, and we were forced to do the same, so throughout the night of Christmas Eve we had our rifles going and did not stop till it was daylight.

But the rifle fire was not the only sound of warfare that was heard—there was the sharp booming of artillery. The field batteries were hard at it and we knew they must be doing fearful mischief amongst the Germans. The night became truly awful; but how dreadful we did not know till Christmas Day itself, then, the firing having ceased, we saw that the ground in front of us, not very far away, was littered with the German dead.

A Merry Christmas!

The very men who had sent the greeting to us were lying dead within our sight, for the Germans had started to change their position and the British shells had shattered them. Something like two hundred and fifty of the Germans were lying dead upon the field, and sorry indeed must the dawn of Christmas Day have been to those who were left.

Peace on earth! There *was* peace of a sort, for as we looked on the German dead from our trenches we saw two Germans appear in full view, holding up their hands, to show us that they were unarmed.

You can imagine what a solemn spectacle that was—what a Christmas Day it was which dawned upon us in the trenches. We knew instinctively what was wanted—the ground was littered with the German dead and the Germans wanted an armistice so that they could bury them.

One of our officers went out and talked with the two Germans who were holding up their hands—covered by British rifles. He soon learned what they wanted, and the armistice was granted.

It was about three o'clock in the afternoon of Christmas Day when the Germans set to work to bury their dead, and as they did so we left our trenches and stood on the open ground and watched them. We saw them perfectly clearly, because the main German trench was not more than 120 yards away, and the burial took place a few yards behind this.

I have seen a photograph of British and German soldiers fraternising on Christmas Day; but there was nothing of this sort with us. The only incident I witnessed was a British officer shaking hands with a German officer. That was all. I did not shake hands with them—and I had not the least wish to do so, though I bore them no ill-will on that sad Christmas Day.

I was thankful when Christmas was over and we had settled down to ordinary routine work, killing and being killed, for it is astonishing how soon you get accustomed to the business of firing on and being fired at.

The trenches had got from bad to worse. When I first went into them there was eighteen inches of water and five inches of mud; but now it was a matter of standing almost up to the waist in water. They became so bad that instead of using the communication trenches, which you might almost call tunnels, it was decided that we should cross the open country to get to our fighting-place, the main trench— indeed, we had no option, because the communication trench was almost impassable.

On a mid-January night, and very bad at that, we began the journey to the trenches. If there had been just ordinary honest darkness we should have been all right and quite satisfied; but though there was darkness enough there was plenty of light—the uncanny brightness which came from the starshells.

Star-shells were going up all along the line and bursting. They are a sort of firework, giving a brilliant light, and as they exploded they showed us up almost as clearly as if we had been in daylight.

We had only a very short distance to go, but the star-lights made the journey to the trenches a desperate undertaking.

In single file, a little bunch of ten of us, crouching down, holding our loaded rifles and carrying all we possessed—we went along, losing no time.

From the stealthy way in which we started on our little trip you might have thought that we were burglars or villains bent on some fearsome job, instead of ordinary British soldiers getting back to their trenches.

We went with caution, and had not covered more than ten yards when what I take to be machine-gun fire was opened on us.

All at once, without the slightest warning, a real hail of bullets struck us, and of the ten men of us who were advancing in single file three were killed and four were wounded. The three who were shot down in the ghastly glare of the star-shells were ahead of me.

When that happened we were ordered to keep well apart and open out, but there was not much chance for those of us who were left; at any rate, no sooner had we obeyed and were making a little headway than I was struck myself on the head.

For half-an-hour or so I was unconscious; then I recovered and picked myself up and found that I was all alone. I crawled a few yards to a trench and got into it; but finding it full of water I thought I might as well be killed as drowned, so I got out, and not caring in the least for the German bullets or the star-shells, I made my way as best I could to the nearest dressing-station, and received attention. After that I found myself in a motorcar, and later at a clearing-station and on the boat for home.

You can see the scar of the wound here; but I don't bother about that. I suffer terribly from sleeplessness—and too often I see again the German soldiers who had wished us a merry Christmas—and were buried at the back of their trenches on the gloomy afternoon of Christmas Day.

CHAPTER 9

Sapping and Mining

In blowing up bridges, repairing the ravages of the enemy, in throwing pontoons over rivers, and in countless other ways, the Royal Engineers have contributed largely to the actions of the British operations in the war. These men, known a century ago as the Royal Sappers and Miners, have not only worked with the greatest energy since the war began, but they have also seen some hard fighting. This story of Sapper William Bell, 23rd Field Company, Royal Engineers, gives a picture of the many-sided operations of the corps whose mottoes are "Everywhere" and "Where right and glory lead."

Sheer hard work was the order of the day for our chaps from the time I landed in France from an old Irish cattle-boat till the day when I was packed off back to England suffering from rheumatic fever.

We worked excessively hard, and so did everybody else. Wherever there was an obstacle it had to go, and the infantry themselves time after time slaved away at digging and clearing, all of which was over and above the strain of the righting and tremendous marching. It was a rare sight to see the Guards sweeping down the corn with their bayonets—sickles that reaped many a grim harvest then and later.

It was during the early stage of the war that bridges were blown up in wholesale fashion to check the German advance, and the work being particularly dangerous we had some very narrow escapes. A very near thing happened at Soissons.

We had been ordered to blow up a bridge, and during the day we charged it with guncotton, and were waiting to set the fuse until the last of our troops had crossed over. That was a long business, and exciting enough for anybody, because for hours the men of a whole division were passing, and all the time that great passing body of men, horses, guns, waggons and so on, was under a heavy artillery fire from the Germans.

At last the bridge was clear—it had served its purpose; the division was on the other side of the river, and all that remained to be done was to blow up the bridge. Three sections of our company retired, and the remaining section was left behind to attend to the fuse.

Very soon we heard a terrific report, and the same awful thought occurred to many of us—that there had been a premature explosion and that the section was lost. One of my chums, judging by the time of the fuse, said it was certain that the section was blown up, and indeed it was actually reported that an officer and a dozen men had been killed.

But, to our intense relief, we learned that the report was wrong; but we heard also how narrowly our fellows had escaped, and how much they owed to the presence of mind and coolness of the officer. It seems that as soon as the fuse was fired the lieutenant instinctively suspected that something was wrong, and instantly ordered the men to lie flat, with the result that they were uninjured by the tremendous upheaval of masonry, though they were a bit shaken when they caught us up on the road later. This incident gives a good idea of the sort of work and the danger that the Royal Engineers were constantly experiencing in the earlier stages of the war, so that one can easily understand what is happening now in the bitter winter-time.

An engineer, like the referee in a football match, sees a lot of the game, and it was near a French village that we had a fine view of a famous affair.

We had been sent to the spot on special duty, and were resting on the crest of a hill, watching the effects of the enemy's field-guns.

Suddenly in the distance we saw figures moving. At first we could not clearly make them out, but presently we saw that they were Algerian troops, and that there seemed to be hosts of them. They swarmed on swiftly, and took up a position in some trenches near us.

The Algerians, like our Indian troops, hate trench fighting, and long to come to grips with the enemy. We knew this well enough, but we realised the peril of leaving cover and advancing towards an enemy who was very close, and who was sweeping the ground with an uncommonly deadly fire.

Putting all fear aside, remembering only their intense desire to come to grips, giving no thought to what must happen to them, the Algerians with enthusiastic shouts sprang from the trenches and bounded, across the shell-swept zone that separated them from the annihilating gunfire of the enemy.

What happened was truly terrible. The Algerians were literally mowed down, as they charged across the deadly zone, and for a piece of sheer recklessness I consider that this attack was as good—or as bad—as the charge of the Light Brigade.

The Algerians were cut to pieces in the mad attempt to reach the German batteries, and the handful of survivors were forced to retire. To their everlasting credit be it said that, in withdrawing under that terrible fire, they did their best to bring their wounded men away. They picked up as many of the fallen as they could and slung them across the shoulder, as the best way of carrying them out of danger.

I shall never forget the scene that met my eyes when we returned to the village. Women were weeping and wringing their hands as the survivors carried their wounded through the streets—for the French are deeply attached to their Colonial troops—and the men of the place were nearly as bad; even some of our chaps, who are not too easily moved, were upset.

While in this locality we had a very warm time of it, for we were continuously under artillery fire. We were in a remarkably good position for seeing the battle, some of our batteries being on our right, some on our left, and the German guns in front. It was really hot work, and when we were not hard at it carrying out our own duties, we took cover on the other side of a hill near the road; but some of our men got rather tired of cover, and found the position irksome; but if you so much as showed yourself you were practically done for. One day our trumpeter exposed himself, just for a moment; but it was enough. He was instantly struck and badly wounded.

At another time we were in our sleeping-quarters in a schoolhouse, and had an escape that was truly miraculous. We had settled down and were feeling pretty comfortable, when the Germans suddenly started shelling us; suddenly, too, with a terrific crash, a shell dropped and burst in the very midst of us.

Theoretically, the lot of us in that schoolhouse ought to have been wiped out by this particular shell, but the extraordinary fact is that though everyone was badly shaken up, only one of our men was wounded—all the rest of us escaped. Luckily we had the hospital men at hand, and the poor chap who had been knocked over was taken away at once to the doctors.

We had had a very hard, hot time, and were glad when the French came and relieved us, and gave our division a bit of rest and change. The Germans in that particular part were thoroughly beaten, and a batch of 500 who were covering the retreat were captured by the French.

They had started for Paris, and were very near it when they were bagged. I dare say they got to Paris all right. So did we, for we entrained for the city, but stayed there less than an hour. I had a chance of seeing something of the thorough way in which Paris had been prepared for defence, and on my way to Ypres I noticed how extensively the bridges that were likely to be of any use to the Germans had been destroyed. The loss in bridges alone in this great war has been stupendous.

When we entered Ypres it was a beautiful old cathedral city; now it is a shapeless mass of ruins, a melancholy centre of the longest and deadliest battle that has ever been fought in the history of the world. We had a rousing reception from the British troops who were already in the city, and a specially warm greeting from our own R.E. men, who gave me a huge quantity of pipes, tobacco and cigarettes from home, to divide amongst our company.

We were soon in the thick of the fiercest and most eventful part of the fighting. We were put to work digging trenches for the infantry and fixing up wire entanglements. The wire was in coils half a mile long, and what with that and the barbs and the weight, the carrying and dragging and fixing was a truly fearsome job.

And not only that, but it was extremely dangerous, because we were constantly under fire—sometimes we were fixing up wire within a few hundred yards of the German lines. Before getting to Ypres we had covering parties of infantry to protect us from snipers and sudden attacks; but at Ypres this protection was rarely given, because of the very heavy pressure on the firing line. We were ceaselessly sniped; but on the whole our casualties were remarkably few—but we were always known as the "Lucky Company."

In addition to doing this hard and dangerous work, we were roughing it with a vengeance. Our sleeping-quarters were dugouts in a wood, and were lined with straw, when we could get it. The enemy always make a special point of "searching" woods with shells, and we were so situated that we were pestered day and night by the German gunners, who were hoping to draw our artillery fire and so locate our own batteries. Anything like rest was utterly out of the question owing to these artillery duels, which were the bane of our life.

"We had a very warm time of it"

Silence was essential for our work, and we used muffled mauls—our big wooden mallets.

One moonlight night we were going to our usual duties when a shell flew past, exploding with terrific force within ten paces of us. We took it to be one of the Germans' random shots, but after going a short distance we had more shells bursting about us, and bullets whizzing, telling us that the enemy's snipers were at it again. Once more we justified our nickname of the "Lucky Company," for we had only one man hit—a fine chap, whose fighting qualities were well known to us, so we grinned when he said to me, after being struck on the shoulder, "I should like to have a look at that German, Bill!"

In the moonlight we offered a first-rate target to the hidden German snipers, and they certainly ought to have done more with us than just hit one man. I have mentioned this little affair chiefly by way of showing the constant danger to which field engineers are exposed.

The Germans at that time had their eyes on us properly, and the very next day they did their level best to make up for their sorry performance in the moonlight.

We had been told off to dig trenches for the infantry on our left, and we started out on the job. Rain had been falling heavily, the ground was like a quagmire, and we had to struggle through marshy ground and ploughed fields.

This was bad enough in all conscience, but to help to fill the cup of our misery the German snipers got at us, and gave us what was really a constant hail of bullets. We floundered on, doing our dead best to reach a certain wood. After floundering for some time, we were ordered to halt. By that time we had reached the wood, and the fire was truly awful.

Behind our tool-carts we usually fasten a big biscuit-tin, which is a big metal case, and as the sniping became particularly furious, four of our men bolted for shelter behind the biscuit-tin. I don't know what it is in the British soldier that makes him see the humour of even a fatal situation, but it happened that the rest of us were so tickled at the sight of our comrades scuttling that we burst out laughing.

But we didn't laugh long, for shells as well as bullets came, and we saw that the Germans were concentrating their fire upon us. They were going for all they were worth at the wood, and our only chance of safety lay in securing cover. We made a dash for the trees, and I sheltered behind one.

Then an extraordinary thing happened. A shell came and literally chopped down the tree. The shell spared my life, but the tumbling tree nearly got me. Luckily I skipped aside, and just escaped from being crushed to death by the crashing timber.

The firing was kept up for a long time after that, but we went on with our work and finished it, and then we were ordered to occupy the trenches we had just dug. We were glad to get into them, and it was pleasant music to listen to our own infantry, who had come into action, and were settling the accounts of some of the German snipers.

Later on we were told to get to a farmhouse, and we did, and held it for some hours, suffering greatly from thirst and hunger, in consequence of having missed our meals since the early morning. Some of our tool-carts had been taken back by the infantry, and this was a far more perilous task than some people might think, for the carts are usually filled with detonators, containing high explosives like guncotton, and an exploding shell hitting a cart would cause devastation.

The farmhouse was ranked as a "safe place," and we reckoned that we were lucky to get inside it; but it proved anything but lucky, and I grieve to say that it was here that my particular chum, an old schoolmate, met his death. We had scarcely reached the "safe place" when the cursed shells began to burst again, and I said to myself that we were bound to get some souvenirs. And we did.

My comrades had brought their tea to a hut, and I went there to get my canteen to take to the cookhouse. No sooner had I left the hut than I heard a fearful explosion. One gets used to these awful noises, and I took no notice of it at the time; but shortly afterwards I was told that my chum had been hit, and I rushed back to the hut. Terrible was the sight that met me. Eight of our men were lying wounded, amongst them my friend. With a heavy heart I picked him up, and he died in my arms soon afterwards. Two other men died before their injuries could be attended to—and this single shell also killed two officers' chargers.

It was soon after this that I went through what was perhaps my most thrilling experience. Again it was night, and we were engaged in our usual work, when suddenly we heard the sound of heavy rifle fire. Throwing down our tools, we grabbed our rifles. We had not the slightest idea of what was happening, but looking cautiously over the parapet of the trench which we were working on, we could dimly see dark figures in front, and took them to be Germans.

We were ordered to fire, the word being passed from man to man to take careful aim; but owing to the darkness this was not an easy thing to do. We fired, and instantly we were greeted with terrific shouting, and we knew that the Germans were charging. Not an instant was lost. With fixed bayonets, out from the trench we jumped, the infantry on our right and left doing the same.

Carrying out a bayonet charge is an experience I shall never forget. One loses all sense of fear, and thinks of nothing but going for and settling the enemy. For my own part I distinctly recollect plunging my bayonet into a big, heavy German, and almost instantly afterwards clubbing another with the butt of my rifle. It was only a short fight, but a very fierce one. The Germans gave way, leaving their dead and wounded behind them.

When the charge was over we went back to our trenches, taking our wounded with us. Our company's casualties numbered about a dozen, the majority of the men suffering from more or less serious wounds; but we were pretty well satisfied, and felt that we had earned our sleep that night.

The next day I had another close shave, a shell bursting very near me and killing twelve horses belonging to the 15th Hussars, who were on patrol duty.

After seven weeks of this famous and awful fighting at Ypres, I was taken ill with rheumatic fever—and no wonder, after such work, and sleeping in such places as we were forced to occupy. After a spell in the hospital at Ypres, I was moved on from place to place, till I made the final stage of the journey to England.

A remarkable thing happened during one of the heavy bombardments that we endured. A shell came and fell plump in the midst of us, and it really seemed as if we were all doomed. But the shell did not explode, and on examining the cap, it was found to bear the number "23." That, you will remember, is the number of my own company, so you can understand that we felt more justified than ever in calling ourselves the "Lucky Company."

CHAPTER 10

Royal Horse Artillery's Stand

Not one of the almost numberless valiant deeds of the war has proved more exceptional than the exploit of L Battery, Royal Horse Artillery, at Nery, near Compiègne, on September 1st, 1914. After greatly distinguishing itself at Mons, the battery helped to cover the retreat of the Allies, and fought a heavy rearguard action. On the last day of the retirement the battery unexpectedly came into action at very close range with an overwhelmingly superior German force. So destructive was the fire which was brought to bear on the battery that only one British gun was left in action, and this was served, until all the ammunition was expended, by Battery-Sergeant-Major Dorrell, Sergeant Nelson, Gunner H. Darbyshire and Driver Osborne, all the rest of the officers and men of the battery having been killed or wounded. At the close of the artillery duel the Queen's Bays and I Battery came to the rescue, and the shattered remnant of L Battery came out of the tremendous fray. This story is told by Gunner Darbyshire, who, with Driver Osborne, was awarded the distinction of the Médaille Militaire of France, while the sergeant-major and Sergeant Nelson for their gallantry were promoted to second-lieutenants, and awarded the Victoria Cross.

As soon as we got into touch with the Germans—and that was at Mons—they never left us alone. We had a hot time with them, but we gave them a hotter. Mons was a terrible experience, especially to men going straight into action for the first time, and so furious was the artillery duel that at its height some of the British and German shells actually struck each other in the air. In less than an hour we fired nearly six hundred rounds—the full number carried by a battery of six guns. But I must not talk of Mons; I will get to the neighbourhood of Compiègne, and tell of the fight that was sprung on the battery and left only three survivors.

All through the retreat we had been fighting heavily, and throughout the day on August 31st we fought till four o'clock in the afternoon; then we were ordered to retire to Compiègne. It was a long march, and when we got to Nery, near Compiègne, early in the evening, both horses and men were utterly exhausted and very hungry. As soon as we got in we gave the horses some food—with the mounted man the horse always comes first—and made ourselves as comfortable as possible.

Outposts were put out by the officers, and the cavalry who were with us, the 2nd Dragoon Guards (Queen's Bays), were in a small field on the side of a road which was opposite to us. That road was really a deep cutting, and I want you to bear it in mind, because it largely proved the salvation of the few survivors of the battery at the end of the fight. For the rest, the country was just of the sort you can see in many places in England—peaceful, fertile and prosperous, with farms dotted about, but nobody left on them, for the warning had been given that the German hordes were marching, and the people had fled in terror.

Having made all our dispositions, we went to sleep, and rested till half-past three in the morning, when we were roused and told to get ready to march at a moment's notice.

The darkness seemed to hang about more than usual, and the morning was very misty; but we did not pay much attention to that, and we breakfasted and fed the horses. We expected to be off again, but the battery was ordered to stand fast until further notice.

In war-time never a moment is wasted, and Sergeant-Major Dorrell thought that this would be a good opportunity to water the horses, so he ordered the right half-battery to water, and the horses were taken behind a sugar factory which was a little distance away. The horses were watered and brought back and hooked into the guns and waggons; then the left half-battery went to water.

Everything was perfectly quiet. Day had broken, and the landscape was hidden in the grey veil of the early morning. All was well, it seemed, and we were now expecting to move off. A ridge about 600 yards away was, we supposed, occupied by French cavalry, and a general and orderly retreat was going on in our rear. Then, without the slightest warning, a "ranging" shot was dropped into the battery, and we knew instantly that the Germans were on us and had fired this trial shot to get the range of us.

Immediately after this round was fired the whole place was alive with shrapnel and maxim bullets, and it was clear that the battery was almost surrounded by German artillery and infantry. As a matter of fact, the French cavalry had left their position on the ridge before daybreak, and a strong German force, with ten guns and two maxims, had advanced under cover of the mist and occupied the position, which was an uncommonly good one for artillery.

We were taken completely by surprise, and at first could do nothing, for the "ranging" shot was followed by an absolute hail of shrapnel, which almost blew the battery to pieces.

The very beginning of the German fire made havoc amongst the battery and the Bays, and the losses amongst the horses were particularly severe and crippling. But we soon pulled ourselves together, with a fierce determination to save the battery, and to do our best to give the Germans a vast deal more than they were giving us.

"Who'll volunteer to get the guns into action?" shouted Captain Bradbury.

Every man who could stand and fight said "Me!" and there was an instant rush for the guns. Owing to heavy losses in our battery, I had become limber gunner, and it was part of my special duty to see to the ammunition in the limbers. But special duties at a time like that don't count for much; the chief thing is to keep the guns going, and it was now a case of every one, officer and man, striving his best to save the battery. The officers, while they lived and could keep up at all, were noble, and worked exactly like the men. From start to finish of that fatal fight they set a glorious example.

We rushed to the guns, I say, and with the horses, when they were living and unhurt, and manhandling when the poor beasts were killed or maimed, we made shift to bring as heavy a fire as we could raise against the Germans. The advantage was clearly and undoubtedly with them they were in position, they had our range, and they had far more guns and men, while we had half our horses watering by the sugar mill and shells were thick in the air and ploughing up the earth before we could get a single gun into action.

Let me stop for a minute to explain what actually happened to the guns, so that you can understand the odds against us as we fought. The guns, as you have seen, were ready for marching, not for fighting, which we were not expecting; half the horses were away, many at the guns were killed or wounded, and officers and men had suffered fearfully in the course literally of a few seconds after the "ranging" shot plumped into us.

The first gun came to grief through the terrified horses bolting and overturning it on the steep bank of the road in front of us; the second gun had the spokes of a wheel blown out by one of the very first of the German shells, the third was disabled by a direct hit with a shell which killed the detachment; the fourth was left standing, though the wheels got knocked about and several holes were made in the limber, and all the horses were shot down. The fifth gun was brought into action, but was silenced by the detachment being killed, and the sixth gun, our own, remained the whole time, though the side of the limber was blown away, the wheels were severely damaged, holes were blown in the shield, and the buffer was badly peppered by shrapnel bullets. The gun was a wreck, but, like many another wreck, it held gallantly on until the storm was over—and it was saved at last.

In a shell fire that was incessant and terrific, accompanied by the hail of bullets from the maxims, we got to work.

We had had some truly tremendous cannonading at Mons; but this was infinitely worse, for the very life of the battery was in peril, and it was a point-blank battle, just rapid, *ding-dong* kill-fire, our own shells and the Germans' bursting in a fraction of time after leaving the muzzles of the guns.

As soon as we were fairly in action, the Germans gave us a fiercer fire than ever, and it is only just to them to say that their practice was magnificent; but I think we got the pull of them, crippled and shattered though we were—nay, I know we did, for when the bloody business was all over, we counted far more of the German dead than all our battery had numbered at the start.

The thirteen-pounders of the Royal Horse Artillery can be fired at the rate of fifteen rounds a minute, and though we were not perhaps doing that, because we were short-handed and the limbers were about thirty yards away, still we were making splendid practice, and it was telling heavily on the Germans.

As the mist melted away we could at that short distance see them plainly—and they made a target which we took care not to miss. We went for the German guns and fighting men, and the Germans did all they knew to smash us—but they didn't know enough, and failed.

As soon as we got number six gun into action I jumped into the seat and began firing, but so awful was the concussion of our own explosions and the bursting German shells that I could not bear it for long. I kept it up for about twenty minutes, then my nose and ears were bleeding because of the concussion, and I could not fire any more, so I left the seat and got a change by fetching ammunition.

And now there happened one of those things which, though they seem marvellous, are always taking place in time of war, and especially such a war as this, when life is lost at every turn. Immediately after I left the seat, Lieutenant Campbell, who had been helping with 'the ammunition, took it, and kept the firing up without the loss of a second of time; but he had not fired more than a couple of rounds when a shell burst under the shield. The explosion was awful, and the brave young officer was hurled about six yards away from the very seat in which I had been sitting a few seconds earlier. There is no human hope against such injuries, and Mr. Campbell lived for only a few minutes.

Another officer who fell quickly while doing dangerous work was Lieutenant Mundy, my section officer. He was finding the range and reporting the effects of our shells. To do that he had left the protection of the shield and was sitting on the ground alongside the gun wheel. This was a perilous position, being completely exposed to the shells which were bursting all around. Mr. Mundy was killed by an exploding shell which also wounded me. A piece of the shell caught me just behind the shoulder-blade. I felt it go into my back, but did not take much notice of it at the time, and went on serving the gun. Mr. Mundy had taken the place of Mr. Marsden, the left-section officer. The latter had gone out from home with us; but he had been badly wounded at Mons, where a shrapnel bullet went through the roof of his mouth and came out of his neck. In spite of that dreadful injury, however, he stuck bravely to his section.

I am getting on a bit too fast, perhaps, so I will return to the time when I had to leave the seat of the gun owing to the way in which the concussion had affected me. When I felt a little better I began to help Driver Osborne to fetch ammunition from the waggons. I had just managed to get back to the gun with an armful of ammunition, when a lyddite shell exploded behind me, threw me to the ground, and partly stunned me.

I was on the ground for what seemed to be about five minutes and thought I was gone; but when I came round I got up and found that I was uninjured. On looking round, however, I saw that Captain Bradbury, who had played a splendid part in getting the guns into action, had been knocked down by the same shell that floored me. I had been thrown on my face, Captain Bradbury had been knocked down backwards, and he was about two yards away from me. When I came to my senses I went up to him and saw that he was mortally wounded. He expired a few minutes afterwards. Though the captain knew that death was very near, he thought of his men to the last, and repeatedly begged to be carried away, so that they should not be upset by seeing him or hearing the cries which he could not restrain. Two of the men who were wounded, and were lying in the shelter of a neighbouring haystack, crawled up and managed to take the captain back with them; but he died almost as soon as the haystack was reached.

By this time our little camp was an utter wreck. Horses and men were lying everywhere, some of the horses absolutely blown to pieces; waggons and guns were turned upside down, and all around was the ruin caused by the German shells. The camp was littered with fragments of shell and our own cartridge-cases, while the ground looked as if it had been ploughed and harrowed anyhow. Nearly all the officers and men had been either killed or wounded.

It is no exaggeration to say that the Germans literally rained shrapnel and bullets on us. A German shell is filled with about three hundred bullets, so that with two or three shells bursting you get as big a cloud of bullets as you would receive from a battalion of infantry.

The Germans had ten of their guns and two machine-guns going, and it is simply marvellous that every man and horse in our battery was not destroyed. Bear in mind, too, that the German artillery was not all field-guns—they had big guns with them, and they fired into us with the simple object of wiping us out. That is quite all right, of course; but they never gave a thought to our wounded—they went for them just as mercilessly as they bombarded the rest.

There was a little farmhouse in our camp, an ordinary French farm building with a few round haystacks near it. When the fight began, we thought of using this building as a hospital; but it was so clear that the place was an absolute death-trap that we gave up that idea very quickly, and got our wounded under the shelter of one of the haystacks, where they were pretty safe so long as the stack did not catch fire, because a good thick stack will resist even direct artillery fire in a wonderful manner. But the Germans got their guns on this particular stack, and it was a very bad look-out for our poor, helpless fellows, many of whom had been badly mangled.

As for the farmhouse it was blown to pieces, as I saw afterwards when I visited it, and not a soul could have lived in the place. Walls, windows, roof, ceilings—all were smashed, and the furniture was in fragments. A building like that was a fair target; but the haystack was different, and the Germans did a thing that no British gunners would have done. At that short distance they could see perfectly clearly what was happening—they could see that as our wounded fell we got hold of them and dragged them out of the deadly hail to the shelter of the stack, about a score of yards away, to comparative safety. Noticing this, one of the German officers immediately concentrated a heavy shell fire on the heap of wounded—thirty or forty helpless men—in an attempt to set fire to the stack. That was a deliberate effort to destroy wounded men. We saw that, and the sight helped us to put more strength into our determination to smash the German guns.

The Germans were mad to wipe us out, and I know that for my own part I would not have fallen into their clutches alive. My mind was quite made up on that point, for I had seen many a British soldier who had fallen on the roadside, dead beat, and gone to sleep—and slept for the last time when the Germans came up. On a previous occasion we passed through one place where there had been a fight—it must have been in the darkness—and the wounded had been put in a cemetery, the idea being that the Germans would not touch a cemetery. That idea proved to be wrong. One of the German aeroplanes that were constantly hovering over the battery had given some German batteries our position, but we got away, and the German gunners, enraged at our escape, instantly dropped shells into the cemetery, to wipe the wounded out. If they would do that they would not hesitate to fire deliberately on our wounded under the haystack—and they did not hesitate.

It was not many minutes after the fight began in the mist when only number six gun was left in the battery, and four of us survived to serve it—the sergeant-major, who had taken command; Sergeant Nelson, myself, and Driver Osborne, and we fired as fast as we could in a noise that was now more terrible than ever and in a little camp that was utter wreckage. There was the ceaseless din of screaming, bursting shells, the cries of the wounded, for whom we could do something, but not much, and the cries of the poor horses, for which we could do nothing. The noise they made was like the grizzling of a child that is not well—a very pitiful sound, but, of course, on a much bigger scale; and that sound of suffering went up from everywhere around us, because everywhere there were wounded horses.

It was not long before we managed to silence several German guns. But very soon Sergeant Nelson was severely wounded by a bursting shell, and that left only three of us.

The Bays' horses, like our own, had been either killed or wounded or had bolted, but the men had managed to get down on the right of us and take cover under the steep bank of the road, and from that position, which was really a natural trench, they fired destructively on the Germans.

British cavalry, dismounted, have done some outstanding work in this war, but they have done nothing finer, I think, than their work near Compiègne on that September morning. And of all the grand work there was none more so than the performance of a lance-corporal, who actually planted a maxim on his own knees and rattled into the Germans with it. There was plenty of kick in the job, but he held on gamely, and he must have done heavy execution with his six hundred bullets a minute.

This rifle and maxim fire of the Bays had a wonderful effect in silencing the German fire, and it helped us greatly when we came to the last stage of the duel.

I don't know how many of the Bays there were, but it was impossible for them to charge, even if they had had their horses, owing to the fact that the road in front of us was a deep cutting. If the cutting had not been there the *Uhlans*, who alone considerably outnumbered us, would have swept down on us and there would not have been anyone left in L Battery at any rate.

By the time we had practically silenced the German guns the three of us who were surviving were utterly exhausted. Osborne, who was kneeling beside a waggon wheel, had a narrow escape from being killed. A shell burst between the wheel and the waggon body, tore the wheel off, and sent the spokes flying all over the place. One of the spokes caught Osborne just over the ribs and knocked him over, backwards.

I looked round on hearing the explosion of the shell, and said, "I think Osborne's gone this time," but we were thankful to find that he was only knocked over. One of his ribs was fractured, but we did not know of this till afterwards.

Meanwhile, the men who had gone to water the horses of the left-half battery had heard the firing? and had tried hard to get back to help us; but they were met on the road by an officer, who said that the battery was practically annihilated, and it would be useless for them to return. The Germans had seen them watering the horses, and had begun to shell the sugar factory. This caused the remaining horses of

"Planted a maxim on his own knees and rattled into the Germans."

the battery to gallop away, and a lot of them were killed as they galloped, though a good many got away and were afterwards found in the neighbouring town of Compiègne, wandering about. As for the men, they "mooched" in any direction as stragglers, and eventually we came up with them.

The three of us had served the gun and kept it in action till it was almost too hot to work, and we were nearly worn out; but we went on firing, and with a good heart, for we knew that the Germans had been badly pounded, that the Bays had them in a grip, and that another battery of horse-gunners was dashing to the rescue. On they came, in glorious style—there is no finer sight than that of a horse battery galloping into action.

Two or three miles away from us I Battery had heard the heavy firing, and knew that something must be happening to us. Round they turned, and on they dashed, taking everything before them and stopping for nothing till they reached a ridge about 2000 yards away; then they unlimbered and got into action, and never was there grander music heard than that which greeted the three of us who were left in L Battery when the saving shells of "I" screamed over us and put the finish to the German rout.

In a speech made to I Battery Sir John French said—

> No branch of the Service has done better work in this campaign than the Royal Horse Artillery. It is impossible to pick out one occasion more than another during this campaign on which I Battery has specially distinguished itself, because the battery has always done brilliant work. Your general tells me that you were in action continuously for ten days....

We had been pretty well hammered out of existence, but we had a kick left in us, and we gave it, and what with this and the Bays and the bashing by the fresh battery, the Germans soon had enough of it, and for the time being they made no further effort to molest us.

At last the fight was finished. We had—thank God!—saved the guns, and the Germans, despite their frantic efforts, had made no progress, and had only a heap of dead and wounded and a lot of battered guns to show for their attempt to smash us in the morning mist. We had kept them off day after day, and we kept them off again. We had been badly punished, but we had mauled them terribly in the fight, which lasted about an hour.

Three of our guns had been disabled, two waggons blown up, and many wheels blown off the waggons.

Some strange things had happened between Mons and Compiègne, and now that the duel had ended we had a chance of recollecting them and counting up the cost to us. Corporal Wheeler Carnham was knocked down while trying to stop a runaway ammunition waggon, and one of the wheels went over his legs. He managed to get on his feet again, but he had no sooner done so than he was struck on the legs by a piece of shell. At Compiègne two gunners were blown to pieces and could not be identified. Driver Laws had both legs broken by a waggon which turned over at Mons, and afterwards the waggon was blown up, and he went with it. Shoeing-Smith Heath was standing alongside me at Compiègne when the firing began. I told him to keep his head down, but he didn't do so—and lost it. The farrier was badly wounded, and the quartermaster-sergeant was knocked down and run over by an ammunition waggon. Gunner Huddle, a signaller, was looking through his glasses to try to find out where the shells were coming from, when he was struck on the head by a piece of bursting shell.

Our commanding officer, Major the Hon. W. D. Sclater-Booth, was standing behind the battery, dismounted, as we all were, observing the fall of the shells, when he was hit by a splinter from a bursting shell and severely wounded. He was removed, and we did not see him again until we were on the way to the base. As far as I remember, he was taken off by one of the cavalry officers from the Bays.

Lieutenant Giffard, our right section officer, was injured early in the fight by a shell which shattered his left knee, and he was taken and placed with the rest of the wounded behind the haystack, where in a very short time they were literally piled up. As soon as the officers and men fell we did the best we could for them; but all we could do was just simply to drag them out of the danger of the bursting shells. Luckily, this particular haystack escaped fairly well, but very soon after the fight began nearly every haystack in the camp was blazing fiercely, set on fire by the German shells.

The first thing to be done after the fight was to bury our dead and collect our wounded, and in this sorrowful task we were helped by the Middlesex Regiment—the old "Die-Hards"—who have done so well and suffered so heavily in this war. They, like I Battery, had come up, and we were very glad to see them. Some of our wounded were beyond help, because of the shrapnel fire.

We buried our dead on the field where they had fallen, amidst the ruins of the battery they had fought to save, and with the fire and smoke still rising from the ruined buildings and the burning haystacks.

Another thing we did was to go round and shoot the poor horses that were hopelessly hurt—and a sorry task it was. One waggon we went to had five horses killed—only one horse was left out of the six which had been hooked in to march away in the mist of the morning; so we shot him and put him out of his misery. We had to shoot about twenty horses; but the rest were already dead, mostly blown to pieces and scattered over the field—a dreadful sight.

When we had buried the dead, collected our wounded, and destroyed our helpless horses, the guns of our battery were limbered up on to sound waggon limbers, and a pair of horses were borrowed from each sub-section of I Battery to take them away. Everything else was left behind—waggons, accoutrements, clothing, caps, and so on, and the battery was taken to a little village about four miles from Compiègne, where we tried to snatch a bit of rest; but we had no chance of getting it, owing to the harassing pursuit of big bodies of *Uhlans*.

From that time, until we reached the base, we wandered about as best we could, and managed to live on what we could get, which was not much. We were in a pretty sorry state, most of us without caps or jackets, and we obtained food from other units that we passed on the road.

We were marching, dismounted, day and night, till we reached the rail-head, where I was transferred to the base and sent home. The sergeant-major and Osborne came home at the same time, and the sergeant-major is now a commissioned officer. So is Sergeant Nelson.

After such a furious fight and all the hardships and sufferings of Mons and the retreat, it seems strange and unreal to be back in peaceful London. I don't know what will happen to me, of course, but whatever comes I earnestly hope that some day I shall be able to go back to the little camp where we fought in the morning mist in such a deadly hail of shell, and look at the resting-places of the brave officers and men who gave their lives to save the battery they loved so well.

CHAPTER 11

Sixteen Weeks of Fighting

Indomitable cheerfulness and consistent courage are two of the outstanding features of the conduct of the British soldier in the war, and these qualities are finely shown in this story of some of the doings of the 1st Battalion Queen's Own Royal West Kent Regiment, which has greatly distinguished itself and suffered heavily. Private Montgomery is a member of a fighting family, for he has a brother in the Royal Navy, two brothers in the Rifle Brigade, one in the Army Service Corps, and one in the Royal Army Medical Corps, so that there are six brothers serving their country.

I don't know whether you have seen the picture of the retreat from Moscow, showing everybody going along in a drove, this, that, and the other way. You know it? Well, that wasn't a patch on some parts of the great retirement on Paris; but there was this enormous difference, that the retreat from Moscow was just that and nothing more, while our retirement was simply the beginning of what was to be a splendid victory.

It led up to the present tremendous fighting and this terrific trench work; and let me say that it is impossible for anybody who has not taken part in that trench warfare to realise what it means. Words and pictures will enable you to understand the life to some extent, but only by sharing in it will you fully realise its awful meaning.

But I'm not grumbling—I'm only stating a fact. Trench life is hard and dismal work, especially in a winter like this (1914-1915); but everything that it has been possible to do for the British soldier by the folk at home has been done.

Look at this—one of the new skin coats that have been served out to us. This is the way we wear it—yes, it certainly does smell, but it's goat-skin, and might have done with a bit more curing—and I can tell you that it takes a lot of even the wet and wind of the Low Countries to get through the fur and skin. These coats are splendid, and a perfect godsend.

I won't attempt to tell you about things exactly as they happened; I'll talk of them just as they come into my mind, so that you can understand what the Royal West Kents have done.

I can speak, I hope, as a fully-trained soldier, for I served eight years with the colours and two years in the Reserve before I was called up, and I did seven years abroad, in China, Singapore, and India; so I had got into the way of observing things that interest a soldier.

Well, one of my first and worst experiences was when at about ten-thirty at night the order for a general retirement was given, but through some mistake that order did not reach a sergeant and fourteen of the West Kents, of whom I was one, and it was not until just before four o'clock in the morning that we got the word, and began to try and pull ourselves out of it.

The Germans were then not more than eighty yards away from us, and our position was desperate. To make matters worse, the bridge by which we had to get across a neighbouring canal had been blown up, but as it happened the detonator on the overhead part of the bridge had not exploded, so that there was still a sort of communication across the water.

The bridge was full of wire entanglements and broken chains—a mass of metal wreckage—and the only way of crossing was to scramble along the ruins and crawl along what had been the iron parapet, which was only eight or nine inches wide. You will best understand what I mean if you imagine one of the iron bridges over the Thames destroyed, and that the principal thing left is the flat-topped iron side which you often see.

Under a terrible fire we made for the parapet and got on to it as best we could. I was the last man but one to get on to it. Just in front of me was Lance-Corporal Gibson, and just behind me was Private Bailey.

With the Germans so near, so many of them, and keeping up such a heavy fire on us, you can imagine what it meant to crawl along a twisted parapet like that. The marvel is that a single one of us escaped, but a few of us did, which was no credit to the German marksmanship.

The bullets whizzed and whistled around us and very soon both the man in front of me and the man behind were struck.

The corporal was knocked straight over and disappeared. Bailey was shot through the instep, but he managed to hold on to the parapet, and to make a very singular request.

"Mont," he said, "come and take my boot off!"

I turned round and saw what had happened to him; but, of course, it wasn't possible to do what he asked, when it needed every bit of one's strength and skill to hang on to the parapet and keep crawling, so I cried back, "Never mind about taking your boot off—come on!"

It was no use saying anything; poor chap, he would insist on having his boot off, so I said, "For Heaven's sake get along, or we shall all get knocked over!" And with that I started to crawl again, and to get ahead as best I could.

The corporal, as I have said, had gone; he had been hit right between the shoulder-blades, and I just saw him roll over into the horrible barbed-wire entanglements.

What exactly happened to poor Bailey I don't know. I hadn't a chance of looking back, but I heard afterwards that both he and the corporal were found lying there, dead, with their faces spattered with blood.

At last, after what seemed like a miraculous escape, I got clear of the parapet, with a few more, and landed safely on the other side of the canal, looking for the West Kents; but it had been impossible to re-form any battalion, and regiments were walking about like flocks of sheep. Efforts were being made to re-form our own men, but at that time there was no chance of doing so.

It was the sight of these disorganised and wandering soldiers that brought to my mind the picture of the retreat from Moscow.

It was not until we reached Le Cateau that the handful of us rejoined the regiment, and so far as fighting went we merely changed from bad to worse.

At Le Cateau the West Kents held the second line of trenches, and the Yorkshire Light Infantry were in the first line, so that we were supporting them. We had the 121st and 122nd Batteries of the Royal Field Artillery in front of us—and no troops could wish for better gunners than the British.

We got into the trenches at about four-thirty on the morning of the 26th, and remained in them for something like twelve hours, and during that time we took part in what was probably the fiercest battle that had ever been fought up to that time, though there was worse to follow in the Ypres region. We were rather unlucky, as it happened, because we were forced to lie in the trenches and watch the other regiments and our artillery shelling the enemy without our being able to fire a shot, for we were so placed that we could not do anything effective against the enemy just then.

The Yorkshire Light Infantry retired, and then came the order for the West Kents to go. It was an order that needed the greatest care and courage to carry out, but it had been given, and, of course, the West Kents always do just what they are told to do. We did so now, with the result, I am proud to say, that we carried out Colonel Martyn's command to the letter.

"Don't get excited in any way," he said. "Just go off as if you were on battalion parade."

And we did, and the colonel showed us how to do it, for he walked off just as he might have walked off the barrack square, though all the time we were under heavy shell fire and our men were falling. We lost a fair number, but not many, considering the nature of the fire upon us.

We got as far as St. Quentin, which is a big town, trying to find out where our regiment had gone; but we got cold comfort, for a man came up and said: "It's no good going in there. The town's surrounded. The best thing you can do is to put down your arms and surrender."

We didn't relish the surrender suggestion, and we started to make inquiries. A sergeant who spoke French went up to a *gendarme* who was at the side of the railway station, and asked him if it was true that the town was surrounded.

The *gendarme* replied that he didn't know, but he believed the statement was true; anyway he advised us to remain where we were.

Not satisfied with that, about half a dozen of us went up to a French cavalry officer and put the question to him.

The cavalry officer, like the *gendarme*, said he didn't know, but told us that the best thing we could do was to go on to a place, which he named, about eight miles away, and off we went; but before we reached it we came across a cavalry division, and learned that it was not safe to go farther. Again we were advised to remain where we were, and we did for the time being.

It was not until later that we discovered what a narrow escape we had had, for three German cavalry divisions had been ordered to pursue the retiring troops hereabouts, but through a blunder the order had miscarried and the *Uhlans* did not follow us.

In such a serious business as this we had, of course, lost heavily, and we continued to lose. Major Buckle, D.S.O., one of the bravest men that ever stepped in a pair of shoes in the British Army, lost his life in attempting to distribute the West Kents. That is merely one of many instances of officers and men who were killed under fire.

Sometimes men were lost in the most extraordinary manner, especially owing to shell fire. At one time about six big shells burst, and in the wreckage caused by one of the explosions ten men were buried.

Men volunteered to go and try to dig these poor fellows out, but as fast as the volunteers got to work they, too, were shelled and buried, so that in the end about thirty men were buried—buried alive. It was useless to attempt to continue such a forlorn hope, and it was impossible to dig the men out, so they had to be left. It was hard to do this, but there was nothing else for it.

Bodies of men were lost, too, as prisoners, when overpowering numbers of Germans had to be met, or when the Germans rushed unarmed men and left them no alternative to capture. A doctor and twenty-five men of the West Kents who were acting as stretcher-bearers were taken. Very splendid work is done by the stretcher-bearers, who go to the trenches every night to collect the wounded, and bring them in to the hospitals. All sorts of buildings and places are used as hospitals, and in this case it was the cellar of a house in a village that was utilised. The men were not armed, as they were acting as members of the Royal Army Medical Corps, to render first aid.

Just about midnight the Germans broke through the line and surrounded the village, and rushed in and captured the stretcher-bearers, and took them off, no doubt thinking they had gallantly won a very fine prize.

I remember this particular occasion well, because on the following morning we were reinforced by some of the native Bhopal Infantry, from India, and that took me back to the time I spent in that country. Little did I think in those days, when we were associated so much with the troops of the Indian Army, that the day would come when, in the heart of winter, we and the Indians would be fighting side by side in the awful Low Countries.

I got used to the heat of the day and the cold of the night in India, but it wasn't easy to become accustomed to the sweltering heat of the earlier days of the war, or the bitter cold of the winter.

One day, not long before I came home, we had six miles to do, after a very heavy fall of snow. We ploughed through the snow in the daytime, and at night we travelled in the transport, but what with the snow by day and the bitter freezing by night, we were fourteen hours covering that short distance—which works out at something under half a mile an hour. And that was the roundabout way we had to go to get at some enemy trenches which were only about fifty yards away from us. But, in spite of this terrific weather, we had only one or two cases of frost-bite.

A change on trench work and actual fighting came with my being told off as an ammunition carrier. There are two ammunition carriers to each company, and our duty was to keep the firing line well supplied with ammunition. This we fetched from the pack-mules, which were some distance away, and we took it to the men in the firing line in bandoliers, which we filled from the boxes carried by the mules. It was lively work, especially when the mules turned awkward and the firing was hot; but we got through it all right—Lance-Corporal Tweedale and myself.

One night, when the shell and rifle fire was very heavy, we went up to the firing line with ammunition, which was badly wanted, and we had such a hot time of it that the officer in charge advised us to remain for a couple of hours, till the firing slackened or ceased; but we had a feeling that it would be more comfortable in the rear, and as the matter rested with us we started off to get back.

This was one of the most uncomfortable bits of journeying I ever undertook, for in order to shelter from the fire of the Germans, which threatened every second to kill us, we had to crawl along a ditch for fully three-quarters of a mile. We crawled along in the darkness, with the bullets whizzing and shells bursting; but we lay low, and at last got out of it and landed back at the rear, which was certainly more agreeable than being in the very thick of the firing line.

I am proud to be one of the Royal West Kents, because they have done so well in this great war. "Give 'em a job and they'll do it," a general said of us, just after Le Cateau.

One day another general said, "What regiment is that coming out of the trenches?"

The answer was, "The Royal West Kent, sir," and the general promptly said, "For Heaven's sake give them a rest—they've earned it!"

But we hadn't gone more than two hundred yards when a staff officer told us to get into position in a field and dig ourselves in—and we were the last out of action that day.

At another time, when we had been hard at it, a general said: "Come on, West Kents! In another half-hour you'll be in your billets." And we went on, for that sounded very cheerful; but, instead of going into billets, we had half-an-hour's rest for a drop of tea—then we went on outpost duty for the night, and woke in the morning in a big scrap.

I am mentioning these things just to show how unexpectedly disappointments came at times; but we soon got into the way of taking these set-backs as part of the day's work.

When the winter advanced, the strain became uncommonly severe, but we were able to bear it owing to the first-rate system of relief we had—a relief which gave us as much change as possible on the confinement and hardship of the actual trenches.

Some very strange things happened in the trenches, and none were stranger than those cases of men being in them for long periods under heavy fire and escaping scot free, to be succeeded by others who lost their lives almost as soon as they got into their places.

There was one youngster—he could not have been more than seventeen or eighteen—who had been in France only about a fortnight. He was having his second day in the trenches, and, like a good many more who are new to the business, he was curious to see what was going on. This was particularly dangerous, as the Germans were only sixty yards away, and any seen movement on the part of our men brought instant fire.

The officer kept telling the youngster to keep down, and more than once he pulled him down; but the lad seemed fascinated by the port-hole of the trench—the loop-hole, it is generally called—and he looked through it again; once too often, for a German marksman must have spotted him. Anyway, a bullet came through the port-hole and struck the lad just under the eye, went through his brain, and killed him on the spot.

I will give you another curious instance, that of Sergeant Sharpe. It was his turn to be in reserve, but he had volunteered to go up to the trenches, to look round. He had scarcely had time to put his feet in them before a shot came and struck him between the eyes, killing him instantly.

I specially remember the sad case of the inquisitive youngster, because it happened on the very day I was wounded, and that was December 16. I was in a trench, sitting over a coke fire in a biscuit tin, when a bullet struck me on the chin—here's the scar—then went to the back of the trench, where it struck a fellow on the head, without seriously hurting him, and came back to me, hitting me just over the right eye, but not doing any serious mischief. After that I was sent into hospital, and later on came home.

On the way back I came across two very singular cases. One was that of a man who had had his arm amputated only a fortnight previously, and he was not used to it. He used to turn round and say, "I keep putting up my hand to scratch the back of it—and the hand isn't there!"

I saw another poor fellow—quite a youngster—who was being carried on a stretcher to the train. Both his legs had been blown off by a shell. I was right alongside when he said, "For Heaven's sake cover up my feet—they're cold." He lived for about half an hour after that, but never reached the train.

There is one thing I would like to say in finishing, and that is to thank our own flesh and blood for what they have done for us. I'm sure there never can have been a war in which so much has been done in the way of sending presents like cigarettes and tobacco; but I think that too much has been sent at one time, and that friends would do well to keep some of the good gifts back a bit. They will all be wanted later on.

CHAPTER 12

A Daisy-Chain of Bandoliers

In this story we become acquainted with a brilliant bit of work done by the brave Gurkhas, fresh from India, and we learn of a fine achievement under a deadly fire the sort of act for which many of the Victoria Crosses awarded have been given. The teller of this story was, at the time of writing, home from the front. He is Private W. H. Cooperwaite, 2nd Battalion Durham Light Infantry, a fine type of the Northerners who have done so much and suffered so heavily in the war.

I was wounded at Ypres—badly bruised in the back by a piece of a "Jack Johnson." There is nothing strange in that, and people have got used to hearing of these German shells; but the main thing about this particular customer was that it was the only one that burst out of eighteen "Jack Johnsons" I counted at one time. If the other seventeen had blown up, I and a lot more of the Durhams would not have been left alive. That same shell killed two of my comrades.

We went into action very soon after leaving England. We had had plenty of tough marching, and on the way we grew accustomed to the evidences of the Germans' outrages.

In one place, going towards Coulommiers, we came across tracks of the German Army. They had destroyed wherever they had passed, and amongst other sights our battalion saw were the bodies of two young girls who had been murdered. The men didn't say much when they set eyes on that, but they marched a good deal quicker, and so far from feeling any fear about meeting the Germans, the sole wish was to get at them.

After a four days' march we got to Coulommiers, where we came up with the French, who had been holding the Germans back and doing fine work. That was in the middle of September, when the

Battle of the Aisne was in full swing. On the 19th we went into the trenches, and after a spell in them we were billeted in a house. We had settled down nicely and comfortably, when crash came a shell, and so tremendous was the mischief it did that we had only just time to make a rush and clear out before the house collapsed.

It just sort of fell down, as if it was tired out, and what had been our billet was a gaping ruin. That was the kind of damage which was being done in all directions, and it told with sorry effect on those who were not so lucky as we had been, and were buried in the smash. All the cellars were crowded with people who had taken refuge in them, and they lived in a state of terror and misery during these continuous bombardments by German guns.

After that lively bit of billeting we returned to the trenches, and on Sunday, the 20th, with the West Yorkshires on our right, we were in the very thick of heavy fighting. The artillery on both sides was firing furiously, and the rifles were constantly going. Our own fire from the trenches was doing very heavy mischief amongst the Germans, and they were losing men at such a rate that it was clear to them that they would have to take some means of stopping it, or get so badly mauled that they could not keep the fight going.

Suddenly there was a curious lull in the fighting and we saw that a perfect horde of the Germans were marching up to the West Yorkshires, carrying a huge flag of truce.

It was a welcome sight, and we thought, "Here's a bit of pie for the Tykes—they must have been doing good." They had lost heavily, but it seemed from this signal of surrender that they were to be rewarded for their losses.

A large party of the West Yorkshires went out to meet the Germans with the flag, and I watched them go up until they were within fifty yards of the enemy. I never suspected that anything wrong would happen, nor did the West Yorkshires, for the surrender appeared to be a fair and above-board business.

When only that short distance separated the Germans and the West Yorkshires, the leading files of the surrender party fell apart like clockwork and there were revealed to us, behind the flag of truce, stretchers with machine-guns on them, and these guns were set to work at point-blank range on the West Yorkshires, who, utterly surprised and unprepared, were simply mown down, and suffered fearfully before they could pull themselves together.

Now, this dastardly thing was done in full view of us; we could see it all, and our blood just boiled. What we would have liked best of all was a bayonet charge; but the Germans were too far off for the steel, and it seemed as if they were going to have it all their own way.

They had given us a surprise, and a bad one; but we had a worse in store for them—we also had machine-guns, and they were handy, and we got them to work on the dirty tricksters and fairly cut them up. The whole lot seemed to stagger as our bullets showered into them. That was one of the games the Germans often played at the beginning of the war; but it did not take the British long to get used to them, and very soon the time came when no risks were taken, and the stretcher dodge was played out.

That Sunday brought with it some heavy fighting, and some very sad losses. There was with us an officer whose family name is very particularly associated with the Durham Light Infantry, and that was Major Robb, as good and brave a gentleman as ever breathed.

After that proof of German treachery he received information that the Germans meant to attack us again; but Major Robb thought it would be better to turn things about, and let *us* do the attacking. I dare say he was burning to help to avenge the losses of the West Yorkshires, the poor fellows who were lying dead and wounded all around us.

To carry out an attack like that was a desperate undertaking, because the Germans were six hundred yards away, and the ground was all to their advantage. It rose towards them, and they were on the skyline, so that it became doubly difficult to reach them.

Well, the order was given to advance, and we got out of our trenches and covered most of the distance in good order. Bit by bit we made our way over the rising ground towards that skyline which was a blaze of fire, and from which there came shells and bullets constantly.

There could be no such thing, of course, as a dash, however swift, towards the skyline; we had to creep and crawl and make our way so as to give them as little to hit as possible; but it was terrible—too terrible.

We fell down under that deadly blast, and though I am not a particularly religious man, I'll own that I offered up a prayer, and the man on my left said something of the same sort too. Poor chap! He had scarcely got the words out of his mouth, when over he went, with a bullet in his neck, and there he lay, while those of us who were fit and well kept up and crept up.

At last we were near enough to the skyline to give the Germans rapid fire, and we rattled away as fast as we could load and shoot, till the rifles were hot with firing. After that rapid fire we crept up again, and it was then that I saw Major Robb lying down, facing us, and smoking a pipe—at least he had a pipe in his mouth, just as cool as usual. He sang out to my platoon officer, "How are you feeling, Twist?"

Lieutenant Twist answered, "Oh, I'm about done for." I looked at him and saw that he was wounded in the chest and arm. We had to go on, and we could not take him back just then.

The lieutenant had scarcely finished speaking when I saw Major Robb himself roll over on his side. A poor lad named Armstrong, with four more of our men, crept up to attend to the major, but a piece of shrapnel struck the lad on the head and killed him—and other men were falling all around me.

There was no help for it now—we had to get back to our trenches, if we could; that was our only chance, as the Germans were hopelessly greater in number than we were. So we made our way back as best we could, and we took with us as many of the wounded as we could get hold of.

Time after time our men went back for the wounded; but, in spite of all we could do, some of the wounded had to be left where they had fallen.

We got back, the survivors of us, to the trenches, and we had hardly done so when we heard a shout. We looked up from the trenches, and saw Major Robb on the skyline, crawling a little way.

Instantly a whole lot of us volunteered to go and fetch the major in; but three were picked out—Lance-Corporal Rutherford, Private Warwick, and Private Nevison.

Out from the trenches the three men went; up the rising ground they crawled and crept; then, at the very skyline, Rutherford and Nevison were shot dead, and Warwick was left alone. But he was not left for long. Private Howson went to help him, and he actually got to the ridge and joined him, and the two managed to raise the major up; but as soon as that had been done the officer was shot in a vital part, and Warwick also was hit.

More help went out, and the major and Warwick were brought in; but I grieve to say that the poor major, who was loved by all of us, died soon after he reached the trenches.

That furious fight had cost the Durhams very dearly. When the roll was called we found that we had lost nearly 600 men, and that in my own company only one officer was left. This was Lieutenant Bradford, one of the bravest men I ever saw. At one time, when we had lost a young officer and a man with a machine-gun, Lieutenant Bradford worked the gun himself. I am sorry to say that he was killed in another battle later on.

Now I am going to leave the Valley of the Aisne and get round to Flanders, where we found ourselves near Ypres, faced by a big force of Germans.

Again we were with our friends the West Yorkshires—they were on our right, and on our left we had the East Yorkshires, so that there were three North-country regiments together. Near Ypres we soon had to carry out a smart bit of work which, in a way, proved very pathetic. The Durhams were ordered to take a small village, and we went for it. We reached a farmhouse, and there we found about a score of women and children. Some of our men were sent into the house, but they could not make the women and children understand English. The poor souls were terrified; they had had to do with Germans, and as they were not familiar with our uniforms they thought we were Germans too—another lot of the breed from which they had suffered so much.

We fetched Captain Northey to explain things to the women, and as he entered the house a shell burst near him and took off part of one of his trouser-legs, but without hurting him. The captain took no notice of this little drawback, and into the house he went, and made the women understand that we were English troops; and I can assure you that when they realised that they simply went wild with joy, and hugged and kissed us.

We had gone out to learn, if we could, something about the enemy's strength, and we got to know that there were about 30,000 Germans in front of our brigade, and that they were entrenched.

The Sherwood Foresters, who were in reserve to us, were ordered to relieve us, and it was wonderful to see they way in which they came into the village we had taken, smoking cigarettes as if they were doing a sort of route-march, although they came right up against a hail of bullets, with the usual shells. In face of such tremendous odds they had to retire; but, like good soldiers, they prepared another lot of trenches near the village, and later on we went into them.

In such fighting as this war brings about there are many, many sad incidents, and one of the saddest I know of occurred at this particular village. There was a fine young soldier named Matthews, who came from West Hartlepool, I think it was. He was struck by shrapnel, and we saw that he was badly hurt. We did what we could for him, but it was clear that he was mortally wounded, and that he knew it. His last thought was for home and wife, and he said he would like his cap-badge to be sent to her, to be made into a brooch. I believe that a comrade, who was also a neighbour of his, undertook to do this for him.

It was my good fortune to see the Gurkhas rout the enemy, who had attacked them, and to give the Germans a most unpleasant shock.

The Germans had been shelling the East Yorkshires, who were now on the right of the Durhams. The enemy had the range almost to an inch, and the effect of the shelling was terrible. Hour after hour this shelling was kept up pitilessly, and the German aeroplanes—"birds," we called them—swooped about and saw the havoc that was being done. This sort of thing went on till after dark, and the Durhams wondered if any of the East Yorkshires were left.

There was a surprise in store for us at dawn next day when we awoke, for the East Yorkshires' trenches were full of Gurkhas, who had slipped in during the night. The Germans knew nothing of this. All they knew was that their shells had been pounding on the East Yorkshires for hours, and doubtless they had satisfied themselves that no troops on earth could stand such a gruelling.

The Germans came on pretty confidently, after dawn, to the position of the East Yorkshires—came on in a cloud. That was after we had repulsed an attack on ourselves, but not finally, owing to the vast numbers of the Germans. Perhaps they expected to find the trenches filled with English dead and wounded, and certainly to us it seemed as if the trenches must be in that condition, for the Gurkhas let the Germans come on without showing a sign of life.

The Germans gave enough warning—as they always do. Bugles sounded, and they rushed on, shouting and yelling; but still there was no sound from the trenches, no sign of life was seen. Even we, who had a fine view of the trenches, could see nothing. We were intensely interested, though we had plenty of hard work to do ourselves in firing at the enemy.

When the Germans got to within about forty yards of the trenches on our left, the little fellows, who had been lying so low, sprang up and simply poured over the tops of the trenches. That performance was one of the most extraordinary things seen in the war. The Gurkhas never even attempted to fire; they just seemed to roll over the ground, gripping their long, curved knives.

We were too far off to see exactly what sort of expression came on the Germans' faces when the trenches, which were supposed to be choked with dead and wounded Britons, vomited these Indian warriors; but we saw the whole shouting, yelling line of Germans pull up sharp.

The Germans made a half-hearted effort to come on, then they wavered badly, and well they might, for by this time the little Gurkhas were on them with fury, and the blades flashed like lightning about the mass of startled Germans.

Stunned by the unexpectedness and swiftness of the Indian onslaught, terrified by the deadly wielding of the knives, the Germans made no real effort to withstand the rush from the trenches, and they broke and ran like rabbits, throwing down their rifles as they scuttled, with the Gurkhas leaping after them and doing fearful execution.

It was truly great, and as the victorious little warriors came back we gave them a cheer that was a real hurrah. We were as pleased as the Gurkhas were, and they showed their joy as they came back wiping their knives. They seemed all grin and knife as they returned, and we felt all the better for it, too, especially as we gave the broken, flying Germans a heavy peppering.

Only the Germans who were behind got away, or had a chance. Those in front, who had had to meet the Indians' swift, fierce spring, were done for as soon as the curved blades were whirling amongst them.

I had had a pretty good innings by this time, and had escaped serious injury, but I was very soon to be bowled out. The Durhams were supporting the West Yorkshires, who had been badly cut up. We received word that the West Yorkshires had run short of ammunition, and that fresh supplies were urgently wanted. We advanced with supplies, and found that we had to cover about fifty yards of open ground. The Germans had got the exact range of this open ground, so that it was impossible to advance over it, except singly. The shell and rifle fire was particularly heavy, and it seemed as if nothing could live on that exposed stretch.

One by one we made a dash across that awful space towards the trenches where the Yorkshiremen were hungering for fresh ammunition, and each of us carried a full bandolier for the Tykes. A good many of our men fell, but a lot got through and took part in a very strange bit of work.

I got through myself, after being blown down by the force of a shell explosion near me—thank Heaven it was the force and not the shell itself that knocked me over for the moment! It was terrible going, for we soon found, after we began to make the journey, that we could not quite reach the Yorkshires' trenches.

There were some haystacks on the open ground, and we dodged behind them and dashed from one to the other, every dash meaning a shower of bullets from the Germans.

There was still the last fifty yards I have mentioned to be covered; but now it meant almost sure destruction to be seen, so we threw the bandoliers to the end man in the trenches, the man nearest to us; but a full bandolier is a heavy thing, and there was not much chance of taking aim. We were almost at our wits' end, but we tried another way. We made a sort of daisy-chain of several bandoliers, and paid this out as best we could towards the trenches.

The nearest man in the trench—a plucky chap he was—slipped out and made a dart for the end of the chain. He just made a mad grab and got it. Then he dashed back to his trench, and it seemed as if the business was all over, and that the daisy-chain would be safely hauled in; but to the grief of all of us the chain broke when a few yards of it had been pulled in.

This was a dreadful disappointment, but still something had been done, some rounds of ammunition, at any rate, had been got into the trenches, and we were determined that the Tykes should have some more. We had to wait a bit, for as soon as the Yorkshireman had shot back to his trench, the ground that he had scuttled over was absolutely churned up by shells, and if he had been caught on it he would have been blown to rags. We lost no time in making other efforts, and at last the ammunition was safely delivered to the West Yorkshires in the trenches, and they did some rattling good business with it.

I have mentioned "Jack Johnsons," and I want to speak of them again by way of finish. It was at Ypres that I was bowled out. These "J.J.'s" were falling heavily, but many of them were what you might call dumb—they didn't speak. As I have said, I counted eighteen as they came, and out of the whole of that number only one exploded. But it was enough. I have already told you what happened to two of my comrades, and as for myself it settled me for the time being by badly bruising my spine and back.

And that's the reason why I was invalided home.

CHAPTER 13

Despatch-Riding

Particularly hard and responsible work has been done for the British Army by motorcycle despatch-riders. Many members of this fine branch of our fighting men abandoned very promising careers in civil life to go to the seat of war, Amongst them is Corporal Hedley G. Browne, Captain of the Norfolk Motor Cycle Club, who when war broke out volunteered for active service and became a motor cycle despatch-rider, attached to a signal company of the Royal Engineers. It is his story which is here retold. Of the work of the motor cycle despatch-riders Sir John French has spoken in terms of high praise, and when the king visited the front recently a number of the riders were specially brought to His Majesty's notice.

I was in Ypres, billeted in a brewery, when that beautiful old city was still intact; I was there when the first German shell came and began the ruthless bombardment which has laid the city in ruins and added one more to the list of heavy debts which the Germans will have to pay when the war is over. The sooner that time comes the better, especially for those who have been at the front since the beginning, and have had to endure things which people at home cannot possibly realise. Five days ago I left the front for a flying visit home, and now I am on my way back. It has seemed a very short spell, and a big slice of the time has been eaten up in travelling. A nice batch of us came over together, and here we are assembling again, though it's a good hour before the boat-train starts.

We go to Boulogne, and then we shall get into motor lorries and be trundled off back to the fighting line. This is the kit we work and live in—even now my revolver is loaded in every chamber. No, so far, I haven't used it on a German; but it's shot a pig or two when we've wanted pork, and really there isn't much difference between the two. It is hard to believe that human beings committed some of the acts of which I saw so many during those four months at the front. The astounding thing is that the Germans don't realise that they have done anything wrong, and quite lately I was talking with some German prisoners who spoke English, who not only did not see this, but were also quite sure that the war will end in favour of Germany. By this time, however, they are changing their tune.

When I got to the front I was attached to a signal company, which consists of establishing communication between headquarters and three brigades, and that meant when we were on the march riding through about seven miles of troops, guns, waggons and hosts of other things. When in action we had to go quite up to the firing line, and very soon I hardly knew myself, as I got quite used to the bursting of shells and to the shocking condition of the killed and wounded. It was astonishing to see how soon men, who had been used to every comfort at home and who knew nothing of war in any shape or form, got accustomed to the hardships of campaigning and developed a callousness which is altogether foreign to their real nature.

One of the most amazing things about the war is the way in which it changes a man and makes him callous. I know that before I had anything to do with the army I was so sensitive in some ways that the mere thought of blood was almost enough to make me ill, yet now, after being for more than four months in the war, and having seen the havoc of the most terrific battles the world has ever known, I tear along the lonely roads and remain almost unmoved by the most dreadful sights. The dead pass unnoticed, and as for the wounded, you can do nothing, as a rule. You have your orders, and they must be obeyed without loss of time, because a motor despatch-rider is always on the rush.

I well remember the very first German I saw lying dead. He was an *Uhlan*, and was on the roadside. I was greatly distressed at the sight of him, there was something so sad about it all, but now there is no such sensation at the sight of even great numbers of the dead. A strange thing happened in connection with the *Uhlan*. I took his cap as a memento, and brought it home, with several other German caps and helmets, chunks of shell, clips of cartridges, and relics of altar-cloths; and now, for some cause which I can't quite fathom, the *Uhlan's* cap has turned a queer sort of yellow.

That strange callousness comes over one at the most unexpected times, and often enough a motor despatch-rider has to dash through a crowd of refugees and scatter them, though the very sight of the poor souls is heart-breaking. When Ypres was bombarded, the men, women and children thronged the roads, and all that was left to them in the world they carried in bundles on their backs; yet they had to be scattered like flocks of sheep when the motor despatch-riders rushed along.

There was, however, one pleasing feature in the matter, and that was that these poor people knew that we were tearing along in their interests as well as our own, and that we did not mean to hurt anybody—which was different, indeed, from the spirit of the enemy, whose policy was to spread terror and havoc wherever he could, and to destroy mercilessly. When I first went into Ypres it was a beautiful old city, very much like Norwich, but I saw the German guns smash the place and the shells set fire to glorious old structures like the cathedral and the Cloth Hall. The two pieces of altar-cloth which I brought home were taken from the cathedral while it was burning.

Though you soon get used to war, still there are always things coming along which are either particularly interesting or very thrilling. Perhaps the most exciting incident I can call to mind is the bringing down of a German aeroplane by a British brigade. That was on October 27th, when I was with the brigade. It was afternoon, and the aeroplane was flying fairly low, so that it was a good target for the rain of bullets which was directed on it.

Even when flying low, an aeroplane is not easy to hit, because of its quick, dodging movements, but this machine was fairly got by the brigade. Suddenly there was an explosion in the aeroplane, flames shot out and the machine made a sickening, terrible somersault. I took it that a bullet or two had struck the petrol tank and blown the machine up—anyway, the airman was shot out and crashed to earth with fearful speed.

You wanted to look away, but an awful fascination made you keep your eyes on what was happening. At first the man looked like a piece of paper coming down, then, almost before you could realise the tragedy that was taking place, the piece of paper took the form of a fellow-creature—then the end came. The man himself smashed to earth about two hundred yards from the spot where I was watching, but the machine dropped some distance off. That was really one of the sights that no amount of war will accustom you to, and I shall never forget it as long as I live.

At first the weather was very hot, which made the work for the troops very hard. The machine I had was left to be handed over to the *Kaiser* as a souvenir; and several other machines in like manner. When a machine went wrong, it was left and a new one took its place—the list of casualties for motors of every sort is an amazingly heavy one; but casualties were inevitable, because in many places the roads that we had to take were perfect nightmares.

It was very hard going till we got used to it. During the first month at the front I had my boots off about three times—I am now wearing my fourth pair, which is an average of one a month—and we reckoned that we were lucky if we slept in a barn, with straw; if we couldn't manage that we turned in anywhere, in our greatcoats. When I say sleep, I mean lying down for an hour or two, as sometimes we did not billet till dark. Then we had some grub, anything we could get, and after that a message. Next day we were off, five times out of six, at 3.30 to four o'clock, and got long, hard days in.

Amongst the messages we had to carry there were none more urgent than those which were sent for reinforcements, the men upon whose coming the issue of a battle depended. It was tear and scurry all along, but somehow the message would get delivered all right and the reinforcements would hurry up and save the situation. Often enough a message would be delivered at midnight to a tired officer who was living in a dugout, and I scarcely ever reached one of these warrens without being invited to take something of whatever was going—it might be a drink of hot coffee, with a biscuit, or a tot of rum, which was truly grateful after a bitter ride. That is the only thing in the way of alcoholic drink at the front, and very little of it.

The shell fire was so incessant that it was soon taken as part of the day's work. At first it was terrible, though one got used to it. My first experience of rifle fire did not come until I had been at the front for some weeks, and then I was surprised to find what a comparatively small thing it is compared with shells—it is not nearly so bad.

It was getting dark, and it was my duty to go down a lane where snipers were hidden in the trees. This was just the kind of lane you know in England, and you can easily picture what it meant. Imagine leaving your machine, as I did, in a tree-lined lane at home, and going down it, knowing that there were fellows up the trees who were on the watch to pot you, and you will realise what it meant; but you will have to picture also the sides of the lane being littered, as this was, with dead and wounded men. Well, I had to go down that lane, and I went—sometimes walking, sometimes running, with the bullets whizzing round and the shells bursting. But by good luck I escaped the bullets, though a piece of shell nearly nailed me—or would have got me if I had been with my machine. The fragment struck the cycle and I picked it up and brought it home with the other things as a souvenir.

That escape was practically nothing. It was a detail, and came in the day's work; but I had a much more narrow shave a few days later. It was a Saturday and I had had a pretty hard time—amongst other things I had done a thirty-mile ride after one o'clock in the morning—the sort of ride that takes it out of you.

There was one of our orderlies with a horse near me and I was standing talking to him. We heard a shrapnel shell coming, and ducked our heads instinctively to dodge it—but the shell got at us. The horse was killed and the orderly was so badly hit that he died in less than an hour. He was buried in the afternoon, and very solemn the funeral was, with the guns booming all around. I was deeply shocked at the time, but war is war, and in a very short time the incident had passed out of my mind. Our fellows told me that I was one of the lucky ones that day.

That was the beginning of one of the most awful periods of the war, especially for the despatch-riders, for we were at it night and day. The roads were hopelessly bad, and as we were not allowed to carry any lamps at night the danger of rapid travel was greatly increased. We were, however, relieved to some extent by mounted men. The fighting was furious and incessant, and we were in the thick of a good deal of it. After a very hard spell I was quartered all day in a little stable, and it proved to be about the most dangerous place I had come across. On October 29th the Germans went for the stable with high explosives and the everlasting "scuttles." For some time these big shells came and burst in the locality, and two houses within a score of yards of us were blown to pieces and enormous holes were driven in the ground.

From the stable we went to a house, and then we fairly got it. Four huge shells came, one after the other, and one came and ripped the roof just like paper. We were amazingly lucky, however, for the worst thing that happened was that a fellow was wounded in the leg. I was thankful when the order came to pack up and stand by, for there were in that little place about twenty of us from different regiments, and a single explosion would have put us all well beyond the power of carrying either despatches or anything else. For a while we could not understand why the enemy should so greatly favour us, but we soon learned that they were going for some French guns near us. So the firing went on, and when we went to sleep, as we did in spite of all, bullets ripped through the roof, coming in at one side of the building and going out at the other, and four more big shells paid us a most unwelcome visit.

I was thankful when we moved out of those unpleasant quarters and took up our abode in a large farmhouse about three hundred yards away. This was one of the very few buildings that had escaped the ravages of the German artillery fire. We made the move on the 30th, when the cannonade was very heavy, yet the only casualties were a pig and two horses.

We were now much better protected from the Germans' fire, though the very house shook with the artillery duel and the noise grew deafening and almost maddening. I wrote home pretty often, and I remember that at this time I got behind a hedge to write a letter, and as I wrote bullets whizzed over my head, fired by German snipers who were up some trees not very far away. They were going for our chaps in the trenches a mile away.

Mons had been bad, and there had been many harrowing sights on the retreat, but at the end of October and the beginning of November the climax of horror was reached. The Germans, mad to hack their way through to the coast, and perhaps realising that they would never do it, stuck at nothing. They were frantic, and I saw sights that would sicken any human being. No consideration weighed with them, they simply did their best to annihilate us—but they are trying still to do that and not succeeding.

We had left the farmhouse and gone into a large chateau, which served as headquarters, and here, on November 2nd, we had a ghastly experience. It is likely that the Germans knew the particular purpose to which the *château* had been devoted; at any rate they shelled it mercilessly, and no fewer than six staff officers were killed, while a considerable number were wounded. Again I was lucky, and came out of the adventure unscathed. On the following day, however, I was nearly caught. I had taken a message to headquarters and was putting my machine on a stand. To do this I had to leave a house, and go about fifty yards away, to the stand.

I had scarcely left the building when two shells struck it fair and plump, and killed two motorcyclists and wounded three others. Like a flash I jumped into a ditch, and as I did so I heard the bits of burst shell falling all around me. When I got out of the ditch and went back along the main road I saw a huge hole which a shell had made. It was a thrilling enough escape, and shook me at the time, because I knew the two poor fellows who were killed. That was the kind of thing we went through as we jogged along from day to day.

I am not, of course, giving a story of the war so much as trying to show what it means to be a motorcycle despatch-rider at the front. He is here, there and everywhere—and there is no speed limit. He is not in the actual firing line, yet he sees a great deal of what is going on. Sometimes he is very lucky, as I was myself one day, in being allowed to witness a fight that was taking place. I had taken a despatch to an officer, and perhaps conveyed some cheering news. Anyway, I had the chance to go to an eminence from which I could view the battle, and I went, and it was wonderful to see the waging of the contest over a vast tract of country—for in a war like this the ordinary fighter sees very little indeed of the battle.

At this special point I had the rare chance of witnessing a fight as I suppose it is seen by the headquarters staff, and one of the strangest things about it was the little there was to be seen. There were puffs of smoke and tongues of flame—and the everlasting boom of guns; but not much more. Men are killed at long distances and out of sight in these days.

War is excessively wearing, and it was a blessed relief when a day came which was free from shells and bullets. That, indeed, was the calm after the storm. It came to us when we were snug in a farmyard about a mile away from a big town, with our motorcars, cycles and horses so well under cover that the German aeroplanes did not find us out. Thankful indeed were we for the change, because the whole region where we were had been pitilessly bombarded, and there was nothing but devastation around us. Shells had done their work, and there was a special kind of bomb which fired anything it touched that was inflammable. A great many petrol discs, about the size of a shilling, were discharged by the Germans, and these things, once alight, did amazing mischief. Villages were obliterated, and in the big town where we were billeted the engineers were forced to blow up the surrounding houses to prevent the entire place from being destroyed.

The glad time came when our division was relieved for a time. We got a bit of rest, and I crossed the Channel and came home for a short spell. One of the last things I saw before I left the front was the Prince of Wales making a tour. At that time he was about fifteen miles from the firing line.

What was the most noticeable thing that struck me when I came back over the Channel? Well, that is not easy to say, but I know that I particularly noticed the darkness of the London streets.

"The men were told to lay hands on anything that would float."

CHAPTER 14

The Three Torpedoed Cruisers

Within a few minutes, on the morning of Tuesday, September 22nd, 1914, three large British cruisers, sister ships, foundered in the North Sea, after being torpedoed by German submarines, and nearly 1,500 officers and men perished. The ships were the 'Aboukir,' 'Cressy' and 'Hogue.' Each was of 12,000 tons, with a speed of twenty-two knots, and each cost £750,000. The vessels were fine warships, but almost obsolete, and before the war it had been decided to sell them out of the navy. The 'Aboukir' was torpedoed, and while the 'Hogue' and 'Cressy' had closed, and were standing by to save the crew, they also were torpedoed. All three ships speedily sank. The boats were filled, and, later, destroyers and other vessels came up and rescued many of the survivors, amongst whom was C. C. Nurse, an able seaman of the 'Hogue,' whose story is here retold. The casualties were very heavy; but, said the Admiralty, the lives lost were "as usefully, as necessarily, and as gloriously devoted to the requirements of His Majesty's service as if the loss had been incurred in a general action."

The three cruisers, sister ships, were on patrol duty in the North Sea early on the morning of September 22nd. They were alone, protecting our own merchant ships and on the look-out for vessels that were minelaying. The weather was nice, with a rather heavy swell on the water. There had been plenty of bad weather, and this was the first good day we had had for a week.

I had done my twelve years in the navy and had been called up from the Royal Fleet Reserve. We had settled into our stride and had been in at the tail-end of the scrap in the Heligoland Bight, where the *Hogue* got hold of the *Arethusa* and towed her away. At that tune the *Arethusa* had been commissioned only about two days. We knew that she was just beginning her life; but we little thought that the *Hogue* was ending hers.

It was my watch below, and I was asleep in my hammock when the bugles sounded the *réveillé*, and we were shaken up and told that one of our ships was going down. We had turned in all standing, and lost no time in rushing on deck. Then I saw that the *Aboukir*, which was about six hundred yards away, was heeling over, and that we were steaming up to her assistance. At first we thought she had been mined; but we quickly learned that she had been torpedoed by German submarines. We were very soon alongside of her, and were doing everything we could to save the survivors. It was very clear that she was sinking, that a good many of the crew had been killed by the explosion, and that a lot of men, who were far below, in the engine-room and stokeholds, would have no chance of escaping.

We instantly started getting out the few boats that were left in our ship. There were only three, because we were cleared for action, and as it was wartime the great majority of them had been taken away. This has to be done so that there shall be as little woodwork as possible to be splintered by shells. With extraordinary speed some of the *Aboukir's* men had got to the *Hogue*, and some, who were badly hurt, had been taken to the sick-bay and were being attended to. The attack had come swiftly, and it was for us the worst of all attacks to guard against; but there was nothing like panic anywhere, and from the calmness of things you might have thought that the three ships were carrying out some ordinary evolution.

I was standing on the starboard side of the after-shelter-deck of the *Hogue*, and could see a great deal of what was going on. With remarkable smartness and speed our two lifeboats were got away to the *Aboukir*, our men pulling splendidly on their lifesaving errand. Our main derrick, too, was over the side and had got the launch out. The launch was a big rowing-boat, which would hold about a hundred men, and not a second had been lost in getting her afloat under the direction of Lieutenant-Commander Clive Phillipps-Wolley. He worked the derrick to get the launch out, though he was not in the best of health, and only a little while previously he had been ill in his bunk. He was near me on the after-bridge, which was above the shelter-deck, and I saw and heard him giving orders for the getting out of the launch. That was the last I knew about him. He was one of the lost.

The launch was afloat, and the men were ready to hurry up to the *Aboukir*; but before she could get away the very deck under my feet was blown up. There was a terrific explosion, and a huge column of wreckage rose. I was stunned for a moment by the force of the explosion. I thought we had been mined; but almost instantly there was a second explosion under me, and I knew that we had been torpedoed. The *Hogue* had been badly holed, and she began to heel over to starboard immediately.

It is only telling the plain truth to say that there was practically no confusion, and that every man was cool and going about his business as if no such thing as a calamity like this had happened. War is war, and we were ready for all sorts of things—and the discipline of the British Navy always stands firm at a crisis.

There was naturally a good deal of noise, shouting of orders, and orderly rushing to and fro as men carried them out; but everything was done with wonderful coolness, and the splendid courage of the officers was reflected in the men. A noble example was set, and it was magnificently followed. The men waited until they got their orders, just as they did at any other time.

The captain was on the fore-bridge, and I heard him shouting; but as I was so far aft I could not clearly make out what he said. I know, however, that he was ordering every man to look after himself. The men were told to take their clothes off, and to lay hands on anything that would float. They promptly obeyed, and at the word of command a lot of them jumped overboard. There was then hope that we could all get to the *Cressy*, which was still uninjured, standing by and doing all she could to rescue the survivors of her two sister ships. Soon, however, she herself was torpedoed, and in a few moments it was perfectly clear that the three ships were going to the bottom of the sea.

All the cruisers shared the same fate, and were doomed. They were the only British ships at hand, and we did not expect the enemy, being Germans, to do anything for us. But everything that skill and resource could do was done by our own survivors without a moment's loss of time. In the sea there was an amazing collection of things that had been thrown overboard—tables, chairs, spars, oars, handspikes, targets and furniture from the officers' cabins, such as chests of drawers. And everything that could float was badly wanted, because the sea was simply covered with men who were struggling for dear life, and knew that the fight would have to be a long and terrible one.

It takes a long time to talk of what happened, but, as a matter of fact, the whole dreadful business, so far as the loss of the ships was concerned, was over in a few minutes. As far as I can reckon, the *Hogue* herself was struck three times within a minute or so. The first torpedo came, followed almost immediately by a second in the same place, and by a third about a minute afterwards. The war-head of a torpedo holds a very big charge of gun-cotton, which, when it explodes against the side of a ship, drives an enormous hole through. An immense gap was driven in the *Hogue's* side, and there seems to be no doubt that the first torpedo struck her under the aft 9.2 in. magazine. That fact would account for the fearful nature of the explosion.

As soon as the *Hogue* had been torpedoed, she began to settle by the stern; then she was quite awash aft, and began to turn turtle. Our ship sank stern first before she heeled over. There was a frightful turmoil as the four immense funnels broke away from their wire stays and went over the side, and the sea got into the stokeholds and sent up dense clouds of steam.

The Germans boast about the work having been done by one submarine, but that is nonsense. No single submarine could have done it, because she could not carry enough torpedoes. I am sure that there were at least half-a-dozen submarines in the attack; certainly when I was in the water I saw two rise. They came up right amongst the men who were swimming and struggling, and it was a curious sensation when some of the men felt the torpedoes going through the water under their legs. I did not feel that, but I did feel the terrific shock of the explosion when the first torpedo struck the *Cressy*; it came through the water towards us with very great force.

We had a fearful time in the cold water. The struggle to keep afloat and alive, the coming up of the submarines, and the rushing through the water of the torpedoes all that we had to put up with. Then we had something infinitely worse, for the *Cressy* spotted the submarines, and instantly opened a furious fire upon them. The chief gunner, Mr. Dougherty, saw one of them as soon as her periscope appeared, and he fired, and, I believe, hit the periscope; then he fired again and again, getting three shots in from a four-pounder within a minute, and when he had done with her, the submarine had made her last dive—and serve her right! The Germans played a dirty game on us, and only a little while before we had done our best to save some of them in the Heligoland Bight, but never a German bore a hand to save the three cruisers' men from the water. Of course, a sailor expects to be hit anyhow and anywhere in a straight piece of fighting, but this torpedoing of rescue ships was rather cold-blooded, and I don't think British submarines would have done it.

There were some awful sights—but I don't want to dwell too much on them. Men had been torn and shattered by the explosions and falling things, and there was many a broken leg and broken arm. Great numbers of men had been badly hurt and scalded inside the ship. In the engine-rooms, the stokeholds, and elsewhere, brave and splendid fellows who never left their posts had died like heroes. They never had a chance when the ships heeled over, for they were absolutely imprisoned.

When once I had reached the shelter-deck I never tried to go below again; but some of the men did, and they were almost instantly driven out by the force of the huge volumes of water which were rushing into the side through the gaping holes.

One man had an extraordinary escape. He had rushed below to get a hammock, and had laid hands on it when the ship heeled over. It seemed as if he must be drowned like a rat in a trap, and would have no chance, but the rush of water carried him along until he reached an entry-port—one of the steel doorways in the ship's sides—and then he was hurled out of the ship and into the sea, where he had, at any rate, a sporting chance, like the rest of us, of being saved.

I saw the three ships turn turtle, and a dreadful sight it was. The *Hogue* was the first to go—she was not afloat for more than seven minutes after she was struck; then the *Aboukir* went, but much more slowly—she kept afloat for rather more than half an hour; and the last to go was the *Cressy*. The *Cressy* heeled over very slowly and was quite a long time before she had completely turned turtle. When that happened the bottom of the ship, which was almost flat for most of its length, was where the deck had been. And on this big steel platform, which was nearly awash, the captain was standing. I saw him quite clearly—I was not more than forty yards away—and I had seen men walking, running, crawling and climbing down the side of the ship as she heeled over. They either fell or hurled themselves into the sea and swam for it; but the captain stuck to his post to the very last and went down with his ship. It was the old British Navy way of doing things, though probably he could have saved himself if he had taken his chance in the water.

One thing which proved very useful in the water, and was the means of saving a number of lives, was a target which had been cast adrift from the *Cressy*. Targets vary in size, and this was one of the smaller ones, known as Pattern Three, about twelve feet square. It was just the woodwork without the canvas, so it floated well, and a lot of the survivors had something substantial in the way of a raft to cling to. Many of them held on gamely till the end, when rescue came; but other poor chaps dropped off from sheer exhaustion, and were drowned.

It must be remembered that not a few of the men had had an experience which was so shattering that, perhaps, there has never been anything like it in naval warfare. They were first torpedoed in the *Aboukir*, then they were taken to the *Hogue* and torpedoed in her, and then removed to the *Cressy* and torpedoed for the third time. Finally they were cast into the sea to take their chance, and, in some cases, they had to float or swim in the water for hours until they were rescued. No wonder it became a question of endurance and holding on more than a matter of swimming.

The sea was covered with men who were either struggling for life or holding on to wreckage. The boats were packed, and well they might be, because no effort had been spared to get struggling men into them. The men who were in the best of health and good swimmers were helping those who could not swim, and in this way many a man was saved who would have been lost.

When I was in the water I did not utter a word to anybody—it was not worth it, and you needed all your breath; but I never abandoned hope, even when I saw the last ship go down, because I knew that we should have assistance.

Wireless calls were made, and appeals for help were being sent out all the time, and when I looked around at all, it was in the hope of seeing some of our own ships tearing down to the rescue. My mind was easy on the point—I knew that the call must have been made, and it was merely a question of time for the response to come.

I was supported by a plank and clung to it with all my strength, though from time to time I endured agony from cramp. In spite of the torture I never let go. I gripped my plank, but I saw men near me forced to let go their hold of things they had seized, and they were drowned. In many cases cramp overcame them, and quite near to me were poor fellows who were so contracted with it that they were doubled up in the water, with their knees under their chins. I could see their drawn faces and knotted hands—and in several cases I saw that the grip which was on the floating objects was the grip of death. I floated past these poor chaps, and it was pitiful to see them. Thank God some of the struggling in the water did not last long, because many of the men had been badly burnt or scalded, or hit by heavy pieces of wreckage, and these soon fell away exhausted, and were drowned. Some, too, were dazed and lost their nerve as well as their strength, so that they could not keep up the fight for life. For long after the cruisers had sunk, carrying hundreds of men with them, the sea for a great space was covered with floating bodies—dead sailors, as well as those who had managed to live.

Whenever a boat came up I tried to help a man into it; but it was not possible to do anything except with the aid of the boats. The two cutters acted splendidly, picking up all the men they could. Captain Nicholson, of the *Hogue*, was in charge of one of them, and he did some rousing rescue work.

There were some fine deeds of courage and unselfishness that sad morning in the North Sea. The launch and the cutter were packed, of course, and seeing this, and knowing that there were men in the water who were more badly wanting a place in the boat than he was, a Royal Fleet Reserve man, named Farmstone, sprang into the sea and swam for it, to make room for a man who was exhausted.

I was thankful indeed when I saw smoke on the horizon—black clouds which showed that some ships were steaming up as hard as they could lick. Very soon, some of our own destroyers—blessed and welcome sight—came into view, and as they did so, I believe, they potted at submarines which were slinking away, but I can't say with what result. The destroyers came up. The *Lucifer*, a small cruiser, came up too, and the work of rescue began as hard as it could be carried out, every officer and man working with a will. There were two or three other ships about, two Lowestoft trawlers—which did uncommonly good work—and two small Dutch steamers, one called the *Titan* and the other the *Flora*. The next thing that I clearly remember was that I had been hauled out of the bitter-cold water and lifted on board the *Flora*, and that she was soon packed with half-dead men like myself.

The *Flora* was a very small Dutch cargo boat, and with so many men on board she was crammed. It is impossible to say how some of the men got on board, and they could not explain themselves, they were so utterly exhausted. The Dutch could understand us, though words were hardly necessary, and they shared everything they had—clothes, food, drink and accommodation. They wrapped their bedding round us and gave us hot coffee. The stokehold was crowded with men who had gone down into it to get dry and warm. Some of the men were suffering dreadfully from burns, wounds and exhaustion, and one of them died on board the *Flora*. He was my next messmate,

Green. He lived for only about an hour. I saw him in one of the seamen's bunks, and he was then in great agony. I think he had been struck very badly in the explosion. We took him away from the bunk, laid him on the fore-hatch and covered him with a tarpaulin, where he lay till about five o'clock in the afternoon, when we landed at Ymuiden. Poor Green was buried there with full honours, the British chaplain at Amsterdam conducting the service.

One very strange incident of the disaster was the way in which the ensign of the *Hogue* was saved. I don't know how it happened, but one of the stokers who had managed to escape got hold of the ensign when he was in the water, and hung on to it all the time he was in—two or three hours. He had the ensign with him when we were in Holland, and had his photograph taken with it in the background.

Another remarkable fact is that four brothers, who came from the Yorkshire coast, I think, were in the *Hogue*, and all of them were saved!

Talking of photographs, I was one of a group which was taken at Ymuiden, when we were rigged out in the kit of Dutch bluejackets. There I am, in the back row. At that time I was wearing a beard and moustache, as there was neither much time not inclination for shaving.

We had lost everything we had, and were almost naked, so we were very glad of the clothes that were given to us by the Dutch. These people were kindness itself to us, and did everything they could to make us comfortable and happy. I was taken to a small cafe and went to bed.

A Dutch soldier was in charge of us, but he had no fear of us doing any harm. Next evening they took us by train to a place in the north of Holland; then we had a sixteen miles' tramp along the level roads to a concentration camp where there were some Belgian prisoners, who gave us a cheer.

We marched those sixteen miles whistling and singing. Had we not been snatched from death?

We had to rough it, of course, but that came easy after such an experience as ours. There was only one blanket amongst thirteen men, and we had to sleep on straw, and eat with our fingers. We had plenty of food, though—rough, but very nice, and we were very glad of it, and thankful to get a drink of water.

Next morning, when we left the straw and solitary blanket, it was very raw and cheerless, and there was a heavy mist. The Belgian pris-

"Good swimmers were helping those who could not swim".

oners had a football, and we borrowed it and played a game, and got warm. We were covered with straw, and our clothes were filled with it when we woke, but we soon shook it clear when we got going with the ball. We enjoyed a basin of coffee and a big lump of brown bread which the Dutch cook gave us, then we got the time on by turning our tents out, and were quite in clover when the British Consul supplied us with knives, forks, spoons, towels, overcoats and boots.

We spent the first morning washing and drying our socks, and wondering what was going to be done with us. We kept on wondering, but soon knew that we were not going to be detained in Holland, but were to be sent home. On the Friday we had definite news that we were to go back to England, and on the Saturday morning we left, and did the sixteen miles' tramp again; but it was easier this time, because we were prepared for it. We stopped at a farm, and they gave us milk and food, cigars and cigarettes, and before entering a special train for Flushing, the Dutch gave us milk again, and cake, bread and apples.

From Flushing we came on to Sheerness, and then we went on leave—and here I am; but I go back in a day or two. I don't know what will happen, for owing to the explosion the sight of my left eye has practically gone. Besides that, I seem to have been completely shattered in nerves, though I reckoned that I was one of those men who have no nerves—I have been a steeple-jack since I left the Navy, and just before I was called up I was cleaning the face of Big Ben.

It is when I wake in the middle of the night, as I often do, that the whole fearful thing comes back with such awful vividness, and I see again the dreadful sights that it is better to forget.

Yes, the Germans got three good hauls in the cruisers; but I don't think they'll have another chance like it.

CHAPTER 15

The Runaway Raiders

In the German raid on Scarborough, Whitby, and the Hartlepools on December 16th, the Huns killed more than a hundred men, women, and children in the Hartlepools alone, and altogether the casualties numbered more than six hundred. This story is based on the narrative of Sapper W. Hall, R.E., one of the few English soldiers who have been under an enemy's fire on English soil. Sapper Hall was badly wounded.

It is just a fortnight today since the German warships came up out of the mist, bombarded Hartlepool, wrecked many of the houses, killed a lot of defenceless women, children and men, and then tore away into the mist as hard as they could steam. Our own warships nearly got up with them, and if it had not been for the mist, never one of those vessels which were so valiant in bombarding helpless towns would have got back to Germany.

A great deal of confusion has been caused in telling the story of the raids on the Hartlepools, the two places being hopelessly mixed up, They are, as a matter of fact, quite separate towns, with separate mayors and corporations.

Hartlepool itself, where we now are, is on the coast, facing the sea; West Hartlepool is two miles inland. Both towns were bombarded, but it is hereabouts that most of the damage by shells was done, and many children and grown-up people killed. It was just over there, too, that eight Territorials were standing on the front, watching the firing, when a shell struck them and killed seven of the men and wounded the eighth.[1]

---

1. I saw the "eighth" man not far from the spot where he and his comrades were standing when the shell burst. He had been wounded by (continued next page),

It was soon after eight o'clock in the morning when we rushed out of our billets into the streets, and, looking seaward, we saw warships firing.

In our billets we had heard the booming of guns, and supposing that it was our own warships practising or fighting, we had hurried out to see the fun. A few seconds was enough to tell us that there was no fun in it, but that this was a bombardment in deadly earnest by the enemy.

The German ships were easily visible from the shore, and did not seem to be very far away—about two miles. They were firing rapidly, and there was a deafening noise as the shells screamed and burst—the crashing of the explosions, the smashing of immense numbers of window-panes by the concussion, and the thudding of the shells and fragments against walls and buildings.

Coming so unexpectedly, the bombardment caused intense excitement and commotion, and men, women and children rushed into the streets to see what was happening—the worst thing they could do, because the splinters of shell, horrible jagged fragments, were flying all about and killing and maiming the people they struck. A number of little children who had rushed into the streets, as children will, were killed or wounded.

As soon as we realised what was happening, we rushed back and got our rifles and hurried into the street again, and did what we could; but rifles were absolutely useless against warships, and the incessant bursting of shells and the scattering of fragments and bullets made it most dangerous to be in the open.

Shells were striking and bursting everywhere, wrecking houses, ploughing into the ground, and battering the concrete front of the promenade.

The houses hereabouts, overlooking the sea, were big and easy targets for the Germans, who blazed away like madmen, though they must have been in terror all the time when they thought that their cannonading was sure to fetch British warships up. How thankful they must have felt for that protecting mist!

The Hartlepool Rovers' Football Ground is very near the sea and the lighthouse, and it came under heavy fire. One of our men, Sapper

---

shell splinters on the head, which, when I saw him, was bandaged. The effect of the explosion, he said, was terrible. He declared that the German warships were flying the British white ensign, and that he could distinguish their flags quiet clearly.—W. W.

Liddle, was near the wall of the ground when a shell burst and mortally wounded him, injuring him terribly. It was not possible to get at him and bring him into hospital for a long time, but when he was brought here everything that was humanly possible was done for him. He lingered for a few hours, then died.

Meanwhile, death and destruction were being dealt out all around us, and the land batteries were making such reply as they could to the Germans' heavy guns. This reply was a very plucky performance, for Hartlepool is not a fortified place in anything like the real meaning of the word, and our light guns were no match for the weapons of the German battle-cruisers.

As it happened, no damage was done to the guns; but fearful mischief was caused to buildings near us. A shell struck the Baptist Chapel fair and square on the front, and drove a hole in it big enough for the passage of a horse and cart; then it wrecked the inside and went out at the other end of the chapel, again making a huge hole.

House after house was struck and shattered, in some cases people being buried in the ruins. Some of the houses are very old, and pretty well collapsed when a shell struck them and burst.

While the bombardment was in progress we were doing our best, but that could not be much. There was not much cause for laughter, but I remember that a shell came and burst near us, and made us see the humour of a little incident. The explosion itself did no actual damage, but the concussion and force of it were so violent that a sapper was jerked up into the air and came down with a crash. He picked himself up and scuttled as hard as he could make for shelter.

The firing was so sudden and so fierce that it was begun and finished almost before it was possible to realise that it had taken place. Most of the men of Hartlepool were at work when the bombardment started, and some of them were killed at their work, or as they were rushing home to see to their wives and children, while some were killed as they fled for safety.

The streets were crowded with fugitives during the bombardment, and it was owing to this that so many people were killed and wounded. The shells burst among them with awful results.

While the Germans were firing point-blank at the buildings facing the sea, and deliberately killing inoffensive people, they were also bombarding West Hartlepool, and doing their best to blow up the gasworks, destroy the big shipbuilding yards there, and set fire to the immense stacks of timber which are stored in the yards.

People were killed who were five or six miles from the guns of the warships, and in one street alone in West Hartlepool seven persons, mostly women, were killed. Several babies were killed in their homes, and little children were killed as they played in the streets.

A good deal has been said about the number of shells that were fired from the German warships, and some people had put down a pretty low total; but from what I saw, I should think that certainly five hundred shells of all sorts were fired by these Germans, who knew that they were perfectly safe so far as the shore was concerned, and took mighty good care not to be caught by British ships of their own size and power; but that will surely come later, and the men of the North will get their own back.

I cannot say anything about the actual defences, or what the military did; but the few troops who were here did their best, and a couple of destroyers bore a brave part in the affair.

A shell fell in the lines of the Royal Engineers, and several dropped in the lines of the 18th Service Battalion of the Durham Light Infantry.

It was very quickly known, as I have mentioned, that seven out of eight men of the Durhams, who were watching the firing—thinking, like everybody else, that it was some sort of battle practice, till they learned the real truth—had been killed by the explosion of a shell, and that the eighth man had been wounded; but there were several other cases of men being wounded which were not known about until later, because of the great difficulties of discovering the men amongst the ruins which the shellfire had caused.

From the moment the bombardment began there was an awful commotion, and the noise grew until it was simply deafening. The whole town literally shook, and while the firing lasted there was a tremendous and continuous vibration—everything shivered and rattled. One shell struck the wall of the football ground, which faces the sea; not far away a hole was dug in the ground by one of the very first of the shells that were fired; the fine old church of St. Hilda was damaged, and the side of the rectory was simply peppered by a bursting shell.

In the particular place where I and my chums were, the shells were coming in a shower, and doing enormous mischief. We could see that plainly enough. But it was not until later, when the German warships had steamed away as hard as they could go, that we knew how great the damage had been, and how many lives had been lost and people wounded.

The German ships fired from one side to begin with, then they turned round and continued the bombardment from the other side, so they must have been ready loaded all round. The size of the shots varied from the 12-inch shells, perfect monsters, to the small ones which came so fast and did so much havoc. The fact that some of the huge shells were found unexploded after the bombardment proves that ships of great size took part in the raid.

Some time after the firing began I felt a blow on my thigh, and fell to the ground, helpless, though I did not know at the time what had happened. At last, when the firing—which continued for about forty minutes—ceased, stretcher-bearers and volunteer ambulance workers set about collecting the wounded, and I was picked up and brought to the hospital here.

It was then found that I had been struck on the thigh by part of the cap of a shell, and that I had sustained a compound fracture. The piece of metal was still sticking in me you can see it later. It was taken out, and I was promptly and most kindly looked after, as were all our men who had been wounded and were brought in. Poor Liddle, as I have told you, was not discovered for some time; then he was found and brought here, and died late at night, in spite of all the efforts that were made to save him. He had a real soldier's funeral—just as had the rest of the soldiers who had been killed.

As soon as the bombardment was over the people set to work to collect the dead as well as save the wounded, and both were heavy tasks; but there were many willing hands. Even in half-an-hour a wonderful difference had been made in the streets, and those people who had been rushing towards the country for safety began to return. They brought in reports of losses which had been suffered in the outskirts through shells; but, as I have said, the worst cases of all were just about here.

One house was completely demolished, and the father, mother, and half-a-dozen children were killed, so that home and family were wiped out in an instant. One part of the Old Town is so utterly destroyed that it is called "Louvain," and if you look at the houses there you will find that they are just heaps of rubbish and ruins, with beds and furniture and so on, buried.

Shells had exploded in the streets, in houses, fields, at the gasworks, in shipyards—anywhere and everywhere—and one big thing stuck itself in a house and is kept as a relic. Another crashed through four railway waggons, and another shell, which travelled low on the ground,

"THE 'HOGUE' BEGAN TO TURN TURTLE. THE FOUR IMMENSE FUNNELS BROKE AWAY"

went through several sets of the steel metals on the railway, which shows the fearful penetrative power of the projectile.

If the Germans had had their way, no doubt this place would have been wiped out altogether. They made a dead set at the gasworks, but did not do a great deal of mischief there, though it meant that that night a lot of people had to burn candles instead of gas. And though more than a hundred people were killed, and the Germans fondly supposed that they had struck terror into the place, they had done nothing of the sort.

The residents were soon clearing up the ruins and settling down again as if nothing had happened. The most pitiful of all the tasks was that of dealing with the dead and wounded children, and the remembrance of the sad sights will be the best of all inspirations for some of our fellows when the day comes on which they will get their own back from the Germans.

It was not long before we learned that at about the same time as we were being shelled at Hartlepool, German warships had appeared off the entirely undefended places of Whitby and Scarborough. They call these old fishing ports fortified, but that is an absolute untruth, and they know it. But the Germans were out to kill and destroy, and they did both in a manner which showed that they had made calculations to a minute, and that their spies had been long at work.

At Scarborough the raiders did a lot of damage before they ran away. They had prepared one of their boasted surprises for us, and we got it; but that was nothing to the surprise we gave them on Christmas morning at Cuxhaven—a real fortified place—and nothing, I hope and believe, to the surprises that our navy has in store for the German naval runaways.

You ask how long shall I be in hospital.

That is hard to tell; but I have been here two weeks already, and I suppose that I shall be here for at least six weeks longer.

I keep the piece of shell which struck me, in a bit of brown paper in the cupboard near the head of the bed. I cannot rise to get it myself, but if you will open the little door you will find it. It's the sort of thing which caused such havoc in the Hartlepools when the German warships came and bombarded us.

CHAPTER 16

Campaigning With the Highlanders

The Highland regiments have made a great impression upon the Germans since the war began, and the kilted troops have added to their laurels in the field. This story of fighting with the Highlanders is told by Private A. Veness, 2nd Battalion Seaforth Highlanders, who was wounded and invalided home.

I have served eight years in the Seaforth Highlanders. To begin with I was a bandsman, but when the war broke out and I was recalled to the colours, I became an ordinary private, and the only music that the Germans heard me play was the rattle of my rifle. When we landed in France and marched off to the front the girls seemed to have a special fancy for the kilted men—at any rate they crowded up and hugged and kissed those they could get hold of; so we went off in very good spirits, singing and whistling popular tunes, not forgetting the *Marseillaise* and "Tipperary."

Being a strange country we saw a good many things that were new and very strange to us till we got used to them. One amusing incident happened as soon as we were in Belgium, and that was the sight of a big fat man being pulled in a little cart by two dogs. It was funny, but still it made us angry, for we rather looked upon it as cruelty to animals; so we shouted, "Lazy brute!" "Get out and give the dogs a ride!" and so on, and I daresay the man was greatly surprised, though he didn't know what we were saying. In a little while we understood that dogs are extensively used for haulage purposes in Belgium and we ceased to take any special notice of them.

It was not long after landing before we were told to be ready for the Germans, but that proved a false alarm. We were, however, to get our baptism of fire in a dramatic fashion, and that baptism naturally dwells in my mind more vividly than many of the far bigger things which happened later in the war.

A terrific thunderstorm broke, and a party of us were ordered to billet in a barn. We climbed up into a loft and began to make ourselves comfortable and to make some tea. We had scarcely got the welcome tea to our lips when the hurried order came to clear out of the building, and into the thunderstorm we dashed. Then the German shells began to fly and burst, and in a few minutes the barn was struck and shattered, so that we had a very narrow escape.

It was at this stage that we had our first man killed. He was a chum of mine, a bandsman, named Dougal McKinnon. While we were having our tea Dougal was under cover in the trenches, in front of the barn, with his company. They were under shell fire, and he was killed by bursting shrapnel. He was buried close to the spot where he fell, and being the first of our men to be killed in action we felt it very deeply. Many times after that, when our chums were killed, we had to leave them, because we had no time to bury them.

We got on the move, and when night came it was awful to see the whole countryside lit up with the flames of burning buildings—farms and houses and other places which had been set on fire by the Germans. There was a farm which was blazing furiously and I shall never forget it, for the good reason that in marching we managed to circle it three times before we could get properly on the march and go ahead.

We pushed on to Cambrai, where the cannonading was truly terrible. My company was in support of another company in advance. We lay behind a bank, sheltering, for a few hours. At the back of us was a British howitzer battery, in a bit of a wood, so that we were between two awful fires. It was indescribable—the deafening din, which never ceased or lessened while the duel raged, the excitement, the danger, and the nerve-strain; yet there was something fascinating in watching the firing and wondering what was going to happen.

It is wonderful to think of the working of the human mind at such a time, and strange to recall the odd things one does. In our own case, as we had to go on sheltering and watching, we amused ourselves by counting the number of shells that dropped within a certain area which was well under our observation. The area was, roughly speaking, about 200 yards square, and in three-quarters of an hour no fewer than seventy-six shells exploded over that particular spot. They were shrapnel and high explosive and never struck the ground—they burst in the air, and at one time I counted six shells bursting in the air together. That gives you some idea of the tremendous nature of the German shell fire. Luckily a great number of the shells did not explode at all, or few if any of us could have got away.

It is impossible to praise too highly the British artillery's work. To my own personal knowledge there was one battery that day—I don't know which it was—which was under fire for at least seven hours continuously without shifting; and during the whole of that time they were replying to the German guns.

After that shattering experience we camped in a cornfield at night, and were settling down to sleep when were we ordered to move again. For hours, worn and weary though we were, we were on the march, and thankful we were when we halted in a village and got a box of biscuits from the French as a midday snack. We had been forced to part with most of our equipment and many of the greatcoats were thrown away; but I felt that I should want mine and I stuck to it—and I am wearing it now. It has had plenty of rough usage—and here are the holes made by a piece of flying shrapnel.

I am proud to say that the general in command of our division congratulated the regiment on its splendid marching, and I think we did a fine thing, for in about twelve hours we covered about thirty-two miles—actual marching, with just a halt here and there. The Germans had done their best to trap us, but they had not succeeded, and we escaped, to turn the tables on them with a vengeance.

That night I had to report sick—there was something wrong with my ankles. I was unable to march, so I got a lift on a limber-waggon of the 88th Battery of the Royal Field Artillery. During the ride, which lasted all night, I went through some of the finest country I ever saw. It was particularly beautiful because of the time of the year, late autumn, and the clear light of the full moon. This moonlight ride on a limber will be always associated in my memory with the grandest spectacle of its sort I saw during the war.

The battery was travelling along a switchback road, and I was wrapped up in the beautiful and peaceful scenery—it was hard to believe that this calm landscape was the scene of war and that the splendid British gunners I was with had been dealing death and destruction amongst the Germans so lately.

Not far away was a river, winding like a silver thread over the face of the country, and suddenly, from the river, there rose an immense mass of flame and smoke, followed quickly by a thunderous rumbling roar.

I knew at once that a bridge had been blown up. I cannot tell you who destroyed it—Germans or French; all I know is that I saw the sight and it was the most remarkable of its kind that I witnessed—and I saw four splendid bridges destroyed in this manner.

At one time we had crossed a fine bridge and as soon as we had done so a hole was dug and a mine was laid in the centre. Then our cyclist section was sent out to report what was going to happen and the bridge was blown up. In this case we were the last to cross before the explosion occurred.

At an early stage of the operations I was lucky enough to see a very fine fight in the air, a duel between a French airman and a German airman. I was able to follow the duel for miles. The men in the aeroplanes were firing revolvers at each other and we could hear the crack of the shots, though we could not see any definite results, because the duel got too far away. This was the first fight in the air that I saw, and I watched it with extraordinary interest, especially as we all keenly hoped that the German would be brought down, because he had been flying over our lines and quickly directed shell fire on us owing to his signals. For fully twenty minutes I watched this air fight. It was wonderful to see the swiftness with which the machines dived and dodged. The Frenchman circled over the German in the most skilful and daring manner and time after time threatened his existence.

Another remarkable incident I witnessed at this time was the escape of a German cavalryman. He was an *Uhlan*, a scout, I take it, and quite alone. We were on the march and had been told that the German cavalry were in large numbers near us, and so that we should be ready for them we took up a position, with some Irish infantry to the left of us.

We were lying in position on a hill, and in front of us was three or four miles of good flat country, so that we should have had a fine view of cavalry in force. We watched and waited, but the threatened cavalry did not come—all we saw was this solitary *Uhlan*, a mere speck on the wide plain.

As soon as the *Uhlan* was seen the rifles rattled and it was expected that he would be potted; but he seemed to bear a charmed life. The Irish battalion gave him a particularly heavy fire—the Seaforths were too far off to reach him with the rifle; but the *Uhlan* galloped gaily on, and it was quite amusing to watch him. No doubt he thoroughly enjoyed himself—at any rate he galloped unscathed across two or three miles of open country, and got away.

It was not until we were within about eighteen miles of Paris that the retirement ended and we began the offensive. We had had a very hard time, and were to have a few days' rest, but we never got it. Yet in spite of the hardships we had some very pleasant times, because of the beauty of the country and the season.

Joyful indeed was the day when we began to drive the Germans back, and it was the more joyful because the advance was almost as swift as our retirement had been.

On that wonderful advance we saw some horrible things—I will not dwell on German barbarities, though there were many proofs of them—including great numbers of horses which had been killed or wounded and left just where they had fallen. No attempt had been made to dispose of the decaying carcases and many a poor brute had died a lingering death.

I was greatly struck by the Germans' cruelty to their horses, in leaving them like this; but that was one proof of the hurriedness of the enemy's retreat—the Germans who had got so near Paris and were then flung right away back from the city. I need hardly say that whenever a sign of movement was noticed in a horse a man was sent to put the poor thing out of its misery.

There was still plenty of hardship to put up with, but that did not matter so much when we were driving back the Germans.

I remember very well one day and night of uncommon wretchedness. It was raining heavily and continuously, and in the deluge I and three more men were sent on outpost—to observe and keep our eyes open, and so that we could do that to the best advantage we took up a position on the top of a hayrick. A perfect hurricane was blowing, and the almost solid rain was fairly driven into us; but we stuck it through, and hung on to the top of the haystack till it was dark, then we thankfully got down and went into an open shed for shelter—a building that was just a protection for wheat-stacks.

I had had my turn of picketing and was lying down to get a snatch of sleep when I was ordered to go up a road about a mile and a half away, to find out whether our relief had come. So out into the darkness and the wind and rain I staggered and fought my way through what was the worst night for weather that I ever saw. On and on I and my comrades went, looking hard for our relief, but we never saw it, and we waited there till next morning, when we rejoined our brigade.

Those were times when there was little rest for the Seaforths, or anybody else.

The aeroplanes gave us little chance of rest, and at times they had an uncanny knack of finding us.

One day, after a long, hard march, we put into a wood for shelter. A French supply column was already in the wood and doubtless the Germans knew of or suspected this; at any rate a German aeroplane came over us, with the result that in a few minutes we were shelled out. We rested in another part of the wood till it was dark, then we were taken on to billets, but we had to make another move, because we were shelled out again. That was the sort of thing which came along as part of the day's work; and as part of the day's work we took it cheerfully.

When we got the Germans on the move we took prisoners from time to time. I was on guard over a few prisoners, part of a crowd, when one of them came up to me and to my amazement I recognised him as a German who had worked in Soho Square and used often to go to the same place as myself for dinner—a little shop in Hanway Street, at the Oxford Street end of Tottenham Court Road. The prisoner recognised me at once and I recognised him. To show how ignorant the Germans were of the enemy they were fighting, I may tell you that this man said to me, "If we had known we were fighting the English, I would never have left London!"

Was it not strange that the two of us, who had so often met as friends for dinner in the little foreign shop, should meet again as enemies on the banks of the Marne?

I am now coming to a sorrowful personal incident—the loss of my chum, Lance-Corporal Lamont. We had been together from the beginning of the war and had shared everything there was, even to the waterproof sheet. He would carry the sheet one day and I would carry it the next, and whenever such a thing had to be done as fetching drinking-water, often a very dangerous task, we would share that too.

Throughout one awful night of ceaseless rain, which soaked us to the skin, the two of us were in the trenches—we had dug ourselves in, with just ordinary head cover. We lay there till next morning, when an officer came along my platoon and asked if we had any drinking-water.

We told him that we had not.

The officer said, "If you care to risk it, one of you can go and fetch some water."

We decided to take the risk, which was great, because to get the water meant getting to a farmhouse just behind us, under a heavy fire.

My chum volunteered to go, and, taking the water-bottles, he left the trench and started to cross the open ground between us and the farmhouse. While he was doing this the order came for us to advance—and I never saw him again.

It was soon my turn to be put out of action. A pretty stiff fight was going on and the fire was so heavy that it was very dangerous to be in the open; but it was necessary for me and a few more men to cross a bit of open ground, and we made a start. We had not gone far when a shell came between me and another man who was at my side. The shell struck him fair on the arm and shattered it. He fell over on his side, and as he did so he said, "For Heaven's sake cut my equipment off!"

I took out my jack-knife and slit the equipment across the shoulders and let it drop away from him.

He crawled off and I was told afterwards that while he was trying to creep to shelter he was struck again and killed.

I crawled as best I could up to the firing line, but when I got there I found that there was no room in the trenches for me, so I had to lie in the open. I had not been there long before a fellow next to me asked me what time it was. I took out my watch and told him it was about eleven-fifteen—and the next thing I knew was that I felt as if someone had kicked me on the top of the head.

I turned round and said, "Tommy, I'm hit!" I became unconscious for some time, then, when I recovered, I said, "Tommy, is it safe to crawl away?"

"No," said Tommy, "it's risky. It's a bit too hot!"

"Never mind," I answered. "If I stay here much longer I shall collapse. I'm going to have a shot at it—here goes!"

I began to crawl away, but I must have taken the wrong direction, for I was soon under two fires. I was approaching the mouths of two or three of our own guns, which were in front of a farmhouse.

I soon found that this was a bit too warm for me, and so I turned and took what I supposed was the right direction. I had had enough of crawling, which was very slow work. I wanted to get out of it, and I made up my mind to rise and run. That does not sound very brave, but it was the better part of valour.

I started to run, as best I could; but I had hardly got going when a bullet struck me, as I supposed, and I collapsed alongside some of my own comrades.

Stretcher-bearers came up, in time, and I was carried to the field hospital. Then a curious discovery was made, which was, that a bullet had gone through four or five pleats of my kilt and had stuck in my leg, high up. This is the place where it struck and stuck and here's the bullet, which the doctor easily pulled out with his fingers, for it had not penetrated deeply, owing, I think, to the resistance of the pleats of my kilt. Apart from this bullet wound I was struck by shrapnel four times, but I managed to keep going.

I left the field hospital the next day and joined an ambulance column which was shelled by the Germans as it went along. I escaped myself, but one of the waggons was completely wrecked.

Having recovered from my wound to a certain extent I went back to the regiment, but after a few days I had to be invalided home, and I have had a long and tedious spell in hospital.

There is one more incident I would like to mention by way of closing. We halted in a village in France where we saw some of the Turcos, one of whom was very noticeable because he was proudly wearing the greatcoat of a German officer which he had secured on the battlefield, after killing the officer.

While we halted, a batch of German prisoners was brought into the village, and they were put into a courtyard between two rows of cottages. No sooner had this been done than an old man rushed out, and if it had not been for the guard he would have hurled himself upon the prisoners and done his best to thrash them.

The act was so strange that I inquired the reason for the old man's fury. And the answer I received was, "He remembers 1870."

"A BULLET STRUCK HIM IN THE BACK AND KILLED HIM"

CHAPTER 17

Transport Driving

It was estimated that, early in the war, no fewer than 10,000 vehicle workers were serving with the colours 3000 taxicab drivers,—3000 tramway men, and 4000 motor-'bus drivers. These trained men went from London and the provinces, some being Reservists, and others joining various regiments; but a very large number went into the Transport Section. From this story by Private James Roache, Mechanical Transport Section, Siege Artillery Brigade, we learn something of the heavy and perilous work that falls to the lot of the Transport Section, and can realise the enormous extent to which the army depends upon its transport.

I got into Ypres about seven days after the Germans had left the city, and I learned from a schoolteacher who spoke English that they had commandeered a good many things, and had pillaged the jewellers' shops and other places of business.

At that time the Germans did not seem to have done any exceptional damage; but they made up for any neglect later on, when they acted like barbarians in bombarding and destroying the beautiful old city, and smashing its priceless ancient buildings into ruins. That is part of the system of savagery which they boast about as "culture."

We had been in Ypres about a week when the first German shell came. It was the beginning of a fearful havoc. That was about ten o'clock in the morning. The shell dropped plumb into the prison. There were a good many civil prisoners in the gaol at the time, but I do not know what happened to them, and I cannot say whether any of the helpless creatures were killed or wounded.

At that time I was helping to supply the Siege Artillery Brigade, the guns of which—the famous 6 in. howitzers—were a mile or so out of the city. We had four cars, each carrying three tons of lyddite—twelve tons in all—standing in the Market Square, and exposed to the full artillery fire of the enemy.

It was a perilous position, for if a shell had struck that enormous amount of lyddite probably the whole city would have been wrecked, and the loss of life would have been appalling. We had to wait for several hours before we could move, because of the difficulty in communicating with the brigade; but when the order did at last arrive, we lost no time in getting to a safer place than the Market Square.

It was while we were standing under fire that I saw a mother and her child—a girl—struck by a fragment of a bursting shell. They were the first people to be wounded in Ypres.

The shell—a big brute—burst on the roof of a house, and the fragments scattered with terrific force all around. People were flying for their lives, or hiding, terror-stricken, in the cellars; and the woman and her daughter were struck as we watched them fly

Some of us rushed up and found that one of the boots of the woman had been ripped open, and that the child had been struck on the face and badly cut.

I picked her up, and saw that she was unconscious; but I got at my field-dressing and did all I could for her, and was thankful to find that she soon came back to her senses, though she was suffering terribly from shock and began to cry bitterly.

The mother also was dreadfully upset, but not seriously hurt. We lost no time in getting them into the underground part of a *café* near at hand, and there we had to leave them. I don't know what became of them, but I suppose they were taken away. I often wonder what has happened to the poor little soul and her mother, victims, like so many thousands more, of the German invaders. I am glad to know that with our field-dressings we were able to help a good many civilians who were wounded.

The four cars I have mentioned were big transport-lorries, made specially for the war, and very fine work can be done with them. But how different the work is from that which we used to do at home as motor-drivers!—and I had a fair experience of that before I joined the Transport Service. There was as much difference between the two as there is between this war and the South African War, in which I served in the Imperial Yeomanry.

These lorries carried immense quantities of ammunition, and so the Germans made a special point of going for them, in the hope of bringing about a destructive explosion; but, taken on the whole, they had very poor luck that way.

When the order came to us in the Market Square at Ypres to march, we left the city and travelled along the roads till it was dark; and after that we returned to the city, taking the stuff with us. No sooner were we back in Ypres than the Germans started shelling again, after having ceased fire for about four hours.

What we carried was wanted for the guns, but we could not reach them, owing to the excessive danger from the German fire. It is a strange fact that as soon as any stuff was going through by transport the Germans started shelling it, which seems to show that they had word when transports were on the move. They shelled us constantly, and we got to take the thing as a very ordinary part of the day's work.

It was only when some uncommon explosion occurred that we were roused to take notice; and such an event took place one day when one of the very biggest of the German shells burst in the air not far away from me with a tremendous crash, and made an immense cloud of awful smoke and rubbish as the fragments struck the ground.

This explosion was so near and so unusual that I thought I would get hold of a souvenir of it. And so I did. I secured a piece of the base of the shell, and meant to bring it home as a trophy; but I had to leave it, for the weight of the fragment was 95 lb., and that's a trifle heavy even for a transport-driver. This was certainly one of the very biggest and most awful of the German shells of the immense number I saw explode.

There is, or was, a skittle-alley in Ypres, near the water-tower, and some of the Munsters were billeted there. I was near the place when some very heavy shelling was going on, and I saw one shell burst on the building with a terrific report. I knew at once that serious damage was done, and that there must have been a heavy loss of life, for I saw wounded and unwounded men rushing into the street from the ruined building. Some of the men were bandaging themselves as they rushed out. I knew that there must be a shocking sight inside the building; so when the commanding officer said, "Would you like to go inside and look at it?" I replied that I would rather not. And I was glad afterwards, for I learned that six poor fellows had been killed. That was the sort of thing which was constantly happening to our fighting men, and it was bad enough; but it was infinitely worse when the victims were women and children, as they so often were, and it was the sight of these innocent sufferers which was the hardest of all to bear. Some of our youngsters were particularly upset.

There was a little trumpeter of the Royal Garrison Artillery, to which we were attached, and a fine youngster he was, about sixteen years old. We called him "Baggie." He used to stick it very well, but at times, when he saw women and children hurt, he gave way and cried. But that kind-heartedness did not prevent him from being always eager to come with us when we took the ammunition up to the guns in the firing line. "Baggie" never knew fear for himself, but he felt it badly when others were hit or hurt, and that took place day after day.

There was another little trumpeter of the Royal Engineers who got badly upset for the same reason. He was billeted in a timber-yard, and I saw a shell fall in the yard and burst and send the timber flying in all directions. It seemed as if tremendous mischief had been done, and that there must have been a heavy loss of life; but, as a matter of fact, only one man was injured on the head and face by splinters.

The trumpeter rushed out, and I went up and talked with him to cheer him up a bit.

"It's no good!" he said. "I can't stick it any longer! I try to be brave, but I have to give way!"

Then he broke down and fairly cried, and a very pitiful sight it was, for he was only a kiddie, fifteen or sixteen years old.

I was always troubled myself when I saw how these little chaps were upset; but they did not break down through anything like fear—they were not afraid, and were splendid when they were with the men—it was the suffering and the fearful sights they saw that bowled them out.

These trumpeters—mere lads—went through all the marching and fighting that led up to the fearful business at Ypres, and they came out of the business brilliantly. Little "Baggie," for example, was right through it from the Aisne, and was up and down with the Siege Artillery all the time. He was present when one of the lieutenants was killed, and when I last heard of him he was still on the move and well; and I sincerely hope that he is all right now, and will come safely home.

I mention these things about the youngsters particularly, because they struck me as being out of the common, and so you notice them more than the ordinary matters.

While speaking of the earlier days of the war, I might say that, after the Marne and the Aisne, when we were going back over ground that we knew and on which we fought, we saw some sickening slaughter scenes, and realised to the full what an awful thing a war like this is.

One very peculiar incident which comes into my mind was the finding of a dead *Uhlan* in a wood. He had evidently been badly wounded, and had made his way into the wood for safety, but he had died there. When we found him he was sitting in a crouching position. On examining him, we found two postcards which he had written. We could not read them, but, as far as we could tell, they were addressed to women of the same name, but living in different places. We buried the *Uhlan* in the wood, and handed the postcards to a German officer who had been made prisoner, and he gave us to understand that he would see that they were sent to their destinations when he got a chance to despatch them. That incident was only one of many similar sights we came across in our part of the business.

Transport work, as a rule, was very uncomfortable, because it was mostly done at night, when the roads were very dark, and we had to do as best we could without lights. Anything like an ammunition or supply column was a particular mark for the Germans, and whenever they got the chance they would do their best to find us out; and a favourite way of doing this was to fire a few shots in one place and a few in another, in the hope that we should be drawn and reveal our position. But we didn't give the show away quite so easily as that.

I had many opportunities of seeing the fine work which was done by our armoured trains, and I saw something of the performances of the aeroplanes. I witnessed several air fights, but there was not really a lot to see, because there was so much swift manoeuvring. There was plenty of firing at the aircraft, but they are most difficult things to hit. One of the German aeroplanes dropped a bomb on Ypres. It fell on a doctor's house near the town station and exploded, but it did not do any great amount of mischief. It broke the front door and shattered the windows and knocked the place about, but I fancy that it did not hurt or kill anybody.

What was the finest sight I saw while I was at the front? Well, I think the best thing I ever saw was the way some of our lancers scattered a far superior body of *Uhlans* and made them fly. That was on the retirement from Mons. It was a very bad time, and there were some fearful sights, for the roads leading from the town were crowded with fleeing women and children. In any case it was bad enough to get along the road, but it was infinitely worse to make our way along through the crowds of refugees with our motor-lorries, especially in view of what we carried. To make matters worse, we had got on the wrong road, and it was necessary to turn back. To do this we had to turn round, and, as there were eighty cars, I need not tell you what a business that meant, especially with the enemy harassing us, and I dare say fondly thinking that they had us in a proper grip. The Germans were quite close to us, and firing, and we were ordered to get down and defend the cars. The road at this point was very narrow, and it seemed as if we were trapped, though we were covered by cavalry.

The country thereabouts did not seem very favourable for cavalry work, but it was all right from the point of view of the *Uhlans*, who, from their horses, potted at us from the brow of the hill on which they stood. The weather was miserable, dull, and it was raining, and, altogether, it was not an exhilarating business. The *Uhlans* seemed to be having it all their own way; then the scene changed like magic, and that was when the gallant 9th Lancers appeared, to our unspeakable joy. I can claim to understand something in a modest way about cavalry, as an old Imperial Yeoman, and I do know that there was no finer sight ever seen than the spectacle of those splendid fellows of the 9th, who, without any sound of trumpet or any noise, came up and charged the *Uhlans*. One body of *Uhlans* was on the brow, two more bodies were in a wood. But these two did not take any active part in the fighting; they seemed to wait till their comrades on the brow had paved the way with us, so that they could swoop down. But the *Uhlans* did not get a chance to swoop, though they were three to one against our lancers.

Jumping a ditch and galloping across the country, our cavalry were after the *Uhlans* like the wind. But the *Uhlans* never stopped to face the lance; they vanished over the brow of the hill, and the fellows who were watching and waiting in the wood vanished, too. They bolted, and must have been thankful to get out of it. All they knew, probably, was that our men came along a road in the wood till they got to a clear part, and that through that opening the 9th were on them like a flash, without firing a shot. They managed to get in amongst the first line of the Germans with the lance and empty some of the saddles, while they themselves had only one or two men bowled over.

I had a splendid view of this brilliant little affair—I should think there were not more than 120 of the 9th—and I shall never forget the way in which the lancers went for the enemy, nor the swiftness with which the boasted *Uhlans* scuttled off behind the brow. It was an uncommonly fine piece of work, and it saved our column.

The *Uhlans* had another shot at us two or three days later. They were at quite close range, not more than four or five hundred yards away, but we managed to keep them off and go about our business, which was to reach the Marne and the Aisne, and then start back. We had about a month on the Aisne without making much progress, though our troops were hard at it all the time.

I had got out of Ypres—thankful to go—and had gone towards another town. It was about midday, and we had halted. The hot weather had gone away, and the cold had come. I was walking up and down to keep myself warm. Shells were falling and bursting, as usual, but I did not pay much attention to them. At last one burst about fifty yards away, and a fragment struck me and knocked me round, after which I fell. At first I thought I had been struck by a stone or a brick which somebody had thrown, and it was not for some time that I realised that I had been wounded in the thigh by a piece of shell. I was sent to England in due course, and here I am, in a most comfortable hospital at the seaside, ready to leave for home in two or three days.

My own experience with regard to the wound is not uncommon. It is not easy to say how you have been hit, and I have known men who have been shot through the body and have been quite unable to say whether the bullet went in at the front or the back.

CHAPTER 18

British Gunners as Cave-Dwellers

Sir John French has repeatedly praised the outstanding work of the Royal Artillery during the war and glowing tributes to the courage and resourcefulness of British gunners have been paid by the other branches of the army. Many a critical battle has been turned into a success by the artillery, some of the batteries of which have particularly distinguished themselves. Amongst them is the 134th, of whose officers and men no fewer than five were mentioned in Sir John French's list, published on February 18th 1915, of names of those whom he recommended for gallant and distinguished conduct in the field. This story of some of the work of our gunners is told by Corporal Ernest Henry Bean, of the 134th Field Battery, who was severely wounded and invalided home.

You cannot exaggerate anything in this war. I am of a cheerful and hopeful disposition, but I never thought I should live through the awful business; yet here I am, cheerful still, though shot through both feet, and forced to hop when I want to get from place to place.

I have had some strange adventures during the last few months, and one of the oddest was in this good old Yarmouth. That was when the Germans came and bombed us. But I will tell you about the air raid later. Here are two eighteen-pounder shells, not from the front, but from practice-firing, and it was such shells as these that made havoc amongst the German troops, especially when we got to work on big bodies of them.

The war came upon us so suddenly that even now it seems amazing that I left peaceful England on a summer day and went straight into the very thick of things. There was no waiting, for I sailed from Southampton on the day after Mons was fought, and when we got into action it was at Le Cateau. We had had a short spell in a rest camp, then we had some hard marching. Throughout the whole of one night we kept at it, and soon after breakfast next morning we were in the thick of one of the most terrible artillery fights that has ever been known. For six mortal hours we were under an incessant shellfire. The experience itself was enough to leave its mark for ever on your mind, but I shall always remember it because of what happened to our horses. They were not used to this awful business and they stampeded, galloping all over the place, and defying every effort of the drivers to control them. The horses bolted with the waggons and tore madly over the country, taking pretty nearly everything that came in their way. The drivers were on the horses, but they were powerless to control the frightened animals.

The battery itself was in action. I was with the teams—on an open road with half-a-dozen of them, and no protection whatever, for the road ran between open fields. We were a fine target for the Germans, and they saw it and began to shell us hell for leather. The fire was deadly and there is no wonder that the horses bolted.

What was to be done? What could be done except make a dash for shelter? I did my level best to get out of the open and seek shelter. But shelter seemed far away, there was nothing near at hand, but in the distance I saw something that seemed hopeful, so I galloped towards it with my teams. We went furiously along, and as I got nearer to the object I could make out that it was a long brick wall which separated an orchard from the road.

For about a mile, under a constant and furious fire, I dashed on; then I got to the wall, and instantly I drew in as many of the bolting horses as I could lay hands on. It all happened so swiftly that it is not easy to tell how this was done; but I know that I was safely mounted on my own horse when the stampede began, and that I dashed at the bolting animals and grabbed as many as I could, and that I hurried them to the shelter of the wall, and I fancy that they were just about as glad of the protection as I was. The gallop was a mad affair, and very likely it would never have ended as it did if all the shells the Germans fired had burst; but some of them did not explode, though I did not know of this till later, when I picked some of them up from the ground.

While I was in the thick of this exciting business Farrier-Sergeant Scott was rushing about and securing other runaway teams, and he did so well and his work was considered so brilliant and important that the French gave him the decoration of the Legion of Honour.

For the best part of an hour I was under cover of the wall, doing the best I could with the horses, and it was a funny old job to keep them anything like quiet with such a heavy fire going on all the time; yet so complete was the protection that practically no damage was done, the worst that occurred being the shattering of a pair of wheels by a bursting shell.

By the end of the hour both myself and the horses were pretty well settling down; then things calmed down a bit. The Germans appeared to be tired of pounding at us, and perhaps they thought that they had blown us to pieces. At any rate we began to get out of it, and we had no sooner started to do that than the firing instantly re-opened.

There was a village not far away and we made a dash for it; but we were forced to clear out, for the enemy's artillery set the little place on fire and all the stacks and buildings were in flames. There was a good deal of confusion and mixing up of all sorts of troops. I had lost touch with my own lot and was ordered by a captain to join another column for the night, and this I did. I joined the 2nd Brigade Ammunition Column and next day I was with my own battery again, thankful to have got safely through a very dangerous business.

Next day we picked up another position, and had no sooner done that than information came that immense bodies of Germans were on the move in our direction. The outlook was serious, because we were in the open and there was nothing for it except a fight to the death. The Germans were expected along a certain road and we made ready to fire at what is practically point-blank range, using Fuses 0 and 2, so that at 500 and 1000 yards the masses of the enemy would have had the shells bursting amongst them.

We had been through some tough times; but not in any situation which was as unpromising as this. We knew that we could make a long stand, and mow down the Germans as they swept along the open country; but we knew also that in the end vastly superior forces must tell against us; but we held our ground and the stern order went round, "Each take charge of your own gun—and God help us!"

How long that awful strain lasted I cannot tell. It could not have been long, but it seemed an eternity. While it lasted the strain was almost unendurable; then it suddenly snapped, an immense relief came over us and even the bravest and most careless amongst us breathed more freely when we knew that the prospect of almost sure annihilation had passed, for the German hosts, instead of coming by the expected road, had gone another way.

With lighter hearts we limbered up, and day after day, night after night, for eleven days, we kept hard at it, marching and fighting, and whenever we got into action it was against very heavy odds. I was with my own special chum, Sergeant Charlie Harrison, and often enough, especially in the night-time, we would walk alongside our horses and talk as we dragged ourselves along—talk about anything that came into our minds, and all for the sake of keeping awake and not falling down exhausted on the road; yet in spite of everything we could do we would fall asleep. Sometimes we would continue walking while practically asleep—we wanted to save our horses as much as we could—and more than once, when I was riding, I went to sleep and fell out of the saddle. There was one good thing, however, about the shock—it acted as a very fine wakener-up. As for sleeping, when we got the chance of it, we could do that anywhere—in ploughed fields, deep in mud and water, and on the road itself.

All sorts of strange and unexpected things happened. While I was with the Ammunition Column the Engineers were putting all their smartness and skill into the building of a pontoon, and the Germans were specially favouring them with "Coal Boxes." This was my introduction to these big brutes of shells, and it was not pleasant, especially as the column was not more than twenty-five yards from the spot where they were exploding with a terrific roar.

I was standing by my horse, feeling none too comfortable, when a big shell burst and made awful havoc near me. A piece of it came and struck me. I thought I was done for, then I looked around at myself, and found that the two bottom buttons of my greatcoat had been torn away, but that no further damage had been done. I was glad to have got off so easily, and just as pleased to find that the horses had escaped.

At this time we were wanting food pretty badly, so that every ration became precious. We were bivouacked when a file of infantrymen brought in a German prisoner. Of course we gave him a share of pretty well everything there was going, hot tea, bread, biscuits and bully beef, and he did himself well. The prisoner was not exactly the sort to arouse compassion, for he looked well fed and was dressed in a very smart uniform. An officer came up, saw the captive, and said, "Do you think this fellow looks as if he wanted anything?" Truth to tell, the fellow didn't, and as we did want things badly, he was sent somewhere else, and we were not sorry to see him go.

After being kept so constantly on the rack, we had a welcome and remarkable change—we became cave-dwellers. We spent five days and nights in some of the famous caves at Soissons, and had a thoroughly comfortable and happy time. We had a fine chance of resting and enjoying ourselves, and we made the most of it.

Originally these caves were occupied by very primitive people; lately they were used as a French hospital, and the French made all sorts of interesting pictures and carvings on the outsides, by way of decoration, then the British took them over as billets. By nature the caverns were queer gloomy places, but a good deal had been done to make them habitable, such as fitting in doors and windows. There had been a lot of fighting near the caves, with the result that there were graves at the very entrances of some of these uncommon billets; but this had no effect on our spirits. We did not allow ourselves to be depressed. What is the use of that in wartime? The British soldier has the happy knack of making himself at home in all kinds of odd places, and so we did in our billets in the rocks and hillside. We called one of our caves the "Cave Theatre Royal," and another the "Cave Cinema," and many a cheerful performance and fine sing-song we had. The only light we had came from candles, but you can sing just as well by candle-light as you can by big electric lamps, and I don't suppose that ever since the caves were occupied they rang with more cheerful sounds than were heard when the British soldiers were joining in a chorus of the latest popular song from home.

Another great advantage of the caverns was that they gave splendid cover to our guns, and protection to ourselves, so that these five days and nights gave us a real rest and complete change, and we were very sorry when we left them and resumed the work of incessant fighting and marching. We were constantly at the guns, and by way of showing what a fearful business the artillery duels became at times, I may tell you that from a single battery alone—that is, half-a-dozen guns—in one day and night we fired more than 4000 rounds.

It was a vast change from the comfort and safety of the caverns, where never a German shell reached us, to the open again, but we got our quiet times and little recreations still, and one of these intervals we devoted to football. We were at Messines, and so was a howitzer battery, and as we happened to be rather slack, we got up a match. I am keen on football, and things were going splendidly. I had scored two goals and we were leading 3-1, when the game came to a very sudden stop, for some German airmen had seen us running about and had swooped down towards us, with the result that the howitzer chaps were rushed into action and we followed without any loss of time. We took it quite as a matter of course to let the football go, and pound away at the Germans, who had so suddenly appeared. It was getting rather late, so we gave the enemy about fifty rounds by way of saying goodnight. We always made a point of being civil in this direction; but our usual dose for goodnight was about fifteen rounds.

Talking of football recalls sad memories. On Boxing Day, 1913, when I and an old chum were home on leave, I played in a football match, and at the end of the game a photograph was taken of the team. On last Boxing Day, if the roll of the team had been called, there would have been no answer in several cases—for death and wounds have claimed some of the eleven. Little did we think when we were being grouped for the picture that it was the last muster for us as a team.

We had got through the tail end of summer and were well into autumn, and soon the gloom of November was upon us, then came my change of luck and I was knocked out. It was November 2, and almost as soon as it was daylight we were in the thick of an uncommonly furious artillery duel, one of the very worst I have seen. The Germans seemed to be making a special effort that morning. They had got our position pretty accurately, and they fired so quickly and had the range so well that we were in a real hell of bursting shrapnel, indeed, the fragments were so numerous that it is little short of a miracle that we were not wiped out.

We had not been long in action when a shell burst on the limber-pole, smashed it in halves, penetrated through the wheel, blew the spokes of the wheel away and shot me some distance into the air. For a little while I had no clear idea of what had happened, then I found that three of us had been wounded. My right boot had been blown to shreds, and there was a hole right through the left boot. So much I saw at once—a mess of blood and earth and leather; but of the extent of my wounds I knew very little, nor did I trouble much about them at the time. The first thing I did was to get into the main pit by the side of the gun, the captain and one or two chums helping me, and there, though the pain of my wounds was terrible, I laughed and chatted as best I could, and I saw how the battery kept at it against big odds.

Number 1, Sergeant Barker, who was in charge of the gun, had been struck by a piece of shrapnel, which had fractured his leg; but though that was quite enough to knock him out of time, he never flinched or faltered. He held on to his gun, and went on fighting pretty much as if nothing had happened. Number 2, Gunner Weedon, had been wounded through the thigh, a bad injury about three inches long being caused; but he, too, held gamely on.

I tried to crawl out of the pit; but could not do so, and I passed the time by trying to cheer my chums, just as they did their best to help me to keep my own spirits up.

The sergeant found time occasionally to turn round and ask how I was getting on.

"It's all right, old Bean," he shouted cheerily. "Keep quiet. We can manage without you." And he went on firing, while the officers continued to give orders and encourage the men.

I was getting very thirsty and craved for a drink; but I saw no prospect of getting either water or anything else at such a time.

The sergeant noticed my distress and gave me the sweetest drink I ever tasted, and that was a draught from his own canteen. He managed to stop firing for a few seconds while he did this—just long enough to sling his canteen round, let me take a pull, and sling it back. I learned afterwards that throughout the whole of that day, in that inferno of firing and bursting shells, the sergeant stuck to his gun and kept it at. For his courage and tenacity he has been awarded the Distinguished Conduct Medal, and no man has ever more fully deserved it.

I was lying in the gun pit for about an hour, then a doctor came and my wounds were dressed, but there was no chance of getting away for the time being, so I had to wait till the firing ceased. At last a stretcher was brought, and I was carried into a barn which was at the rear of our battery. One of the bearers was Sergeant E. Leet, the right-back in our battery team. He left the fight to bear a hand with me, and as soon as I was safely in the barn he returned to his post. He had no sooner done that than he too was struck down by a wound in the ankle and had to be invalided home.

When I was carried away the major and the sergeant-major said goodbye, and I rather think they expected that that was the last they would ever see of me. I certainly felt bad, and I daresay I looked it; but I was quite cheerful. I particularly felt it when I passed my chum, Charlie Harrison, because for more than six years we had kept together without a break. We shouted goodbye as we passed, and I did not know whether I should ever see him again.

When I reached the barn I wanted to get back to the battery, to be at my own gun again, to bear a hand once more in the fighting that was still going on and seemed as if it would never stop; but when I

"We were in a real hell of bursting shrapnel"

tried to stand up I collapsed, through pain and loss of blood. Soon after this I heard that Charlie Harrison too had been wounded. He was struck on the neck just after I was carried away from the gun pit and had shouted goodbye to him; but he bandaged himself and refused to leave the battery.

What became of him? Why, he got home from the front a day or two ago, and you've just seen him. There he is. And let me show you this shattered foot, to let you see how it is that I'm forced to hop when I want to get about.

And now to get back to the air raid on the East Coast, which to me and other soldiers from the front who saw it, was an extraordinary experience, though I fancy that we took it more or less as a matter of course, because you so soon get used to that kind of thing.

I had scarcely settled down at home when one night there was a fearful commotion, caused by dull explosions. I was a bit taken aback, for I knew what the sounds meant, and thought that I had done with the Germans and righting for a spell at any rate.

As soon as the sound of the explosions was heard, people rushed into the streets—the most dangerous thing they could do—to see what it all meant, and there were cries that the Germans had come.

So they had. They had come in a gas-bag or two, and were dropping bombs on the good old town, which was lighted as usual, though that was soon altered.

I hopped into the street—hopping is the only thing I can do at present—and there I found that there was intense excitement and that women in particular were badly scared. But really the thing did not upset me at all—it was mere child's play compared with what I had been through, so I made myself useful, and hopped away and bought some brandy, which suited some of the scared people very well—so well that there wasn't a drop left for myself.

The raid was soon over, and so was the scare, and I hopped back to the house. There have been several frantic alarms since then, and more than once I have been shaken out of my sleep and told that the Germans have come again; but all I have said has been that it will take something far worse than a German gas-bag raid to make me turn out of bed in the middle of the night.

CHAPTER 19

With the "Fighting Fifth"

One of the battalions which composed the 5th Division of the British Expeditionary Force was the 1st East Surrey Regiment. It was on the 5th Division that so much of the heavy fighting fell on the way to the Aisne, and in that heavy fighting the East Surreys suffered very severely. This story is told by Private W. G. Long, who rejoined his regiment from the Reserve. He has been wounded by shrapnel, and has permanently lost the use of his right arm.

When I went out with my old battalion, the Young Buffs, we were more than 1,300 strong. When I came back, after six weeks' fighting, we had lost more than half that number. This simple fact will show you what the East Surreys have done during the war, as part of the famous "Fighting Fifth" which has been so greatly praised by Sir John French.

I had got up to start my day's work after the August Bank Holiday; but that day's work was never done, for the postman brought the mobilisation papers, and off I went to Kingston, after kissing my wife and baby goodbye. Many a fine fellow who marched off with me is sleeping in or near a little forest which we called "Shrapnel Wood." That was near Missy, where we crossed the Aisne on rafts.

We lost our first man soon after we landed in France, and before we met the Germans. That was at Landrecies, where we went into French barracks, and were told off into rooms which we called rabbit-hutches, because they were so small—no bigger than a little kitchen at home. We were crowded into these, and the only bed we had was a bit of straw on the floor. The nights were bitterly cold, but the days were hot enough to melt us; so we had a bathing parade, and had a fine old time in the canal till one of our men was missed.

I looked around, and saw that one of our fellows was having artificial respiration tried on him. He came round, and then he told us that another man had gone under the water. Then began a really first-class diving display, many of our chaps plunging into the canal to try to find the missing soldier.

At last one of the divers rose and shouted, "I've got him!" And, sure enough, he had brought a poor chap to the surface. Lots of strong arms were stretched out, and in a few seconds the rescued man was got on to the bank, and every effort was made to bring him back to life. But nothing could be done. The man was drowned, and we buried him. This little tragedy threw quite a gloom over us till we moved away.

I am going to tell of a few of the things that happened and affected me personally. They took place mostly when we were retiring, and some of them occurred in the early days, when we were forging along in fearfully bad weather. We were soaked to the skin, and at night did our best to get some sort of shelter by building up the stacks of corn that had been cut for drying, but it was no use. The rain came through so heavily that we gave the task up, and waited for daylight again. When the day came it brought another rain of shells and bullets with it. The place got too warm for us, so we had to leave and retire again. We went on, getting as much shelter as we could; and then we had to halt, and here the sorry discovery was made that we had not a round of ammunition left. At this time there were advancing towards us some men in khaki, and our sergeant, thinking they were our own men, told us not to fire at them.

The order was not necessary, seeing that we had nothing to fire with. As soon as these men got level with us on our flank they opened fire, and then we knew that they were Germans, who had stripped some of our men, or had picked up British caps and greatcoats which had been thrown aside.

In this desperate position a man who belonged to the Cornwall Light Infantry was shot just below the left ear. He was knocked down, but got up, and kept saying, "Help me! Help me!"

I shouted to him to lie down and keep under cover, but he took no notice, and kept on calling for help. He came up to me, and when he was near enough I pulled him down and forced him to lie on the ground. All this time there was a very heavy fire. We were getting shots from the front and on our flanks, and there was nothing for it but to get away as best we could.

I could not bear the thought of leaving this Cornwall man where he was, so I took him up and began to carry him, but it was very slow going. It was all uphill, the ground was sodden with rain, and I had to force a way through a field of turnips, which were growing as high as my knees. It was bad enough to make one's own way through such a tangle as that; but I am young and strong, and I managed to make progress, although I was hit five different times—not hurt, but struck, a shot, for instance, hitting my cap, another my water-bottle, and another the sleeve of my coat.

After going a long distance, as it seemed, and feeling utterly exhausted, I put my man down under what I thought was safe shelter. I wanted to give him a drink, but I could not do so, as the shot-hole in my water-bottle had let the water run to waste.

At last we reached a roadway, where we saw some more of our men, who had got there before us, and had commandeered a horseless cart and filled it with wounded men.

I got the wounded man into the cart, and then off we all went. It was as much as we could manage to get the cart along, for it was such a great big thing; but we worked it willingly, the officers taking their turn in the shafts.

We dragged the cart along the heavy roads, but it was such hard going that we saw that we should be forced to get a horse from somewhere; so we looked around at the first farm we came to—and a sorry place it was, with everything in confusion, and the animals about suffering terribly and starving—and there we found a horse of the largest size.

With great difficulty we got together bits of harness, string and rope, and tied the horse in the shafts with the ropes for traces, and when we had finished we did not know whether we had harnessed the horse or tied the cart on to it. Anyway, we got along very well after that.

The cart had amongst its wounded an infantry officer who had been saved by one of our fellows, though the officer belonged to another regiment. He had got entangled in some barbed wire, and, as he had been wounded in the leg, he could not move either one way or the other. He was absolutely helpless, and under a heavy fire.

Our fellow went out and got to the helpless officer, and, by sticking at it and doing all he could, being himself pretty badly cut in the operation, he freed the officer from the entanglement, and carried him safely up to the cart. We were getting on very nicely with our little contrivance when we ran into the 2nd Dragoons, but we soon left them behind us, and found ourselves amongst some of our own transport. We joined up with it, adding another and a very strange waggon to the column, and on we went until we reached a large town and halted.

During the whole of this time I had been carrying a canteen which had belonged to a Frenchman. It was quite a big canteen, and I kept it filled with apples, of which we got an enormous number, and on which at times we had practically to live for two or three days together.

We had reached a stage of fighting when we had to make continuous short rushes against the Germans, under hails of shrapnel. In making these rushes it often happened that we sheltered behind a little sort of earthwork which we threw up. We just made a bit of head cover and lay behind that; but sometimes this head cover could not be made, and that was where I scored with my Frenchman's canteen.

During one of our rushes shrapnel burst right over my head, and one fellow said to me, "I wouldn't carry that thing, George, if I were you." But, having kept it for so long, I was not going to throw it away.

Away we went. I was carrying the canteen in my left hand, and my rifle in the right; but I changed them over, and I had no sooner done that than crash came a shell, and, in bursting, a fragment hit the canteen, and took a great piece out of it. I should have been badly wounded myself, but I had filled the canteen with earth, and so it had protected me and acted as a first-rate cover. The man who was on my right received a nasty wound.

After this we had to advance over open country, where there was not so much as a blade of grass for cover. We went on till we reached a ditch, which was full of water. Some of us had to wade through it, but others, by going farther back, were able to cross a tiny footbridge—one of those narrow planks which only allow one man at a time to cross. The Germans had a machine-gun trained at this little bridge so we lost no time in getting off it. It was here that our captain was mortally wounded by a shot, and we had other casualties in crossing the bridge.

From this point we had to climb to the top of a hill, which was so steep that we had to dig our fixed bayonets into the ground to help us up. There was a wood at the top of the hill, and there we took shelter; but we had no sooner got amongst the trees than the shrapnel was on us again, causing many casualties.

There were many funny incidents at this place, and one I particularly remember was that there were three of us in a sort of heap, when a piece of shell dropped just alongside. There was not any great force in it, because before falling the piece had struck a tree; but, as it dropped, fellows started turning up the collars of their coats, and rolling themselves into balls—just as if things of that sort could make any difference to a bursting shell; but it is amusing to see what men will do at such a time as that.

From this wood we got into what seemed a wide roadway between two other woods, and here we were under a never-ending rain of bullets, which hit the trees, sending splinters all over us, cutting branches off and ploughing up the ground on every side. One of our officers said, "Keep your heads down, lads," and he had scarcely got the words out of his mouth when he was shot in the body and killed, and we had to leave him where he fell.

So heavy and continuous was the fire that we could not get on between these two woods, and we had to try another way; so we started to go through a vineyard, but we were forced to lie down. We sheltered as best we could amongst the vines, with bullets coming and actually cutting off bunches of grapes. Like good British soldiers, we made the best of the business, for we were both hungry and thirsty, and we devoured a good many of the bunches that were knocked off by the German bullets.

After this we got into an orchard, but we did not remain there long, as the place was later on blown to smithereens. We hung on to the orchard till it was dark, then we advanced farther into the wood, and again got through into the open, and lay down to try and get some sleep; but that was almost impossible, because it was raining and perishingly cold, and we had nothing at all for cover. Then, in whispers, we were ordered to get out as silently as we possibly could.

At first I could not understand the meaning of this secrecy, but it soon became known that we had been actually sleeping amongst the enemy, though we were not aware of this until we were again on the move. We crept about like a lot of mice, till we reached a village, where we were to get some breakfast.

We were settling down, and making ourselves comfortable under a wall which gave us some cover. There were some men from another regiment with us, and we thought we were going to have a good time, for we had got hold of some biscuits and jam. Then over the wall came a shell, which exploded and wounded about seven men from the other regiment. We did not stop for any more breakfast, and some of the men who had had nothing to eat did not trouble to get anything, and they went without food for the rest of the day.

We went back to the wood, and there we soon again found the Germans, and plenty of them. We fired at them for all we were worth, after which we advanced a little, and came across so many dead that we had to jump over them every pace we took. One thing which particularly struck me then, and which I remember now, was the great size of some of these German soldiers. At a little distance they looked just like fallen logs.

After that our officer called us together to wait for reinforcements. I thought I would have a look around me, and while I was doing so I saw one German running off to our left, about fifteen yards away. I took aim and fired, and down he went. I got down on my knee and unloaded my rifle, when I saw another German going in the same direction. I was just getting ready to take aim again, but this time I did not fire—in fact, I did not even get to the aim, for I felt something hit my arm.

For the moment I thought that some chap behind me had knocked me with his rifle or his foot. I turned round, but there was no one behind me, so I concluded that I had been hit. I stood up, and then my arm began to wobble, and the blood streamed out of my sleeve.

Someone shouted, "You've got it, George."

And I replied: "Yes; in the arm somewhere, but where I don't know."

I did my best to get back again, and then a fellow came, and ripped the sleeve open and dressed my arm, and there was all my elbow joint laid open, and some of the bones broken. This chap wanted to take me back to the village, but I said I was all right, although in a sense I was helpless. We started going back, and we got to the first house, where we saw a poor old man and his daughter who had been there all through the fighting. The place was filled with wounded, and the two were doing their best for them.

I asked for a drink, for I was almost dying of thirst, and I got some whisky. While I was drinking it a shell burst in the middle of the road, and sent the mud and stones everywhere; so I shifted my quarters, and went along to a big house which had been a fine place, but it had been pulled to pieces, and was now being used as a hospital. The place itself gave no protection, but we found a cellar and crowded into it, and there we watched the Germans blowing the temporary hospital to pieces.

The night came, and it was terrible to hear the poor chaps moaning with pain. I was in pain myself now, but my sufferings were a mere nothing compared with those of some of the men around me. It seemed as if the day would never break, but at last it came, and by that time some of the poor fellows who had been making such pitiful noises were no more. Sometime after that, however, I got away in a field ambulance.

When we were at Le Cateau many spies were caught. I saw several of them. They were young chaps, dressed up as women and as boys and girls, and it was not very easy to detect them. One was disguised as a woman, with rather a good figure. I saw this interesting female when she was captured by our artillery. The gunners had their suspicions aroused, with the result that they began to knock the lady about a bit, and her wig fell off. Then her figure proved to be not what it seemed, for the upper front part of it was composed of two carrier-pigeons! I did not see the end of that batch of spies, but a battery sergeant-major afterwards told me that they had been duly shot.

One of the most extraordinary things I saw was the conduct of a man who had had his right arm shot off from above the elbow. I was standing quite near him, and expected that he would fall and be helpless. Instead of doing that, he turned his head and looked at the place where the arm should have been. I suppose he must have been knocked off his balance by what had happened. At any rate, he gave a loud cry, and instantly started to run as fast as I ever saw a man go. Two or three members of the Royal Army Medical Corps at once gave chase, with the object of securing him and attending to him. The whole lot of them disappeared over some rising ground, and what happened to them I do not know.

I saw many fellows who had queer tales to tell of what had happened to them. One chap, a rifleman, who was in the ship coming home, was so nervous that the slightest noise made him almost jump out of his skin. And well it might, for his nerves had been shattered. A shell had buried itself in the ground just in front of him and exploded, blowing him fifteen feet into the air, and landing him in a bed of mud. He was so completely stunned that he lay there for about eight hours, scarcely moving, though he was not even scratched. He came round all right, but was a nervous wreck, and had to be invalided.

"I TOOK HIM UP AND BEGAN TO CARRY HIM"

Chapter 20

The Victory of the Marne

One of the most moving statements in the earlier official reports dealing with the war was that about the fighting at Mons and elsewhere, which cost us 6000 men, and no paragraph was more stirring than that relating to Landrecies, a quiet little French town on the Sambre. "In Landrecies alone," the report said, "a German infantry brigade advanced in the closest order into the narrow street, which they completely filled. Our machine-guns were brought to bear on this target from the end of the town. The head of the column was swept away, a frightful panic ensued, and it is estimated that no fewer than 800 to 900 dead and wounded Germans were lying in this street alone." The story of that furious combat and the subsequent operations on the Marne is told by Corporal G. Gilliam, of the Coldstream Guards. On September 6 1914, in conjunction with the French, the British assumed the offensive, and, after a four days' desperate struggle, which is known as the Battle of the Marne, the Germans were driven back to Soissons, with enormous losses."

It was early on the afternoon of August 26 when we entered Landrecies, which is a little garrison town, consisting mostly of a single street in which there are three cross-roads. We were billeted in the people's houses, and for the first time in three days we had a drop of tea and a bit of dinner in comfort, and to crown our satisfaction we were told we could lie down and rest, but we were to have our bayonets fixed and rifles by our sides and kits ready to put on.

We were soon down to it and sound asleep. It was about eight o'clock when some of us woke, and after a smoke were off to sleep again, but not for long, for almost immediately we heard the sound of a motorcycle, and knew that the rider was travelling at a terrific rate.

Nearer and nearer came the sound, and the rider himself swept round the corner of the street. He never stopped nor slackened speed; he simply shouted one word as he vanished, and that was "Germans!" Only one word, but enough.

Rifles in hand, we rushed to the top of the street and lined the three crossroads, lying down. Our officer, who was standing up behind us, said, "Lie still, men"; and we did—perfectly still, not a man moving. All at once, out of the darkness, an officer came and cried in English to our commander, "Surrender!"

"We don't surrender here" our officer answered. "Take that!"—and instantly shot him through the head with his revolver.

Our officer's shot had scarcely died away when crash went a German artillery gun, and a lyddite shell burst right over us. This was our first experience of lyddite, and the fumes nearly choked us.

"Lie still, boys—don't move!" said our officer; and we lay low.

Just then, from the opposite direction, we heard the sound of horses and a waggon, in the distance, it seemed; but soon it was very near, and to our great joy there dashed up the street one of the guns of the 17th Field Battery. There was a shout of "Into action! Left wheel!" And in truly magnificent style that gun was almost instantly laid and ready for action.

Shells now came upon us rapidly, wounding several of our men; but our maxim gunners had got to work, and very soon enormous numbers of Germans were put beyond the power of doing any further mischief.

Many brave things were done that night at Landrecies; but there was nothing finer than the work of our maxim-gunner Robson, who was on our left. Our machine-guns were by now at our end of the town, and they had a solid mass of Germans to go at. Robson was sitting on his stool, and as soon as the officer ordered "Fire!" his maxim hailed death. It literally was a hail of fire that met the packed Germans, and swept down the head of the column, so that the street was choked in an instant with the German dead. Those who lived behind pushed on in desperation—shoved on by the masses still further behind, the darkness being made light by the fire of the maxims and the enemy's rifles. Those behind, I say, pressed on, with fearful cries, but only to be mown down and shattered, so that the street became more than ever glutted with the dead and wounded. The Germans were thrown into frenzy, and if sheer weight of men could have driven the head of the column on to us not a British soldier could have lived that night at

Landrecies.

Meanwhile, we had been ordered to hold our fire. There were only 600 of us opposed to an immense body of Germans; but the maxims were doing annihilating work, and the artillery had got into action.

When the gun of the 17th had got the order to fire we heard a gunner shout: "Watch me put that gun out of action!"—meaning a German gun which had been brought up and laid against us. He fired, and the most marvellous thing happened, for the shell from it went right down the muzzle of the German weapon and shattered it to pieces.

Then we heard a shout, and before we could look round about 4000 German infantry were charging us, with horns blowing and drums beating—adding to the fearful din.

"Don't shoot, boys," shouted our officer, "till I give the word!"

On the living mass of Germans came. They rushed up to within 80 yards of us; then the order rang out: "Fire!"

Again the Germans got it—fifteen rounds to the minute from each rifle, for the front rank men had their loading done for them. As soon as a rifle was emptied it was handed to the rear and a fresh loaded rifle was handed back. In this way the rifles were kept from getting too hot, and an incessant fire was poured into the Germans.

In spite of this hail, a few Germans managed to break through their walls of dead and wounded. One of them, disguised as a French officer, and wanting us to think he had been a prisoner, but had just broken away from the Germans, rushed up to Robson and patted him on the shoulder and said: "Brave fellow!" And with that he whipped round his sword and killed our maxim gunner on the spot; but he himself was instantly shot down by our enraged fellows.

There was another case of treachery, this time, unhappily, from inside our ranks. Our guide, a man claiming to be a Frenchman, at about one o'clock in the morning, turned traitor, and went and told the Germans how many there were of us, and by way of indicating our position he fired a haystack; but he had no sooner done that than two bullets settled him.

One of our corporals dashed away to put the fire out, but before he reached the haystack he was killed. It was at this time that Private Wyatt, of my company, rushed out—everything was done at a rush— and brought in a wounded officer. The colonel, who was on his horse, and saw what had happened, said: "Who is that brave man?" He was told, and afterwards Wyatt was taken before the general and recommended for a decoration.

Hour after hour, all through the time of darkness, and until daylight came, that terrible fight went on. For seven long hours a few hundred British Guards had kept at bay an enormous body of Germans—and at the end of the firing we had killed far more than the whole of our force numbered when the battle began. We had given them wholesale death from our machine-guns, our rifles, and our artillery, and they had faced it they had been driven on to it. Now they were to have the bayonet.

We gave them two charges; but they didn't stop long, for as soon as they saw the cold steel on the ends of our rifles they were off like a shot, throwing down a lot of rifles and equipment. When this happened it was between five and six o'clock on the morning of the 27th, and we then got the order to retire.

We were told that we had lost 126 in killed and wounded. That was a heavy list, but not so big as we had expected, bearing in mind the furious nature of the fight. The marvel was that we had not been wiped out, and we should certainly have been in a very serious state if it had not been for the 17th Field Battery. There is this to be said, too: if the Germans had broken through our lines it would have meant that, in all probability, the whole Second Division of our army would have been cut up.

We fell in and were soon on the march again, retiring, and we marched as fast as we could go till we halted at a rather large town about ten miles from Landrecies. Here we were in clover, in a way of speaking, because we sheltered in a clay-pit where the French had been making bricks, and we all sat down and waited for our tea of German shells.

They soon came and we were on the move again, and we were constantly at it, retiring and fighting, until we halted about thirty miles from Paris; then we were told that after retiring another dozen miles it would be our turn to advance.

Didn't we cheer? It was glorious to hear we were going to chase the Germans instead of their chasing us. At this time we had our first wash for a fortnight, and it was as good as having a thousand pounds given to us.

The fiercest fighting of the war has taken place on Sundays, and it was on a Sunday that the Battle of the Marne began. The Germans had had the biggest surprise of their lives on a Sunday, and that was at Mons. Though we had been kept on the go because they outnumbered us so hopelessly, we mauled them mercilessly on the retreat, teaching them many bitter lessons. When we got to the Marne and were able to tackle them on equal terms, they scarcely had a look in. The Germans had almost reached the forts of Paris, and, I daresay, had their bands ready to play them into the city. Soon, however, they were hurrying back on their tracks a good deal faster than they had come. We heard the German bands playing a good many times, but every time we heard the music it was farther away from Paris.

We covered such big tracks of country, and saw so many great happenings, that it is the most difficult thing in the world to know where to start a story of the Marne; but I will come down to the time just before the battle, when we were still retiring, and had got used to marching twenty or twenty-five miles a day. We had left the Germans very sore for coming too close to us, and we had gone through a small town and entered a great wood.

While we were in the wood I had to fall out. Almost instantly I heard the sound of talking which wasn't English, and in the distance I saw six Germans coming after me as hard as they could. I thought it was all up with me, but I said "Come on, chum, let's clear!"—"chum" being my rifle, which I had placed on the ground. I snatched it up and sprang behind a tree, and felt fairly safe. It's wonderful what a feeling of security a good rifle and plenty of ammunition give you. I waited till the Germans got within a hundred yards of me; then with a good aim I fetched down two; but my position was becoming very critical, as the other four dodged from tree to tree, watching for a chance to pot me, and it looked very much as if they wouldn't have long to wait. I don't know what would have happened, but to my intense relief three men of the 17th Field Battery, which was passing, rushed up and shouted, "Don't move. We'll have 'em!"

By this time the four Germans were within about fifty yards, continually sniping at me—how I blessed them for being such bad shots!—and at last they came out into the open and made straight in my direction. But they only dashed about twenty yards, for my rescuers put "paid" to the four of them, and saved me from being made a prisoner and worse, far worse, for by that time we had seen proof enough of the monstrous things they did to men they captured—things you might expect from an opponent, but certainly not from soldiers.

The last day of our retirement was September 4, and on that day we never saw the enemy. We had crossed and recrossed the River

Marne, and had blown up bridges as we retired; but the Germans threw their own bridges over the river with amazing speed, and kept up the pursuit. Sometimes they overdid their zeal, and were a trifle too quick for their own comfort.

We had blown up two bridges that crossed the Marne, one a railway bridge and the other a fine stone structure. I was one of the last of our men to cross the stone bridge before the engineers, who had made it ready for destruction. The bridge ran between two high banks, so that it was a considerable height above the water. When the explosion took place there was a tremendous shattering roar, almost like a salvo of Black Marias, then a crashing and grinding and thudding as the middle of the bridge was utterly wrecked, and fell into the river, leaving an immense gap between the banks. The work of months, costing thousands upon thousands of pounds, had been smashed in a few seconds.

I was looking back at the ruins when I saw a motorcar, with several Germans in it, tearing after us, meaning to cross the bridge as we had done. The car came on at a tremendous speed, and the Germans in it must have had eyes only for us and none for the road in front of them, for they rushed on right into the blank space, and before they knew what was happening, the car was in the river.

We had had battle after battle, each one in itself enough to make a long story. We had fought and marched in the fearful August heat, and had been thankful when we could lie down with a little heap of sand or a sheaf of corn as a pillow. At last we were so near Paris that the forts opened fire, and that was the beginning of what I'm sure will be the end of the Germans.

Now at last we were in touch with the French, and we got the Germans in a proper grip. The French got round the Germans and turned them towards Coulommiers, a town on the Marne; then the British took the job on and drove the Germans through the town. That part of the work fell largely on the Guards, and what we were doing was being done, of course, over an enormous stretch of country by other British and French troops.

We had got to the night of September 5 and were lying in trenches which we had dug along a canal bank about Coulommiers. We waited for the Germans to come, and they came in fine style. It was getting dark and we could make out three of their aeroplanes sweeping in the air like big birds. We had seen a good deal of the German aeroplanes by this time and knew what to expect. These were trying to find out

"Before they knew what was happening the car was in the river."

our positions, so that they could signal to their gunners and give them the range.

Suddenly the aeroplanes dropped some balls of blue fire, and very pretty the fireworks looked; but we hadn't time to admire them, because the German artillery instantly opened fire on us with such fury that we felt the very ground shake as we lay in our trenches.

Under cover of their guns the Germans—the 32nd Infantry Brigade, I think it was—dashed up to the other side of the canal bank and blazed away at us; but we blazed harder at them. We gave them a fair hell of rifle fire and very soon they were forced to clear out, leaving the whole of the canal bank littered with their dead and wounded.

A fine little "tiffey" we had at the Marne was a rearguard action, in which there was one of those British cavalry and infantry charges that have shaken a lot of the Germans to pieces, especially the *Uhlans*, who are a pretty poor crowd in spite of all their boasting.

Our scouts had returned with the news that the Germans were entrenched about a mile and a half away, on the bank of the Marne. We got the order to extend the usual three paces, and our advance guard went out, while our main body lay down. Our advance guard had gone about 900 yards when the German infantry opened fire. We took it up, and there was a ceaseless rattle. We kept the Germans well employed, and our advance guard were pouring in a proper good peppering. But there was a little surprise in store for them. We had with us a couple of the magnificent British cavalry regiments—the Scots Greys and the 16th Lancers, and they swept on till they got to a little wood, where they had the Germans on the left wing of their rearguard, fairly at their mercy.

When they were ready for the charge the signal was given to our advance guard, and, with a perfect roar of cheering, the British cavalry and infantry hurled themselves on the Germans, a tremendous weight of horse and man. The Greys and the 16th fairly thundered over the earth, and the Guards rushed up in splendid style, though we had our heavy packs, and in such hot weather a big weight adds enormously to the terrific work of charging. But you don't think of heat or weight at such a time—you feel only the thrill and excitement of the battle and have the joy of knowing that you are settling the account of a suffering and outraged nation.

Cavalry and Guards got in amongst the Germans and fairly scattered them. I got one German in the back and another sideways, and all around me chums were doing the same, while the cavalry were cutting the Germans down everywhere. Limbs literally flew about as they were lopped off with the sword, and Germans in the open and in the trenches—for we routed them out—fell to the bayonet.

That was a fierce and bloody "tiffey," and there have been many like it. At the end of it we had settled that particular German rearguard and had a nice bag of prisoners. A lot of these prisoners were glad to be out of the business; most of the Germans we captured seemed to feel like that, and I remember hearing one of them—an officer—say, in good English, "Thank God I'm caught! Now I shall not starve any more!"

Talking of charges, I might tell you that there is a great difference between the British and the German ways of doing it. The Germans make as much noise as possible—a perfect devil of a row, with drums thumping and trumpets sounding, and, of course, their banners flying. We carry no colours into action (we leave them at home), we have no drum-thumping and no bugles sounding—often enough the signal for a charge is just something like a hand wave or a word of command; but that answers all practical purposes and starts us on the business as quickly and full of fire as any amount of noise.

When we had got through our first rearguard action we thought we had driven the Germans to the other side of the Marne and got them fairly on the move back to Berlin; but to our surprise we were attacked by a strong force of their cavalry, who had been in ambush not a thousand yards away. The German horsemen came on us at a full gallop and swept on until they were about two hundred yards away. At this particular spot there were Guards, Worcesters, and Camerons, and it looked very much as if the Germans would dash up and do a lot of mischief.

The commander of the Worcesters shouted, "Fix bayonets! Make sure of your men."

On came the German cavalry, with a roar and a rattle, until they were less than a hundred yards away; then we let go and the troopers tumbled out of their saddles like ninepins. The going was too hard for German cavalry, and as one of their officers shouted an order, they wheeled round and made off, rushing, as they supposed, for a safe place and a way out; but they galloped straight up to a spot where some French artillery were in position.

The Germans thundered on towards their fancied safety; then there were crashes from the French artillery, and shells went plump into the horsemen and practically annihilated them. Horses and men were shattered, and of those who escaped the French took about one hundred and fifty prisoners. It was a fine little performance, and helped us to fix in our memories the first meeting with the Frenchmen on the Marne.

The artillery fire on the Marne was awful in its destructiveness and earsplitting in its noise—sometimes the very air seemed to be solid matter that was broken into chunks and knocked about you; but we soon got used to it all, and laughed and smoked and joked in the trenches, where, at the back, we had dugouts which we called rabbit-hutches, These were shelter-places, well covered at the top, and were most useful protections against shells. When the enemy's fire became too hot we would go into our rabbit-hutches.

About noon on the 6th we had re-formed and advanced to the bank of the river, and there we found that we were opposed to a large body of Germans and that they had howitzer batteries with them. These howitzers do deadly mischief, and the fumes from their lyddite shells are perfectly poisonous—they spread through a good big patch of air and suffocate the men. It was about four o'clock in the afternoon when the Germans began to pour into us a fearful fire, and we were enfiladed; but our trenches gave us some fine shelter, and the Germans did not have their own way for long, nor did they do much damage at that point. Here again the British had ready one more of the many surprises that the Germans met with on the banks of the Marne. One of our batteries of short howitzers, four guns, went along the river bank and hid in some bushes on the right of the German howitzers, while a battery of our field artillery dashed up and took a commanding position which got the Germans between two fires. Then the command was given, "Ten rounds rapid fire!"

But ten rounds were not needed—only four were fired before the German battery was put to rest. But the crippling of the German howitzers did not seem to have much effect on the enemy at that point, for they rushed up more of the infantry, which, brought along by immense numbers of trains and motors, literally swarmed over the countryside.

At this time we renewed our acquaintance with some of the Germans who were known to us as the "drop-shots." I believe there is only one brigade of them in the German Army, and I will do them the justice to say that they are very good at the game. They kneel down, and putting the butt of the rifle on the thigh, fire in the air at an angle of about forty-five degrees. The bullet makes a big arc and drops right on top of you in such places as trenches. These "drop-shots" were about four hundred yards away, but they hadn't got just the right range of us and the bullets plugged into the wrong places.

The "drop-shots" tried their queer game on us for about half an hour, but finding that they could not damage us, they stopped, especially as we were beginning to shift them out of their positions. There was some furious rifle firing between the troops entrenched on both banks of the Marne, and often enough the reddened water bore away many a dead soldier.

The righting was always most fierce when the Germans were in masses and hurled their regiments against us in their attempt to hack their way through to Paris. Any street fighting that came about was sure to be terrific, and one of the most furious of the fights took place in the streets of Coulommiers, a town similar to Reading.

Coulommiers, of course, was almost entirely given up to troops, for the inhabitants had been warned by us to leave and get as far away from the Germans as they could go. Poor souls, they did not need much persuading, knowing what they did of German "culture," and, carrying with them only such few oddments as they could quickly collect, they fled, the roads leading to Paris being thick with them. During this fighting in Coulommiers there was such brilliant moonlight that you could see almost well enough to shoot a rabbit.

It was about eight o'clock at night when we got to Coulommiers. We were just going to stop to have some food when the Germans put two big shells into us, killing four of our men, and wounding fourteen. We jumped up, fixed bayonets, and rushed for the Germans; but we were brought up by some more shells, and for a couple of hours the guns were banging at us. Fortunately the shells had a bit too long a range, and instead of hitting us they went over the back of us.

We lay down until ten o'clock, when the order was given to prepare to charge. Up again we sprang—we were getting used to charging—and made another rush, running as hard as we could down the street for a hundred yards, then lying flat in the roadway.

All this time the Germans were pouring in on us a fire which, if it had been accurate, would have swept us out of existence. But it was very poor stuff, and we were lucky enough to escape with the loss of a very few men. We were lying down for five minutes, then we were up and off again, dashing along the main street.

It was a rousing bit of work, and we gloried in it, especially when, from every doorway in the street, Germans dashed out and made a bolt for their lives. They had been firing at us from bedroom windows, and tore frantically downstairs and out of doorways when they saw that we were fairly on the job and after them.

That bolting gave us just the chance we wanted. We drove after the flying Germans as hard as we could go, and being big and powerful men, with plenty of weight in us, we literally picked some of them up on the bayonets. We rushed them through the town and out of it; then we came across a gang of Germans who were no good at all. They had looted all the wine-shops and soaked themselves with liquor. Many a German from Mons to the Marne was drunk when he died or was made a prisoner.

When we had dashed through Coulommiers we had to halt, because the Germans had four batteries of guns and a division of cavalry waiting for us. So we retired to the cross-roads in the middle of the town, and had to take up almost exactly the same position as we did at Landrecies, where the Coldstreamers wiped out a strong German force in the street. We waited at Coulommiers till our heavy howitzer batteries were fetched up, then we lined the cross-roads, two howitzers were placed at the end of each street and we were in at the finish of the fight.

It was about midnight when the Germans started shelling us again, and the town blazed and boomed with the awful gunfire. We did not suffer much damage, but the houses were wrecked, and bricks and stones and pieces of timber were flying all about. A few of the bricks struck us, but we paid no heed to trifles like that. The Germans kept up the firing till about half-past two in the morning. Then, to our great surprise, they charged down the street.

"Lie still, boys, and let them come!" our officers shouted.

We lay perfectly quiet, and let the Germans rush on till they were almost upon us; then the sharp order came: "Ten rounds rapid fire! "

There was an absolute fusillade, and the ten rounds were fired in less than a minute, and simply struck the Germans down. Their dead and wounded were lying thick in the roadway and on the pavements when we sprang up and were after the survivors with the bayonet. This time we chased them up to the very muzzles of the guns, where we had a splendid bit of luck. The German gunners flew when they saw us, and we were on top of them and on top of the infantry. We dashed straight through the batteries, the enemy flying before the bayonet, and there, in the moonlight, which was almost as strong as daylight, I accounted for two of them with my own steel.

For fully three miles that furious chase was kept up, the Germans flying in all directions. It was a long and fierce fight in the moonlight, but at the end of it Coulommiers was ours, and six batteries of German guns and a thousand prisoners were ours, too, to say nothing of the killed and wounded.

You might have thought that enough had been done, but we had scarcely settled down to have a little drop of something hot to drink—and we needed it badly—when the cry arose, "Come on, boys; let's get after them again!" We emptied our canteens, which were full of hot coffee and rum, and were after the Germans again as hard as we could go. By daylight we had put the finish on them at Coulommiers. We were well pleased, too, with the fine haul of guns.

We had fought fiercely, and had not spared the Germans—no one could have any mercy on them who saw the proofs, as we had seen them, of their barbarities. When we advanced into Coulommiers we saw the bodies of two little girls who had been murdered and mutilated in a shocking manner. There were in that locality alone scores of such atrocities committed by the brutes.

I had a fair innings at the Marne, and saw a good deal of the beginning of the fight which started the Germans on the run. I had two days and nights of it; then I was bowled out by a piece of shell which struck me on the thigh and went off with a piece of flesh. I felt as if a brick had hit me, and when I saw the blood I thought it was all up with me. The doctor told me that this might easily have happened if the wound had been a little deeper. He was Lieutenant Huggin, of the Royal Army Medical Corps, a kind and brave gentleman, who was soon afterwards killed while doing his duty under fire. He was mentioned in despatches, with other officers who did so much. I remember one of them, a field officer of the Coldstreamers, during a very hot fight standing with his hands in his pockets watching to see how things were going, and saying, "Men, this is beautiful! We shall soon be on the other side of the river."

And we soon were—though to cross the Marne meant that we had at one time to fight waist deep in its waters.

The Battle of the Marne was hard, long work, following a long and terrible retreat; but it was a glorious victory. We had many privations, but also many compensations, and we were always cheerful, and very often singing. "Tipperary" was an easy first.

Sir John French used to come into the trenches with his hands in his pockets and take no more notice of the German shells and bullets

"Cavalry and guards got in amongst the Germans and fairly scattered them".

which were bursting and flying about than if they were peas shot by little boys.

One morning Sir John came round the trenches, and said, as usual, "Is everything all right, men? "

"Well, sir," he was told, "we want a drop of water, please." And we did want it, badly, because the weather was so fearfully hot, and we were almost boiled in our uniforms and heavy kits.

"Certainly; I'll see to that at once," replied the field-marshal. He immediately turned round, called to some men of the transport who were at hand, and told them to bring us some water at once.

General Joffre, too, was a great favourite. He speaks English well. Once when he came into the trenches he asked if there was anything we should like. Well, we wanted some cigarettes badly, and told him so, and he promptly took a box of about a hundred from his pocket, and handed them round.

I am now well enough to be back at the front, and I'm keen to get into the firing line again, and rush along in some more bayonet charges—for those are the swoops that roll the Germans up as much as anything we do.

I have been a Coldstreamer for more than a dozen years, and have always been proud of it; but I never felt prouder than I do now, after reading what our chief has said about us in despatches.

We have sometimes been called feather-bed soldiers; but we're known as "Coldsteelers" now, and try to live up to the reputation of our motto—"*Second to none.*"

CHAPTER 21

An Armoured Car in Ambush

Sir John French, in one of his despatches, expressed his great admiration of the glorious work which has been done at the front by our Territorials—that work, indeed, by this time has become almost equal to the glorious achievements of our Regular troops. The first of our Territorials to go into action during the war were the Northumberland Hussars, and this story is told by Trooper Stanley Dodds, of that corps, who was serving as a despatch-rider and on being wounded was invalided home. He afterwards returned to the front. Trooper Dodds is one of the best-known motor cyclists in the North, and winner in the competition of the summer of 1914 promoted by the North-Eastern Automobile Association. This was decided in North Yorkshire, over difficult country.

I fancy there are people in England who imagine that the life of a despatch-rider is one long unbroken joy ride. They seem to think that he gets somewhere near the front, and spends all his days careering over beautifully kept military roads between headquarters and the firing line, and seeing and enjoying everything that goes on; but I can assure such people that in practice despatch-riding does not work out like that at all.

I am only a humble member of the fraternity, but I have had a fair share of despatch work, and I do know that I have not had a single joy ride since I took the business on, and I can vouch for the fact that beautifully kept roads do not exist anywhere near the front, at any rate in Flanders. Even some of the so-called roads have never been roads—they were simply tracks to start with, and when military traffic had been going over them for some time they had lost all resemblance to roads, and you could scarcely tell the difference between them and the ordinary countryside.

The fact is that the life of a despatch-rider, though exciting enough to satisfy the cravings of any ordinary man, is largely an endless battle amongst bad roads, bullets and shell fire, want of sleep, and the hundred-and-one other things which often wreck the nerves; but the life is well worth living, all the same.

In work like this there is a good deal of nerve-racking riding and all sorts of difficult jobs have to be tackled. One of the worst I had to carry out while I was at the front was riding back to a patrol which was in our rear, and which had been lost sight of in the strain and turmoil of a rapid retirement.

The patrol had been left at a corner where there were some forked roads, and in order to reach them it was necessary to go through a village.

The Germans were everywhere and keenly on the look-out for a chance of sniping, so that there was plenty of excitement in the affair, especially as it was night and there was a darkness which was literally black.

This made the task doubly dangerous, for in addition to the ordinary risks of being shot there was the great danger of coming to serious grief on the road—a road which you could feel but scarcely see. I don't mind saying that when I started in the pitch darkness on this expedition I did not feel any too comfortable.

It is the custom at such times to ride without lights, because lights serve as targets, but in spite of this I was forced to light up, because it would have been utterly impossible to ride without some sort of guide.

After a good deal of trouble and a lot of risk I reached the village and then I had a most unpleasant shock, for a Belgian peasant told me that the Germans were actually occupying some of the houses.

That was a startling announcement, but the added danger forced me to set my wits to work to decide what it was best to do. At last I determined to make tracks down a side street.

I was riding very slowly and carefully when I was pulled up short with a sharp cry of "Halt" and I knew that a loaded rifle was covering me not far away.

I did halt—I didn't need to be told twice, not knowing what fate had in store for me; but thank heaven I quickly found that it was a British sentry who had spoken.

I rapidly told him what I was out to do, and I was very glad to have his help and advice.

The sentry told me that the patrol, like wise men, had acted on their own initiative and had fallen back on the village—and that was joyful news, because it meant that my work was practically done.

Being greatly relieved I could not resist the temptation to tell the sentry that I might have scooted past him and got clear, but my humour vanished when another British soldier from the darkness said grimly, "Yes, you might have got past *him*, but *I* should have put a bullet into you!"

I have not the slightest doubt that this smart fellow spoke the truth—anyway, if he had missed me I should doubtless have been potted by a chum of his, because there were four sentries posted at short distances from this place. I could not see a sign of them, but of course they had my light as a target and they were as keen as mustard, knowing that the Germans were in the village.

There were a good many little thrilling experiences for all of us which came in as part of the day's work, and most of them were thoroughly enjoyable—a few in particular I would not have missed for worlds. One of these was a little jaunt with an armoured motorcar.

Incidentally, this experience showed me that we have learnt a good deal from the South African War. It is pretty common knowledge by this time that the Germans sprang something of a surprise on the world with their big guns; but our own armoured cars came on the Germans with even more stunning effect. It was the South African War which to a great extent gave us the most useful knowledge we now possess of armoured cars and armoured trains.

The armoured car is a development of the idea of the armoured train, with this enormous advantage, that you can get your car pretty nearly anywhere, while the train is limited in its operations to the lines on which it runs. Remarkably good motorcar work at the front has been done by Brigadier-General Seely and Commander Sampson. Some of these cars are extremely powerful and fast, with huge wheels, and in the hands of skilful drivers they can overcome almost any obstacle.

In order to meet the exceptional demands which a war like this makes upon them the cars have to be specially protected and strengthened. The body itself is protected with toughened steel, which has so much resistance that bullets simply make no impression on it, and light guns can therefore be mounted behind the metal which can do enormous execution amongst bodies of the enemy's riflemen or troops who are not protected by anything but rifles. If you want excitement, therefore, you can get it to the full by being associated with these machines. Whenever they go out they simply look for trouble—and they can afford to do so, because they despise ordinary cavalry and infantry tactics. Their chief gain has been *Uhlan* patrols, which they have wiped out with the greatest ease.

Scouts bring in word of enemy patrols on the road; off swoop the cars straight to the spot, and the fun begins.

My own little job was not actually in an armoured car, but accompanying one. Very often, in the case of a retreat, the cars remain behind the main line, to do the work of wiping out as many of the enemy's advanced guards as they can get under fire, and an affair of this description took place during the retreat from Roulers.

I happened to be there, armed with my rifle, which I carry in preference to a revolver, because I have found it more useful.

I stayed behind to keep in touch with the armoured car. This was at a corner of one of the roads, and a prominent feature of the district was a brewery, the entrance to which commanded the approach by road.

Matters at that particular time were very lively and the car was swiftly run into the yard, where with astonishing skill and speed it was disguised as much as possible and then it was ready to give the Germans a surprise.

I left my machine round the corner, and made my way into one of the nearest of the houses. Rushing upstairs, I entered a bedroom and went to the window, where I took up a position with my rifle, and kept properly on the alert, for you never knew from which quarter a bullet would come and settle your account for ever.

There was every reason to believe that the enemy would come—and they did. They came along as if they were satisfied that nothing could happen to them—certainly the German body that was making its way along the road had no idea that a disguised motorcar was ready to give it a welcome as soon as it got within striking distance of the entrance to the brewery. Being Germans, doubtless their thoughts, when they saw the brewery, were more concentrated on beer than on the British troops in ambush.

On the Germans came, and one could not help feeling how awful it was that they should be advancing utterly unsuspectingly into a perfect death-trap.

From behind my bedroom window, rifle in hand, I watched them come up to their doom. They got nearer and nearer to the innocent-looking brewery entrance and to the houses and other places where the unseen rifles were covering them; then, just at the right moment, the maxims from the armoured car rattled and the rifles kept them company.

The German ranks were shattered and scattered instantly. It was a swift and destructive cannonade and the Germans went down in the fatal roadway just like ninepins. I do not think I exaggerate when I say that practically the whole of the enemy's advanced guard was wiped out in a few moments.

This little affair was as short as it was brilliant and decisive, and almost before there was time to realise fully what had happened the car was stripped of its disguise and was triumphantly driven out of the brewery yard and back to the British lines.

When I saw the car going I took it as a signal that I had better make tracks myself, so I hurried away from the bedroom, got clear of the house, jumped on to my machine, and lost no time in following it.

This fine performance, typical of a great number of such deeds done in the war by resourceful men of which nothing has been heard and perhaps never will be, strikes me as being a very good illustration of doing exactly those things which the enemy does not expect you to do. Personally, I have always made a point of putting this principle into practice. If the enemy is waiting for you to take the highroad, the obvious thing, it seems to me, is to take to the fields, especially as in bad weather, in a country like Flanders, there is very little difference between the fields and the roads.

There is one interesting point which I may mention, and it is that so far I have had no difficulty in finding petrol. Nearly all the Belgian farmers use gas-engines, and their stores are very useful for motor cycles. I need hardly say that I never saw any want of willingness on the part of Belgian farmers to help the fighters who are doing their best to get the country back for them.

At present I am not a bit useful as a fighting man, because when I was going into the trenches I heard the ping of a German bullet and found that blood was running down my arm.

When I was actually struck I felt only a numb sensation, and did not for some time know what had happened; but later it was discovered that the bullet had struck me between the wrist and elbow of the right arm and had gone clean through, leaving a hole on each side of the arm.

Strange though it may seem, I felt little pain at any time, in spite of the fact that one of the bones of the arm was broken, and I am glad to say that this wound—and there have been an enormous number like it since the war began—is making a first-class recovery, and I shall soon be all right again.

A man does not go to war for fun, but there is a bright side to the grim business, as I found when I reached a Belgian hospital. I spent three very comfortable days there, and when I was sent off to England the nurse who was attending me very gravely made me a little present, which I as gravely accepted. She paid me three-halfpence! I did not know what it meant, but I concluded that I had received the Belgian's rate of daily pay as a soldier, and his keep. I was perfectly satisfied, and I hope my excellent nurse was the same.

Chapter 22

Exploits of the London Scottish

"*Eye Witness*," *in his descriptive account of November 4th 1914, dealing with the first phase of the desperate fight for Ypres, said that a special feature of the battle was that it formed an epoch in the military history of the British Empire, and marked the first time that a complete unit of our Territorial Army has been thrown into the fight alongside its sister units of the Regulars. That unit was the 14th (County of London) Battalion London Regiment, better known as the London Scottish. Its ranks contained many prominent men who gave up everything at their country's call and went to the front. Amongst them was Mr. J. E. Carr, Managing Director of Scremerston Colliery, Northumberland, a well-known breeder of Border Leicester sheep, a keen rider to hounds and a thoroughly good sportsman. Private Carr served with the London Scottish until he was wounded and invalided home and it is his story which is here retold.*

It is very difficult to keep within defined limits the varied experiences that are crowded into a few months at the front in a war which is waged on such a vast scale as the present conflict. Every day has its own fresh and particular excitements which are worth remembering, and one can scarcely pick out, off-hand, the most startling or interesting phases of the campaigning. However, the earliest impressions undoubtedly cling most tenaciously, and I have vivid recollections of the thrill I experienced when our transport swung to her moorings and the London Scottish disembarked on the other side of the Channel.

I should like to say here that the London Scottish have been the subject of a good deal of comment, mostly favourable, I am glad to know; but there has been undue exaltation. The blame for this certainly does not rest with the London Scottish, but in other perfectly well-meaning quarters.

I am proud indeed to belong to the London Scottish, because they are good boys to be amongst, so good that there was no reason whatever why people should have expressed surprise that the first Territorials to go into action did so well. I don't think there was any reason for astonishment, for the London Scottish had been a well-trained body of Volunteers before the Territorial system came into being. And if they pulled through, as they did, when the actual fighting began, do not let it be forgotten that they had some glorious examples to follow. On their left and on their right were some of the very finest soldiers in the world, and it was for the London Scottish to prove that they were worthy of fighting with these truly splendid fellows. Troops like the Coldstream Guards, the Scots Guards, the Black Watch and the Cameron Highlanders are men with whom it is indeed an honour to be associated.

Our landing on the Continent was an event which I shall remember all my life. It meant that we were many miles nearer to the band of heroes who had held the Germans up at Mons and had completely disarranged a whole plan of campaign. Whenever I meet a man who fought in that greatest of rearguard actions I want to take off my hat to him.

It was not long after the war began that we found ourselves on the lines of communication and began to feel that we were really bearing a hand in the things that mattered. This was in September, and the weather being good we found it no great hardship to guard railways, escort prisoners, run up ammunition for the fighting lines and do any odd job that came along. There was not a man amongst us who did not put his back into the business, realising that it was all a part of the tremendous game that was being played, monotonous and unexciting though the duties might be, and with every day that passed we got fitter and keener and better able to meet the heavy calls that came upon us later. We felt that we were really "in" and part of the great adventure. In various ways we did a good deal of wandering, and some of us went as far south as Nantes.

This was about harvest time, and we saw the old men of France and the women and the boys gathering in the sheaves. Later on we saw even the women ploughing, and very good job they did. One thing which particularly astonished us was their courage in working on the land quite close up to the fighting line. They were often well within shell fire, but they did not seem to be in the least disturbed.

I suppose they thought that if their husbands and sons and brothers could fight for France at rifle and bayonet range they could go on working for their country in spite of a stray shell or two.

A few weeks later we moved up to the firing line, and then we had the opportunity of seeing how gloriously the Scottish Regular troops were doing their work and maintaining the traditions of the Highland regiments.

People have become so used to amazing happenings in this war that it is not easy to realise that only a very few months ago the mere sight of an aeroplane was a novelty, and it was a thrill indeed for us when, near Béthune, we had a splendid view of a fight in the air between British, French and German airmen. The German, in a machine which looked exactly like an enormous bird in the sky, came scouting over our lines, to find out what was going on. The mere sight of him was enough to fetch along a British 'plane and a Frenchman followed. This happened on a clear, peaceful Sunday morning, and it was truly wonderful to see how the three machines were manoeuvred to get the top position and so spell doom to the lowest 'plane. By extraordinary daring and skill, and because his very life hung in the balance, the German managed to get away, in spite of the most desperate efforts of his opponents to bag him.

One of our first experiences of real fighting came when we were ordered to charge at Messines. I do not care to say much about that charge, because I think too much has been said of it already; so I will not go beyond saying that it was hot and sanguinary work with the bayonet and that we lost many good fellows. I cannot help thinking that the London Scottish got too much praise for Messines, and they are the first to admit that; but this was due to the fact that correspondents and others spread themselves out on the charge and gave special attention to the matter because of the fact that up to that time practically nothing had been heard of Territorials in action.

The praise that was given to the regiment had the effect of making us rather unpopular with the Regulars, and naturally enough, too, seeing that they had been constantly doing the same sort of work ever since the beginning of the war. It was pride enough for us to be in the same brigade as the Coldstreamers, the Scots Guards, the Black Watch and the Camerons, and to feel that we had done just what we were told to do. It was, of course, a source of great satisfaction to us afterwards to be congratulated by General Munro on what he was good enough to term our "steadiness as a battalion." Now that is all I am going to say about the charge of the London Scottish at Messines.

Speaking generally the fighting from November until the time I was wounded can be divided into two distinct parts, the actions around Ypres and the affairs at La Bassée. At Ypres about fifty men of our regiment were in the city during the siege, and a very exciting time we had. Shells were constantly bursting all around and no matter where the people were they did not seem to be able to keep clear of danger. Even the cellars, in which large numbers of men and women and children sought refuge, were at times blown in and there were some very distressing and unpleasant sights. Personally, I was uncommonly lucky, because I escaped being hurt.

I had the good fortune to sleep for two nights in the beautiful and famous Cloth Hall, of which the story is told that it was particularly spared by the German artillery because the *Kaiser* meant to enter it in state at the head of his victorious troops. But when I was in it the shells came pounding on the walls and roof of the hall, doing grievous damage, though our own men had the good luck to escape. Not so lucky were some men of the Suffolk Regiment who followed us, for one afternoon a huge shell came through and burst and killed five of the Suffolks and wounded a number of other men of that fine regiment.

So much has been said of the enormous German shells which have become known as Jack Johnsons that people have almost ceased to be affected by their performances; but nothing that I have heard or read conveys any real idea of the extraordinarily destructive nature of these awful engines of war when they explode—and that, luckily, does not always happen. One afternoon, however, we counted no fewer than thirty of them which *did* explode, and the results were absolutely devastating.

When the Germans really set to work to bombard Ypres, the Cloth Hall and the splendid cathedral were soon practically destroyed; but one of the most noticeable things in connection with this destruction was that many sacred objects were undamaged whilst there was ruin all around them. Take the case of the crucifix of Ypres Cathedral—it is literally true that this was found entire and upright amongst such general ruin that it seemed as if only a miracle could have saved it. In several other places I saw crucifixes hanging uninjured on walls of houses although the structures themselves had been practically wrecked. On the other hand, while we were in the trenches I saw a little nickel crucifix with a bullet-hole right through it.

With the King's Royal Rifles on their right, the London Scottish were in some furious fighting in the earlier days of November, and the coming of Christmas brought more hot work. On December 22nd we marched about twenty-six miles with the brigade, and the Coldstreamers, went straight into action after their arrival. They did fine work that day, and paid for it accordingly. There followed a rest at Béthune and then we went into more trouble in the neighbourhood of Givenchy.

Very little of what may be called spectacular fighting was seen hereabouts; it was mostly trench work, and this was all the more difficult because the German trenches were so close to our own, and the real old-fashioned way of conducting a battle was out of the question. But all the same we got some variations, and one of these was a fight for a brickfield which was a good hot performance while it lasted.

At this period we made a change on the usual form of trench by lining our own trenches with bricks, which were handy for the purpose. These trenches were more comfortable than the general type, but they were more dangerous, because when a shell burst near us the bricks splintered, so that the flying bricks had to be added to the dangers and discomforts of the flying metal fragments.

One of the brick splinters struck my hand and poisoned it, and another unwelcome attention that was paid to me was a piece of shrapnel in the back of the neck; but these were really very minor details compared with the injuries that were received by other members of the London Scottish, and I am not for a moment complaining, nor can I, for when I came home my company had only twenty left out of 119. There had been the casualties in the charge and in other affairs, and a number of men had been killed and wounded in the trenches.

At Givenchy we had to endure as best we could that most unpleasant engine of war which is called the trench mortar. This affects high-angle fire and plumps a shell into the trenches when the aim is good. One shell dropped into a trench of ours and exploded, killing one man and wounding five others—a round half-dozen fine fellows as toll to a single German shot.

There were the snipers, too, pests who are intensely disliked by the British soldier. These fellows find a lodging in what seems to be an impossible sort of place, often enough high up a tree, and being well supplied with food and ammunition they can go on potting for a long time without going down from their perch. It was always matter for rejoicing when one of these queer birds was winged.

I spent Christmas 1914 in the trenches, with the boys. It is odd to be talking about Christmas at this time of the year, but that season was an outstanding feature of the experiences of the London Scottish, just as the New Year was. Christmas Day was comparatively comfortable because there was a lull in the fighting. New Year's Day was unforgettable to those who saw it in and did their best to keep up the national custom.

I think that of all the strange incidents that have been recorded in connection with this war, and they have been many—and some of them have proved how soon soldiers become impervious to the most terrible happenings of campaigning—one of the strangest must have been the sight we saw on New Year's Eve.

When the New Year actually came in we fired three rounds rapid, and the pipes of the Black Watch rose on the night, while our own voices broke into "Auld lang syne." Wonderful and affecting it was to hear the pipes and the dear old tune and many of us were deeply moved.

The effect on the Germans was very curious. Apparently they judged from the sounds of the pipes and the roll of the song that the Scots were going to pay them a special visit with the bayonet, and by way of being ready for it and giving us a welcome, they sent up star-lights, and these, bursting in the air, gave a sinister illumination of the landscape and would have shown us up if we had had in mind the purpose of an assault on the German trenches. But we had no intention of letting the New Year in upon them in such an unfriendly manner, although later in the day we were of necessity hard at it again in the ordinary way of firing.

From day to day the London Scottish kept at it, doing their best, I hope; then, on January 25th a spell of uncommonly hard work came along. The Coldstreamers, who had held out successfully against great odds, had to withdraw from their trenches owing to an overwhelming attack by the enemy. For the time being the Germans had scored and no doubt they were exulting in their best manner, but the London Scottish were sent up to reinforce the Coldstreamers. Later in the afternoon the Black Watch, with the Sussex Regiment and the Royal Rifles, came up too, and the combination proved too much for the Germans, who, after a brilliant attack, were sent flying back to their own trenches.

I have heard that many old and young Germans have been taken prisoners at various parts of the immense battle-front of the Allies; but those that I saw pass through our lines were neither very old nor very young. Occasionally we observed signs that they required a good lot of leading, that is to say, "leading" from behind; but generally speaking they seemed to be the best men that Germany had and on the whole they were undoubtedly good fighters.

While talking of German prisoners I am reminded of a particularly ugly incident. When I was taken to the hospital I was with a number of German prisoners.

The hospital rule is that everything shall be taken away from the patient until the time comes for him to be discharged. Well, when one of these prisoners was searched I learned to my amazement, disgust and anger, that he carried with him a bomb which was powerful enough to blow up the whole place but prompt steps were taken to prevent him from making any use of it. How on earth he had got so far from the lines with the deadly thing I cannot understand; but he had it with him all right.

We got a good deal of amusement and help from a new set of "*Ten Commandments for Soldiers in the Field*," which were duly but not officially published. I will quote one or two by way of showing their character and indicating that incorrigible British cheerfulness which the German, with all his "culture," cannot understand. Number Three ran: "*Thou shalt not use profane language except under extraordinary circumstances, such as seeing thy comrade shot or getting petrol in thy tea.*" Number Four was worded: "*Remember that the soldier's week consists of seven days. Six days shalt thou labour and do all thy work, and on the seventh do all thy odd jobs!*" "*Honour thy King and country,*" was the Fifth. "*Keep thy rifle oiled, and shoot straight, in order that thy days may be long upon the land the enemy giveth thee.*" Then we had, "*Thou shalt not steal thy neighbour's kit,*" and "*Thou shalt not kill—time!*" By Number Nine it was enjoined, "*Thou shalt not bear false witness against thy comrade, but preserve discreet silence on his outgoings and incomings.*" Last of all came Number Ten, full of a wonderful hope for the lowly: "*Thou shalt not covet thy Sergeant's post, nor the Corporal's, nor the Staff-Major's, but do thy duty and by dint of perseverance rise to the high position of Field-Marshal.*"

★★★★★★

This is one of the first detailed stories to be told of some of the achievements of the London Scottish at the front, and its modest vein is in keeping with the general point of view of the members of this distinguished corps. It has been for others, not of the London Scottish, to tell us something of what the regiment really did at Messines and elsewhere in those early days of the Ypres fighting on which such vast issues depended. What happened at Messines was this: The regiment was in reserve when unexpectedly the order came to hurry up to the support of the hard-pressed Regular troops, who were being fiercely assailed by very much superior German forces. Crowding on to motor-buses the London Scottish were hurried along in the course of the afternoon and while some of them spent the night in deserted cottages others bivouacked in the streets, waiting for daylight.

After much marching and wandering, the zone of fire was entered, and the fine battalion which not many weeks before had marched along London streets after being embodied made acquaintance with the German shells and got ready to show what the British Territorials could do with the rifle and the bayonet.

The regiment was amused and interested in the antics of a windmill the sails of which turned constantly and oddly, although there was no wind. It was not until later that the phenomenon was explained and that was when the windmill was visited and a German spy was caught in the act of signalling, by means of the sails, the position and movements of the British troops.

It was at Hollebecke and at Messines, between Ypres and Warneton, that the British lines were hard pressed owing to the determined attempts of the Germans to break through and hack their way to Calais, and it was here that the London Scottish went to support the Cavalry Brigade who were holding the trenches.

Forming up under the crest of a hill they advanced over the crest and found themselves right in the battle line. Hurrying down the slope, struggling over heavy ground which was made all the harder because of beet crops, the regiment went into a most destructive artillery and rifle and machine-gun fire.

Many a fellow was shot down before he could use his own rifle, and others were wounded; but nothing could stop the advance. By short rushes, and taking cover, the men in time reached the trenches and had to encounter an overwhelming assault of Germans with the bayonet.

These Territorials, fresh from civil life, hurled themselves with the bayonet upon the finest troops of Germany. They were thrown back. Again they charged, only to be driven off once more; but the regiment was not to be denied or beaten and with a final furious rush the Germans were scattered and the day was won for the British. No wonder that Colonel J. H. Scott, late of the Gordon Highlanders and formerly adjutant of the London Scottish, wrote on hearing the news: "Hurrah for the London Scottish! From my knowledge of them I knew they would do it!"

CHAPTER 23

The Rout of the Prussian Guard at Ypres

The official writers have told us of the almost superhuman efforts made by the Germans to break through to Calais so that they might, from that place, either raid or bombard England. For a whole month a little British army round Ypres held its ground against the repeated onslaughts of overwhelming German hosts. These actions were divided into two phases, the first lasting from October 20th to November 2nd, and the second from November 3rd to 17th 1914. German infantry of the Line having failed to win success, the Prussian Guard was hurried up, only to be thrown back and broken. This crushing of the crack corps of Prussia was a bitter blow to the Kaiser and the German people, who believed it to be invincible. In these unexampled contests the Seventh Infantry Division bore the brunt of battle, and the tale of the first phase is told by Private H. J. Polley, 2nd Battalion Bedfordshire Regiment. Lieutenant-General Sir H. S. Rawlinson, commanding the division, said in an order: "You have been called to take a conspicuous part in one of the severest struggles of the war. . . . The Seventh Division has gained for itself a reputation for stubborn valour and endurance in defence." When the Glorious Seventh was withdrawn from the firing line only forty-four officers were left out of 400 who had sailed from England, and only 2,336 out of 12,000 men.

All the world knows now how furiously the Germans tried to hack their way through to Calais, so that they could have their fling at the English. It is known too that they were held and hurled back. I am going to tell you something of the way in which this was done, for I belong to the Bedfordshire Regiment, the old 16th Foot, and the

Bedfords were part of the Glorious Seventh Division, and did their share in keeping back the German forces, which included the Prussian Guards, the *Kaiser's* pet men. They had been rushed up to this position because it was thought that no troops could stand against them.

These idols of the German nation are picked men and brave fellows, and at that time had an absolute belief in their own invincibility; but events proved that they were no match for the British Guards and the rest of the British troops who fought them at Ypres, and practically wiped them out. I saw these Prussian Guards from Berlin mown down by our artillery, machine-gun and rifle fire, and I saw them lying dead in solid masses—walls of corpses.

The *Kaiser* had planned to enter Ypres as a conqueror, at the head of his Guards; but he hurried off a beaten man, leaving his slaughtered Guards in heaps.

Originally in the 1st Battalion of the Bedfords, I later went into the 2nd, and I was serving with the 2nd in South Africa when the European War broke out. It is an interesting fact that nearly all the battalions which formed the Seventh Division came from foreign service—India, Egypt, Africa and elsewhere—which meant that many of the men of the Seventh had seen active service and were veteran fighters. They had not learned their warfare at peace manoeuvres in Germany. Our division consisted of the 1st Grenadier Guards, the 2nd Scots Guards, the 2nd Border, 2nd Gordon Highlanders, 2nd Bedfordshire, 2nd Yorkshire, 2nd Royal Scots Fusiliers, 2nd Wiltshire, 2nd Royal West Surrey, 2nd Royal Warwickshire, 1st Royal Welsh Fusiliers, 1st South Staffordshire, and the Northumberland Hussars; and we had a pom-pom detachment and horse, field and garrison artillery. We were under Major-General Sir T. Capper, D.S.O.

We had been sent to help the Naval Division at Antwerp, and early in October we landed at Zeebrugge—the only division to land at that port. But we were not there long, for we soon learned that we were too late, and that Antwerp had fallen. We were sorry, but there was no time for moping, and we were quickly on the move to the quaint old city of Bruges, where we were billeted for a night. Sir Harry Rawlinson had moved his headquarters from Bruges to Ostend, so next day we marched towards Ostend and took up outpost. Then we had a forced march back to Bruges, and from Bruges we started marching, but we did not know where we were going till we got to the city of Ypres.

So far we had not had any fighting. We had been marching and marching, first to one place, then to another, constantly expecting to come into action, and very nearly doing so, for the Germans were swarming all over the countryside. We had to be content with being on outpost and guarding bridges, and so on—hard and necessary work, we knew; but we wanted something bigger—and we eventually got it.

There was practically only the Seventh Division available for anything that turned up. The Northumberland Hussars were able to give a very good account of themselves, and were, I believe, the first Yeomanry corps to go into action. The few *Uhlans* I saw while I was at the front had been taken prisoners by these Hussars, who brought them in, lances and all. But there is very little to say about cavalry work; it was mostly a matter for the infantry, and, of course, the artillery.

While we were around Ypres, waiting for the Germans to come and break through, we heard a good deal, indirectly, of what was going to happen to us and to England. The Germans had all sorts of monster guns, and with these they were going to bombard England across the narrow Channel when they got to the French coast, and they were going to work all sorts of miracles with their airships and aeroplanes.

We soon heard, too, that the *Kaiser* himself was in the field; but the only effect of that information was to make us more keen to show what we could do. Truth to tell, we were far from being impressed by the presence of either the *Kaiser* or his Guards.

It was on October 31st—which has been called *the* decisive day of the fight for Ypres, and which was certainly a most terrible day in every way—that the Seventh Division was ordered to attack the German position. The weather was very fine, clear and sunny, and our spirits were in keeping with it. We were thankful to be on the move, because we had had nearly three weeks in the trenches, and had been billeted in all sorts of queer places—above and below ground under an everlasting shell fire, which became unendurable and was thoroughly nerve-destroying.

We knew what a desperate business the advance would be, because the Germans greatly outnumbered us, and they had planted vast numbers of guns. They had immense bodies of men in trenches, and in a large number of the houses and buildings which commanded the ground over which we had to advance they had placed machine-guns, with their muzzles directed on us from bedroom windows and holes which had been knocked in walls.

From start to finish the advance was a terrible business—far more terrible than any words of mine can make you realise. The whole Division was on the move, stretching along a big tract of country; but of course no man could see much of what was happening, except in his own immediate locality. Neither had he much chance of thinking about anything or anybody except himself, and then only in a numbed sort of way, because of the appalling din of the artillery on both sides, the crash of the guns and the explosions of the shells, with the ceaseless rattle of the rifles and the machine-guns.

At the beginning, the regiments kept fairly well together, but very soon we were all mixed up, and you could not tell what regiment a man belonged to, unless he wore a kilt; then you knew that, at any rate, he wasn't a Bedford. Some of us had our packs and full equipment. Others were without packs, having been compelled to throw them away. But there was not a man who had let his rifle go: that is the last thing of all to be parted from; it is the soldier's very life. And every man had a big supply of ammunition, with plenty in reserve. The general himself took part in the advance, and what he did was done by every other officer present. There was no difference between officer and man, and a thing to be specially noticed is the fact that the officers got hold of rifles and blazed away as hard as any man.

Never, during the whole of the war, had there been a more awful fire than that which we gave the Germans. Whenever we got the chance, we gave them what they call the "Englishman's mad minute"—that is, the dreadful fifteen rounds a minute rapid fire. We drove it into them and mowed them down. Many a soldier, when his own rifle was too hot to hold, threw it down and snatched the rifle of a dead or wounded comrade who had no further use for it, and with this fresh, cool weapon he continued the deadly work by which success could alone be won. I do not know what the German losses were, but I do know that I saw bodies lying around in solid masses, while we passed our own dead and wounded everywhere as we advanced. Where they fell they had to stay; it was impossible to do anything for them while the fighting continued.

The whole of the advance consisted of a series of what might be called ups and downs—a little rush, then a "bob down." At most, no one rush carried us more than fifty yards; then we dropped out of sight as best we could, to get a breather and prepare for another dash. It was pretty open country hereabouts, so that we were fully exposed to the German artillery and rifle fire, in addition to the hail from the machine-guns in the neighbouring buildings. Here and there we found little woods and clumps of trees and bits of rising ground and ditches and hedges—and you may take it from me that shelter of any sort was very welcome and freely used.

A remarkable feature of this striving to hide from the enemy's fire was that it was almost impossible to escape from the shells and bullets for any appreciable time, for the simple reason that the Germans altered their range in the most wonderful manner. So surely as we got the shelter of a little wood or ditch, they seemed to have the distance almost instantly, and the range was so accurate that many a copse and ditch became a little graveyard in the course of that advance.

At one point as we went along I noticed a small ditch against a hedge. It was a dirty, uninviting ditch, deep in water; but it seemed to offer promising shelter, and so some officers and men made a rush for it, meaning to take cover. They had no sooner scrambled into the ditch and were thinking themselves comparatively safe than the Germans got the range of them with machine-guns, and nearly the whole lot were annihilated. In this case, as in others, the enemy had been marvellously quick with their weapons, and had swept the ditch with bullets. I don't know what happened to the fine fellows who had fallen. We had to leave them and continue the advance.

The forenoon passed, noon came, and the afternoon was with us; still the fighting went on, the guns on both sides crashing without cessation, and the machine-guns and the rifles rattling on without a break. The air was filled with screaming, bursting shells and whistling bullets, and the ground was ploughed and torn everywhere. It was horrible beyond expression, yet it fired the blood in us, so that the only thing that mattered was to put the finish to the work, get up to the Germans, and rout them out of their positions.

At last, after endless spells of lying down and jumping up, we got near enough to make it possible to charge, and the order went round to get ready. We now saw what big, fine fellows we had to tackle. Clearly now we could distinguish the Prussian Guards, and a thing that particularly struck me just then was that their bayonets looked very cruel. The Guards wore cloth-covered brass helmets, and through the cloth we could see the gleam of the brass in the sunshine.

The nearer we got, the more clearly we saw what splendid chaps they were, and what a desperate business it would be when we actually reached the long, snaky blades of steel—much longer than our own bayonets—with longer rifles, too, so that the Germans had the pull of us in every way. But all that counted as nothing, and there was not a man amongst us who was not hungering to be in amongst them.

The order to fix bayonets came quietly, and it was carried out without any fuss whatever, just as a part of the day's work. We were lying down when the order came, and as we lay we got round at our bayonets, drew them and fixed them, and I could hear the rattle of the fixing all along the line, just as I had heard it many times on parade or at manoeuvres—the same sound, but with what a different purpose!

A few of the fellows did not fix their bayonets as we lay, but they managed to do it as we ran, when we had jumped up and started to rush along to put the finish to the fight. There was no bugle sound, we just got the word to charge, an order which was given to the whole of the Seventh Division.

When this last part of the advance arrived we started halloaing and shouting, and the division simply hurled itself against the Prussian Guard. By the time we were up with the enemy we were mad. I can't tell you much of what actually happened—and I don't think any man who took part in it could do so—but I do know that we rushed helter-skelter, and that when we got up to the famous Guards there were only two of my own section holding together—Lance-Corporal Perry and myself, and even we were parted immediately afterwards.

The next thing I clearly knew was that we were actually on the Prussians, and that there was some very fierce work going on. There was some terrific and deadly scrimmaging, and whatever the Prussian Guard did in the way of handling the steel, the Seventh Division did better.

It was every man for himself. I had rushed up with the rest, and the first thing I clearly knew was that a tremendous Prussian was making at me with his villainous bayonet. I made a lunge at him as hard and swift as I could, and he did the same to me. I thought I had him, but I just missed, and as I did so, I saw his own long, ugly blade driven out at the end of his rifle. Before I could do anything to parry the thrust, the tip of the bayonet had ripped across my right thigh, and I honestly thought that it was all up with me.

Then, when I reckoned that my account was paid, when I supposed that the huge Prussian had it all his own way, one of our chaps—I don't know who, I don't suppose I ever shall; but I bless him—rushed up, drove his bayonet into the Prussian and settled him. I am sure that if this had not been done I should have been killed by the Prussian; as it was, I was able to get away without much inconvenience at the end of the bayonet fight.

This struggle lasted about half-an-hour, and fierce, hard work it was all the time. In the end we drove the Guards away and sent them flying—all except those who had fallen; the trench was full of the latter, and we took no prisoners. Then we were forced to retire ourselves, for the ample reason that we were not strong enough to hold the position that we had taken at such a heavy cost. The enemy did not know it then, though perhaps they found out later, that we had nicely deceived them in making them believe that we had reinforcements. But we had nothing of the sort; yet we had stormed and taken the position and driven its defenders away.

We were far too weak to hold the position, and so we retired over the ground that we had won, getting back a great deal faster than we had advanced. We had spent the best part of the day in advancing and reaching the enemy's position; and it seemed as if we must have covered a great tract of country, but as a matter of fact we had advanced less than a mile. It had taken us many hours to cover that short distance; but along the whole of the long line of the advance the ground was littered with the fallen—the officers and men who had gone down under such a storm of shells and bullets as had not been known since the war began.

Retiring, we took up a position behind a wood, and were thinking that we should get a bit of a rest, when a German aeroplane came flying over us, gave our hiding-place away, and brought upon us a fire that drove us out and sent us back to three lines of trenches which we had been occupying.

By this time our ambulances were hard at work; but ambulance or no ambulance, the pitiless shelling went on, and I saw many instances of German brutality in this respect. The ambulance vehicles were crowded, and I saw one which had two wounded men standing on the back, because there was not room enough for them inside. Shells were bursting all around, and a piece struck one of the poor chaps and took part of his foot clean away. He instantly fell on to the road, and there he had to be left. I hope he got picked up by another ambulance, though I doubt it, for the shell-firing just then was heavy, and deliberately aimed at helpless ambulances by people who preach what they call culture!

We made the best of things during the evening and the night in the trenches. The next day things were reversed, for the Germans came on against us; but we kept up a furious fight, and simply mowed them down as they threw themselves upon us. We used to say, "Here comes

"I MADE A LUNGE AT HIM, BUT JUST MISSED, AND I SAW HIS OWN LONG, UGLY BLADE DRIVEN OUT"

another bunch of 'em!" and then we gave them the "mad minute." We had suffered heavily on the 31st, and we were to pay a big bill again on this 1st of November, amongst our casualties being two of our senior officers.

The battalion was in the peculiar position of having no colonel at the head of it, our commanding officer being Major J. M. Traill. I should like to say now, by way of showing how heavily the Bedfords suffered, that in one of Sir John French's despatches, published early in the year, seven officers were mentioned, and in the cases of six of them it had to be added that they had been killed in action. Major Traill and Major R. P. Stares were killed not far from me on the day I am telling of—and within two hours of each other.

We were lying in trenches, and the majors were in front of us, walking about, and particularly warning us to be careful and not expose ourselves. Their first thought seemed to be for us, and their last for themselves.

Just at that time there was some uncommonly deadly sniping going on, and any figure that was seen even for a fraction of time was a certain target. The sniper himself was a specially chosen German, and he had as a companion and look-out a smart chap with field-glasses, to sweep the countryside and report to the sniper anything promising that he saw in the way of a target. Working in pairs like this, the snipers were able to pick off the two majors as they walked up and down directing and encouraging us. They were shot, and, as far as we could tell, killed instantly. We felt their loss very greatly.

Major Stares had very much endeared himself to his men, and he was a great favourite in South Africa before the war began. We were all eager to get to the front, of course, and were constantly talking about what we should do, and wondering what would happen when we met the Germans. The major was never tired of explaining what we ought to do in tight and dangerous corners, and asking us what we should do. I have known him stop us in the street to ask us these questions, so keen and anxious was he for our welfare.

The second day of the fighting passed and the third came. Still we held on, but it became clear that we were too hopelessly outnumbered to hope for complete success at the time, and so we were forced to leave the trenches. Withdrawing again, we took up positions in farmhouses and woods and any other places that gave shelter. All the time there was a killing fire upon us, and it happened that entire bodies of men would be wiped out in a few moments. A party of the Warwicks got into a wood near us, and they had no sooner taken shelter than the German gunners got the range of them, shelled them, and killed nearly all of them.

There was not a regiment of the Glorious Seventh that had not suffered terribly in the advance during the three days' fateful fighting. The Bedfords had lost, all told, about 600, and it was a mere skeleton of the battalion that formed up when the roll was called. But there was one pleasant surprise for me, and that was meeting again with Lance-Corporal Perry. We had lost sight of each other in the hand-to-hand fighting with the Prussian Guard, and met again when we were reorganised at an old *château*; and very thankful we were to compare notes, especially as each of us thought that the other was a dead man. There were a good many cases of soldiers turning up who were supposed to be either killed or wounded, or, what is worse, missing. In the inevitable disorder and confusion of such a battle they had got separated from their own regiments and had joined others; but they turned up in due course in their right places.

I had become a member of the grenade company of the battalion, which was something like going back to the early days of the army, when the grenadier companies of the regiments flung their little bombs at the enemy. So did we, and grim work it Was, hurling home-made bombs, which had the power of doing a great amount of mischief.

I was with the grenade company, behind a brick wall close to the trenches, and was sitting with several others round a fire which we had made in a biscuit-tin. We were quite a merry party, and had the dixie going to make some tea. There was another dixie on, with two or three nice chickens that our fellows had got hold of—perhaps they had seen them wandering about homeless and adopted them.

Anyway, they found a good home in the stew-pot, and we were looking forward to a most cosy meal. As a sort of change from shelling by batteries in the ordinary way, we were being shelled from an armoured train, but were taking little notice of it, being busy with the tea and chickens.

The Germans were close enough to fling hand-bombs at us. They gave us lots of these little attentions, so that when I suddenly found myself blinded, and felt a sharp pain in my left hand, I thought they had made a lucky shot, or that something had exploded in the fire in the biscuit-tin.

For some time I did not know what had happened; then I was able to see, and on looking at my hand, I found it to be in a sorry mess, half the thumb and half a finger having been carried away.

I stayed and had some tea from the dixie, and my chums badly wanted me to wait for my share of the chickens; but I had no appetite for fowls just then. I made the best of things till darkness came, and under cover of it a couple of stretcher-bearers took me to the nearest dressing-station.

I suffered intensely, and lockjaw set in, but the splendid medical staff and the nursing saved me, and I was put into a horse ambulance and packed off home. And here I am.

CHAPTER 24

The British Army at Neuve Chapelle

On the road from Béthune to Armentieres, four miles to the north of La Bassée, is the little straggling frontier village of Neuve Chapelle, which first came into notice in October during the British advance to the north of La Bassée. At that time the village was held by the Germans, but on October 16th they were driven out by the British. As a result of the tremendous efforts of the Germans in trying to reach Calais we were not able to hold the village, which again was held by the enemy at the beginning of November. The British were driven back and for more than four months they remained near Neuve Chapelle; then, on March 10th they began an attack which ended in the village being retaken by us and held. The German Westphalian Army Corps in October and November had forced the British out of Neuve Chapelle. What the battle meant and how it was fought is told by Sergeant Gilliam, 1st Battalion Coldstream Guards.

The Battle of Neuve Chapelle began at half-past seven o'clock on the morning of March 10th, and ended at about half-past nine on the night of the 12th. Earlier on the morning of that famous day our battalion was ordered to stand to, as supports of the 1st Brigade. We were told to be ready to turn out at ten minutes' notice; and we *were* ready, for we were longing to have a settlement with the Germans, who had dug themselves in at Neuve Chapelle, and made themselves very comfortable and thought that no power on earth could drive them out. But we had a big surprise in store for them, and we sprung it on them like a thunderbolt when our massed guns roared soon after sunrise on that early day in March. Whatever advantages the Germans might have had at the beginning of the war we had been getting the better of them, and we were certain that we were now much superior to the enemy in every way. We knew that the British Army was becoming too much for them, and we were anxious to prove it that morning, when the biggest bombardment the world has ever known began, and along a tremendous front there came into action hundreds of the largest and the smallest guns that we had out in France.

I am sure that every man who was in at the beginning of this war, from Mons to the Marne and the Aisne, as I was, till I was invalided home wounded, will agree with me that there had been nothing like the British artillery fire at Neuve Chapelle. It was truly fearful. Something like five miles away, nearly five hundred British guns were bombarding the village, the batteries being on a front four or five miles in extent, so that there was only a few yards space between each gun. The result was that an immense wall of fire was seen where the artillery was in position, while the village itself was a target on which shells rained and made havoc. Nothing could withstand that awful cannonading—houses and buildings of every sort were shattered, and often enough a single shell was sufficient to destroy an entire house. When we got into the place at the end of the battle it looked as if some tremendous earthquake had upheaved it and thrown it down in a mass of wreckage

It was almost impossible to tell where the streets had been, and so enormous was the power of some of the shells that were fired and burst in the ground, that the very dead had been blown up from their resting-places in the churchyard, only to be re-buried by the falling walls around. The bombardment was bad enough for those who were out of it; for those who were in it the effect of the shell fire was paralysing. The Germans had had nothing like it, and more than one prisoner declared that it was not war, it was murder. We didn't quite see how they made that out; but it was near enough for the Germans, and we told them that we were only getting a bit of our own back for Mons.

The roar of these massed guns was so deafening, and the noise of the exploding shells was so incessant, that we could not hear one another speak. The air was all of a quiver and you could see the heat in the atmosphere just as you see it when looking at the horizon in a tropical country, and as I saw it many times when we were in Egypt. The heat from the shells made the day for all the world like a hot summer day, and the fumes and flashes caused a strange mist that looked like rain, though the sun was shining.

The bombardment was grand and terrible beyond description; but there was one good thing about it, and that was that the Germans did not reply very often—they seemed numbed and stunned—and when they did, their fire was very slight and feeble, and so far as I could tell not one of their shells did any serious damage amongst the British forces.

For half-an-hour the British artillery bombarded the enemy's first line of trenches, and this fire to the Germans must have seemed as if hell had been let loose, because everything that was in the line of fire was blown away or levelled to the ground—walls, trees, buildings, sandbags, even the barbed wire entanglements were carried away by shell splinters and shrapnel bullets, though unfortunately some of the entanglements escaped injury, and became deathtraps for a number of our fine fellows who were hurling themselves upon the Germans.

Perhaps I should explain, so that my story is quite clear, that Neuve Chapelle, or what is left of it, stands on perfectly flat ground, with plenty of enclosed gardens and orchards and some wooded country near. The Germans had dug themselves into very complete trenches, and had built some strong breastworks near the highroad into which they had put a large number of machine-guns. In houses and elsewhere these weapons had been planted, and in some places they fairly bristled. Our object was to rout the Germans out of their trenches and houses and barricades, and in view of the deadly nature of machine-guns and rifles the work was bound to be long and heavy and costly. How desperate the assault was has been shown by the losses of some of our line battalions.

When the bombardment of the first line of trenches was over, the way had been paved for the infantry, who were lying in their trenches, not far from the village. They were waiting eagerly for the order to advance, and when it came, they sprang out of their trenches with such shouts that you might have thought a lot of lunatics had been let loose. They dashed forward, and almost before it was possible to realise what had happened they were in the nearest German trench.

Then it was, even so soon after the battle had opened, that we knew how destructive the fire of our guns had been, for when the trench was reached there was hardly a German left to tackle. Our shells had landed plump into the enemy, and the result was that the trench was full of dead and wounded Germans. The few survivors did not hesitate to explain that they felt as if they could shake hands with themselves and to marvel that any one of them had come out of such a fire alive.

Our men were full of joy at such an ending to their rush, full of satisfaction to feel that they were making such a fine score, then came one of those misunderstandings and mishaps which are part and parcel of a fight in which the artillery cannot always see what it is doing—our own poor fellows suddenly found themselves under the fire of our gunners, who had started bombarding the trench again under the impression that it was still held by the Germans.

Imagine, if you can, what it meant to be in a trench like that, at such a time—a long narrow pit which had been knocked about by shells and was crowded with debris and killed and wounded men, and then to be under our own shell-fire. With unerring aim the shells came into the trench, causing consternation. Above the cries of the wounded and the shouts of the men came the loud voices of the officers, saying, "What is our artillery thinking of? What are they doing?" And at the same time doing their dead best to get their men out of it and back to their own trenches.

The order was now given to retire to our old position, and at last the order was carried out, but still some of our men were puzzled to know what had taken place, and they shouted, "What's wrong?" "What's happened?" and so on, while there were many cries for help and water. It was soon seen that there had been a mistake, and the best was made of it, though that was not much consolation for poor chaps who had been badly mauled and knocked about by fire that was meant for the enemy.

Noon came round on that first day of the battle and the chief thing we knew was that what we thought was finished had not been done, and we had to start afresh. Suddenly our artillery restarted. They knew by this time what had happened, and I think they must have felt pretty savage, judging from the nature of their fire. We could see the destructive effects of it from our trenches, and it was a wonderful yet awful sight to watch the Germans being blown out of their trenches into the air, some of the bodies being shot twenty or thirty feet high. I am not going to dwell on the havoc that was caused amongst men; but you can imagine how dismembered parts were scattered by such a continuous bursting of shells.

The bombardment stopped abruptly, and in the strange calm that followed it we went off again. This time we were lucky; there was no mishap, things went well and right, and by half-past two we had made ourselves masters of the first line of the German trenches.

This line was piled up with the German dead, and the first thing we did was to get to work to clear some of the bodies away, so as to make a bit of room for ourselves to stand, keeping at the same time well under cover in case the enemy tried to get their own back; but they had been too badly shaken, and nothing of this sort took place. The Germans believed that Neuve Chapelle could not be taken, as it was so strongly fortified, and we now had a chance of seeing how much ground they had for their belief. A particularly strong defence was the barbed wire entanglements, which had been made uncommonly thick and complicated. This was the reason why even our destructive fire did not cut through the entanglements and why some of our infantry suffered so heavily.

The Liverpool Regiment lost terribly, as so many of the officers and men were caught in the wires and had no chance of escaping from the fire which the Germans mercilessly directed upon them. The Liverpools were caught between the cross-fire of two German maxims as they tried to cut through the barbed wire, just in front of the German trenches. It was real heroism on the part of the Liverpools and it was a ghastly sight to see the brave fellows being cut down like flies.

In our captured trench, which was nothing more than a huge grave, we began, when we had made ourselves secure, to snatch a few mouthfuls of food; but we had no sooner started on this pleasant task than down came the order to prepare to advance.

"That's right!" the men shouted. "The music's started again! Let's get at the German pigs!" Not very polite, perhaps, but in this war a good deal has been said on both sides about swine.

We sprang out of our trench and went full swing for the second trench—there were four trenches to storm and take before our object was accomplished. Very soon we were in amongst the Germans in the second trench, and it was a fine sight to see them being put through the mill.

Just in front of us, amongst the enemy, the shells from our own guns were bursting—a wonderful instance of the accuracy of modern artillery fire—and it was fascinating to see the shells sweeping every inch of the ground, and marvellous that human beings could exist in such a deadly area. Every now and then in would go one of the German parapets, and the almost inevitable accompaniment was the blowing into the air of limbs and mangled bodies. These things were not a laughing matter, yet often enough, as we watched a shell burst and cause havoc we laughed outright—which shows how soon even the most dreadful of happenings are taken as matters of course.

Now came the order for us to assault and away the infantry went, right into the German trench, with such a rush and power that the enemy seemed to have no chance of standing up against the onslaught.

The men of the Leicestershire Regiment hurled themselves into the thick of the bloody fray, not once, nor twice, but five times in succession did they rush the Germans with the bayonet—and at the end of that tremendous onslaught they had not a single German prisoner! Never while a German lives who survived the charges of the Leicesters will he forget what happened in the trenches at Neuve Chapelle—and what the Leicesters did was done by the Irish Guards. No prisoners—and no man who has been through the war from the start will blame them, for he knows what the Germans have done to our own brave fellows, not in fair fight, but when they have been lying helpless on the roadside, especially in the retreat from Mons.

The long and thrilling day was ending, darkness was falling, and we pulled ourselves together and prepared for a lively night. We fully expected a counter attack, but no—it seemed to be the other way about, for on our left we had our famous Gurkhas and Sikhs, and they were getting ready for work.

It was quite dark, about half-past nine, when suddenly there was a shout in the German trenches, and as it rose in the night a pair of our starlights burst, like bright, beautiful fireworks in the sky, and showed us what was happening. It was this—the Indians had moved swiftly and silently in the night, they had crept and crawled up to the German position, and before the enemy knew what was taking place the heavy curved knife, which is the Gurkha's pride, was at work, and that is a weapon against which the German soldier, especially when in the trenches, seems to have no chance whatever.

It is almost impossible to get over your surprise at the way in which these brave little Indians cover the ground in attacking. They crawl out of their trenches at night, lie flat on their stomachs, with the rifle and the bayonet in the right hand, and wriggle over the ground like a snake and with amazing speed. Having reached the enemy's trenches they drop the rifle and bayonet and out come the knives—and woe betide the Germans that are within reach. The Gurkhas are born fighters, the love of battle is in their very blood, and they fight all the more readily and gladly because they believe that if they are slain they are sure to go to heaven. If a German makes a lunge at him, the Gurkha seizes the bayonet with the left hand and gets to work with the knife. The plucky little chaps get their hands badly ripped with the German bayonets, and many came into Neuve Chapelle with half their left hands off.

The Germans hate the sight of these Indians, and those who could do so escaped from the trench. They lost no time in going—they fled, and no wonder, for they had suffered terribly, not only from the Indians, but also from the Black Watch, who had been at them with the bayonets. The Highlanders took a large number of prisoners; but the German dead were everywhere, and the trench was packed with them—indeed, all the trenches at the end of the battle were filled with Germans.

During the 10th and 11th we made such good progress that we had taken three of the four trenches; then came the worst day of all, the 12th, for on that we were ordered to take the fourth trench which the Germans held. This was on the outskirts of the village and was strongly fortified. There was a strong blockhouse at the back of the trench which added greatly to the security of the position.

We were up and ready early—at half-past six—and as soon as day had broken the guns began their dreadful booming, and very solemn they sounded in the cold grey light, which is always so cheerless. The guns cleared the way again and did some excellent work in smashing away the wire entanglements and blowing up German works; then came the order to charge.

I was not in at the actual taking of this last trench, but I was lucky in being close enough to be able to see what was going on, and what I saw was some of the most furious fighting in the whole of the battle. The first charge was made with all the dash and courage of the infantry, who had already done so well. Our men rushed at the Germans; but so withering was the fire with which they were met and so hopeless seemed the obstacles that they were repulsed with heavy loss, and I know of nothing more heart-breaking to us who were watching than the sight of these soldiers being sacrificed and suffering as they did without, apparently, winning any success. Again the artillery shelled the German position, then, across the ground which was littered with our dead and dying our brave fellows charged again. They sprang up from the shelter of their trenches, and with even greater fury than before threw themselves upon the enemy, only to be beaten back for the second time, by the cross fire of the machine-guns.

In spite of all these losses and the awful odds against them our men kept their spirits up and vowed that they would still drive the enemy completely out of Neuve Chapelle, and get their own back for Mons and the rest of it, and so, while our artillery took up its tune again the men got a breather, and after a bombardment which lasted at least three-quarters of an hour there were shouts of "Now, boys, again! Let 'em have it!" And up the infantry sprang once more and dashed across the fatal ground. The men who were nearest to me were the 2nd Black Watch, and it did one's heart good to see the way the kilties swung towards the enemy's position.

But it all seemed in vain, for at this point there was the blockhouse to be reckoned with. It was right in the centre and was a veritable little fortress which seemed a mass of flame and sent machine-gun and rifle bullets like hail. No troops could live or stand against such a fusillade, and so our men had to fall back even once more to the protection of the trenches.

By this time the position and danger of the blockhouse were known, and our artillery got the range of it, and that having been done, the end was merely a matter of time. A battery of British guns was trained on the blockhouse and the fire was so accurate that the fourth shell went through the left corner and the building was riddled with shrapnel and put out of action.

It was about this time that our fellows spotted an observation-post on the church in the village. As you know, churches and houses are objects that the British always avoid firing upon if they can, though the Germans have wantonly destroyed large numbers of both. There was the observation-post, plainly to be seen, and as the Germans were directing their artillery fire from it and the post was a danger and a nuisance to us and hindered our progress, a special effort was made to wipe it out. And the effort succeeded, for the British gunners got on it a "Little Harry," a shell that puts to shame even the Jack Johnsons and the Black Marias of the enemy. "Little Harry" settled the observation-post swiftly and finally, and then the fourth and last charge for Neuve Chapelle was made.

And what a charge it was! Every bit of strength and courage that was left seemed to be put into it, and while the infantry dashed on with the bayonet and put the finish to the stubborn German resistance in the trenches and got the enemy fairly on the run, the Gurkhas and the Sikhs and Bengal Lancers hurled themselves on the flying regiments and cut them down with lance and sword. It was a wonderful swirl of fighting. This time the blockhouse was stormed by the 2nd Middlesex and the Royal Irish Rifles.

All at once the guns had finished, and with wild cheers the old

"THE INFANTRY DASHED ON WITH THE BAYONET."

"Die-Hards" and the Irishmen rushed to the German trench and would not be driven back. By about half-past three the blockhouse was taken, and then it was seen that it had been defended by no fewer than half-a-dozen machine-guns and two trench mortars, to say nothing of rifles. These weapons and thousands of rounds of ammunition were captured and the Germans who had not been killed were found hiding under cover as best they could and they were thankful to surrender.

While this splendid piece of work was being finished our Indians on the left were doing heavy execution. The Bengal Lancers were driving the fleeing enemy straight through the village, if that could be called a village which was now an almost shapeless mass of burning and smoking ruins. And spies and snipers had to be searched for in the shattered buildings, while we had to leave the captured trenches for two reasons, because they were filled with dead, and at any moment we might be blown out of them by mines which the Germans had laid. So we had to set to work, even while the fight was being finished, to construct new trenches, and we worked hard on these so as to make ourselves secure in case of a counter attack.

It was not long before we saw the victorious Indian cavalry returning. At about six o'clock we heard the thud of horses' hoofs, and looking up from the new trenches that we were making we saw the Bengal Lancers coming back from their pursuit of the Germans. They had chased the enemy right through the village and into a big wood on the other side of Neuve Chapelle, and what they had done was shown by their reddened lances and the helmets and caps that were stuck on the steel. There were about six hundred of these fine horsemen and not one of them had less than two trophies on his lance, while I saw one of them with no fewer than eight skewered on, and he was smiling all over his dark handsome face. So were the rest of them—they were all delighted with the success that had crowned their work, and we cheered them mightily and laughed too, for somehow we couldn't help doing both.

Meanwhile we were being shelled from a spot which we could not locate for some time, then we learned that the firing came from a fort on the left of the village which was known as Port Arthur. We were in the direct line of fire from it, and our position became very uncomfortable. The Germans who were in Port Arthur were a plucky and stubborn lot, for they refused to surrender when they were asked to do so, and declared that they would not cave in either for British or French or Russians. That showed a fine and right spirit, but at last these chaps had to stop, because our gunners got two or three "Little Harrys" into Port Arthur, and it came tumbling down about the defenders' ears.

It was now dark, past nine o'clock, and it seemed that the enemy was a long time making up his mind to attack us; but at about twenty minutes past the hour they began firing with their artillery. The very first shell they sent came right into my two sections of trenches, and killed one man and wounded half-a-dozen of us, including myself. The poor fellow who was killed had his head completely taken off his shoulders. I helped to bandage the other five before I troubled about myself. Then I looked around again and found that the Germans were well into the night attack; but they never got within fifty yards of our trenches.

What happened after that I am not able to tell you. I was sent to the field ambulance to have my wounds dressed, then I learned that I had got two shrapnel bullets in me, one in the left thigh and one on the other side, to keep it company.

In the ambulance train I went to Béthune, then on to Boulogne, then, on a Sunday afternoon—the 14th of March—I landed at an English Channel port and once again had experience of the care and kindness of friends and nurses in the hospitals at home.

For the second time I had been sent home wounded from the front. I was proud enough when I felt that I had tried to do my duty in the glorious rearguard fighting after Mons and in the battles of the Marne and Aisne; but I was prouder still to know that I had shared in the Battle of Neuve Chapelle..

"Several villages have been destroyed in the interests of the defence my heart bleeds when I think of the number of innocent persons who have lost their homes and their goods."—The Kaiser, in a telegram to President Wilson.

CHAPTER 25

How Trooper Potts Won the V.C. on Burnt Hill

As part of the operations in Gallipoli, it was decided to bombard and attack a very strongly fortified Turkish position near Suvla Bay—a sector stretching from Hill 70 to Hill 112. The frontal attack was a desperate enterprise, as the Turks had dug themselves in up to the neck in two lines of trenches of exceptional strength. The attack was made on the afternoon of August 21st, 1915, after a bombardment by battleships and heavy land batteries. It was in the course of this advance that the teller of this story, Trooper Frederick William Owen Potts, of the 1/1st Berkshire Yeomanry (Territorial Force), was struck down, and later performed the unparalleled act for which he was awarded the Victoria Cross. For nearly fifty hours Trooper Potts remained under the Turkish trenches with a severely wounded and helpless comrade, "although he could himself have returned to safety," says the official record. Finally the trooper, in the extraordinary manner which he now describes, saved his comrade's life. Trooper Potts is only twenty-two years old, and is the first Yeoman to win the most coveted of all distinctions.

I saw a good deal of the Turks before we came to grips with them near Suvla Bay. I had gone out to Egypt with my regiment, the Berkshire Yeomanry, and for about four months we were doing garrison work and escort work for Turks who had been captured in Gallipoli and the Dardanelles and sent as prisoners of war to Egypt. Our place was not far from Cairo. I was greatly struck by the size and physique of the Turks. There were some very fine big men amongst them—in fact, I should think the average height was close on six feet.

We had taken our horses out to Egypt with us, and all our work in that country was done with them; but as the weeks went by, and no call came to us for active service, we became disappointed, and got into the way of singing a song which the poet of the regiment had specially composed, and of which the finish of every verse was the line—

The men that nobody wants,

—this meaning that there was no use for us as cavalry in the fighting area. But when the four months had gone, the order suddenly came for us to go to Gallipoli. By that time we had got acclimatised, a point we appreciated later, as the heat was intense and the flies were very troublesome.

From Alexandria we sailed in a transport, which occupied four days in reaching Gallipoli. Here we were transhipped to trawlers and barges, and immediately found ourselves in the thick of one of the most tremendous bombardments the world has ever known. Battleships were firing their big guns, which made a terrific noise, and there was other continual firing of every known sort. We were very lucky in our landing, because we escaped some of the heaviest of the gunfire. The Turks could see us, though we had no sight of them, and whenever a cluster of us was spotted, a shell came crashing over. Thus we had our baptism of fire at the very start.

We were in an extraordinarily difficult country, and whatever we needed in the way of food and drink we had to carry with us—even the water. Immense numbers of tins had been filled from the Nile and taken to Gallipoli in barges, and this was the water we used for drinking purposes, as well as water which was condensed from the sea, and kept in big tanks on the shore. Every drop of water we needed had to be fetched from the shore, and this work proved about the hardest and most dangerous of any we had to do after landing and taking up our position on a hill. Several of our chaps were knocked over in this water-fetching work.

While we were at this place we were employed in making roads from Suvla Bay to Anzac, and hard work it was, because the country was all rocks. We had landed light, without blankets or waterproofs, so that we felt the intense cold of the nights very much.

We had a week of this sort of thing, under fire all the time. I think it was on a Sunday we landed, and a week later we heard that we were to take part in the attack on Hill 70, or, as we called it, because of its appearance, Burnt Hill. There were immense quantities of a horrible sort of scrub on it, and a great deal of this stuff had been fired and charred by gunfire. I little knew then how close and long an acquaintance I was to make with the scrub on Hill 70.

It was about five o'clock in the evening when the news came. We were to be ready at seven, and ready we were to be in it. We did not know much, but we understood that we were to take our places in some reserve trenches. Night comes quickly in those regions, and when the day had gone we moved round to Anzac, marching along the roads which we had partially made. We reached Anzac at about two o'clock in the morning, in pitch darkness.

We had a pick and two shovels to four men, and took it in turn to carry them. Each man also carried two hundred rounds of ammunition, so that we were pretty well laden. When we reached Anzac Cove we moved in right under the cliffs, which go sheer down to the sea; but there is practically no tide, so that the beach is safe. The only way to reach the shore was to go in single file down a narrow, twisting pathway.

We were on the beach till about two o'clock in the afternoon, when we were ordered to be ready with our packs, and we went up the cliff, again in single file, forming up when we reached the top. Then we went a mile or so along the road we had marched over the night before—all part of the scheme of operations, I take it. Then we cut across to our right and saw a plain called Salt Lake, where we watched a division going into action under heavy shrapnel fire.

We were now in the thick of the awful country which I was to know so well. The surface was all sand and shrubs, and the great peculiarity of the shrubs was that they were very much like our holly trees at home, though the leaves were not so big, but far more prickly. These shrubs were about three feet high, and they were everywhere; but they did not provide any real cover. There were also immense numbers of long creepers and grass, and a lot of dust and dirt. The heat was fearful, so that you can easily understand how hard it was to get along when we were on the move. These obstacles proved disastrous to many of our chaps when they got into the zone of fire, for the shrapnel set the shrubs ablaze. This meant that many a brave fellow who was hit during the fighting on Hill 70 fell among the burning furze and was burned to death where he lay.

As we were waiting for our turn, we could see the other chaps picking their way through this burning stuff, and charging on towards the Turkish trenches. When our own turn came, the scrub was burn-

CHOCOLATE HILL,

ing less fiercely, and to some extent we were able to choose our way and avoid the blazing patches. We ran whenever we got the chance, making short rushes; but when we got into the real zone of fire, we never stopped until we were under the protection of Chocolate Hill.

For half an hour we rested at the foot of this hill. From our position we could not see the Turks, who were entrenched over the top; but their snipers were out and bothering us a good deal. It was impossible to see these snipers, because they hid themselves in the bushes, and had their faces and rifles painted the same colour as the surrounding objects. However, we levelled up matters by sending out our own sniping parties.

We were on the move again as soon as we had got our breath back. We still understood, as we moved to the left of Chocolate Hill, that we were going to occupy reserve trenches. We went through a field of ripe wheat. About two yards in front of me was a mate of mine, Reginald West. I saw him struck in the thigh by a sniper's bullet, which went in as big as a pea, and came out the size of a five-shilling piece. It was an explosive bullet, one of many that were used against us by the Turks, under their German masters. In a sense West was lucky, because when he was struck down he fell right on the edge of a dugout, and I heard one of the men shout, "Roll over, mate! Roll over! You'll drop right in here!" And he did.

The rest of us went on, though in the advance we lost a number of men. Some were killed outright; some were killed by shells and bullets after they had fallen wounded, and some had to lie where they had fallen and do the best they could. We pushed ahead till we struck Hill 70 again.

When we got to the reserve trenches I asked a chap how far away the Turks were, and he answered, "About a thousand yards," but I don't think it was as much as that.

Now we began to ascend Hill 70 in short spurts, halting from time to time. We had fairly good cover, because the scrub was not on fire, though several parts had been burnt out. During one of these halts we were ordered to fix bayonets.

We had found shelter in a bit of a gulley, and were pretty well mixed up with other regiments—the Borders, Dorsets, and so on. We first got the idea that we were going to charge from an officer near us; but he was knocked out—with a broken arm, I believe—before the charge came off. He was just giving us the wheeze about the coming charge when a bullet struck him.

How did the charge begin? Well, an officer shouted, as far as I can recollect, "Come on, lads! We'll give 'em beans!" That is not exactly according to drill-books and regulations as I know them; but it was enough. It let the boys loose, and they simply leapt forward and went for the Turkish trenches. It was not to be my good fortune to get into them, however; in fact, I did not get very far after the order to charge was given.

I had gone perhaps twenty or thirty yards when I was knocked off my feet. I knew I was hit. I had a sort of burning sensation; but whether I was hit in the act of jumping, or whether I jumped because I was hit, I do not know. What I *do* know is that I went up in the air, came down again, and lay where I fell. I knew that I had been shot at the top of the left thigh, the bullet going clean through and just missing the artery and the groin by an eighth of an inch, as the doctor told me later.

Utterly helpless, I lay there for about three-quarters of an hour, while the boys rushed round me and scattered in the charge. This happened about a quarter of a mile from the top of the hill. I propped myself up on my arm and watched the boys charging.

I heard later, from a man who was with me in hospital at Malta— he had been struck deaf and dumb, for the time being, amongst other things—that the boys got into the Turkish third trench and that the Turks bolted. He told me that when they reached this third trench there were only seventeen Berkshire boys left to hold it. The enemy seemed to get wind of this; then it looked as if all the Turkish army was going for the seventeen, and they had no alternative but to clear out.

After the charge I saw this handful come back down the hill, quite close to where I was lying. I had fallen in a sort of little thicket, a cluster of the awful scrub which was like holly, but much worse. I was thankful for it, however, because it gave me a bit of shelter and hid me from view.

I had been lying there about half an hour when I heard a noise near me and saw that a poor wounded chap, a trooper of the Berkshires, was crawling towards me. I recognised him as a fellow-townsman.

"Is that you, Andrews?" I asked.

He simply answered "Yes." That was all he could get out.

"I'm jolly pleased you've come," I said, and Andrews crawled as close as he could get, and we lay there, perfectly still, for about ten minutes. Andrews had been shot through the groin, a very dangerous wound, and he was suffering terribly and losing a great deal of blood.

We had been together for a few minutes when another trooper—a stranger to me—crawled up to our hiding-place. He had a wound in the leg. We were so cramped for space under the thicket, that Andrews had to shift as best he could, to make room for the newcomer. That simple act of mercy saved his life, for the stranger had not been with us more than ten minutes when a bullet went through both his legs and mortally wounded him. He kept on crying for water; but we had not a drop amongst the three of us, and could not do anything to quench his awful thirst.

That fearful afternoon passed slowly, with its grizzling heat and constant fighting, and the night came quickly. The night hours brought us neither comfort nor security, for a full moon shone, making the countryside as light as day. The cold was intense. The stranger was practically unconscious and kept moving about, which made our position worse, because every time he moved the Turks banged at us.

I was lying absolutely as flat as I could, with my face buried in the dirt, for the bullets were peppering the ground all around us, and one of them actually grazed my left ear—you can see the scar it has made, just over the top. This wound covered my face with blood. Was I scared or frightened? I can honestly say that I was not. I had got beyond that stage, and almost as a matter of course I calmly noted the details of everything that happened.

Throughout the whole of that unspeakable night this poor Bucks Hussar chap hung on. He kept muttering, "Water! Water!" But we could not give him any. When the end came he simply lay down and died right away, and his dead body stayed with us, for we could neither get away nor move him.

During the whole of the next day we lay in our hiding-place, suffering indescribably. The sun, thirst, hunger, and our wounds, all added to our pain. In our desperation we picked bits off the stalks of the shrubs and tried to suck them; but we got no relief in that way.

The whole of the day went somehow—with such slowness that it seemed as if it would never end. It was impossible to sleep—fighting was going on all the time, and the noise was terrific. We could not see anything of our boys, and we knew that it was impossible for any stretcher-bearers to get through to us, because we were a long way up the hill and no stretcher-bearers could venture out under such a terrible fire.

Night came again at last, and Andrews and myself decided to shift, if it was humanly possible to do so, because it was certain death from thirst and hunger to remain where we were, even if we escaped from bullets. So I began to move away by crawling, and Andrews followed as best he could. I would crawl a little way and wait till Andrews, poor fellow, could crawl up to me again. We wriggled like snakes, absolutely flat on the ground and with our faces buried in the stifling dirt.

We managed to wriggle about three hundred yards that night—as near as I can judge. Starting at about a quarter past six, as soon as the day was done, it was about three in the morning when we decided to rest, so that if we had really done three hundred yards we had crawled at the rate of only thirty-three yards an hour!

A great number of rifles were lying about—weapons which had been cast aside in the charge, or had belonged to fallen soldiers; but most of them were quite out of working order, because they were clogged up with dust and dirt. I tried many of them, and at last found one that seemed to be in good working order, and to my joy I came across about fifty rounds of ammunition. Another serviceable rifle was found, so that Andrews and myself were filled with a new hope.

"We'll die like Britons, at any rate!" said Andrews. "We'll give a good account of ourselves before we go!" And I agreed with him.

We were now some distance from the Turks, and I was terribly anxious to shoot at them; but Andrews was more cautious. "If you fire they'll discover us, and we shall be done for!" he said. Then we shook hands fervently, because we both believed that this was the last of us.

We had managed to crawl to a bit of shelter which was given by some burnt-out scrub, and here we tried to snatch some sleep, for we were both worn out. We went to sleep, for the simple reason that we could not keep awake; but I suddenly awoke, because the cold was intense and I was nearly frozen. Luckily there were a lot of empty sandbags lying about, and I got two or three of these and put them on top of us; but they were really no protection from the bitter air.

When the morning came we made a move, and for the first time we were able to get some water; but only by taking the water-bottles from the poor chaps who had been knocked out.

Then we crept back to our shelter, finding immense relief from drinking the water we had got, though it was quite warm.

We slept, or tried to sleep, there for the rest of that night, and stayed in the place till next morning. We must have been in what is called "dead ground," a region which cannot be seen or touched by either side, and so it proved to be, for in the early morning there was a real battle and the bullets were singing right over our heads.

"There's more lead flying about than there was yesterday," said Andrews; and really some of the bullets were splashing quite close to us—within six feet, I think, though there were not many that came so near.

Andrews was bleeding terribly—every time he moved he bled; but I did the best I could for him with my iodine—I dressed him with mine, and he dressed me with his, and splendid stuff it is. Though we had nothing to eat we did not really feel hungry now—we were past the eating stage. I was very lucky in having four cigarettes and some matches and I risked a smoke, the sweetest I ever had in my life.

Again we stuck the awful day through.

I was terribly anxious to move and get out of it all at any cost; but still Andrews was very cautious. "No, we won't try till it gets dark," he said. I felt that he was right, and so we waited, as patiently as we could, for the night. Three or four yards from us was an inviting-looking bush, and we crawled towards it, thinking it would help us to get away and give us shelter; but at the end of our adventure we discovered that we had done no more than crawl to the bush, crawl round it, and get back to our original hiding-place; so we decided to give up the attempt to get away just then.

When the third night on the hill came we were fairly desperate, knowing that something would have to be done if we meant to live, and that certain death awaited us where we were. We had nothing to eat, and the only drink was the water, which was frightful stuff. But though it was, we were thankful to have it. The water was warm, because of the heat, and was about the colour of wine.

We did not for a moment suppose that we should live to reach the British lines, which we believed to be not far away; but we risked everything on the effort, and in the moonlight we began to wriggle off. We had managed to get no more than half a dozen yards when Andrews had to give it up. I myself, though I was the stronger and better of the two, could scarcely crawl. Every movement was a torture and a misery, because of the thorns that stuck into us from the horrible scrub.

We had kept the sandbags, and with my help Andrews managed to get them over his arms and up to his shoulders. I fastened them with the pieces of string they have, and these gave him a good deal of protection, though the thorns got through and punished us cruelly. I was picking them out of my hands for three weeks afterwards.

Water supply at the Dardenelles

Having crawled these half-dozen yards, we gave up the attempt altogether, and did not know what to do. We could see a cluster of trees not far away, about a hundred yards, and there was one that looked fairly tall.

"If we can get to that tree," said Andrews, "I could lie there, if I had some water, and perhaps you could strike some of our chaps and bring help." I had little hope from such an effort as that. Then Andrews unselfishly urged me to look after myself; but, of course, I would not dream of leaving him. I offered to carry him, and I tried, but I was far too weak.

What in the world was to be done? How were we to get out of this deadly place? There seemed no earthly hope of escape, when, literally like an inspiration, we thought we saw a way out.

Just near us was an ordinary entrenching shovel, which had been dropped, or had belonged to some poor chap who had fallen—I can't say which, but there it was. I crawled up and got hold of it, and before we quite knew what was happening, Andrews was resting on it, and I was doing my best to drag him out of danger.

I cannot say whose idea this was, but it is quite likely that Andrews thought of it first. He sat on the shovel as best he could—he was not fastened to it—with his legs crossed, the wounded leg over the sound one, and he put his hands back and clasped my wrists as I sat on the ground behind and hauled away at the handle. Several times he came off, or the shovel fetched away, and I soon saw that it would be impossible to get him away in this fashion.

When we began to move the Turks opened fire on us; but I hardly cared now about the risk of being shot, and for the first time since I had been wounded I stood up and dragged desperately at the shovel, with Andrews on it. I managed to get over half a dozen yards, then I was forced to lie down and rest. Andrews needed a rest just as badly as I did, for he was utterly shaken and suffered greatly.

We started again at about a quarter past six, as soon as the night came, and for more than three mortal hours we made this strange journey down the hillside; and at last, with real thankfulness, we reached the bottom and came to a bit of a wood. Sweet beyond expression it was to feel that I could walk upright, and that I was near the British lines. This knowledge came to me suddenly when there rang through the night the command: "Halt!"

I obeyed—glorious it was to hear that challenge in my native tongue, after what we had gone through. Then this good English sentry said, "Come up and be recognised!" not quite according to the regulation challenge, but good enough—and he had seen us quite clearly in the moonshine.

Up I went, and found myself face to face with the sentry, whose rifle was presented ready for use, and whose bayonet gleamed in the cold light.

"What are you doing?" said the sentry. "Are you burying the dead?"

I saw that he was sentry over a trench, and I went to the top of it and leaned over the parapet and said, "Can you give me a hand?"

"What's up?" said the sentry, who did not seem to realise what had actually happened—and how could he, in such a strange affair?

"I've got a chap out here wounded," I told him, "and I've dragged him down the hill on a shovel."

The sentry seemed to understand like a flash. He walked up to the trench, and when I had made myself clear, three or four chaps bustled round and got a blanket, and I led them to the spot where I had left Andrews lying on the ground. We lifted him off the shovel, put him on the blanket, and carried him to the trench. These men were, I think, Inniskilling Fusiliers, and they did everything for us that human kindness could suggest. They gave me some rum and bully beef and biscuit, and it was about the most delightful meal I ever had in my life, because I was famishing and I was safe, with Andrews, after those dreadful hours on the hillside, which seemed as if they would never end.

When we had rested and pulled round a bit, we were put on stretchers and carried to the nearest dressing-station. Afterwards we were sent to Malta, where Andrews is, I believe, still in hospital.

The granting of the Victoria Cross for what I had done came as a complete surprise to me, because it never struck me that I had done more than any other British soldier would have done for a comrade.

I never lost heart during the time I was lying on Hill 70. All the old things came clearly up in my mind, and many an old prayer was uttered, Andrews joining in. We never lost hope that some way out of our peril would be found—and it seemed as if our prayers had been answered by giving us this inspiration of the shovel.

CHAPTER 26

A Prisoner of War in Germany

For nine weary months, including the whole of an uncommonly bitter winter, the teller of this story, Corporal Oliver H. Blaze, 1st Battalion Scots Guards, was a prisoner of war in Germany. Corporal Blaze was on outpost when he was severely wounded and captured. Corporal Blaze is a fine type of the splendid Guardsmen who have done so much in this great war to add to their own glory and the noble reputation of the British Army.

I hardly know where to begin my story, but perhaps I might start with a little tale of an air fight, because a night or two ago I happened to be in the streets when German airships raided London, and I could not help recalling the difficulty of hitting even a huge object like a Zeppelin in the night-time.

In the early days of September 1914, when we had got used to fighting, the battalion was on the march when a German aeroplane, decorated with two Iron Crosses, was sighted. At that time we were more than a thousand strong, and the lot of us opened fire with our rifles, rattling away with rapid fire, so that we soon accounted for about fifteen thousand rounds. At the same time another battalion not far away was on the job, so that a perfect fusillade was going on. The firing was tremendous, but it seemed as if the machine would not be touched. At last, however, the aeroplane was brought down, the observer being dead and the other man severely burnt and wounded. I do not know whether it was our battalion or the other which got the machine; but I called to mind the great difficulty of hitting an aircraft when I watched the raid on London. I was walking along, too pleasantly occupied to be thinking of war, and did not know of the affair until I reached a street corner and saw the people craning their necks skywards, watching the airship and the shells that were bursting under it.

Mons, Cambrai, the Marne and the like make an old, old story by this time, so I will get on to the tale of my nine months' captivity in

Germany, as a prisoner of war.

It is common knowledge now that the Germans never lost a chance of trying to do something by treachery and trickery and not playing the game. Killed and wounded English soldiers were robbed of their coats by the Germans, who took them for their own use; and dressed in these coats the enemy on several occasions tried to get near us, to their heavy cost, when we got accustomed to the dodge.

One day, early in September, not long after we had gone out with the Expeditionary Force, a German machine-gun brigade came along, dressed in our uniform. We thought they were reinforcements, so we let them get very close and they occupied a ridge on our left. Ten minutes afterwards they opened fire on us; but our garrison artillery soon shifted them with sixty-pounders. The Germans killed a lot of the Coldstreams that day by this trick.

It was not long after this that we had one of those experiences which have been so often known in this great war. We were marching along in brigade column, with the Black Watch or Coldstreams, I am not sure which, leading. We were going through an area which had been reported all clear, and had got to a bend in the road, when the Germans started shelling us. It was one of those swift happenings which cannot be avoided in such a war as this, and before we fully realised what was taking place, a shell had burst and killed four stretcher-bearers of the Coldstreams, the N.C.O. who was in charge, and a wounded man who was being carried on a stretcher; and the same shell wounded a man in our front section of fours. That one shell did a fair lot of havoc, and it was quickly followed by several more; but these did not do much mischief.

What struck me most in this little affair was the coolness of our CO., Colonel Lowther, now a brigadier-general. He personally conducted every company from the left of the road into a ditch on the right of the road.

"Keep cool, men," he said, "and come this way." And we did keep cool, for the colonel took the direction of everything, in spite of the shelling, just as calmly as if he was carrying out a battalion parade at home—a really wonderful performance at a time like that, and one which completely steadied the lot of us, though we had got pretty well used to things.

But the Germans did not have a look in for long, for the Kilties got hold of the gunners and chased them off. I did not see much of it, except in the distance; but we heard the shouting as the Jocks got to work with their bayonets.

As we were going along the road we saw where the Germans had put out of action a whole battery of our artillery which was standing at the side of the road. The weather was dull and it started to drizzle, so that it was not easy to distinguish troops. While the battery was being knocked out some of our fellows—the Loyal North Lancashire, I think—were advancing across a field. To protect themselves from the rain they had covered themselves with their waterproof sheets. Seeing them, and not being able to tell who they were, but believing them to be Germans, our gunners opened fire on them; but what damage they did I don't know. That was another of those things that will happen in war, and it could hardly be helped, for about this time it was a common dodge of the Germans to disguise themselves in British uniforms and attack us before we could tumble to the trick.

When we had crossed the Aisne and had got into the hills we had grown wary, and in crossing fields and open spaces we went in artillery formation, or "blobbing," as it is called. This "blobbing" was a splendid way of saving the lives of men when we were under fire, for it kept us in platoons closed, but 200 yards between each platoon, and so enabled us to escape a good many of the bursting shells.

We went along a whole stretch of country till we reached a small village and billeted there. In the morning we were on the move again, driving the Germans from one crest to another, but their position was too strong for us to shift them any farther, and then it was a long monotonous job of hanging on and waiting. They are practically in the same place now.

We did a lot of bayonet work from time to time; but I can't say much about it. I know that in one affair I saw a German. I stuck and he stuck—and I don't remember any more—one goes insane. I got a bang on the back of the head from somebody, though I thought at the time that a stone had been thrown and had struck me. I remember that day well—September 14th—because in addition to the charge I saw a Jack Johnson for the first time, though we christened them Black Marias and Coal-boxes then. This monster burst amongst some French Algerian troops, and shot a lot of them up into the air, literally blowing the poor devils to pieces.

On October 19th we marched away and moved by train, finally getting to Ypres. We dug trenches in a ditch on the night of the 22nd and occupied them, and on the morning of the 23rd I went on outpost duty, little dreaming of the fate that was in store for me. At that time shells were dropping very heavily between our line of trenches and a village not far away which was supposed to be occupied by the French.

It was about six o'clock in the morning when I went out with my patrol, of which I was corporal in charge. There were four of us altogether, and we were put on outpost duty in what proved to be a very warm corner. The shelling went on all day, and we were looking forward to our relief; but it did not happen to come, and so we had to hold on. The day passed and the night came, and it was not long after darkness that we knew that a strong rush was being made on us by the enemy—they proved to be the 213th Landwehr Battalion of Prussian Infantry.

I saw that we were being rushed, and I knew that our chance of escape was hopeless. I thought very swiftly just then, and my thought was, "We can't get away, so we may as well stick it. If we bolt we shall be shot in the back—and we might just as well be shot in the front; it looks better."

They were on us before we knew where we were, and to make matters worse, they rushed upon us from the direction of the village where we supposed the French to be.

There was a scrap, short and sweet, between our outpost and the Germans, and almost in the twinkling of an eye, it seemed, two of my men were killed, one got away, and I was wounded and captured.

A bullet struck me in the right arm and I fell down, and the Germans were on me before I knew what was happening. I still had my equipment on, and to this fact and the prompt kind act of a wounded German—let us be fair and say that not all Germans are brutes: there are exceptions—I owe my life, for as soon as I fell a Prussian rushed at me and made a drive with his bayonet. Just as he did so, a wounded German who was lying on the ground near me grabbed me and gave me a lug towards him. At this instant the bayonet jabbed at me and struck between the equipment and my wounded arm, just touching my side. The equipment and the wounded German's pull had prevented the bayonet from plunging plump into me and killing me on the spot, for the steel, driven with such force, would have gone clean through my chest. That was the sort of tonic to buck you up, and I didn't need a second prick to make me spring to my feet.

I jumped up, and had no sooner done so than a second bullet struck me on the wounded arm and made a fair mess of it, and I knew that this time I was properly bowled out.

I had fallen down again and was lying on the ground, bleeding badly; and the next thing I knew was that I was being stripped. Everything I had on me, my equipment and my clothing, was taken away; not for the purpose of letting a doctor examine me, as one did later, but as part of a system of battlefield plunder which the Germans have organised.

The very first thing the doctor said when he saw the wounds was *"Donnerwetter!"* I was taken to a barn and left there till morning. I had treatment, then I was moved into another barn. The Germans were decent over the business, and there was no brutality or anything of that kind. I had been taken from the second barn, and was being carried across a field, when the ambulance was stopped by a German doctor who was on horseback. He looked at my arm, and instantly said that it would have to be amputated right away, as mortification had set in; and so, lying on the stretcher, which had been put down in the field, and round which a small green tarpaulin had been rigged to keep the wind and cold out, my arm was taken off. Injections had been made in the arm, and I felt no pain during the operation, which I watched with great interest. The doctor who performed it had studied at Guy's Hospital and spoke English well. When I had been removed to a German hospital in Belgium he saw me every morning, noon, and night, and I had exactly the same food as the Germans, while the old inspector of the hospital used to give me custard and fruit now and again, when he thought no one was looking; and I had cigarettes and cigars issued to me just the same as to their own men.

I was in this hospital in Belgium for a fortnight, and was then moved into Germany, being sent to Münster, in Westphalia, with a lot of wounded Germans. It seemed as if, in leaving Belgium, I had said goodbye to civilisation, in view of what happened during my imprisonment in Germany.

I very soon made acquaintance with German brutality to British prisoners of war—brutality and cowardice, of which I saw constant signs in my captivity; I say cowardice advisedly, because only a coward will hit and bully a man who can't hit back. On that point, however, there is some consolation. It was practically a death matter to strike a German soldier, even under great provocation; but if you were struck first, you had your remedy, and nothing pleased a British soldier more than to be struck, because that gave him his chance, and many a hard British fist got home on a fat German jowl. I shall always be thankful to know that I got one or two in on my own account, though I had only my left arm to work with. I did not, of course, strike until I had been struck first; but when I did hit out I got my own back, with a lot of interest.

That is getting off the track a bit, so I will go back. At Münster I was taken into a disused circus which had been turned into a hospital for prisoners, and when I got there the doctor examined my wound. It was all raw, but he messed about to that extent that I fainted. Two mornings afterwards—they only dressed us every two mornings—I was lying on a table, to be dressed. The job was to be done by a young German student, a born brute, for I tell only the plain truth when I say that he deliberately cut the flesh of my only arm with his lancet and scissors.

"English swine!" he said. "He's had one arm off, and he ought to have the other off, too!"

This was the type of fellow who was let loose on wounded helpless British prisoners of war.

Those dressings were horrible experiences, as a rule, for I was held down on the table by German orderlies, who had about as much feeling and compassion as the table itself.

Let me give another illustration of the German way of treating wounded British soldiers. Just after Christmas I was moved into an open camp at Münster, and the only covering I had was a tarpaulin, the result being that I caught cold in my wound, and on January 2nd I was moved back into another hospital. I knew nothing whatever about the regulations of the place, so that I saw nothing wrong in walking along an ordinary looking passage. As I did this there came towards me a man who corresponds in rank to our regimental sergeant-major. I was suffering greatly from my stump, and was quite helpless; yet this fellow seized me by the scruff of the neck and the seat of the trousers and threw me out of the passage—and it was not till later that I learned that the passage led to the operating-room, and that patients were not allowed to use it. Such a thing could not possibly happen in a British military hospital containing wounded German soldiers. It is only fair to say that the food we got in hospital was good.

Though my wound was not healed, I was sent away from the hospital and back to the camp. That was bad in some ways, but it had a fine compensation, for I was attended by two of our own medical officers of the Royal Army Medical Corps who were also prisoners—Captain Rose and Captain Croker. I believe they have been exchanged now. I need not say what a joy it was to be looked after by our own splendid

A BRITISH SOLDIER HELPING A WOUNDED GERMAN PRISONER

doctors.

Time passed slowly and very wearily, and the monotony became deadly. It was bitterly cold, and snow fell heavily and constantly till about April. We did our best to keep cheerful and fit, and were always thankful when we could get a chance of playing games. Sometimes we played football with our sentries; but they were sorry sportsmen, and could not endure being beaten, even in fair football. There were some Royal Welsh Fusiliers amongst the prisoners, and three footballs had been sent out to them. These footballs reached the camp safely, and everybody was hugely pleased with them. We got up a match between a British team and the German sentries, and beat them six to one. It was a straightforward, honest match, and a fair and square win; but the Germans could not stomach it, and for three days our smoking was stopped. No reason for the stoppage was given; but we knew well enough what the cause was, especially as the order applied only to the British prisoners of war.

I will give another instance of the utter smallness of the German spirit. On the night of the day when Italy declared war on Austria we were sitting outside our wooden huts singing our own National Anthem, the "*Marseillaise*," "Rule, Britannia," and lighter compositions such as "Hi! Tiddley hi ti!"—in fact, anything that came to mind, just to keep things moving and cheerful. Then the news of Italy's decision came and fairly struck the Germans dumb.

No reason was given for the steps they took against us—though we knew perfectly well what the cause was—but our smoking was stopped for seven days. Some of us were locked in the lavatories for twenty-four hours, and for twenty days our meat was stopped, so that we were almost starved. And on top of all this, two Englishmen and a Belgian were sent to a punishment camp. God knows what happened to them.

During all this bitter winter weather we were accommodated in wooden huts, which we had been put to build ourselves. We did not mind that in the least, because we were thankful to be employed. But it was almost impossible to keep warm in the huts, owing to our scanty clothing and the small number of stoves. There were two stoves in each room, but we were only allowed one small box of coal—sometimes coke—daily for each. Generally speaking, the British prisoners could not get near the stoves because of the foreign prisoners who crowded around them, all day long, swathed in a pair of blankets. To add to the misery of the life, the bedding was horribly verminous, and we were only allowed to have one wash a day. That solitary wash was early in the morning, and we could not get any more, because the wash-house was closed after 7 a.m.

The food was very poor, and there was not enough of it. There was plenty of soup of a sort—and well there might be, for it was mostly water—and there were solids of a kind for which an Englishman has no liking—chestnuts, potatoes and horse beans—poor stuff. The drinks were as bad as the solids. We had what was called coffee given to us; but there was not much difference between the coffee and the soup. As for clothing, no real attempt was made to supply us, though in so many cases we had been stripped naked when captured. When I went out of camp, just after Christmas, I had only a pair of trousers and a pair of *sabots*, wooden shoes, and I should have fared badly if I had not been lucky enough to receive an old cycling jacket which my mother had sent out to me.

The following statement will show exactly how and when we were fed each day:—In the morning, at six o'clock, we had "coffee," made from burnt rye, but nothing to eat; at twelve noon, soup, with a plentiful supply of water in it and any one of the following ingredients: chestnuts, potatoes, horse beans, sauerkraut, acorns. At 12.30 to 1 p.m. there was an issue of bread, the loaves being about 2½ in. by 6 in. by 2 in. At 3 p.m. there was "coffee," as at 6 a.m., but nothing to eat; and at 6 p.m. there was soup, as for dinner, but no meat, fish or cheese. By this you will see that we had nothing to eat from 6 p.m. till noon the following day—a period of eighteen hours. We had a small piece of meat three times a fortnight, cheese once a week, and two raw herrings a week.

As for passing the time, it was one long dreary "roll on, night." Cards, draughts, football, and causing as much trouble as we dared to the Germans, with a little singing, formed our only means of keeping sane. Nearly everybody had to work at something or other, the hours of work being 7 a.m. to 11.30 a.m. (empty stomachs), and 2 p.m. to 6 p.m.

There was only one occasion when we had a little change from the bad treatment, and that was when a batch of German prisoners of war, who had been in England and exchanged, returned. They must have told how well they were treated in English hospitals—which, as I know, are paradise compared with German hospitals—for we were better fed and looked after for a time. This improvement did not last long, however, and we went back to the old ways. Germans can't keep a good thing going.

German cunning and lying soon made themselves evident, for under the guise of voluntary work a lot of the prisoners of war were obliged to work in mines and ironworks, and by being forced to do these things they were really helping to fight their own people.

The way the trick was done was this—Germans came round and asked prisoners to volunteer to act as waiters, and a lot of us readily agreed, because any sort of employment was better than awful idleness. But the "waiters" soon learned that they had been shamefully deceived, for they were sent into mines and ironworks and on to farms. It was no use to protest, because it was a case of work or no food. There was so little to eat in the ordinary way that poor fellows could not face actual starvation, and so they worked unwillingly. I was asked to go and work in the fields, but I was quite incapable of doing this, and so I told the camp commandant, who put me into the office.

I had had experience of orderly-room work with the Guards, and felt quite at home at this job—and it was interesting, too, for I was in the extraordinary position of being a sort of censor!

My duty was to handle letters from England for the prisoners, and see that no news, or cuttings from newspapers, or other forbidden things got through. There were three of us doing this work—two sergeants and myself, one sergeant being in charge of the parcels. I naturally did the best I could for the prisoners. This office work was both interesting and exciting, and helped to get the time along.

As for our privations generally, there was nothing for it but to make the best of them and grin and bear it. The American Consul at Münster paid two visits to the camp while I was there, but no good came of them. Again the crafty German was prepared. It was known on each occasion that the consul was coming—known two days before he arrived—so things were ready for him. He inspected only a few of the rooms, and the principal result of the first visit was that our dinner was two hours late. We made complaints, but nothing came of them, so when the consul visited us for the second time and asked if there were any complaints to make, we bluntly answered, "No, it's no good making them, for nothing's done." The Germans instantly published in the local paper the statement, "The English are satisfied. They have no complaints."

Constant attempts were made to escape, and I fancy that some of the prisoners gave up the whole of their time to plotting and planning ways of clearing out. The chance of getting away was small, because at night the camp, buildings as well as compounds, was brilliantly lighted by big electric arc lamps, and there were sentries and barbed wire entanglements everywhere. But in spite of all precautions several Belgians and a few Englishmen and Frenchmen escaped, and we were immensely pleased when we heard that one Belgian had got away by stealing the commandant's motorcar and bolting in it. I did not hear what became of him.

Brutal punishments were inflicted for the most trivial offences, such as smoking in forbidden places, and a common method was to tie a prisoner to a post, with his feet deep in snow, and leave him there for two hours, with an armed sentry over him. The poor wretch dare not move, if he did the brave warrior with the gun kicked him—the German is a fine hand at hitting when the other chap can't hit back. This savage cruelty had a terrible effect on some of the victims, and helped to make them the life-long wrecks that they now are.

From Münster I was sent to Brussels for exchange. We were quartered in the Royal Academy, and naturally enough the Belgian women and children tried to give us things. When this was seen, the German wounded who were in the building were ordered to turn the hose on, and they did. It was a great laugh, though, for it took them four hours to fix the hose—and then it would not work properly.

The authorities suddenly decided that I should not be exchanged, because I was a non-commissioned officer, and I was sent to Wesel on the Rhine, where I stayed six weeks. I had to go into hospital again, because my wound would not heal—it never got a sporting chance. Ill treatment continued, and for reasons, mostly revenge, which Britishers would scorn. The chief of this hospital was an old man whose only son had been lost in a submarine that had been sunk by the British. I saw that something was wrong as soon as he appeared in the morning, and I felt that we should get it hot, though I did not know how.

The old doctor had all the English prisoners sent for, and incredible as it may seem, every wound that was healed was deliberately reopened and plugged, while wounds that were not healed were probed inside and all the newly-formed flesh was destroyed. Many of us suffered terribly for a long time as the result of the visit to us of the old man who had lost his son in fair fight.

My wound was finally healed on July 25th, exactly nine months from the day on which my arm was taken off.

My sole object now was to get away from the horrible country and the more horrible people, and, thank God, I managed to do it. The refusal to exchange me was a bitter blow, but I soon pulled up and set to work to get away. Accordingly, when I reached Wesel, I reported myself as a private, and I was reckoned as a private and put in the list for exchange. I was sent to Aix-la-Chapelle.

Soon after this I came away with other prisoners of war, and one of the most glorious moments of my life was when I set eyes again on Old England.

There is one strange incident that I have kept to the last.

I have said that when I was shot on outpost I was stripped. My jacket must have been thrown aside, for next day a chum of mine picked it up and put it in his pack, thinking I had been killed, and meaning to bring it home, if he lived, as a relic. During many a long day and hard fight he carried that extra burden in his pack—no little thing to do—then he himself was wounded and sent home. He brought my jacket with him, and now I have it, and shall always treasure it as a memento of my war-days. The jacket is smothered in blood.

British soldiers charging through a smoke-cloud.

CHAPTER 27
Gassed Near Hill 60

The conflict at the village of St. Julien, in the region of the famous Hill 60, where many troops fell in repelling the attempts of the Germans to hack their way through to Calais is told by Lance-Corporal R. G. Simmins, of the 8th Battalion Canadian Infantry, 90th Winnipeg Rifles.

When I recall my experiences at the front, I am particularly struck by the circumstance that the thing which stands out most clearly in my mind is not the actual campaigning, not the long and weary times in the trenches, not even artillery, rifle, or bayonet fighting, but the coming of the poison-gas. I myself was gassed in the furious fighting at St. Julien. I will get right at things quickly. Towards the end of April the Canadian Division was holding a line near Ypres, which was not far short of three miles in extent. That line ran north-west from Poelcapelle-Paschendaile Road, and at the end joined up with the French. Three infantry brigades with artillery comprised the division, the first being in reserve, the second on the right of the third, and the third connecting with the French.

We were in the salient of Ypres which was known to be weak, but the holding of which was of vast importance. I am proud to think that I am one of the Canadian Contingent to whom the big task of keeping back the Germans at that point was given, and that I fought with men who gave their lives in stopping the German attempt to find a way through to Calais, so as to have a very near blow at England. Placed as we were placed, it was possible to see the battle being fought on three sides, and this was uncommonly interesting.

We were, of course, in trenches, quite near the Germans, but between us there ran a ridge which is known as a hogback, so that there was a formidable natural barrier between the opposing forces. We were so near to the famous Hill 60 that we heard the explosion there and the subsequent battle when we were in billets at Ypres. The hill had been mined with six or seven tons of dynamite, the explosion of which was enough to change even the appearance of the hill.

There was a smart affair on the night of April 17th, when about a mile of German trenches was taken, and I saw about 2000 German prisoners being escorted away. Their uniforms were shabby, and their equipment was not what it ought to have been, but the men themselves appeared to be remarkably fit and well cared for.

We had gone into the trenches after marching through Ypres, where the chimney-pots were tumbling about our ears, and we were expecting very hot times; but the hogback prevented us from seeing the Germans, and of course kept us out of their sight. But there were German snipers everywhere.

I had charge of a section of bomb-throwers, and we did our best. At first the bombs were homely contrivances, made of jam-tins filled with explosives; but later they were made under War Office control, and were far superior to the primitive articles which we manufactured ourselves.

In such a war and in such a place it is not easy to tell of what was done by individuals, but I call to mind the coolness and resource of my own platoon officer, Lieutenant McLeod. He was dashing all over the place, encouraging his men at every point.

One outstanding performance of his was to run, in broad daylight, from battalion headquarters to the trenches—a pretty brave achievement, when you bear in mind that a running man presents an almost certain target to snipers.

In this connection, I call to mind the case of a section commander who was in a trench. He wished that a certain thing should be done, and by way of indicating his desire he held up his hand, with palm extended. That must have been a small enough target, in all conscience, but it was no sooner in the air than it was pierced by five German bullets. If a hand can be so effectively fired at, what chance to escape has the body of a man?

This trench warfare was uncommonly exhausting. You never knew what was going to happen, or what you would be called upon to do; but it was astonishing to find how soon you could adapt yourself to circumstances.

I recall an occasion when we had been forced to retire at one point and get into a communication trench; we were taken aback by the discovery that it was not deep enough. We had to dig ourselves in. That was not a hard matter for the boys who had their entrenching-tools, but I had lost mine, and the only thing left to do was to try rabbit tactics. So I began to dig myself in with my fingers, and I have a distinct recollection of tearing and scooping at the ground like an animal scuttling for shelter. Luckily the ground was soft and yielding, or I should not have had a chance with such poor tools. As it was, my fingers were torn and bleeding long before the digging-in process was completed.

I have given you a general understanding of the task that fell to the Canadian Contingent to accomplish; but as I have said, it is not the actual fighting that dwells in one's memory.

We soon settled down to the ordinary ways of war, and took them as a matter of course. While in training in England we had heard and read a good deal about the fighting, and had become accustomed to it; while as for any such discomforts as heavy rain and sodden ground, they did not trouble us. Not even Flanders could give us worse trials of this sort than we had known while wintering on Salisbury Plain.

The boys took the fighting and the hardships as part of the day's work, and there was neither grumbling nor protesting; but that state of things was changed with the use of poison-gas.

This poison-gas came upon us unseen, insidiously, and without the slightest warning in the one case; and in the other it rolled down upon us literally as a cloud.

It is hard to speak calmly of this unprecedented form of warfare, but I will try to tell exactly what happened, and I think I can do that, because when I was a medical student I particularly interested myself in chemistry.

It was on Saturday, the 24th, that our brigade had their first experience of gas. We had been shelling the German trenches all day, and were standing to, expecting an attack by the enemy. We naturally looked for the employment of the usual methods, and were ready to receive the Germans when they showed themselves. We were strongly entrenched, and many a keen eye was kept on the hostile ground, watching for the appearance of the enemy. But not a sight of a German was to be had; there was no commotion, no excitement, no appearance of anything uncanny or uncommon, yet there was coming towards us a German weapon—poison-gas. There was nothing to be seen in the air, yet suddenly, and without any apparent cause, we were overpowered by a smell exactly like nasturtium, but infinitely stronger and more pungent. The similarity noticed is remarkable, for doesn't nasturtium come from Latin words which really mean a nose-twister? Anyway, there we were in our trenches, unexpectedly overpowered by a horrible acrid smell and an invisible gas.

A lot of the boys were utterly unable to fathom the mystery, and they seemed to think that it was the kind of pest that had to be taken with the other discomforts of campaigning in the Low Country.

"What the deuce is it?" they asked.

It was not until the whole unspeakable visitation was over that most of the men realised what had happened, and that the Germans had tried to blind us as a preliminary to annihilation. Like so many more of the German hopes, this did not develop on the lines that had been planned.

This was the first poison-gas attack that we experienced, and I am thankful to say that on the whole it was a failure; but when you remember that we were utterly unready for such a filthy form of fighting, and that we had no means of combating it or nullifying its effects, you will realise the extreme disadvantage of the contest from the point of view of the Canadians.

I have said that it was about four o'clock in the afternoon when we had our first experience of the poison-gas. Now that I am talking of the thing it strikes me as a strange coincidence that it was at about four o'clock in the morning when we had our second visitation.

We had got into our stride and settled down to hard hammering and what you might call routine campaigning. Then came the morning of Saturday, April 24th, when the sun rose ten minutes before five o'clock, which means that at about four o'clock day was breaking.

Most of us were asleep; but in war time there is no such thing as universal rest for men, and our sentries were posted and keeping watchful eyes upon the German lines. It is said that the darkest hour comes just before the dawn, and I think there is no doubt that man's lowest vitality is reached at that particular period. At any rate, the Germans probably thought so, for they planned a specially fatal attack upon us in the grey hours of this April morning.

While looking round in the cheerless dawn one or two of our sentries saw a yellowish kind of cloud coming towards us, over the hogback, and travelling pretty fast. The sight was unusual enough to be noticed, but no one who saw it had the slightest idea what it really was, until we were enveloped in the filthy folds; then we knew that it was poison-gas.

The cloud rolled on, and as it got quite close to us I noticed that it was about eight feet or twelve feet high, a deep, dense yellow at the bottom, and becoming lighter towards the top, so diffuse, indeed, that it was almost indistinguishable from the atmosphere. It is not easy exactly to convey an understanding of what the cloud really was, because few men have ever seen anything like it; but it might well be described as a moving mass of yellow, fat filth, insufferably loathsome. The poison-gas, the chief constituent of which I took to be chlorine, was about twice as heavy as air, and, consequently, it travelled along the surface of the ground.

I saw the yellow cloud come, I watched it as it enveloped us, and I observed it as it rolled away behind us and went towards Ypres, gradually losing force as it was absorbed in the air. In addition to being so favourably situated, we had just had a rum ration—and plenty of it. I do not know whether the spirit did us any good, but it certainly did not do us the least harm, and may have helped to nullify the effects of the poison-gas.

Our salient, vulnerable and undoubtedly attractive to the Germans, was rushed by them, and they succeeded in breaking through and occupying a trench about a hundred yards away from our own and parallel with it. They came on with wonderful steadiness, advancing just as if they were on parade, scarcely breaking step at all. They came out of their trenches about a dozen at a time, formed two long lines, and literally seemed to walk over into the trench, though we were peppering at them all the time. They kept up an excellent covering fire, with the result that a good many of our own men were shot.

Company Sergeant-Major F. W. Hall, of my company, in spite of a very heavy and at that time fatal fire, rushed out from the shelter of his trench to bring in a wounded man who was lying in the open. He seemed to bear a charmed life, for he got clear of the trench and was untouched by the fire of the enemy.

The sergeant-major managed, by good fortune to get as far as the wounded man; he seized him and started with his burden for safety. In fact he actually got him as far as the trench, then, when the worst seemed over and security was just within his reach, when he was getting over the parapet and men were loudly cheering him because of his success, he was shot and killed. But the uncommon courage of the action had been noticed, and later on, to the real gratification of all the Canadians, and especially those who knew him, the announcement was made that the dead hero had been awarded the Victoria Cross. Hall's men were terribly shattered by the enemy's rifle and machine-gun fire; but in spite of it all they held their ground, and the living remnant won great glory.

It was not long before I dropped. I did not recover till the fight had swept away to my right. Then I reported to an artillery officer who was near, and he showed me the way to Ypres, telling me also to go into the city for hospital treatment.

I cannot close my yarn without mention of Captain Northwood's Company—No. 4. The company was not relieved—it could not be, because of the heavy call on troops—but it fought on doggedly till two platoons were captured. Yet there were no prisoners made except at a bitter cost to the Germans.

There were many heroes that day in No. 4 Company. I cannot name them all, but I must mention two of them who stand out pre-eminent—"Box-car" Kelly (now a King's Corporal), and Corporal Sandford. Kelly did everything in his power to rally some of the British troops who were near him, while Sandford, a section-commander, did as much by his example of courage as any officer I know.

That is my story.

If space permitted I might tell of Corporal Degan and his gallant band of hand-grenaders; how they bravely fought when hemmed in by the enemy; of Lieutenant Owens, who stood with an automatic pistol in each hand, cheering and swearing in the same breath, defending his comrades and destroying the Germans; of Sergeant Nobel (now a captain), who repaired a telephone-wire under an annihilating cannonade from German guns, and a score of other fellows.

A VIEW OF "V" BEACH, TAKEN FROM THE "RIVER CLYDE."

CHAPTER 28

A Linesman in Gallipoli

A vivid understanding of the work which our soldiers did in Gallipoli during the earlier stages of the operations in the Dardanelles, and of the strange happenings which were of daily occurrence in fighting the German-led Turks, is given by this story, which is told by Private John Frank Gray, 5th Battalion Wiltshire Regiment.

Everybody knows how the transport *River Clyde*, with two thousand British soldiers packed in her, was deliberately run ashore on V Beach, at the southern point of the Gallipoli Peninsula. Great holes had been cut in her steel sides, to make doors through which the men could get ashore when she was hard and fast, without embarking in any sort of craft. Land they did, in the end, though they suffered heavily through the Turks' terrific fire. I did not see that happen, but I disembarked, with my regiment, close to the transport while she was still aground. We had almost the same experience as the troops from the *River Clyde* had gone through. We forced a landing, in spite of barbed wire entanglements in the water, traps which had caught many a fellow and held him till the enemy's fire got him. It is odd to talk of wire entanglements in the sea, grabbing and tearing you as you plunge into the water, to wade ashore; but there they were, one more new feature in a war that has been full of strange things. Before we landed in Gallipoli we had experience of transport, trawler, barge and pinnace; and we were no sooner at the end of the voyage from England than we were under deadly fire and in the thick of it.

We went right into the firing-line, and the Turks gave us more than a warm reception—it was hot. We were under fire all the time we were landing, but we had the uncommon good luck to suffer no loss. As we forced our way ashore we saw plenty of evidence of the desperate nature of the assault of the men of the *River Clyde*; but we were too much absorbed in our own affairs to pay much heed to what had happened to other fellows.

We had got ashore on July 16th at Seddul Bahr, and stayed there all night. So that we should be as comfortable as possible we made dug-outs in the face of the cliff. The cliff at that place is very hard, and we had plenty of blasting to do, as well as work with pick and shovel.

My mates and I had put plenty of elbow-grease into our own particular job, and had finished our dugout and got into it, to be cosy for the night. It was very much like animals going to bed. We were worn out, and lost no time in going to sleep. I had gone off soundly and knew nothing till I was roughly roused by some fellows shouting, "Wake up! Wake up! Three of our chaps are buried alive!"

We did not need a second rousing. We all sprang up and rushed to a spot not far away, where we saw that there had been a fall of earth and rock, and we dug harder than we had ever dug before. At the end of it, having dug to a depth of three feet, and thrown the earth and rock away from us, we came across three poor chaps of my company who had been buried by a fall of earth, caused by them digging too far into the ground to give them shelter. They had undermined too much, and the earth-roof had collapsed and crushed them. We saw at once that there was no hope—the men looked as if they had been killed on the spot: they must have been dead an hour—but we put them on stretchers and the field ambulance men did all they could. But it was too late. Next day we dug graves for them and put crosses over. There are some fine graveyards out there, well cared for, and with barbed wire fences to preserve them. While we were burying our comrades the Turks fired on us continuously, and this had to serve as the last volleys over the fallen. That solemn and tragic beginning of my experiences after landing at Gallipoli will never fade from my mind.

Even at this early stage I noticed the extraordinary luck of war. Some of the King's Own Lancasters had been in the trenches for fourteen days, and during the whole of that time they had had only twenty casualties. They left the trenches and came right up alongside of us, on a little bit of a mound. The Turks must have got wind that a lot of troops were on the move, for the shrapnel came bursting over the lot of us, especially the Lancasters, who in less than half an hour lost more than forty men, fourteen being killed and the rest wounded. Four or five of our own mates were hit, so that we escaped lightly, and were able to send our stretcher-bearers to give a hand in getting the wounded soldiers to hospital.

The burying alive of men and the loss of men who had spent a fortnight in the trenches unscathed, were the things I saw when I was spending my first night in Gallipoli, so I can say that we landed right in the thick of it. It was a hot start, and it did not get cooler, for on the following morning, when we were on the way to the trenches at Achi Baba, we were under constant shrapnel fire. We crawled and crept up as best we could, using roads, or rather tracks, which had been made by the 29th Division. It was fearfully hot, we were heavily laden, and there was nothing but prickly scrub and rock and stifling dust about, and bursting shell all the time. But we forged slowly ahead, making the best of it, and thankful when we got into one of the little ravines which abound there, and make natural trenches—thankful because we got shelter without having to dig for it. In this advance some of our chaps fell, and the ravines formed their resting-places. The graves were filled in and crosses put over to tell how the soldiers had died.

An advance like this is a slow business. You go in single file, keeping your heads well down, because of the stray bullets from snipers. The Turkish snipers are dead shots—I will tell you more about them later. At the end of our dodging and ducking and crawling in single file we got into a support trench, and I began to breathe a bit more freely, because I thought that here at any rate I was safe. But we had no sooner reached the front-line trenches than the Turks started shelling us, and very quickly I thought that the very end of me had come. There was a tremendous crash just overhead, then a horrible rumbling, then I was knocked down in a heap, and all I knew was that a shell had burst in the trench and that I was buried in a mass of earth and rock. I was bruised and stunned—so were four of my chums who were near me; but we had had better luck than the three poor fellows who had been buried by the fall of earth above them, and pretty soon we had worried our way out of the heap of muck and were staring at each other—and I shall never forget that incident, if it is only because of the stupid way in which we stared at each other, and never said a word.

We were making tea when the shell burst, and were looking forward to a cosy meal; but here we were, staring at each other in surprise, wondering what the dickens the matter was, till we looked around and saw what sorry objects we were, and that the tea gear had been scattered all over the place. When we had got over our fright—and what's the use of saying that we weren't scared?—we saw the grim humour of it, and laughed and pulled ourselves together, thankful that we were still in the land of the living.

That was part of our early introduction to shell fire, and we very soon learned that you never know what sort of a trick a shell is up to. Shells are very deceiving. You hear their peculiar and horrible whistle and think that they are going to burst anywhere except where they do.

When we had pulled ourselves together we left our shattered trench and went into another part of the trench, to pull round a bit and get out of the shrapnel bombardment. But within three hours we were back again and settled down, wondering what the coming night had in store for us. We were in for another surprise, though at that time, of course, we did not know it.

This surprise took the shape of an attack upon us by hand-grenades, or bombs. It was pitch dark; but the blackness was lit up near us in patches, caused by the explosion of the bombs. We got half a dozen of them, and as it was clear that some Turks had crept towards us from their firing-line, which was only about 200 yards away, we sent out a sergeant and five or six men to hunt the bomb-throwers. You might as well have looked for a needle in a haystack as try to find Turks who were hiding in the darkness in the shrubs or the ravines; at any rate, our chaps did not see or hear anything of the Turks, and they had to come back without doing anything. There was no doubt that the Turks had crept up to us quite close and then hurled their bombs; but we were lucky to escape with only one man slightly wounded, though if the bombers had had any luck we should have been blown to pieces. These intensely dark nights were always very trying because of these attacks.

It was an immense relief when the moonlight nights came, because then the Turks dared not try their tricks on. There was always the guard, of course, two hours on and two hours off. This gave a great sense of protection; but the guard work itself gave you the creeps. You were on the rack all the time, fancying that you saw some one approaching when as a matter of fact there was no one near. There was always the chance, too, of being picked off by a sniper who used horrible explosive bullets. One of our men was struck down, and when we went up to him and removed his helmet we saw at once that an explosive bullet had been used, for the skull was completely shattered. You could always tell when these awful things had been used, from the appearance of the sandbags. The bullets would strike and explode, and smash the sandbags so badly that it took us all our time to make the damage good. You dare not put even a periscope above the trench; if you did a sniper got a bullet through it before you knew where you were.

The system of trenches was amazing, turning and twisting everywhere in the most wonderful manner. We made the most of these complications, too, by naming the trenches Oxford Street, Regent Street, and so on, with Clapham Junction and the like for important junctions of trenches. These names, which were chalked up or put on boards, were most useful in helping you to find your way about, and sometimes very amusing misunderstandings arose.

"Do you know where Oxford Circus is?" a chap asked me one day.

"Rather!" I told him, proud to throw light on his ignorance, and I began to tell him, till he cut me short by snapping that he wasn't talking about London, but the trenches. We got many a good laugh out of these little misunderstandings; for out at the front you are always ready to make the most of the smallest joke. You needed all the cheerfulness you could get, too, because of the awful sights that constantly met you and the endless peril you were in. I shall never forget one of the very first things my eyes saw in those opening days of my campaigning in Gallipoli. We got to the spot at Achi Baba where the Munsters and the Dublin Fusiliers, during an advance, had been enfiladed by machine-gun fire and literally mown down. From the trench we had occupied we could see the men lying just as they had fallen, while trying to take cover. There they were, on the open ground, absolutely riddled with bullets, and with their packs on, and their rifles and bayonets and everything else. They had been lying there for about a fortnight, because it was impossible to do anything in the way of burying them, owing to the enemy's incessant fire and sniping.

Things hereabouts were particularly horrible. We went into a Turkish trench that had been taken, and started to make a fire-trench. We pulled away the old sandbags and dug away at the parapet with our picks. There was a horrible stench, but we were used to smells and did not take much notice of it till we found that the picks had a lot of foul stuff on them which we could not account for; but we soon discovered that the parapet was composed of the dead bodies of Turks which had been piled up and just covered with earth, the sandbags being placed on the top of the wall of corpses.

In this same trench there was a well which had been covered with planks. Naturally enough we began to explore it, not that we expected to get anything to drink from it, and when we had removed the planks we found that the well, which we calculated was ten or twelve feet deep, had a lot of dead Turks in it. We counted six of them, and had enough of the job, so we put the planks back, and felt that our curiosity had been satisfied.

When we had been there four or five days and were getting used to the appearance of the country, we saw a Turk just peeping over the top of a little mound, with his rifle pointing towards us and in the attitude of firing. We felt sure that we had caught a sniper, and two or three shots were promptly fired. The Turk was still there, and it was clear that he had been shot. Later on we were able to get near him, and then we saw that "he was black with flies and had been shot through the eye while sniping; but not shot by us, because when we shook him his head fell off, showing that he had been dead for some time. We saw another Turk who was sitting against a tree. We went up and found that he, too, was dead. He looked a mere skeleton; but he was swathed in clothing and equipment in the most extraordinary fashion. His trousers were all rags, and his tunic was all patches of differently coloured cloths; he had three shirts and two belts on, and we wondered how he had stuck so many clothes in such stifling weather.

I had an exciting adventure one day—a bit too exciting to be altogether pleasant. I and another chap had been sent out to an artillery position which was called Clapham Junction Station, to get some corrugated iron. We had a long way—two and a half miles—to go, and it was necessary to keep to the cover of the trenches whenever we could do so. We were able to do that for most of the way, going through the very trenches which had been dug by the poor chaps of the Munsters and Dublin Fusiliers who had fallen. We got to the end of our journey, quite near the French lines, and then started back with our corrugated iron. Burdened in this way, we found that one of the trenches was too narrow for us to get along, and we were forced to make our way across open country for about 500 yards. As soon as we left the shelter of the trench the sun shone on our galvanised metal and gave the Turks a good target. We promptly had three or four shells bursting near us, and we lost no time in doubling over the open ground, staggering along with the iron sheets, and thankful when we were under shelter again, with a farewell shell or two to show us what a narrow squeak we had had. I picked up one of these shells, which had not burst, and kept it a long time, meaning to bring it home as a souvenir, but I found it a nuisance and had to throw it away.

We were constantly seeing strange sights and learning how cunning the Turks were. One morning I saw some Australians bring in a Turk who was wearing one of our uniforms. The tunics had white patches on them, so that our artillery could distinguish us, and it was one of these that the fellow wore. He had no doubt taken it from a dead British soldier, and so dressed, he had joined a party of Australians who were drawing water at a well. He kept his mouth shut, and might have gone undiscovered, but he and an Australian began quarrelling, then fighting, and that gave him away, because he could not speak English. They shot him, as a spy, the following morning.

At the same place—I am now speaking of W Beach, where we were resting—we saw a Turkish sniper on the top of a hill. We sent out two or three times to try and get him, but failed; but at last he was caught while robbing one of our fellows who was dead. The sniper had shot him, and now he was out for plunder. When we had this sniper in hand we found that we had got hold of a very dangerous customer, a man who had done a lot of mischief amongst our fellows. He had gone about his sniping in a very business-like way, and had established himself in a spot which commanded points which had to be continually passed by our stretcher-bearers and working parties.

A good many of the R.A.M.C. chaps were hit, and it was curious that most of the wounds were about the knee. We discovered that these wounds were the result of the sniper's low firing—he was very near the ground and had pretty nearly complete control of this particular spot. Our fellows used to double round it for all they were worth, but they were not fast enough to dodge the Turk's bullets. When we examined his dugout we found three rifles fixed on tripods, which were always trained on the spots where our fellows had to pass. In addition to that he had a machine-gun, and this he used for firing on our men when he knew that it was meal-time and that they were in clusters. It was a great relief when his account was settled.

Aircraft fighting has developed enormously during the war, and I saw an exciting fight between three of our aeroplanes and two of the Turks. We had got a bit used to aeroplanes, for a Taube had swooped over us and dropped a chance bomb which blew up the quartermaster's stores. Three bombs fell about a hundred yards away, and I noticed that the noise they made when they came through the air was just like the whistle of a railway engine. In the fight I am talking about our fellows brought down one of the Turkish machines, and they made a hard chase after the other, but it got away. It was a really thrilling fight, and our chaps got tremendously excited over it. We had been warned of an attack from the air by three blasts on a whistle, and that was the signal to take shelter and to cover up the guns with tarpaulins, to hide them.

During these attacks you are supposed never to look up, but the fight was so splendid and our chaps got so excited that the warning was forgotten in many cases, and chaps were peeping over the parapets and some were actually standing up on the parapets. Poor fellows! Turkish snipers spotted them and got three with their bullets. I was only about a hundred yards away when they were killed. Their loss, which was a lesson to all of us, cast quite a gloom over our victory in the air.

After being in the trenches at Achi Baba for sixteen days we went back to Lemnos, a big naval base about four and a half hours' distant by transport. We were supposed to have a week's rest, but we were at Lemnos only three days. At the end of that time we went back to the Peninsula and landed at Anzac, and went straight up to the firing-line, which had been made at Chunuk Bahr—and our regiment got absolutely cut up.

We had gone up into the trenches and nothing much happened while we were there. After our spell in the trenches we were taken up into a gulley for twenty-four hours' rest and sleep. We were in high spirits at the prospect of such a change, and we took our equipment off and made a few dugouts and got into them and settled down, and very comfortable and contented we were. But our rest and peace were smashed at dawn on the following morning, when we were thrown into confusion by a heavy Turkish attack. The Turks had advanced into the firing-line on the opposite side of the hill. There were plenty of them and they had machine-guns, while we were quite helpless, having no rifles nor equipment—indeed, many of us had not even our jackets on, as we were taking it easy.

There was quite a stampede for the time being, and some one passed the order, "Every man for himself!" It was a mistake, I am certain, but it added immensely to the confusion. That awful alarm caused some of our unarmed chaps to make a bolt for it, the result of panic.

The adjutant, Captain Belcher, rallied about seventy of the men. He pulled them together, and shouted to them to get their rifles and bayonets and follow him. The little band rallied round the adjutant, and they hurled themselves upon the Turks, and such was the suddenness and fury of their attack that the Turks bolted—and big hefty chaps they were—with our fellows, some of them almost as small as dwarfs, tearing after them with the bayonet. In this furious affair one of our men got wounded and could not walk. The adjutant picked him up and began to carry him away. As he did so the Turks opened fire on him with a machine-gun, and he must have been riddled—I never saw anything more of him. At the same time Lieutenant Ratcliffe, who had been wounded, was being carried off on a stretcher. He seemed to think that the chance of escape was hopeless, and so he said to his bearers, "Put me down and look after yourselves, boys. I shall be all right." It was a hard thing to do, but the men obeyed, and all of us who could do so got away from that fatal spot, which we were far too weak to hold, in spite of the success of the adjutant's rally, and at last we got back to the beach.

It was then that we compared notes and heard of what had happened in various places, and the roll having been called we supposed that every man who could escape had reached the beach. But two nights afterwards we formed a search party, and went back up the hill and were lucky enough to find and bring back with us about a dozen poor fellows who had been lying all that time on the battlefield. From this rescue we supposed that there must be other men alive at the top of the hill; but there was no chance of reaching them in the daytime, and we could not go at night, for the searchlights from our own warships swept the hillside and lit it up so brilliantly that any search party would have been shown up to the snipers. So we did no more, and soon we were forgetting; for we were hard at work on fatigue, helping the Engineers to build a new firing-line, a trench about 1400 yards long. Then happened a thing so strange that it seemed beyond belief, like men rising from the dead.

Fifteen days had passed since the fight, and no one dreamed that there could possibly be survivors, yet there appeared at the beach headquarters two terribly worn and haggard men, Lance-Corporal A. G. Scott of my company, and Private R. Humphries, another of our chaps. We were amazed to see them, and far more amazed to hear their story, which was that they and Private W. J. Head had been up in the hill for fifteen days and nights, unable to get away, and living on the biscuits and water that they had taken from the haversacks and bottles of dead men. The Turks, they said, used to pass them and shake hands with them, but would never give them any food or water. The three used to grope about in the daytime to get food and drink, and the Turks sniped at them whenever they got the chance.

Head was quite unable to escape, having had two bad wounds. Scott and Humphries, desperate at last, crawled away and managed to reach our regimental headquarters and tell their wonderful story, and it was no sooner heard than a search party was organised, and, with Scott and Humphries as guides, went back to the old fighting-place—a slow and dangerous job. On the first night they found nothing, but on the next night the relieving party came across three fellows and brought them down. Head was amongst them—he had been out getting more biscuits and water, and while doing so his right arm was smashed by a machine-gun which was trained on him. The body of the poor lieutenant was found, with several bayonet wounds, and he, like all the other officers who fell, had been completely stripped by plunderers. The bodies had not a thing on them.

The survivors of those awful days and nights on the hillside—from August 10th to August 26th—had such a welcome as can be given only to those who return when they have been given up as lost, and Scott and Head and Humphries have been awarded the Distinguished Conduct Medal. There have been some extraordinary incidents in this war, but not many are stranger than this adventure of this little band of men for what must have seemed an endless fortnight, and none that will stand out more finely in the annals of the Wiltshires.

There was so much to be seen and done in the three months I spent in the Near East that it is not easy to describe everything, and I must now mention only one or two things more. Very clearly in my mind stands out our attack on Chocolate Hill, after the warships had bombarded it for three days. We watched the naval guns at work, and saw the terrible havoc they caused—many a Turk we saw flying up in the air when the shells burst. When we advanced over Salt Lake we had to cross a hayfield, under a very heavy fire. The bursting shrapnel knocked many a fellow down, and we could not stop to help them or pick them up—and that was terribly hard on us, for the hayfield had taken fire and it meant that a lot of helpless men were burned alive. I saw one poor chap, a Yeoman, struck by shrapnel. This made him completely helpless for the time, and the fire got at him and burnt half his left leg off; but I am thankful to say that he managed, by a truly desperate effort, to crawl away, and he got out of it at the finish. We were in the advance, and as the field was catching fire just as we got out of it, we escaped the worst, which was to be caught in the middle, so that even those who were fit and could make a rush were badly burned and suffering intensely before they could get clear of the horrible ring of fire.

I can tell you of an extraordinary incident that happened in the Chocolate Hill attack to a man of the South Wales Borderers. In the second bayonet charge he drove his steel into a Turk—and it broke. Off he dashed without his bayonet, and rushed with his chums to the next trench, where he plumped into a Turk who was crawling through a hole. Knowing that his broken bayonet was useless, he clubbed his rifle and let the Turk have the butt. The blow smashed the butt clean off, and the Borderer tumbled down. The Turk, who was not much hurt, sprang back from his hole, and jumped to his feet with the Englishman fairly at his mercy. Luckily for the Borderer a pal rushed up and saved him by settling the Turk. It was an extraordinary thing that the Borderer first broke his bayonet and then bashed his butt, which came off as clean as a whistle.

Another thing that happened was this: An officer was wounded and fell. One of the men of his regiment heard the report that the officer was missing. "I'll go and find him," he said, and off he went. After an hour's search he found the officer and asked him if he could walk. "No," the officer told him, so the man picked him up and started to carry him—a hard and dangerous job. While the officer was being carried he was wounded again, a bullet striking him. "Put me down," he ordered, "and look after yourself."

"No, sir," said the man; "if you're game, I am." And game he was, too, for he got him safely away, and the officer, to show his gratitude, made the man a present of his revolver and a silver flask. When the soldier rejoined his regiment they took the revolver away; but he kept the flask as a memento, carefully wrapped up in all sorts of things, very proud of the gift from the officer, who had said, "I shall never forget you!" The officer was mortally wounded, and died before they could get him into the hospital ship.

It was round Chocolate Hill that we made our queerest find of all—women snipers. There was a kind of blockhouse which had been a farmhouse, and it had a very fine well, which had some very fine water—a precious thing. There was a big run on the well, and a lot of fellows were shot by snipers who could not be traced, till a fellow in a Welsh regiment swore that he could see some one moving in some trees not very far away. A machine-gun was brought up, and fifty rounds or so were fired into the trees, which dropped some very rare fruit—four men Turks and one woman Turk, all snipers. When we went up we found that they were almost naked, and had their faces and hands and bodies and rifles painted green to match the trees. And there they roosted, like evil birds, potting at our chaps whenever they got the chance, which was pretty often.

This was such a good haul that firing was directed on all the trees, and more snipers were brought down, including several women. Some of the women wore trousers, like the men, and some had a kind of full grey-coloured skirt. They were as thin as rats, and looked as if they had had nothing to eat for months. I think there were six or seven women snipers caught in the trees, and it is said that the Turks have women in the trenches; but I don't know if that is true. I saw one woman sniper who had been caught by the New Zealanders. I don't know what was done with her; but as the men came back they told us they had bagged her in a dugout, where she had a machinegun and a rifle, and that she seemed to have been doing a very good business in sniping.

Dysentery knocked me out in the end, and after spending a fortnight in hospital at Malta I had "H.S.B."—hospital-ship berth—put opposite to my name. I came home in a hospital ship, a foreigner, which made me thankful when I landed at Southampton and entered a good old English hospital train bound for Manchester.

Chapter 29

An Anzac's Adventures

When the German blood-stained Eagle and its vulture-hearted Chief
Made war on little Belgium, they held the fond belief
The British Lion had grown too tame and dared not interfere;
But when old England called the roll, Australia answered,
'Here!'

That is part of one of the marching songs of the Anzacs, and it will go down to history as surely as "John Brown's Body" has descended to our own generation. It was written for a particular Australian battalion, but it applies to all the regiments that have won immortality in Gallipoli. This Anzac's story shows how the sons of the Empire rallied to the call of the Motherland, and helped so much to carry out that unexampled undertaking in the Dardanelles of which our descendants alone can be the fairest judges. The narrator is Trooper Rupert Henderson, of the 6th Australian Light Horse.

I was a sheep overseer when I joined the Australian Light Horse. Before that I was a jackaroo on a twenty-thousand acre station. What is a jackaroo? Well, a cross between a kangaroo and a wallaroo, and applied to a man, it means that he does anything that comes along. My boss's station was twenty-five miles from the nearest town; but that's nothing of a distance in Australia, and we used to have some merry parties when we had a day off, and drove or rode to the town for a change. And it was to the town that we swarmed just after the war broke out—bosses and men, rich and poor. A fine young fellow, a squatter's son, Mr. David McCulloch, wrote and asked me to join the Light Horse, and I gladly did. He tried hard to come, too, but the doctor would not pass him, and to his intense disappointment he was rejected. He came to see me twice while I was training, and both times he tried to pass; but could not get through. That was the spirit which was shown when the call came out to us to go and fight the Germans and the Turks, or anybody else that British troops were up against.

We went into camp at Rosebery Park, Sydney, which is a racecourse. The 1st Light Horse had to sleep in the stables; but we were comfortably camped. The hard floors of the stables were very different from the comfortable beds which had been left; but the fellows were mostly horsemen from the country and didn't mind, because they were used to roughing it.

Horses, saddles, equipment and uniforms were issued to us, and we were soon doing horse and foot drill. After six weeks of this training we went to Holdsworthy, on the George's River, in the bush country. Snakes of all sorts swarm there—tiger snakes, black snakes, copperheads and deaf adders, all poisonous, as well as the carpet snakes, which are sometimes twenty feet long. They are gorgeous things, and look like bright-coloured carpets. They are non-poisonous, and our chaps let them coil round their necks and do all sorts of things. At this place there was the German internment camp, and already there were plenty of both military and civilian prisoners. The camp was not cleared—it was just barbed wire for a guard camp—but the country round it was being cleared.

We were very lucky in our training, and afterwards, too, because we were under Colonel Cox—"Fighting Charlie," we called him—who had seen service in South Africa, and was a fine soldier.

It was midsummer and harvest-time when, on December 17th, we left Holdsworthy for Sydney, and we had the remarkable experience of going through three summers in one year. We started with our own, which we left in the tropics, when we got to Egypt it was the Egyptian summer, and when we landed at the Dardanelles it was the Gallipoli summer.

In Australia, of course, everything had given place to the war, and army lorries and so on had cut the roads up frightfully. They were full of ruts and holes and deep in dust; but luckily a storm came on, and the rain made it possible for us to travel in comfort.

I shall never forget that march to the transport to embark. We marched in the night-time, but all along the route the people were waiting for us. Nobody seemed to have gone to bed, and as we marched along they cheered us and wished us luck. The people gave us drinks, and fruit, and handkerchiefs, and other souvenirs. It was a wonderful and moving sight, and the people kept it up right away to the Wool-

ANZACS AT SUVLA BAY

loomooloo Wharf at Sydney, where we embarked on board the White Star liner *Suevic*. We lay in harbour from Sunday morning till Monday afternoon. I was on guard all the time. We had plenty of visitors, some of them trying to get chaps out for a last spell ashore; but that had to be stopped, of course, and the officers sent the men down to stables. The horses of my squadron, C, were below; but the other squadrons had their horses on deck.

I am not going to dwell on the last parting and send-off. We steamed away, and on Christmas Day we were six days out and two days' sail from Albany, Western Australia. When we got there we picked up a magnificent fleet of sixteen transports and the Australian submarine AE2, which was afterwards lost. Then the war seemed to be really with us, the Anzacs, the famous word which is formed of the initials of the words "Australian and New Zealand Army Corps."

We came through Suez and Port Said, and did not go off the boats till we got to Alexandria. We stayed a night at Ismailia, and there, as the beginning of our fighting with the Turks, we came under their fire, or rather, we heard it. This made us feel that we were getting into things, and we listened with immense interest to the boom of the guns. At the same time we piled up our ship with bales of hay, as a protection, and mounted machine-guns, and fervently hoped that the Turks would come on and give us a chance against them; but we were not molested. They did not interfere with us then, but we soon had plenty to do with them.

It was March 31st when C Squadron disembarked at Alexandria and got into the train, with Major White in charge. We went to Cairo, and then unloaded our horses and took them, walking, to a place ten miles outside the city; and there, practically in the desert, we camped, and for three months we had steady mounted drill, which made us as fit as fiddles. We had real dry heat, and no rain, all the time; but this did not trouble us, being Australians, and used to droughts. But we were glad when, at the end of the three months, the order came for us to pack up our kits and leave for the Dardanelles. We had the infantry kit served out to us, and in the middle of May we were back in Cairo, where we saw a lot of our chaps who had come back wounded from the Dardanelles. We found ourselves once more at Alexandria; and then, in two days we were at the Dardanelles, of which we had heard and talked so much, and where we had been so eager to go.

We had left Egypt on a peaceful Sunday afternoon; now we were in the very thick of a wonderful and exciting war, for we were being towed ashore in pinnaces, each holding about 250 men—half the regiment—and were under heavy fire. Gunboats were booming away, shells were bursting, and aeroplanes were sweeping about the sky. All these things gave us a good idea of what was going on.

How did we take it, not being used to the business? Well, the chaps sat in the pinnaces and looked at one another, to see how they stood it. We were landing in broad daylight, the boats were packed, bullets were dropping all around us, sending nasty little spits of water up; and bullets from rifles and machine-guns were whizzing over our heads. I was watching the impression it was having on the others. Some of our chaps were wearing war medals, and I made up my mind to carry on as they were doing. If they took it all right, so would I.

They did take it all right.

As the bullets dropped round us I heard such remarks as, "By Jove! If that hit a fellow it would hurt him!" Then men would laugh.

Our colonel—I was sitting near him in the pinnace—looked stern and calm. He knew better than most of us what it meant.

We were lucky in our landing, for we had no casualties; but a lot of the other troops who were landing at the same time and in the same way were picked off. We lay off till one of the naval boats got alongside. We all tumbled into her and were taken to the beach for landing.

The Turks saw us landing and gave us five shells, but these did not hurt anybody. We were told to hurry up; but we didn't need telling to do that, and as soon as the boat was at the shore we hopped on to a little wharf and found ourselves in the thick of some Indians who were unloading sheep. So little did we need telling to hurry up, that I well remember how we rushed through the sheep in our eagerness to get to shelter.

We were in fine spirits and made the best of it; but as soon as we landed we realised what we were in for. A shell came and burst amongst a fatigue party, knocking the men about badly and wounding half a dozen, but luckily not killing anybody. This showed us how necessary it was to take cover, and when we had got some distance up the heights and were ordered to dig in, we set to work with a will, and we readily obeyed the order to keep our heads well down, as the shrapnel was bursting over the top of us.

Our regiment was keeping well together. The colonel was in a gulley just below me when a shell burst over us. It seemed to be high, and we did not realise the danger of such explosions. This shell seemed to be harmless; but I soon discovered that a fragment or bullet of it had struck the colonel in the leg. As this was the headquarters the doctor was handy, and he attended to the colonel straight away, and sent him to the beach on a stretcher. Two minutes afterwards, one of the squadron clerks got shot with a shrapnel bullet. This also happened near me, and I saw what happened to him. The bullet struck him just by the right temple—he had the closest possible shave of instant death—and carried the eye away. This chap was put out of action at once, and was sent on to Malta. About ten days later he wrote to us saying what rotten luck he had had. But he was a cheerful soul and made the best of things, though he said, very truly, "I have only had a one-eyed view of Malta!"

We got dug in. There were holes in front of us, about four feet deep, with head covering, about two feet of earth, on top of us; but these did not give much protection from shells that burst just overhead. Some of the men filled empty biscuit-tins with earth and put them alongside to protect their legs from stray and spent bullets, and these proved very useful. When we had dug in we were ordered to eat our iron-rations for tea; then, about eight o'clock, they called the regiment to fall in, as the Turks were going to attack us. We stood up as reinforcements at a place called Shrapnel Gulley—and well it deserved its name, as we soon learned, for there were a terrible lot of casualties there, especially amongst the fatigue parties which had to go to the beach for water.

You will see that we were initiated straight away. We did not know the danger of it at the time, and never thought that we should be so soon put through it after landing. But it was astonishing to see how well the chaps settled down to the business. We had been landed only a few hours, and yet we were standing to arms, waiting for the Turks to come on. We expected them with a rush, for we had been told that Enver Bey, the Minister of War, had ordered that the Anzacs were to be thrown into the sea. Well, we didn't mean to be thrown.

We were standing on open ground. There were two very high hills, and we were in the gulley at the bottom. Some of our troops were dug in on the top of the hills, and the Turks were dug in in front of us, some of them being not more than fifty yards away.

It was a pitch-dark night, and a nerve-racking job waiting for the promised onslaught. Time passed and it seemed as if the Turks would never come; but at three in the morning they let themselves loose.

The word was passed along—"The enemy is advancing in front!"

and we were all ordered to stand fast till two blasts of the whistle had been sounded.

It was hard to make out anything in that inky blackness, even with the eyes of bushmen; but we knew that the Turks had crawled out of their trenches and that they were going to throw themselves upon us. Then two shrill blasts struck the still night, and instantly there was a fearful commotion, for the Turks hopped up from the ground and charged, yelling and firing, and making all sorts of deafening noises, amongst which we noticed a trumpeter doing his best to blow our own call of the "Officers' Mess." They seemed to blow anything that came along, so as to confuse us in the pitch darkness. And a startling business it was, too, to peer into the blackness and see the figures of the Turks by the light of the bursting shells and crackling rifles.

Never while I live shall I forget that fight in the first night we were ashore in Gallipoli. We did our best to see what was going on by looking through the pot-holes in the sandbags of the trenches, though at night you could look over the tops of the parapets; but it was little enough that we could make out in the darkness.

We had our magazines loaded and our bayonets fixed. The infantry alongside were in "possies," as we called them, holes dug in the trenches to keep a man from being exposed. Two men were in each "possy," one firing and the other loading for him, so that a constant fire was kept up. One of our fellows, terribly excited, had crawled up on to the sandbags, and there he stood, just seen in the darkness by the flashes of fire, for about ten minutes, when he was ordered down.

At this time I was a non-combatant, one of the stretcher-bearers, and I was just standing, waiting for somebody to get hit; so I could see everything that was going on. The shells were flying round all the time, making a fearful noise, and an Indian battery above us was doing good work. In a "posy" high above us were the machine-guns, and we could see even in the darkness what havoc they were causing amongst the enemy.

In the loud cries that arose I heard a Scotchman of our regiment shout, "Here comes a big Turk with a brick in his hand!"

We peered into the blackness and saw a big fine Turk crawling on the ground about five yards away, holding in his hand something that looked like a brick. The machine-guns got him just as he jumped up. The bullets fairly smothered him, and he dropped like a thousand of bricks. Later on I had a good look at him, and found that the thing he carried was not a brick but a bomb. He had no boots on, but his feet were wrapped in cloth, so that he made no sound. He had managed to get within ten paces of us.

The din quietened down as daylight came, which was about five o'clock. We looked eagerly around us to see what had been done, and noticed the dead Turks everywhere, many of them in clusters of half a dozen, just as they had been mown down by our machine-guns. Later on we learned that the number of the Turkish dead was 2000, so that the ground was fairly strewn with bodies.

We were ordered back to our trenches, where we had breakfast and a bit of rest; but at ten o'clock we were told to fall in again, as the Turks were making another charge. The enemy did come on, but rather half-heartedly, and they were repulsed without our aid. They had made a fine and brave dash in the night, as we saw. They never got into our trenches, but we were told that they had rushed in farther round, where the New Zealanders were; but they had been bayoneted straight away.

In the afternoon the Turks put up a white flag and asked for an armistice, to bury the dead.

A big old Turk walked towards us, and he was met by Captain R. J. A. Massie, a famous Australian amateur champion, an all-round athlete of splendid physique. The Turk was blindfolded and brought into our trenches and then taken to headquarters, and after he had been questioned an armistice was granted.

The firing ceased, and the Turks came out with all their stretcher-bearers, and our stretcher-bearers and diggers went out, too, and the burials went on—and not before they were necessary, for the stenches were awful.

This sad work was being done, when our artillery observers noticed that the Turks were bringing up guns and reinforcements from the gulley at the back of our chaps, and we were ordered to come in.

That ended the armistice for the time, and the Turks at the back were fired on and their little game stopped. Next morning there was another armistice, for it was absolutely necessary to get on with the burials. The atmosphere was almost unendurable, and, even on landing, the stench from dead mules and so on was so horrible that it nearly made me bilious.

On that second morning I was able to see that a lot of our chaps were lying between our parapet and the Turks' parapet. We made an exchange of bodies, and having got our men's identification discs, we buried them in the small trenches, so that the fighting-places became graves.

All these things that I have told about happened within thirty hours of our landing—and the fortune of war had sent some of the Anzacs to their last resting-place and put others, wounded, on the list for home. Men were sent off, their fighting careers ended, after having been in the enemy's country for only a few hours.

We were pretty philosophical over the business. I remember one of the men in my squadron saying, "If your name's on a bullet you're going to stop it." Soon afterwards a four-point-seven got him.

The Turks used to fire like mad. It was astonishing to see how many bullets they fired, but even at that early stage our men, when off duty, were asleep and taking no notice of them.

At this time we were opposite Lone Pine, attached to the 4th Australian Battalion as infantry. After the fighting we had exactly a month in the trenches, and then relieved some infantry who had had three weeks of solid fighting. We were relieved and went to a rest camp near Gaba Tepi. We had seven days there, with a good deal of excitement one way and another, and plenty of casualties, for we were being called out every day.

It was rumoured that Achi Baba was going to fall, and we were ordered into the firing-line as supports for the 5th Light Horse. The 5th were going out in front to draw the Turks' fire and keep reinforcements from going down to Achi Baba. Some of the 6th and 7th Light Horse were to stand by and act as reinforcements. My troop was in the firing-line.

The 5th hopped out right on the beach, and ran for Gaba Tepi under cover of the ridges. The 7th got up on our left. We were in the middle. A squadron of the 7th ran along under cover of the ridge, in the same direction as the 5th. They went a good while without drawing the fire of the Turks, who did not seem to notice them; but fire was opened at last.

Still the advance continued, more cautiously now, our fellows crawling when they could, for shelter. The Turks got a few lucky shells in amongst the 5th, and the casualties began to come in.

There were some odd incidents.

Our sergeant was peering through a look-out with a pair of glasses, his right hand being round them. Another sergeant said, "Let's have a peep."

Our sergeant pulled his head back and straightened himself, but still held the glasses with his hand in front of the hole.

The other sergeant was just stepping up to take the glasses, when a bullet came through the hole and went clean through the hand that still held the glasses, putting our sergeant out of action. We took him to the dressing-station, and he was not long before he was back in the firing-line, which is more than would have happened if the sergeant had been still bending down and had got the bullet in his head. He was a nice chap—a station-manager from Queensland.

In about two hours volunteers were asked for to bring in wounded Colonials from the front. There were a good many casualties by this time, and plenty for the stretcher-bearers to do.

We got to two men who, we saw at once, were very badly wounded. They were pretty well sheltered, and it was thought better to leave them where they were for the present, and not try to move them. One man had his foot blown off by shrapnel, and he was otherwise very badly wounded. A stretcher-bearer had bound him up roughly and put a tourniquet on to stop the bleeding; and another chap had carried him on his back to shelter. Several of the stretcher-bearers were killed and wounded at this time, but I do not think that the firing on them was deliberate.

The other man was a trumpeter. He was a little chap, and we called him "Scottie," because he had gone out to Australia from Scotland. He was wounded in the abdomen, and was in agony, but we managed to relieve his suffering with half a grain of morphia. The flies were swarming and were terribly troublesome. I tried to keep them off with a wet towel—I had to wet it in salt water—so that they should not annoy him. I noticed that his boots were torn, and I took them off. I then saw that his legs had not been dressed—and he had been lying there for some time. I put iodine on the wounds.

Scottie was rather cheery, and when the *padre* came up and said, "Well, how are you?" he answered, "I'm feeling pretty good now."

When the colonel went up to him, Scottie said, "I'm going to die!"

"Oh no, you're not," said the colonel. "You'll get all right again. Don't let that worry you. You'll soon be playing Christmas Calls for us."

To that Scottie made a reply which I shall never forget. "Yes," he said. "I *shall* die! I can *smell ut!*" That was his real expression, and I suppose he meant that he could smell death.

Scottie wanted the colonel to take charge of some little trinkets and things: his pay-book, and a photograph of two children. "Give these to the wife," he said. Then he broke into "Annie Laurie," and sang a verse of it. He sang the song fairly well. It was a good attempt for a man in the straits that he was in.

At six o'clock he died, and was buried the same night, after sundown, at the place where we were, and that was a big cutting called Chatham's Post, named after one of the officers. It was a deep cutting in the side of the hill. These two chaps were lying there on stretchers, and it was very hard for a bullet to hit them. Scottie was just taken to the back of the parade at the back of Chatham's Post, a place called Shrapnel Green. It was a green field when we first went, but it was soon trodden down and made bare by gun and rifle fire. And there Scottie was laid to rest.

From the burial we went back to the dressing-station and carried the wounded trooper—Lane, they called him—down to the beach. The *padre* asked Lane if he would like a "wad," that is a pannikin, of tea, and Lane said he would. I helped him to sit up, and I held the "wad" for him. He drank the tea cheerfully, though he must have been in awful agony. They took him along the beach. He did not say much, but never complained. When he did speak it was to ask, "Who's that lying there?" or "How is he getting on?" He was the best I saw the whole time I was there.

On the way to the beach there were wire entanglements, to stop the Turkish patrols. The stretcher-bearers fell into the entanglements and dropped Lane; but he never thought about himself. What he said was, "Are *you* hurt?" I am glad to say that he is here in England, like me, and has pretty well got over it, though he has lost his foot. Seventeen men were hit by the shell that knocked Lane out.

We settled down again to the fighting game with the Turks, who kept us very lively, especially with a gun that we called "Beachy Bill." This gun played on the beach whenever there was a sign of our movements, and it became a common thing to say, "Beachy Bill's got somebody again." That Turkish gun caused more casualties than all the rest put together. The monitors used to go for it, and I believe they bombarded it out of existence more than once. A new gun was soon at work again, but to us it was always "Beachy Bill." When we first got to Gallipoli we did not know the tricks of the trade, but everybody soon got fly, and that helped us a lot in tackling "Beachy Bill" and lessening his bag.

There's a lot more to say, but I will only tell you about one more thing, and that is the blowing up of some Turks. Our trenches and

The Dardanelles: carrying wounded to a hospital ship.

those of the Turks almost met in places, and bombs were thrown from one to the other. That was a lively exchange of greetings, but it didn't lead to much. Something more definite was wanted, and so our people began to dig a tunnel at a very narrow junction, so as to blow up the Turkish trenches, and make our own trench-line straight, instead of being, as it was, twisting and zigzag.

It was a real Turk hunt, and just the sort of work that our chaps revelled in.

This affair, like most of our scraps, was done in the darkness, which made it all the more thrilling. Well, we dug and sapped and tunnelled towards the Turks, and when everything had been got ready, powder was packed in sandbags and fuses were put to them. The deeper the sandbags the worse the explosion.

All was ready at last. The powder-bags were packed, the fuses were lit, and then the 11th and 12th Battalions began to finish the work which the artillery had begun. The guns had started at five o'clock, they went on booming till nine, then there was a fearful sound which was louder than the loudest thunder I ever heard, accompanied by an immense mass of red fire in the blackness of the night. I was two hundred yards away, but the very earth on which I stood shook and shivered with the upheaval.

As soon as the crash came our chaps hopped up and rushed the shattered trenches. They found that a big crater had been made by the explosion, and that most of the Turks had been stiffened. Those who were left were either bayoneted or bombed. The Turks did not counter-attack that day. They had had enough of it. We had a good few casualties, but it was an effort that was worth while, because it showed that if we wanted a place we could take it, and at any time we liked. I saw all this very clearly, for I was going backward and forward all the time as a stretcher-bearer.

The Turks gave us no chance and we gave them none; but at the same time they did not do anything that I would call really dirty or out of the way. A lot of them were fine fellows physically. Some of the Turkish diggers we got as prisoners had no fighting gear on them at all. They were just peasants who had been brought up to do the work.

At last I fell ill with dysentery and gastritis, and came home on a huge hospital ship, with four thousand more sick and wounded soldiers. We had a six days' run to Southampton, and had just under sixty deaths on board. They were buried at sea in batches, the biggest being eleven—and very solemn it all was.

Now I have done; but I want to tell of just one more little thing that happened here in England, where I have been in hospital, and where people have been so good to us.

It was Christmas-time, and we were having a Sunday evening service in hospital. We were asked what hymns we would like, and a chap spoke out and said, "Let's have—

We plough the fields and scatter
The good seed on the land.'

The parson was puzzled. He hardly thought we could, because it was Christmas-time and this was a harvest hymn.

"And it's harvest-time now at home in Australia," the chap said.

So we had the good old hymn, and it took us back to home twelve thousand miles away.

I think the Anzacs did what they set out to do.

CHAPTER 30

"Imperishable Glory" for the Kensingtons

"By your splendid attack and dogged endurance on May 9th, you and your fallen comrades won imperishable glory for the 13th London Battalion. It was a feat of arms surpassed by no battalion in this great war." This was the fine tribute paid to the 13th (Kensington) Battalion of the London Regiment by General Sir Henry Rawlinson, commanding the 4th Army Corps, after the Kensingtons had taken part in the British advance in May between Bois Grenier and Festubert. The battalion had already greatly distinguished itself in the Neuve Chapelle operations and elsewhere. This story of some of the doings of the corps at the front is told by a member of the Kensingtons, who wishes to remain anonymous.

The main body of the Kensingtons had gone out in October, and I left England with a draft in January, the dead of winter. We marched up to billets in Laventi, three miles from the firing-line. The place was being heavily shelled by the Germans, and amongst other buildings the church was smashed up; but the men were lucky, and I don't think that any soldiers were hit there. I shall always particularly remember that place, because it was there that I saw for the first time a man who had been killed by the enemy.

I was going along a street near an old ruined house which was being used as a soldiers' club, when I heard the noise of an exploding shell. The crash was very near, and soldiers rushed out from the ruined house to see what had happened. They told me that the shell had burst farther down the street, and that a civilian had been killed. Without any loss of time they took a door down, and using this as a stretcher they carried the dead man away, and as I watched them I realised that we were fairly in it, and I am bound to say that I was very strangely moved and deeply impressed by this little tragedy.

We realised even more fully what it all meant when for the first time at the front we put five rounds of ball ammunition in the magazines and marched off for our first spell in the trenches, between our billets and the firing-line. We started at dusk, so that we should reach the trenches just when it became dark.

There was something very solemn in going away like that towards the enemy; yet there was, of course, intense excitement and curiosity. It was not a very exhilarating start, because the country was in a very bad state, owing to the heavy January rains. There was plenty of water in the trenches when we reached them, and it was bitterly cold. We were only one night in them that time, but it was a useful breaking-in experience, and hardened us a bit for the much longer spells, during which the cold was so intense that the rifles were frozen as they lay on the parapets, if care had not been taken to keep them well oiled after firing.

We got some fine experience and first-rate preparation as a nerve-steadier in carrying out the duties of "listening patrol." When night came we went out of our trenches and made our way to the front of the parapet, working in pairs. This work was both dangerous and ticklish, for we had orders not to fire under any circumstances, as that would have brought the German machine-guns on us; but to use only the bayonet in case we came across parties of the enemy.

The object of the "listening patrols" was to find out, if we could, the German working parties putting up barbed wire entanglements and doing other things for their own protection. One of the pair of men would lie down on the ground and listen, and the other would be on the alert, ready to report instantly any suspicious noise that was noticed. If the Germans were putting up barbed wire, it meant that they were quite exposed and good execution could be done amongst them by our machine-guns; on the other hand, if the enemy heard our "listening patrols" they would instantly open fire with machine-guns and rifles and anything that came handy.

Patrol work was very trying, especially on the intensely cold nights, when it was a hard matter to keep awake, and the man who was lying on the ground was almost frozen stiff.

This sort of work went on for several weeks—until about March, slushing about in the trenches, and often enough, when we went out

Field Artillery near Ypres

of them at night we would fall, in the darkness, into trenches that were full of water. Sometimes men were in it up to the neck, and the only way to get your clothes dry was to let the heat of the body do it—a long business at times, when the body had very little heat to spare. There was no help for it, because the men who came to grief like that could not change at all.

Early in March we were digging trenches on La Bassée Road. This work occupied us for several nights, and though we did not at the time fully understand its meaning, we knew afterwards that the trenches were meant for the massing of our men for the Battle of Neuve Chapelle. These were reserve trenches, and in the open; the consequence being that they were exposed to the German fire, and the digging was very dangerous work. We used to get as many as a dozen casualties in a company while digging, and one spot became known as "Suicide Corner," because of the heavy losses there. Of course, the digging was always done at night; but digging means making a noise, and whenever the enemy heard a noise they went for the place it came from.

It was at "Suicide Corner" that I made my first real acquaintance with the horrors of war. As usual we had gone out to dig. We had been taken to our allotted place by the Engineers, every other man carrying a spade, and our rear being brought up by four or five stretcher-bearers. It was obviously to our interest to dig as hard as we could, to get shelter, and we went at it with a will, being pretty well massed.

There was a man quite close to me, digging for all he was worth. Suddenly he went down, and I felt sure that he must have been shot, because the Germans, doubtless hearing our digging, had opened rapid fire on us. I soon found that the poor chap had been shot through the chest, and I went to fetch up our stretcher-bearers. They came, and a doctor came, and the man was carried to the shelter of a neighbouring hedge, where the doctor and the stretcher-bearers did everything they could for him, by the light of an officer's electric pocket-torch; but he had been mortally wounded in the chest, and he died at the hedge side, in the darkness which was lit only by the light of the torch and the flashes of machine-guns and rifles. The poor fellow was covered up and put on a stretcher and carried back to the billet.

This was the first man I had seen killed in action, and it made a very deep impression on me, especially as it happened at night. That picture of the dying soldier under the hedge, with the doctor and the ambulance men striving by the light of the little torch to save him, will, I think, remain in my memory when many of the bigger happenings of the war have faded and are almost forgotten. It is an early and a very sorrowful impression of the days that came just before the beginning of the furious battle of Neuve Chapelle.

No one who was in those Neuve Chapelle operations will ever forget the massing of the British forces for the fight. The whole countryside was alive with troops of every sort, and there was the incessant rumble of gun-carriages, ammunition-wagons and heavy motor-lorries, and the tramp of hosts of men on the march. There was a great deal of inevitable noise, but at the same time a sinister and impressive quietness. There was the feeling in the air that something very big was going to happen, and everybody felt on the "edge."

The Kensingtons went on in the night until we got into some reserve trenches, which there had not been time to finish properly. They were simply scoopings in the ground, with the earth thrown up on each side, a rough-and-ready sort of arrangement, affording very little cover and with not enough room for us to lie down—indeed, so shallow were they that when the bombardment began in the morning we were actually lying one on top of the other.

The bombardment which opened the Battle of Neuve Chapelle began fairly early, and it is no exaggeration to say that when the immense number of guns began crashing it was hell let loose. The very earth shook, and no part of the country where we were seemed to escape from the shattering effects of the shells of every sort which were bursting all around us, a great many of them in the air. Some shells fell into the reserve trenches, and many of our fellows were hit.

The trenches in front of us were manned by two fine Line regiments, and these troops were ordered to advance towards the Germans and dig them out of their trenches. The Linesmen had a heavy task before them, but they began to carry it out most gallantly, and while they did so we came in for a very furious attack from the enemy's batteries, because, although they could not get at the advancing Regulars, we were well in the zone of their fire. We suffered severely during this bombardment, and were glad when the order came to rush to the trenches that the Linesmen had left and take their places.

To get to the trenches we had to rush over some fields, and as we dashed along we were under a heavy fire, which caused us serious losses, and those of us who reached the comparative shelter of the trenches were thankful when we were able to drop into them and so escape from the open ground. The thing to do was simplicity itself, and that was to get across the open space from one lot of trenches to another. There was no question of doing anything except look after yourself and carry out your orders; there was no chance of helping any one who fell—it was forward all the time, and those who went down had to be left where they fell.

Shells were bursting everywhere and the fragments were scattered all around the battlefield, and men were going down, killed or wounded, on every hand. It was through this real hail of fire that we reached the trenches which had been occupied by the two Line battalions, and then we saw a sight that I, at any rate, shall never forget—a spectacle, too, which proved how terrible the struggle was and how greatly the Regulars had suffered.

I talk of trenches, but no such things were left—the German gunners had smashed them out of all resemblance to ordinary trenches—and owing to one of those inevitable happenings of warfare some of our own British shells also had helped to complete the work of destruction.

The trenches had been blown in on all sides, and the barbed wire entanglements near them had been utterly destroyed, so that what we saw was a confused heap of ruins, or rather an area of shattered ground in which men had been killed and buried at the same time. The real horror of this part of the affair was to see the brave fellows who had done their best, and were now lying dead and shattered in the debris.

I soon had a very bad experience in the trenches that we had taken over, so to speak.

I and another Kensington had been allotted a firing position, and we were doing our best with our rifles when I suddenly became aware that my companion had come to grief. I looked round and saw that he was lying at the bottom of the trench—and I made the terrible discovery that his head had been blown completely off. I would not mention this circumstance except by way of trying to show what the whole of the trench warfare meant. This incident occurred in the open trenches; but a lot of the dugouts were blown in with the men inside, which meant burial alive, and I know of one case in which seven men, so killed, were lying together, and that is only one instance of many of the same sort.

When we got into the trenches that had been occupied by the two Line regiments we were ordered to take up a firing position, and the first thing we did was to try and restore the parapet and to make the trench serviceable, in case the Linesmen were driven back. At this particular time everything gave way to the chief business in hand, which was to fight, and only the stretcher-bearers were allowed to do anything for the men who fell. Here, again, every other man carried a spade, and those who had them had to set to work at once to put the trenches to rights again, as far as it was possible to do so. This work was being done very vigorously when it had to be dropped suddenly, because the order came that we were to advance right up into the village of Neuve Chapelle; and so it happened that we were rushed up just behind the spot where the Regulars had dug themselves in. We rushed up into the village and lay in the open, behind some ruined buildings.

The Germans had arranged a counter attack, and if this had come to anything we should have made a dash for the trenches, which were just in front of the village; but as it was we made for the village itself, or what was left of the place, for by this time there was nothing left but the ruins, and the whole region was an absolute shambles.

Before we made this rush the men of the Line regiments began to bring in German prisoners. These came in batches of fifteen or twenty, disarmed, of course, so that one or two British soldiers were enough for a batch. These prisoners looked as if they had had a terrible time, and, indeed, they said they had been through some dreadful experiences owing to our artillery, and that our guns had given them a shell for each yard of ground they held.

The German attack not having materialised, we were able to retire to the trenches and make them habitable. Before this could be done we had to get the wounded out and bury the dead. As a rule, we had dug a grave for each man, but now there were so many of the killed that we had to put the bodies side by side in long trenches, which we made just behind the line. Quite a cemetery came into existence there, and we did our best to make it nice and worthy to be the resting-place of those who had given their lives for their country.

There is one feature of this great war which has been lost sight of to some extent, and that is the tremendous call which has been made on the physical endurance of the men, quite apart from the ceaseless and excessive strain on the nerves and mind. I will give one illustration on this point.

On the night of March 10th, during the Battle of Neuve Chapelle, the front line ran short of ammunition and the Kensingtons were ordered to take up a supply. First of all we had to load up with our little lot, and, as it was impossible to carry the ammunition in the cases, each man got a score of canvas bandoliers across his shoulders, in addition to his own kit and rifle, and he had to stagger along with this tremendous weight, the filled bandoliers alone representing about eighty pounds; so that with the rifle and standing kit each man carried a burden of considerably more than a hundredweight. That was bad enough, but matters were made infinitely worse by the fact that we had to go along a newly-made road, or rather track. This road had been constructed by the Gurkhas, by the simple plan of putting bricks down almost anyhow—there were plenty of bricks handy from the ruined buildings all around us; so that the road we had to take was rather like the huge teeth of an enormous saw, for there was no steam roller to flatten down the surface.

In the darkness, under constant fire, we staggered and stumbled along with our ammunition; but even the biggest and strongest amongst us could not do more than cover about a hundred yards at a time. If a man did that he was proud and thankful, and having got a bit of rest as best he could—and that was by hunking up and resting on the rifle, for if a man had really got on to the ground he would have been hard put to it to rise again—we forged slowly ahead.

We had been ordered to take the ammunition into a house that was battered, but was more whole than the rest—it was really only a skeleton of a building—and having reached the house we very gladly dumped our bandoliers down in the garden. To reach the garden was quite a simple matter—all we had to do was to dash through a big hole in the side of the house, made by artillery fire, and I give you my word that we lost no time in shedding our burden of bandoliers.

It was a most exciting little performance from start to finish, yet it put a terrific strain on every man who took part in it—load yourself up with more than a hundredweight of stuff and see what it feels like; then you will partly realise what we had to go through—and the excitement was by no means ended when we reached the garden in the darkness, because just as we were getting rid of the bandoliers a shell crashed into the house next to us and smashed it to smithereens, a lot of our chaps being fairly smothered in the flying bricks and rubbish.

That *was* a night, and one that I shall never forget.

There seemed every prospect that we should be fairly mopped up, and when the order came for the N.C.O.'s to take back the men in parties we lost no time in returning, as best we could, to the trenches. Shelling was going on all the time, and just by way of giving a finish to the performance something like thirty star-shells burst together, making the dark night as light as day and giving the Germans a chance to plump more shells into us as we got back. This hurrying up with ammunition to the firing-line is only one of many such things that have been done as part of the day's work by British soldiers at the front.

About two nights afterwards these two Line battalions of which I speak were relieved, and we took over their trenches. There were no dugouts, or any such protections; the trenches were simply breastworks, and we had a very bad time when the wet weather set in, as it did.

When we took the trenches over they were in an unfinished state, and we set to work at once to complete them. One night, or rather about two o'clock in the morning, I was working on the top of the back parapet, with my head and shoulders showing, and half asleep, for I was dead tired. Suddenly the Germans sent up about fifty star-shells, which burst in the sky and made the darkness as light as day and showed us up as clearly as possible. Instantly the enemy opened rapid fire on our trenches and swept us with machine-guns, the bullets whistling over the parapets.

I was roused as swiftly as if the *réveillé* had sounded—perhaps faster, because there are no whizzing bullets when the bugles blow—and I well remember that I wriggled and rolled sideways. I knew that the darkness had become as light as daytime and that the German fire was peppering us, and that the best thing to do was to get out of it as rapidly as I could. So I fell flat, then lay still, then rolled into a trench as best I could. I remember—so soon do we get accustomed to war—that one of our chaps growled, "Why don't you go a bit farther, then you could go through an opening! "Fancy a chap picking and choosing a landing-place when he was clearing out from shell-fire! I knew that in rolling and falling like this there was a risk of landing on top of a fixed bayonet, as some of our fellows did, but I cheerfully took that chance in my eagerness to get under cover.

After this we polished up our bayonet work and went through a lot of routine, at the end of which we were told that we were to take the offensive and that some Regulars were to do the support work—a proud position for Territorials. So we filed into a front trench and relieved men who were only seventy yards away from the Germans, so that we knew we should not have far to rush when the real business came to hand.

I wish I could tell you of what happened on the Ninth of May, when, according to all reports, the Kensingtons did so well and won so much praise from General Rawlinson; but I cannot go into detail, for I was hit at the start, and fell before the German lines were reached. I know that this particular fight began early in the morning, that it lasted all day, and that our chaps were practically surrounded. The order had come that we were to go for the Germans, and I was doing my bit in carrying it out.

We were rushing forward when I was shot through the chest and was knocked completely out. When this happened I was in a trench, and our chaps were cheering loudly, as if no such things as Germans existed.

The bullet that struck me had gone through my left lung, though I did not know this until later, and I had had a very narrow escape; but I did not at the time fully realise how close a call I had had.

After being shot I just managed to get back over the parapet, and I was bandaged up and kept going for the time being.

I felt pretty well until the alarm came that the Germans were starting on the gas tack, and then I wanted to be on the move. Respirators were fixed, and every preparation was made to meet the devilish device. For my own part, being shot and helpless, I naturally wanted to be out of it, so I beseeched the stretcher-bearers to carry me away, so that I should have, at any rate, a sporting chance.

"Will you try and get me out?" I said; "because I know that gas will finish me." And being good chaps two of them came, put me on a stretcher, and carried me down a communication-trench and into safety, under a constant and heavy fire, which lasted all that famous day.

I have been yarning long enough, though I could say a good deal more. By way of finish I will tell you of a little incident of sniping.

Sniping was going on all the time. In many places it was very deadly, especially where the green uniform of the snipers harmonised with the cabbages, so that the snipers could not be seen. We got used to the cabbage-patches whizzing bullets, but we were puzzled by some especially dangerous firing which came upon us from the rear. For a considerable time we could not make this out; then we discovered a haystack, and suspicion was aroused. We kept a strict watch, and made particular inquiry, and were rewarded at the end of it, by finding that what looked like an inoffensive haystack was a place of cunning hiding for a German marksman. This special rick concealed in its very heart a son of the Fatherland, who had been having a truly glorious time in potting us. He knew that he was certain to be discovered; but he went on sniping till we found him and put an end to his performance. He knew that his discovery was certain, and that discovery meant death; but he kept his game up—and he died game.

This was quite fair and square fighting, for sniping is legitimate. I cannot say as much for the German practice, which we fully proved, of using dum-dum bullets in their machine-guns. This they did by taking out the bullets as ordinarily used and reversing them.

CHAPTER 31

Ten Months in the Fighting-Line

It is almost incredible that a man can endure a war like this for the best part of a year without a break; yet there are many British soldiers who have had that experience. At the outset these were mostly the old Regular troops who for efficiency and discipline were unrivalled in the world's armies. The story of one of these long-service Regulars—Private Frederick Woods, 1st Battalion Royal Irish Fusiliers—who served at the front for ten months and was then gassed and invalided home, is told here.

I had ten months at the front with my regiment before I was invalided home, and I think that during that long period I saw every form of fighting except one, and I have just been reading about it. That exception is the use by the Germans of liquid flame, which they sprayed on French troops some time ago and are now sending on to the British. It is a devilish device.

It is natural enough that I should take my mind back to a year ago. How clearly I recollect that morning when I had just finished breakfast and opened my newspaper, and to my astonishment saw that war had been declared and that all Reservists were to report at once, without waiting for the official notice from the depot.

I was a Reservist of the Royal Irish Fusiliers, and had done seven years with the colours, so I at once went to my old home. I will confess that I was a bit downhearted, because my brother, also a Reservist, had come home, too, and he had the pain of saying goodbye to his wife, as well as to our parents. But we made the best of things, and it was the better for the two of us because we both belonged to the same battalion.

How many of us who assembled at Euston Station for the journey to our depot in County Armagh, Ireland, are left, I wonder? Not many, there cannot be, for the Royal Irish Fusiliers have suffered terribly in the war. The old soldiers assembled with brave hearts and were full of fun, and left Euston singing "Tipperary" in fine form. I well remember how much amused we were, when crossing in the boat, at a man who had come from Lancashire. He was wearing wooden clogs, and had a bottle of whisky with him; and he sang and danced and became particularly lively, and we thoroughly enjoyed his performance. At the depot we found our clothes and equipment waiting for us, and next day a big draft of us set out for England, my brother and myself amongst them. It was wonderful to see the draft and realise that here were fully trained soldiers, completely equipped, ready to take the field, and yet only a few hours ago many of the men were in civil life in various parts of the United Kingdom.

I had the strange experience of dealing with German soldiers before we left England, for a score of us were given ammunition and driven to Folkestone Harbour Station to meet a train of German Reservists who were trying to get away by a boat which was lying in the harbour, ready to take them to the Fatherland by way of Flushing. But the German Reservists didn't get off, and they had a big surprise when they saw us waiting for them. We searched them, of course, and found that several of the men were carrying arms. We took them to Christ's Hospital, the beautiful building in Surrey, and I suppose that they are still prisoners of war in England. These men were the usual type of Germans who were so often seen in London—waiters, and barbers, and so on, and I fancy that some of them were not sorry to be just too late to join the German Army. I cannot help thinking how different were these "reservists" to the long-service men who had rejoined the British colours.

I am not going into any details of the earlier part of the war; but I was not long before I saw a few more German prisoners on the other side. We had marched two days without seeing the enemy, then our scouts returned with three prisoners. The scouts told us that they had banged into the Germans, who were retreating fast, and had captured these three fellows. I was deeply interested in the prisoners, because they were the first German soldiers I had seen. They struck me as being somewhat miserable specimens, but that was perhaps because they seemed very hungry. They looked better when we had given them some biscuit, which of course we did at once.

Very soon after that I saw a farm which our artillery had hit, and

Royal Irish Fusiliers in trenches in Gallipoli.

which was in ruins and full of dead Germans. They had not had much of a chance against the British gunners, and I noticed that along the road leading to the farm ammunition was lying in heaps. It was a gruesome place to billet in; but in spite of the German dead we passed quite a comfortable night at the farm. Next day we were on the move again, and reached a river where a bridge had been blown up. This delayed us till the following morning, as our transport could not cross. But we found a way out of that trouble by taking the transport along a railway, and a rough, hard job it was, too, for we needed four horses and men with ropes to do the hauling, as the wheels kept getting stuck between the sleepers. But in spite of all the difficulties we got the transport across, and reached a town which the Germans had passed through; and we did not want telling which way they had gone, as we could see champagne bottles and wine bottles along the road for miles—drink which the Germans had looted from the town.

Drink and outrage and destruction marked the path of the German troops, wherever they had been, in those early unforgettable stages of the war, just as they did afterwards; though I believe that now, when they know that they are outcasts from civilisation, the Germans are disposed to mend their ways, if only to get better treatment when the final reckoning comes.

There comes into my mind as I talk the picture of a dreadful sight I saw near Armentières. We had reached a place and entered it, not knowing that the Germans were so near at hand, though we knew that we had them on the drive and that they were going away from us as hard as they could travel. Suddenly we came to a nunnery, where the nuns showed us the dead body of a little French boy, a mere child about five years old. A glance was enough to show that he had been bayoneted in the stomach, and it was clear that the murder had been done quite recently. One of our officers made inquiries of some nuns, and he was told that a drunken German soldier had killed the child. Can you wonder that when our eyes saw such dreadful evidence, the Royal Irish Fusiliers, at any rate, made up their minds that whenever the chance arose the enemy should be severely punished?

Even in the way of ordinary warfare many innocent women and children have been killed. In one village we passed through one of our men found a woman's head of hair, which had been cut off, and the body itself was found by civilians. The woman had been maltreated and murdered by the Germans, and on every hand there were signs of the enemy's ferocity and inhumanity. Buildings were in ruins and homes were wrecked, doors having been battered down so that the savage soldiery could wreak their maddened will on fellow-creatures and their belongings.

On every hand there was evidence of outrage. I went to a farm in this village to try and buy some milk and eggs. On entering a room which had a big fireplace, I saw in the corner of the fireplace an old man who seemed to be an idiot. A woman, whom I took to be his wife, and could speak broken English, told me that the *Uhlans* had taken him away, with his hands tied behind him.

"Why did they take him? What had he done?" I asked her.

She answered that the man had done nothing, but that the Germans had accused him of firing a shot. He had not done anything of the sort, for the shot had been fired by a French patrol; but in spite of his declarations, protests and appeals, the Germans beat the poor old fellow on the head with their lances and did their best to force him into a confession that he had fired. But he would do nothing of the sort, and at last they let him go—they would not have done that if they had not known that he was perfectly innocent. He managed to get back to his home, covered with blood and almost senseless, and the first thing that was noticed about him was that he had lost his memory. He very soon became the sorry spectacle I saw in the corner of the fireplace, an innocent man who had had the life nearly beaten out of him and had been maltreated into idiocy. It took me some time to understand the real point of the Germans' brutality—that they had let the poor old fellow loose and told him to run, and had battered him on the head and prodded him with their lances because he did not run fast enough.

I recall the sad case of another old lady I saw. She was crying bitterly, and when she was questioned explained that the Germans had taken her son away—and he was never seen again. Like so many more of the inhabitants, he had fallen a victim to German "frightfulness."

If you turn from these sad cases—and I have mentioned only one or two that come into my mind—and try to tell of what was done to ordinary people because they happened to be in the war zone, words almost fail you; but I recollect that at one time we had been relieved by French Alpine troops and had entrained for St. Omer, where Lord Roberts died, while the guns were solemnly booming in battle.

We reached St. Omer and were resting on the square, when a German aeroplane came over and dropped two bombs, killing a woman and a child, but no soldiers. As soon as it was seen that this was happening, one of our own aeroplanes was sent up after the German. Up he went, in glorious style, and brought him down; and when we saw it we cheered for all we were worth. The German dropped between the two firing-lines and was shot. We tried to make him a prisoner, but every time we made a rush to get him the Germans fired on us, not caring in the least about the fate of their own airman. The machine itself was shelled by us and burnt.

When we reached the Aisne we found that a bridge by which we were to cross was blown up; but our engineers soon repaired the bridge, which had not been destroyed properly, so that it was strong enough to carry us. Having crossed the river, three regiments went to the tops of the hills and entrenched—the Warwicks, the Dublin Fusiliers, and the Seaforths, our own regiment being left in reserve at the back of a village.

The French troops were on our left, in front of Soissons, and we used to see their artillery galloping across the plain with ammunition for the guns. The French use mules and not horses for their batteries, and once we saw some artillery galloping in fine style under German fire. When the guns were passing near us four shells landed amongst the limbers, but no one was hurt, and on seeing this we gave the Frenchmen a tremendous cheer, for luck, and they replied with cheers and wild waving of whips as they galloped away and nearer into the fire zone. I remember that day well, because on the night of it we had to go and bury thirty-five of our artillery horses that had been killed.

Next day was our turn for shell fire from the Germans. The shells landed right into us, but we were lucky—only one man was killed though several were wounded. We advanced up the hill, out of the way of the fire; but as we moved the enemy gave us shrapnel, and the shelling became so heavy that half-way up the hill we dug ourselves in.

While we were going up the hill, in short rushes, just like an ordinary field day, and without any confusion, an artillery corporal, whose name I do not know, showed splendid courage and uncommon strength in carrying several of our men to a hospital which the Germans were shelling. For his bravery he received the French *Médaille Militaire*.

Our transport had a very rough time, for out of fifty horses no fewer than forty-two were killed or had to be shot. Twenty men were picked out, myself amongst them, and sent back some distance for new horses, and I am glad to say that we returned safely with the animals.

I was then put on guard over a bridge which was a special favourite with spies. They were always trying to get through, but in most cases they failed, and being caught and found out, there was no waste of time in shooting them, after trial by court martial. After being relieved at this place by French Alpine troops we entrained for St. Omer, the place I have mentioned, and from St. Omer we were rushed in French motor lorries for about sixteen miles, to a village where we rested for the night. Next morning we were told that the Germans were on a hill six miles away.

I shall never forget that day, because it rained in torrents, and it was a sodden regiment that trudged through the mud and mire and swished across drenched fields. It was not exhilarating, but we were soon warmed up by the German fire. We were ordered to lie down, and down we lay in a field of swedes, so we fairly flopped into beds of mud and water, just about completing our discomfort.

The rain was pattering down like tiny bullets, but we also got a shower of the real things, and you could hear the bullets "*zip*" into the leaves of the swedes. It was intensely trying and very miserable to be in such an exposed place, and we were glad when the order came to fix bayonets, ready for a charge. We fixed bayonets, but had to wait some time before the order to charge came; then we heard the word we wanted, and up we rose and off we went. The firing became hotter than ever, and several of our men were killed and wounded before the top of the hill was reached.

There was not much commotion as we advanced, but somewhere a Seaforth Highlander was playing bagpipes, and the skirl helped the boys along.

We expected some stiff work when we reached the top of the hill; but when we got there we were astonished to find that the Germans had gone, taking their wounded with them. We were after the enemy so quickly, however, that they had to leave their wounded, who fell into our hands. A hundred and three of the poor beggars had been left in a convent for the nuns to look after, so you may be sure that they had been well cared for before they became our prisoners.

The Germans at this stage were retiring rapidly, and we kept them on the run. We soon came to a little village, where we found that the Germans had put sandbags in the church tower and had planted a machine-gun in the tower. A French flag which was flying on the tower the day before had been dragged down by the Germans and torn to pieces. We looked upon the flag with sadness, for here again we had evidence of German brutalities—in their retirement the soldiers had maltreated the women, and they had battered down doors and smashed windows in their savage determination to enter houses. They accused the villagers of firing on them—though the villagers had nothing but a few old useless firearms, which we saw. In spite of this they declared that a man had fired on them, and they shot him. The body was taken away by a priest. These things, I can assure you, roused us up properly, and we put plenty of heart into our continued pursuit of the Germans; but they were flying so fast that they were very hard to catch.

We came up with them in the big town of Armentières, and were so close to them that as we entered the town our scouts came back and told us that the enemy were just leaving it at the other end. As we entered the town we were cheered enthusiastically by the French, who seemed to look upon us as deliverers, and so loaded us up with gifts of chocolate bread, matches and so on that we had to throw half the things away.

Going into Armentières on the very heels of the Germans was an exciting and dangerous performance, and as we advanced along the streets we went on each side, not knowing on which side shots would come from windows, but ready for anything that happened, as the men on one side had their rifles handy for any German that appeared on the other. This was a better plan than being on the look-out for trouble from the windows just above your head. Luckily not many shots were fired upon us at this stage; but we soon came to a farm where one of the most desperate little fights that I can call to mind took place.

We were wary in entering the farm, for we saw at once the sort of thing we had to tackle. There were four Germans concealed in a cellar the window of which was on a level with the ground, so they had full control of the yard and the entrance-gate.

Some of our boys, with Captain Carbury, went in and tried to persuade the Germans to surrender, but their answer to the coaxing was a volley which killed the officer and wounded the men. The captain was terribly mutilated, for he had been struck full on the body, not by an ordinary bullet, but an explosive bullet, and the men had been badly hurt. As they lay on the ground they cried for help, and all the time the Germans were firing on them and succeeded in hitting them on the legs and shoulders. Two of our men volunteered to try and save their wounded comrades, and they dashed into the yard, only to be shot and killed as soon as they entered. One of these fine chaps was Lance-Corporal Shield, but I do not know the name of the other.

It was useless to waste further life in the attempt to get the Germans out of their strong little position, from which they could fire without making themselves targets, so our officer sent for some engineers to undermine the farm and blow it up. The Germans were warned what was going to be done, and were called upon to surrender. This they refused to do.

During that night the engineers were working like moles, and I didn't envy the feelings of the Germans who were trapped in the cellar, nor was there any pity for them next morning when the engineers finished their work.

There was a crash and a flame and a shaking of the ground—and when, later, things having settled, we went to see what had happened we found one badly damaged German hanging over an iron girder on to which he had fallen after being blown up. We made a prisoner of him. His three companions had been killed, and we saw that they had been blown to pieces.

The Germans by this time had received big reinforcements, and they entrenched themselves strongly. We entrenched as well, and a warm job it was, as bullets used to whistle past us constantly.

We were in these trenches thirty-seven days before we were relieved, and long, hard days and trying nights they were, putting an uncommonly severe strain on everybody. It was almost certain death for a man to show himself, yet men had to show themselves, because water had to be fetched and rations had to be brought up to the trenches and taken in. Whenever it was possible to do so advantage was taken of the darkness; but we could not always wait for night, and during the daytime some splendid acts of bravery were seen.

I will tell of one particular instance, because the man will be always remembered with pride by the Royal Irish Fusiliers—his valour won for him the Victoria Cross. This was Private Robert Morrow, an Irishman, who literally did not know the meaning of fear. One day we badly wanted some water, and this was to be had only from a farm which was some distance away. To reach the farm it was necessary to leave the trenches and cross open ground, exposed to the German fire, which was very deadly because we were so near the enemy's trenches. These were only about 600 yards away, and not more than 300 yards away were some snipers, in a farm in front of the trenches.

Morrow volunteered to fetch some water, and taking an empty two-gallon stone rum-jar he started on his perilous journey. As soon as he was seen after leaving the trench the Germans did their very best to pot him; but they missed every time, and Morrow reached the farm, filled his jar and began his trip back. And a hard business it was, for a jar like that will hold about fifty pounds' weight of water, then there is the jar and the awkwardness of carrying it when the carrier has to duck and dodge over every yard of the ground. But Morrow was a splendid hand at the game, and he actually managed to reach the trench in safety and was on the point of dropping into it with his precious water, and we were just ready to give him a wild Irish cheer. But at this very moment crash came a German bullet, and the rum-jar was smashed to pieces and the water rained on the ground and was lost.

Morrow was the sort of chap who can't be beaten. Instantly he volunteered to go back to the farm with water-bottles. What can you do with such a man but let him have his way? We handed over the water-bottles, quite a festoon of them, and having slung them round him Morrow left the trench for the second time and began to make his way towards the farm.

As soon as he left the shelter of the trench he drew the German fire on him, and he was under it all the way to the farm, where he filled the bottles, and all the way back. This time he reached the trench safely and dropped into it, bringing the water with him and escaping every German bullet that was meant to kill him. He was a plucky kid and we were proud of him. And the regiment will be proud of him for all time—I say will be, for like quite a number of the heroes who have won the Cross Morrow has been killed.

Now that I am talking of him I recall the fact that only the day before he was killed he went to a well for water, and had a remarkably narrow escape from an odd sort of death—not a soldier's end at all. The Germans had blown the farm to pieces, but there was a lonely chimney-stack standing. When Morrow went to the ruined farm a high wind was blowing, and just as he was passing the chimney a strong gust brought it down in a heap at his very feet. He escaped by just a few inches from being killed and buried in the heap of masonry.

It was on April 12th that Morrow actually won his Cross. At that time we were near Messines, and the trench warfare was being carried on with great energy on both sides. Shell fire from the Germans was shattering and wrecking some of our own trenches, so much so that

British troops were being buried alive in some places.

Several soldiers had been knocked out by shell fire and buried in the fallen earth. You can easily imagine what it means—men are in a trench, which is really a sort of vast open grave, and shell fire shatters the earth which is around and simply buries the men. So it happened on the 12th of April, and Morrow saw and knew it. Just as he had acted when he went and filled the rum-jar and our water-bottles with water, so he acted now—he gave no thought to himself. Out he went, not once, but many times, into a bullet-swept zone, till he reached the trenches which had been knocked out of shape by German shells, and in the rubbish of which his comrades were lying buried and helpless. He dug them out and pulled them out, and one by one he brought the senseless fellows into safety. That was the deed for which Morrow got the Victoria Cross; but in reality he had won the honour time after time. He was killed at "Plug Street," as we called the place. A piece of shell struck him on the head and he died immediately.

The most extraordinary things happened to some of our fellows, and there were escapes from death or capture so strange that you could not credit them unless you saw them. I will mention one particular incident that comes into my mind. I saw one of our motor ambulances going along a road. There was nothing unusual in that, of course, because we have many motor ambulances and there are many roads, but in this case the road led straight into some German trenches. Before it was possible to do anything or raise an alarm the driver had blundered into the very midst of the enemy, and there he was, with his ambulance, just about as much amazed to see the Germans as they were to set eyes on him. They ought, of course, to have bagged both the driver and his vehicle; but he sprang down, restarted his engine and began to run away. The Germans pulled themselves together, and every man who could bring a rifle to bear fired on the retreating ambulance; but luckily the driver had a fair lot of protection, and though hundreds of bullets struck the bonnet of the car not one of them touched him, and he got safely away and went on his journey. It was a remarkable escape, and all who saw it were glad that the plucky chap got so well out of the trouble which had followed his mistake.

One night I was on sentry in the trenches when the sentry next to me gave the alarm. He had no sooner done that than he saw something crawling over the trenches. He did not waste a second—he lunged out with his bayonet, and then found that he had driven it into a German's shoulder. The German was made a prisoner, then it was discovered that he had lost his way in the dark and had got into our trench. When we searched him we found that he had a revolver and a long knife; but he was miserably clad, his feet being wrapped up in newspapers, as he had no socks. He said he was glad to be captured.

Our chaps sometimes make the same mistake—a very easy one, as the German trenches were so close to our own. Two of our men went, one dark night, to get some hot tea in dixies. On their return they got into a communication trench and lost their way; but at last, thinking they were home again, they shouted down a trench, "Hi, Bill, take the tea!"

Instantly bullets were flying around them, and realising that they were not back home at all, but had reached an enemy trench, they dropped the hot tea on the Germans, then ran for it and got safely off.

I had been a long time at the front before I was detailed to go back with the transport and bring up the officers' rations every night. We used to gallop as hard as we could till we came to a bridge, which the Germans could see and did their best to smash with shells. There was a sharp turning which a priest had called the "Devil's Corner," saying it was worse than hell because of the continual shelling. We were forced to take this road, because it was the only way to reach the trenches.

At night the Germans threw a searchlight on the "Devil's Corner," and as soon as ever they saw us appear they shelled us, sometimes as many as four shells coming together; but we dashed on so furiously that they could not get us, nor did they catch us when we ran the gauntlet coming back, though they used to get an average of a wagon a night. In addition to this deadly corner we had three burnt villages to tackle; but we were always lucky, and our men did not come to grief.

We used to go right up to the trenches, only about twenty-five yards from them, with the horses and wagons, and there was one specially dangerous spot which had to be passed. This was where there was a gap in a hedge, which the Germans knew of quite well and could see. They knew that at night our troops went to the gap to get water, and so in the daytime they trained machine-guns on the spot, and when darkness came they blazed away in the hope of wiping some of our men out. I have known these guns whirr for five minutes without a break, sending out a fire so horrible that nothing could live under it. We lost several men at this gap, and were forced to make an opening in the hedge somewhere else.

We got into reserve trenches, and here it was that a "whistling Willy," which is our nickname for a small German shell, went clean through a Seaforth and then killed one of our own men in the trenches. The shell passed through the Highlander intact, and did not explode until it reached the trenches, a circumstance which shows the amazing performances of projectiles in this war. You never know what they will do. At another time one of our chaps, named Steel, was having his hair cut, when a shell exploded near him and a piece of it, six inches long, like a needle, struck him through the heart and killed him on the spot.

The winter was a very rough time for us, as we could not keep the water out of the trenches, and we often had to sleep standing up, during a four days' spell in the trenches. Often enough, at the end of one of these hard spells, we were intensely disappointed because we could not be relieved, owing to troops being moved elsewhere, and we were forced to stick it for an extra four days; but we did not forget to make up for it when we were out, although we had to march a few miles to our billets to rest, and even then we were not free from shell fire.

By the time I had been at the front seven months I think I had seen almost every phase of this tremendous war; but I had yet a lot to learn of what the war means, and I began to learn afresh when we got to Ypres and later on had a dose of poison-gas.

None of the sights I had seen were to be compared with what we witnessed in the famous and beautiful old city, which the enemy had reduced to ruins. They had used shells of every sort, and I saw many evidences of the havoc and death that had been brought about on innocent people.

There was one house, on the left-hand side of the Museum, the home of a poor-class person, which was in ruins. I noticed this specially, as many of us did, because from the ruins there peeped some tiny feet—one of the most pitiful sights I ever saw. We made inquiry and found that a gas-shell had come, shattered the house, and killed and buried in the wreckage the father and mother and three children—a whole family of five, and it was the little feet of the smallest child that we saw amongst the debris. There was nothing for us to do but march on, and become more grimly determined than ever to fight and smash the enemy who had done these things. In cases like these we cannot stop to do anything; but there is the comfort of knowing that our fatigue parties will come up and give decent burial, and that the service will be conducted by a priest of the same faith as the slaughtered victims.

It was on April 26th that the gassing by the Germans began, and we had a repetition of the diabolical business on the 27th and 28th. We were quite taken aback by this development in the warfare, and as we were not prepared for it, not having even respirators, we suffered terribly. The men who got a full dose of the poison died an awful death, turning black in the face and foaming at the mouth, the buttons on our tunics turning rank green; while those who were only half-gassed reeled about like drunken men. I was lucky enough to be amongst the only partially gassed, but what with that and my ten months at the front I was pretty well worn out and was invalided home.

I have said that I have seen every form of fighting except one—the liquid fire. I have certainly been under every sort of fire but that, and I don't think I am saying anything unsoldierly in admitting that the fire I love best is the fire we left behind in dear old England.

CHAPTER 32

A Gunner at the Dardanelles

"Next I come to the Royal Artillery. By their constant vigilance, by their quick grasp of the key to every emergency, by their thundering good shooting, by hundreds of deeds of daring, they have earned the unstinted admiration of all their comrade services." That is the tribute which General Sir Ian Hamilton paid to the gunners in his despatch describing the operations in the Gallipoli Peninsula—a document which is the story of a noble failure. Little has been told of the doings of the artillery, but we can realise what they did from this narrative of Gunner John Evans, 92nd Battery, Royal Field Artillery, who was included in the vast number of soldiers who were invalided home through sickness.

I was in India with my battery when the war broke out. I had been in the country for seven years, and much as I liked it—I thoroughly enjoyed my soldiering there—I wanted to be off to the front. But I was kept in India for six months, training men to fight the Germans, and so doing my bit in that way. Then I came to England, with my battery and after that very pleasant change I was off to the Dardanelles, and went right into a fair hell of fighting. You can imagine a lot as a soldier, but no flight of fancy would ever have made you picture in your mind the things that actually happened. It is all over now, and some of us in hospital have time to think of the brave fellows who are resting in the Peninsula. They could not do what they were set to do, because that was beyond the power of ordinary man; but they did more, I think, than any other troops in the world could have done. To any man who knows what the country and climate are like, and who saw the difficulties and endured the awful discomforts, it seems that almost miracles were performed; and of all the wonderful things none was more wonderful than the withdrawal from Gallipoli.

We went straight into the business. There was no beating about the bush over the job. We got there, to the famous Lancashire Landing at W Beach, and my battery was the first to land on Turkish soil. Looking back on the campaign makes you wonder that we ever got either in or out of Gallipoli.

When our transport got near enough for us to begin our landing operations we were treated to a fine view of the desperate fighting that was going on, to say nothing of being under fire ourselves from the Turkish guns, a proper preparation for the regular hell of fire that we were under when we actually landed ourselves.

The Turks had opened fire on our transport from the Asiatic side as well as the European side, and what was happening to our own ship was happening to a whole fleet of transports and all sorts of other ships. There were warships bombarding the enemy's position, and the din altogether was enough to stagger even a long-service gunner who thought he knew what noise meant.

This happened about half past ten in the morning. At that time the Lancashire Fusiliers were making their magnificent attempt to land, and I shall never forget their pluck and the way they stuck to their deadly job. They were being conveyed ashore in lighters, and the Turks—we could distinctly see them over the edge of the cliff, not a hundred yards from the foreshore—were pouring in a terrible fire at close range. Shells, too, were dropping from the batteries at Achi Baba, miles in the rear, with wonderful precision.

The fusiliers' lighters could not get close to the beach owing to the barbed wire entanglements which had been fixed in the water, so the men were ordered to get out and wade ashore. This they began to do—and it was one of the most awful jobs that a landing party ever undertook.

I could see them quite well from our transport. Without a moment's hesitation the Lancashires clambered over the sides of the lighters and into the water they went, struggling to get ashore. It is hard enough to force your way through water at any time; put to that difficulty a heavy kit and rifle and ammunition, throw diabolical barbed wire in, and you will understand to some extent what it all meant.

As these brave fellows threw themselves overboard dozens of them were shot; a lot more were caught by the barbed wire, and as they were held helplessly, with flesh and clothing torn in their frantic efforts to get free, they were killed or wounded by the Turkish fire.

"W" BEACH, SHOWING CAPE HELLAS

It seemed impossible for any of the fusiliers to survive and get ashore, yet many forced their way through everything and landed on the beach, where they at once formed up roughly, and then without the slightest hesitation they charged up the face of the cliff, which looked to me almost as hard to scale as the side of a house.

As they scrambled up the cliff they were met by a more murderous fire than ever from rifles and machineguns, and numbers were killed or wounded. It seemed to me that for every man who reached the top at least four were killed or maimed. I could see the bodies rolling down the cliff-side on to the beach.

It was only a little band of Lancashire Fusiliers that managed to scramble and rush to the top of that terrific cliff—a few hundreds or so. They must have been exhausted; but their blood was fairly up, and with fixed bayonets they charged with such fury and success that the Turks were fairly taken aback, and I could see them giving way before our boys' cold steel.

Some of the Turks were throwing up their arms, and I could hear their shrill appeals for mercy; but the Fusiliers hadn't too much time to listen after the awful experience they had just gone through.

After they had been driven off the Turks made a counter-attack, and the Fusiliers, being a mere handful, were forced back to the very edge of the cliff and seemed in peril of going down it; but even then they re-formed and again rushed on the Turks with the bayonet and scattered them. Back again the Lancashires were driven, only to recover in the most amazing way and charge with the bayonet for the third time. And this seemed to settle the Turks, who cleared off.

While this thrilling fighting was going on, a sight that can never be forgotten by those who saw it, our brigade was getting ready to disembark. The infantry had had a hard enough business to get ashore; but ours was naturally a lot worse, for we had to tackle our guns and horses, as well as look after ourselves.

There were lighters alongside the transport, and into each of these we got two guns and eight horses, not easy work at any time, but hard now, with such a rush on and shells dropping all around us. Some of the explosions caused havoc amongst the horses, and several shells dropped near our lighter; but I am thankful to say that they were not near enough to do us much damage.

We were towed as near to the shore as we could get, and then we began the uncommonly hard and long job of getting the guns and horses ashore. The lighters were bobbing up and down and "ranging," owing to the run of the sea, and this unsteadiness made it very difficult to get the guns and horses overboard; but every officer and man worked with a will, and we did it. We got them out of the lighter and on to a strange kind of roadway that had been made in the water by putting sandbags tightly down. These sandbags "gave" a fair lot, of course, but we could not have done anything without them, for the wheels would have sunk too deeply in the wet soft sand.

When a gun was ready, from ten to sixteen horses were harnessed to it, and it took these and forty men on the drag-ropes to get one gun over the sandbag road on to the beach. We did our best, we strained every nerve, we were experts at the work, yet it was evening before the battery was ready for action. By that time we had got the guns on the level at the top of the cliff, about forty yards from the edge, after tremendous efforts by horses and men. I never saw such man-handling, even in India.

We had luck in the weather, for a heavy storm came on and the rain fell in blinding sheets. This, with the darkness, when it came, enabled us to take up our position without the Turks knowing of the fact.

Of course, while all this work of ours was going on the infantry were screening us in front. A constant and confused sort of fighting was taking place, and our men were mixed up with the enemy in furious hand-to-hand scraps. It was a regular bedlam, and so that nothing should be left in the way of trouble we were soaked to the skin. But we were so absorbed in the fighting, and so keen to get to work ourselves, that we did not give a thought to the drenching. We longed to get into action, but were kept back by the mixing up of our own men with the Turks, which made it impossible for us to open fire, because we should have killed as many of our own men as Turks.

We stood by till we knew that our infantry had driven the Turks well back, and then it was that the enemy got one of the biggest shocks of the day, for we simply let go at him with shrapnel at point-blank range. So well had we been handled by our officers that the first hint the Turks had of our presence was when we opened fire, and then the muzzles of our guns were almost in amongst them.

During the first few minutes of that tremendous excitement we did not bother much about the gun drill-book—I, for instance, was loading, setting fuses, ranging and doing any other work that came to hand. Despite this there was nothing whatever to grumble about in the way the guns were being served.

In the darkness we could not see what mischief we were doing, but we knew perfectly well that it must be enormous, because of the rapidity of our fire and the goodness of our shells; and when the daylight came we had proof, for ahead of us were piles of Turkish corpses, men who had been killed by our shrapnel.

We went on firing till the Turks had been driven back in complete disorder. We kept the game up throughout the day, but the darkness prevented us from following the enemy's movements.

We, of course, had no observation-posts at that time, as there were no trenches available for the observation officers to get to know the results of our fire.

After this promising start things were fairly quiet till the small hours of the next morning, when the enemy counter-attacked with great fury. The Turks are rare good fighters, they knew the country, and they had German officers driving them on in the rear, brutes who shot them down without mercy time after time, as I saw with my own eyes.

There were some native troops on our right front, and these were so hard pressed that they were forced to give way.

A staff officer who was at hand realised instantly the serious state of the situation, as the line was broken, and he called on some of the gunners in our brigade to fill the gap.

About fifty of our men fell out at once. There were hundreds of rifles with fixed bayonets lying on the ground around us, and grabbing what they wanted of these, our men rushed up and joined in the fray, filling the gap and making good the broken line before the Turks could understand what was happening.

It was a smart little affair, and the enemy was driven back and had to scuttle for shelter to his trenches, where he was left for the time being, for our troops were utterly exhausted and a rest was necessary.

We were thankful for a bit of a break. It was not for long, but we took things fairly easily till just before midday, when another advance was ordered against Seddul Bahr, a village of great tactical importance some hundreds of yards away, on our right front.

Our brigade was ordered to get ready for action.

By this time we were better off than we had been, for we had established the necessary observation-posts, and so we were ready for anything that might happen.

At noon the order came to open fire, and we fairly rained shells into the village—hundreds of rounds of shrapnel—to help the infantry in their advance.

The Turks were just as ready as we were, and they started a bombardment both from Achi Baba and the Turkish forts on the Asiatic side.

Some of these shells were proper "duds," and they made us laugh. It was not necessary to be told that they were made in Germany, for they dropped harmlessly into the ground, without exploding; but of course there were lots that did burst and do mischief. Many of these dropped on to the beach down below, killing mules and causing losses amongst transport drivers and the men of the Army Service Corps. Owing to the luck of war we had not many casualties in our own battery, and the losses were nothing like what you would have expected from such a lot of firing from the Turkish guns.

But we had some sad losses, all the same.

Our major was amongst the few who were killed that afternoon. He was in an observation-trench ahead, and was struck by a piece of shell which burst just near him. The news soon spread that he had been mortally wounded. He was most popular with the men, and as soon as they heard what had happened both officers and men rushed out to his post, to do what they could for him. But you can't do much for a dying man.

The major did not last long. His last words were, "Good luck, boys. Tell my wife I died happy."

There wasn't a dry eye amongst the men who laid him to his last rest.

They say that misfortunes never come alone, and it was all too true of us that day, for in the evening the colonel and the adjutant were done to death through German treachery.

We heard, but not till later, that a German came along a piece of enemy trench, close to the observation-post where the two officers were.

The German shouted, in quite good English, "All officers this way!"

The colonel and the adjutant, who did not suspect anything, got out on to the parapet of the trench, and instantly a hand grenade was thrown from an enemy trench quite close at hand. It exploded and killed both of them.

That's the sort of dirty trick which the Germans know so well how to play. They have a born gift for it—and that reminds me that the Germans who were with the Turkish forces were just as dirty and brutal in their methods as they are, by all accounts, on the Western front.

Looking through a pair of field-glasses, I have seen German officers during an attack by the Turks follow them with revolvers in hand—your German officer doesn't lead, he drives, having a precious regard for his carcase, and no earthly sense of honour—and I have seen them shoot Turkish soldiers who have fallen because they have been shot in the leg or have stooped to pick up a rifle which had been dropped. The German would be about a hundred yards in the rear, and would run up and deliberately shoot the prostrate man. I am talking now not from hearsay, but of what I have seen with my own eyes, and it does not help you to love the Germans.

I once saw a German prisoner, a fair specimen of the Prussian bully—he was a lieutenant—knock down a British sentry who had told him not to smoke in a part of the line where lights were prohibited. It was lucky for the bully that a British captain came along at the moment, or the fellow would have got the full force of the sentry's bayonet.

I heard Turkish prisoners say that the German officers treated the Turks with contempt, and it was a marvel that the Turks had not risen and slaughtered their so-called benefactors wholesale.

While on this point, I would like to say that as a fighter the Turk is a gentleman. We would go for them hammer and tongs in the ordinary way of scrapping; but ten minutes after it was over we would gladly shake hands with them—but we wouldn't do it with the Germans.

The dirty trickery that killed our colonel and our adjutant made our brigade swear that they would never spare the Germans when they met them in the way of fighting.

It was on the third day from the landing that we began the great advance which was meant to sweep the Turks away from the Peninsula, but which failed through lack of men and ammunition.

On that day we moved our guns forward about three hundred yards, and took up a fresh position from which we could bombard the enemy with great advantage.

We were in that place for a fortnight, and during that time the infantry had many a desperate shot at Achi Baba, which was the Turkish stronghold. There were many attacks and counter-attacks, without much apparent advantage to either side; but matters favoured the Turks, who had been strongly reinforced and had prepared very fine defensive positions.

While we were here our brigade lost a fair number of men; but of course the infantry suffered far more.

I am proud to say that our battery was the nearest to the Turks, and was constantly in action.

One night we had a report that the enemy was going to attack us in great force, and on the strength of the report we had to retire to a safer position. We withdrew, not without a lot of grousing among the boys, and when we reached our new point we were heavily bombarded; but no infantry attack followed, as we had been led to expect.

There was a good deal more grousing next morning when we moved forward again, because the Turks began to shell us heavily as we went along the road. This showed how well informed they were as to our movements even since the previous evening; but luckily our losses amounted to only two or three horses.

The next day the great retirement of the British forces began, and the whole of our infantry fell back about two miles to a point which we had nicknamed Clapham Junction, because the two main roads in the Peninsula join there. The artillery did not retire, being supported on the right and in the rear by French troops and the heavy guns.

Everybody knows now that if there had been enough men and ammunition our infantry, instead of retiring, would have taken Achi Baba and driven the Turks out of the Peninsula. Let us hope that if we did not manage to do that, our tremendous losses were not in vain, and helped to spoil any plans for marching on Egypt and India.

Early in June we started business again with the Turks, and that was when the great Battle of Krithia took place. This fight lasted two days, but we did not make much headway, as the enemy had got big reinforcements and had prepared a defensive position of enormous strength.

I had several narrow escapes from death during that great fight.

During a lull I was standing behind a bank with two or three other men, watching the enemy's artillery shelling a water-cart some distance away. The cart was going along a road, and we were wondering whether it would get clear or be blown up. While I was doing that, a shell burst right over us, making a horrible noise and peppering the air with pieces of shrapnel. I ducked my head instinctively, and so kept it on my shoulders. It was lucky for me that I did this, or I should have been killed, because the shell burst very low, so low that I got several shrapnel bullets through the back of my helmet, and the man nearest to me was seriously wounded by flying bits of metal. The third man received a good shaking up, but was otherwise unhurt.

A day or two later I had an even narrower shave with death—one of those extraordinary bits of luck that are so common in a war like this, that you take them almost as a matter of course.

I wanted to be as comfortable as possible, and so I had started to make a dugout for myself. I was under fire, but I did not pay much attention to that. I soon found that the ground I was working on was in a bad and insanitary state, so I gave up the job, and took myself off and began to try my luck at a place about fifty yards away.

I had just got to work on the new pitch when a huge high explosive shell dropped plump on the ground where I had been digging. It burst with tremendous force, and I was pelted with flying clods of earth and got a proper good shaking; but beyond that I was not hurt. But my first pitch was simply shattered, and if I had not cleared out I should have been blown to fragments, as I have seen many a fine chap blown in Gallipoli.

One of the very worst of my experiences was one day when I went to visit a chum who was on duty at the beach. I called at his dugout, just as you might call for a chap at his home, and out he came, smiling, walking up to me to shake hands.

Just at that moment a shell of the enemy dropped short.

I was struck dumb with the shock. When I regained myself I looked for my chum, and a terrible sight met my gaze, for there he lay in little pieces.

I felt right cut up, as I had soldiered with him for years in India, and I was going to visit his home if we had the luck to get through together. So you see we were so near but yet so far in a few seconds, and I am one of the lucky ones to be here to tell the tale. Out of the whole of the officers and men who came from India in my splendid battery, you could almost count those who are left on the fingers of your hands. Fighting and disease have taken nearly all of them.

More than once I was nearly "outed" by snipers; but I managed to keep a whole skin. It must be said in all fairness that the Turkish snipers were both plucky and resourceful—snipers were brought in who were found actually in our own lines; and once I was astonished to see a young and pretty Turkish girl brought in as a prisoner. She was a sniper, and had been hanging about our lines for a fortnight. There was no doubt that she was responsible for the death of several good men. We were greatly interested in this young lady, who was sent off to Tenedos.

These Turkish marksmen took every risk like good sportsmen, and we made their acquaintance right at the start, for when we were carrying out our desperate landing snipers were actually potting us from the beach, where they were covered with sand, so that it was almost impossible to see them. After that we got used to see snipers brought in who had painted themselves green, to match the trees and foliage, and others had decked themselves out with branches. It was funny to see some of the beggars, and as they had played a straight game we could not bear them any ill will. It was the Germans who did the dirty tricks.

Now for a few words on how I left the Dardanelles.

It was about July, when dysentery was at its worst, and quite half my battery were sick with it, all at the same time. It came to my turn to get it, and I was very bad for about three weeks. At last I could stand it no longer, for I could not work without suffering awful pain—it was like two pieces of sandpaper rubbing together in one's inside, with much vomiting; so I was forced to report sick to our doctor, who was a gentleman and a brave man. He was very kind to me, and did all in his power for my benefit. But it was no good. I had to go to hospital. I thought this would be at a place a few miles away, and I was glad at the prospect of being out of the firing, which was awful to a degree, and to get some quietness; but I found myself at a beach hospital, which was composed of tents and was always under fire. Several shells dropped in on us, causing much damage and loss in life and material. So I was pleased enough when I knew that I was to go on board a hospital ship; gladder still when I knew that I was being carried to a place which was a little safer than Gallipoli, namely, dear old England. There was no room for us at two ports on the way home; but I didn't mind that. England was quite good enough for me.

We had a fine though sad voyage. It did one good to see the smiles on the faces of the wounded. Though they were in great pain, they were cheered with the thought that they were leaving a hell on earth for a turn in heaven.

That was the bright side of the case; the dark side was that our engines were continually stopped while one of our dear comrades was committed to the deep, where he could get the rest which he had so hardly won—but it was a godsend after what they had suffered.

I can assure the friends of those who are gone, that they were comforted in their last moments by the chaplain and nurses, and were given proper Christian burial as soldiers who had fought the good fight.

The brave nurses were like mothers with young children, and deserve the highest praise for what they did for us.

Chapter 33

The "Flood"

The following extract from a letter written by Corporal Guy Silk, 2nd Battalion Royal Fusiliers, has been very kindly placed at my disposal. It describes a phase of life in Gallipoli of which little or nothing has been published—the storms and floods with which our troops had to contend in the now abandoned operations.

I have been wondering how you are getting on, and if you have been worrying over the absence of letters. There has only been one chance of sending a letter, and then I sent a card in an envelope to let you know that I was well. We have been through some terrible experiences since I last sent a proper letter, on November 25th.

On the 26th we had one more of those terrible storms, and suddenly, as I was mopping some water from the dugout floor, a "tidal wave" burst in, and I just had time to seize the Company Roll, my diary and letters, Horlick's Malted Milk, and my rifle and bandolier. Then I climbed out of the dugout, on to the parapet! The first, or rather second time I had done so (the first was to pick some tomatoes).

By this time the trenches were completely flooded, and the whole valley was covered with water ankle-deep. As the lightning flashed I saw a group of fellows near me, and they joined me on my mound. All around were similar groups. We laughed and pretended to be enjoying it, so as to keep our spirits up.

The water rose and rose, and when it was knee-deep we started off for a piece of higher ground we saw in the distance. We were in to the waist, and the current was tremendous. We settled down on this mound—the first one we saw proved to be just a clump of weed tops. The regimental sergeant-major joined us, but was nearly unconscious, and suffering with ague. I laid him on my lap, and there we stayed until daylight.

It was bitterly and painfully cold, and a curious sight too, when we first saw the huge mass of water and groups of wet men. I took the S.-M. on to headquarters, and there he was undressed and rubbed and wrapped in some dry blankets. Then our company sergeant-major was brought down, quite delirious, and Jackson and I took him on to the clearing-station.

It was fine to get on to higher ground out of the water. I reckon this walking saved me. I went back to the company, and found the water had gone from the ground in the valley, and the chaps were lying in hastily constructed breastworks behind the rear parapet.

The trenches were like canals, and were acting as drains. The Turks shelled a lot. This was on Saturday. In the evening and early morning of Sunday it snowed and froze, and on Sunday at daybreak we were ordered to find our way to the brigade "dump." At about mid-day we got some food and dry clothes. It was grand, after two nights and a day of sodden and frozen things.

We had a roll-call on Monday, and we were 63—on the Friday afternoon we were 600 odd. I was made corporal—Baldion said I must be, so as to "help to hold the fellows together," and for a few days was acting company S.-M.!

We expected to go to Alexandria, but had to stay to drain the trenches. A big draft joined us, and did most of the work, our feet were too sore. (I spent one whole day rubbing feet—a savoury job, since baths are unheard of.)

On the Thursday after the "Flood "(everything dates from the "Flood" now) we went to find equipment, and the ground was covered with bodies.

We are back on the Achi Baba end now, but have not quite given up hopes of a rest, at least for the "survivors." I am orderly-room corporal now. Nearly all of us are employed at headquarters, so except for shells I am pretty safe, as we don't have to make advances.

We have had no mail since before the "Flood," but hope to get one soon. Please tell Aunt —— I received and enjoyed her parcel (some was lost, buried when the trench fell in), and explain why I haven't answered to thank her for it. Let everyone know I am still alive in spite of the long silence. We heard tonight that no mail is leaving for three weeks from tomorrow. The sketch-book has gone. I found it, but it was "done."

We had a busy time when the "Flood" had abated, and I was continually taking my section out, digging up rifles and equipment, and we were all able to make up our losses in the way of shaving apparatus, knives and forks, etc. It was hard work, as the trench bottoms are knee-deep in mud. We wore waders.

CHAPTER 34

The Belgians' Fight With German Hosts

It is hard, in language, to express the thoughts that come to one in contemplating the achievements of the Belgian Army at the outset of the war. Undoubtedly the coming sure defeat of Germany is largely due to the valiant stand which was made when the would-be all-world conquerors overran and ravaged a little, beautiful and inoffensive neutral state. The knell of Prussian doom was sounded first on Belgium's battlefields. It was believed that at the utmost Belgians could only make a pretence of fighting; but the little army of our brave ally defied and held at bay the Germans in an almost incredible manner. What happened in those fateful days, which seem so far and yet in reality are so near is told by Soldat Francois Rombouts, of the 8th Regiment of the Line, Belgian Army.

I was in the Belgian Army before the war broke out. I was a conscript of the 1913 class, and went to my regiment from the sea. For five years I had been crossing the Atlantic in liners sailing from Antwerp—and how beautiful it was in the summer-time on the blue sea, with the hot sun shining; and how hard and cold in the winter, peering into the grey gales from the crow's-nest! I loved the sea, and I loved my regiment, especially when I had my rifle in my hands and with my keen sea eyes I could make out the Germans and use them as targets. I do not know how many I shot—I hope and believe a big number—because when they fall it may not be always to your own bullet. But I saw very many of them fall before I was wounded and had to lie in bed for sixteen weeks, helpless, like a child.

Look at my right arm. Here, on the inside, a bullet went in. If it had been an ordinary bullet, like the one you show me—you say the cartridge was given to you by a British Guardsman who was at Landrecies and carried it there with him?—it would have gone through the arm and made only a little hole, which would soon have become well; but the bullet was explosive. See, here at the entrance is the small scar; but at the outside of the arm there is this long and ragged blue mark, because the bullet that struck me was what you call a dum-dum. Feel the wound, it does not hurt me now. That hardness is bone. It was carried away from the flesh and broken, and there it has set and will remain. For many weeks my hand was like this—a bunch, you call it?—because I could not open it out. I was hurt in other ways also by German fire; but I am young—only twenty-two years—and very strong, and I may yet again go back to the Belgian Army. If I do, and we get into Germany—as we shall—for every Belgian life that has been taken we shall take one German, and more; for every Belgian home that has been destroyed we shall burn or destroy one, and more, and for all the innocent women and little children and helpless old men that have been murdered we shall make them pay in German soldiers and in German soil.

I have my mother and sisters still in Belgium, where the Germans are; and I do not know the truth of them. I pray that they are well; but if I learn that they have come to harm I will never rest until I have had my revenge in Germany, All Belgians will tell you the same as that. How can it be otherwise when they have seen what I have seen—their country run over and beaten down and taken by these Germans?

How well I remember that night in Antwerp when the war broke out! It was eleven o'clock and the church bells were ringing.

That was the sound of war.

Several days we had been out of barracks, enjoying ourselves; but this night they would not allow us to go out.

My mother and sisters and brothers came, crying. They said, "The Germans will kill you!"

But I said, "Shut up! It will not be so. Besides, I am a single man, and so I do not care. It is not as if I had a wife and children." So they were comforted, and I made myself happy by myself.

We were singing and whistling and dancing all night in barracks; then in the early morning we marched to Brussels, and after being there two days we were ordered to take the train to go to Liège, to keep the Germans back, and as we went along the people shouted,

Devastation in Belgium: Ruins in the floods of Yser

"Good Belgians! Good Belgians!"

We went by train to Liège, fifty miles away. We had got the orders we were waiting for in the evening—the orders to stop the Germans. If we could not stop them there, we were told, they would get through. And how true it proved!

We were in the train all night, singing and whistling, and all what we can do in a train to make soldiers happy.

The regiment that had gone before my own regiment was fighting. We had gone as reinforcements, and when we got to Liège at four o'clock on that August morning and got out of the train, fighting was going on.

I saw the Germans at once—we went straight into the street from the train and fought them.

We were excited, yes, but not afraid. They had come into our little country, where they had no right to be, and our only wish was to drive them away.

We rushed from the train with our loaded rifles. I did not know Liège. It was all strange to me; but all streets are much the same, and it was enough that the Germans were in them and must be driven out.

We fired on them, and they retired; but only a little way and for a little while, because there were so many of them. And in the evening they came back.

We fought them in the streets when they came, and we rushed into the houses and shot them from the windows and doorways.

Even now, so soon, I learned the truth of what I had said to my weeping mother in the barracks at Antwerp. She said, "The Germans will kill you!" and I told her, "No. I am not afraid of anything. The Germans cannot kill me!" And they did not—not then, and not later, though I was shot in the right arm with an explosive bullet and afterwards in the right foot, of which I will tell you.

I do not know whether I killed any Germans at Liège, but I hope I did. You could see them falling over, but could not say who killed them.

We hated them because they had come into Belgium.

We were fighting all night, the rifles crackling because of the constant firing of the magazines.

We chased the Germans into the fields outside Liège. We got at stragglers with the bayonet, and we brought fifteen prisoners in. How amusing it was when we caught them! They said, "Oh, my Belgian brother!" We left them with contempt, and looked after other ones.

Then, when we had got them, they were sent to the station and so to Antwerp.

The Germans came on in such strength that we could not stop them; but in spite of all their guns and regiments we held Liège for twenty-four days. We had only 300,000 Belgians in our army, and the Germans had about a million; but I would not run away from fifteen Germans myself. The Belgians called the Germans "swine," and said, "we will be giving the Germans one presently!"

And we gave them one.

We went into the trenches, and the Germans were bombarding us and smashing the place up. We did as much as we could to keep them back.

Houses were smashed and everybody seemed to be killed or wounded. The shells came on top of you and spread out like an umbrella. A lot of my friends were killed and fell over in the trenches.

When we were in the trenches a man near me was not happy, because he was married and his thoughts were with his wife and children and home; but when we were going on firing I said, "Look! A German has fallen over again!" And then he was happy. He was married and I was single, and that made the difference.

If you had your friend in the trenches you did your best for him, because you liked to take your friend home again; but many friends were left in the trenches.

Did I see General Leman, the defender and hero of Liège? Oh, yes. General Leman was a good man. He came round and saw the soldiers and talked to us and made us happy.

I do not know how many we lost in Liège. We had a lot wounded and killed and missing; but we only knew this from the newspapers.

We were on duty in the trenches for twenty-four hours, then we were relieved. At the end of the twenty-four days for which we held Liège we went to Anden, ten miles away. We retired in the daytime, without any fighting, and were in Anden about fifteen days. We never saw the Germans there.

And now I became a motorcyclist, which gave me many adventures and exciting journeys. I was with a friend, a motorcyclist also, and we were reconnoitring near Anden. We saw a big house, a *château*, standing in its own grounds, with trees. They are beautiful and peaceful houses, and you saw many of them in Belgium before the war.

"There are some Germans here!" my friend said. We looked and listened, and what he said was true. There were Germans in the *châ-*

teau, but how many in number we did not know.

We hurried away to our officer and told him, and he sent three companies of soldiers to attack the *château*. How well they marched up, and how from behind the trees and other points of shelter they fired upon that big house in the trees, with the Germans making themselves happy in it.

I and my friend had acted as guides to the companies, and now we saw the Belgian soldiers firing upon the *château*, and the surprised Germans rushing to the windows and doors and behind the trees to fire back.

It was a furious fight, and it lasted for two hours. Then we got the house—the Germans ran away, and we took it and occupied it. But next day the Germans came back in stronger numbers and retook the *château*; and the day after that we once more got the house and killed all the Germans. We knew that we could not hold it long, because we had not enough soldiers, and when we had been at the *château* for about four hours, and the Germans came up stronger than ever, we had to leave, We had not had many losses—two or three men killed. One was shot through the heart, and another was mortally wounded and lived a few hours.

There is a river at Anden, and when we retired we had to cross a bridge. When we had crossed the bridge we blew it up, so that the Germans should be delayed in pursuing us. Then, when we were retiring, and had seen the bridge destroyed, we were made unhappy because we saw that on the other side of the water, which was now the German side, there was a company of Belgian infantry, which could not cross.

It was terrible and sad. What was to be done? How were our comrades to be saved, to come to us, to be kept from capture or killing by the Germans?

The commander of the company was quick to think and act. He knew that at Namur there were some boats, three or four of them. He ordered a cyclist to go and have the boats sent to Anden, so that the men could cross. And the cyclist went. It seemed so long before the boats came; but they appeared at last, and the soldiers got into them, crowding five and six in one small boat, and then being rowed over the river. All the time the Germans were firing on the company from the big hills which are there; but we could not fire back, and all we could do was to watch our comrades on the other side of the river, walking about and eagerly waiting for the boats. They tumbled into the boats and came across the river to us, and we shouted and laughed when they were near enough for us to get at them, and to help them to jump on to the bank and to say defiance to the German bullets.

There is a railway tunnel at Anden, and we were ordered to go to it. We went. There is a big wood at the tunnel, and from this wood there came a party of *Uhlans*, fifteen of them, commanded by a lieutenant.

Three or four Belgians fired on the cavalry, who were taken by surprise. The lieutenant was shot in the side, next his heart, and he fell from his horse. The soldiers went up to him to make him prisoner of war, but he did not want to be taken, and he fired on them with his revolver. So it was necessary for them to shoot him, and they did.

When he was killed four soldiers carried him on two rifles, one under his back and one under his legs, to the major of the Belgian battalion, who ordered that he should be buried. So a grave was dug and the lieutenant was buried, and planks were put over him, and he was left there to his rest, and we attended to the German wounded.

After what happened by the railway tunnel we were ordered to make trenches; but the Germans came up and forced us to retire to Namur, an old city and fortress.

We saw many refugees who were flying from the Germans, who had come and stolen their land and plundered it and overrun it. There were old men and women and children, and it was pitiful to see them; yet it made us fiercer in our fighting with the Germans.

Near Anden I saw a column of refugees, a little line of about thirty-five people, and at the head of them was a man dressed like a tourist, with a soft hat, breeches and leggings. He was looking under trees and all around him, as if taking care of the refugees.

Then, when we had seen this tourist, a boy came up to me on a bicycle, and said, "There is a German spy."

I called my corporal, and instantly we had soldiers searching in the trees and fields and everywhere; but we did not see another trace of the "tourist," who was the German spy, though we did not suspect it when we saw him leading the refugees like a shepherd leads his flock.

That was sad, to miss him so; but another spy I got at Namur. I saw a man standing amongst the trees, dressed in civilian clothes. He was about fifty-nine years old and had long whiskers, such as you see on many tourists.

I went up to him as he was standing by a tree. I was alert, for I was reconnoitring and expected things to take place.

Before he could understand me and be ready to explain, I rushed at him and had him by the arms and held them to his back. My comrades came up and sent him with his long whiskers to the regiment. I do not know what happened to him. I hope they shot him.

I have here in my pocket an electric lamp with a bull's eye. It gives a fine strong light. No, this is not what I carried in Belgium, because I exchanged mine with an Englishman for his; but it is just the same. And with these pocket electric lamps we used to search the houses for Germans that were hiding from us. We would find them in dark corners and cellars, and when the light was snapped on them they would throw up their hands and cry, "Oh, my Belgian brothers!"

Then we would say, "Come out of it, and we will give you Belgian brothers!" But we always made them prisoners, and did not kill them. It was "Belgian brothers!" when death was on them, but in the trenches they called us "Belgian swine" and "little devils." We gave them "swine" presently.

We had been fighting much and had been in the trenches many days, so that we were very tired, and thankful to get three or four days' rest in Namur. Then, after that blessed change, we went into the firing again, which was shrapnel, and terrible.

Namur was a very strong place and was not expected to fall; but the Germans had made long preparations for the war, and were bombarding with enormous guns—I saw German guns that took twenty-two horses to draw them.

At Namur we lost a lot of men, because of the heavy gun-fire. All the wounded soldiers and prisoners of war were there; but the Germans did not care about that—they fired on the hospital and smashed it up. When we lost Antwerp the prisoners of war were taken away; but when we lost Belgium we could not keep the prisoners, and the Germans got them back again.

After the Battle of Namur the regiment was smashed up, like many others. Every man was looking after himself and trying to find his own regiment, which was not easy.

Here is a photograph of Namur, showing the bridge which crosses the river. I was the last man to cross the bridge when we were forced to leave Namur; and for two nights I was in one of these old houses which you can see here in the picture. When I was over the bridge I met a couple of men of my company, and we watched some firing in the distance and felt happy, because we knew that it was the firing of

French soldiers, who were just outside Namur.

We were stragglers, and I and a corporal joined the Frenchmen. It was now that many Belgians who were caught by the Germans were shot—yes, in threes and fours Belgians were shot by Germans.

There are good Germans and bad Germans; but more bad Germans than good ones.

We crossed the frontier and got into France, and rested ourselves. I found some of my old friends again, but not all, because a lot had been lost.

In France we made up the regiment again. I had got to Le Havre, and from there I went to Ostende. We had two days in Ostende, then I went back to my dear Antwerp, which was before the Germans got there. From Antwerp I went to Conte, where we had a fortnight's rest, after which we went to Malines. There was not much fighting at Malines, but there had been a lot before we got there, and the place had been destroyed. At that time the Germans were holding the town, but we drove them out. Afterwards we lost it, because they came in heavy numbers, and we could not stop the big guns.

We went up to Conte again about four o'clock in the morning, and later we advanced to Termonde, about twenty-five miles from Antwerp. Our 1st battalion had been ordered to attack Termonde, and the 2nd was stopping outside for reserve.

We saw our 1st battalion go and assault the place; and then we saw it come back, and sad it was to see them, because those who returned were mostly wounded men in ambulances. There were many wounded, as the attack had lasted three hours and our comrades had had to cross the river under fire.

Then it was, when the wounded began to come back in the ambulances, that we were ordered to go in and push the Germans back. We had to go over some fields, and crossing them was like walking on rubber, because of the dead bodies. These bodies had been taken from the trenches, when it was no longer possible to have them there, and had been put in the fields. Sometimes they had been in the trenches three or four days, and we had to eat and drink and sleep with them there. And in the fields that felt like rubber, there were arms and legs and heads sticking out. Ah, yes, it was horrible indeed. And this was the war that the Germans had brought into our little country, which had done them no wrong whatever, and where they had no right to be. It will be the same for them when we get into Germany!

In Termonde it was fierce fighting all the time I was there, and that was for six days. And I tell you that we Belgians did fight; for when we went into Termonde, driving the Germans out, we saw the bodies of women and children and old men that they had massacred—and most of us were crying as we passed them. The Germans do what they like in wartime, and these were some of the things they liked.

When we saw the Germans at Termonde, after seeing those murdered women and children and old men, we rushed at them with the bayonet, burning to drive our steel into them.

We rushed up to them in our fury, and I drove my long bayonet at a German soldier. I struck at him blindly, but I do not know where I hit him, because at such a time you look after one German and then after another, so that you shall get many of them; but his own bayonet came at me and cut across my right fingers. You can see the scars here—but they are nothing.

It was hard and fierce work; but I was still well. I was tired and sleepy at the end, and was almost killed by bursting shrapnel. Pieces struck me, and one went through my right boot and between the toes. But that also was nothing.

The evening came, and it was just dark. That was October 1st. I had been in the trenches, and was lying down under some trees, resting. Firing was going on still, but we were indifferent to it, and I did not care until I was struck on the right arm by an explosive bullet, a dum-dum. I was lying there, bleeding, with my badly torn arm, for three-quarters of an hour; then some of my friends came and picked me up and gave me a drink and bandaged my arm. At nine o'clock a doctor came along and sent me to a church, which was being used as a hospital. There I spent the night, waiting for the morning, when I was to have an operation.

The morning came, and brought with it one of the strange adventures of a soldier in the war.

I was taken on a wheeled ambulance to a part of the church which was used as an operating-room, and there my torn arm was treated, without pain to me. A nun, who like her other sisters of mercy was a nurse, had the care of me, and she was wheeling me back to my bed.

There was the big entrance to the church near my bed, and as I was being wheeled I saw in that entrance many German soldiers, who were about to rush into the church and seize it.

Quick as thought my nurse wheeled me back, and rushed with me to a door at the back of the church, and out into the open air. She was quite calm, which was well for me, and she hurried me to an English motor ambulance, which was standing at the door and had one English soldier in.

The nun cried to the chauffeur, saying that the Germans were taking the church, and telling him to help her to push me into the ambulance.

The chauffeur, who was an Englishman, quickly and calmly obeyed, and he and the nun got me inside, on my stretcher; then the chauffeur jumped up into his seat, and the motor ambulance tore away and took me into Antwerp. I was in hospital in my native city two days, when the Germans bombarded the city. I was there during the whole of the bombardment; then when the Germans took Antwerp my mother took me out of hospital. There was much excitement and commotion, and it was not a happy thing to be wounded then; but an English ambulance came, and I was asked if I could speak English. I said "Yes."

"Do you want to go to Ostende?" the man asked, and again I said "Yes."

It was a time for haste. A few minutes more, and if I had not been able to speak English I should have been too late, for the train into which I was put by an English marine was the last to leave Antwerp before the Germans entered the city.

Again the Germans came to where I was, and so I had to leave Ostende. I went from there by train to France, and from France I came to England.

I still stop in England. It is a good country, and I feel safe here. It is strange to see beautiful cities not bombarded and smashed by the Germans, and not to see the worst of all—the murdered little children.

If the Germans were in this country it would be just the same, or worse.

I think much of my country, little but beautiful, as it was; but ruined now.

I am young. When I am old Belgium may be as it was before.

I have an eager wish, and to have it fulfilled would make me very happy indeed—and that is to see Belgian, English, and French soldiers march into Germany!

CHAPTER 35

A Blinded Prisoner of the Turks

This is a simple, unaffected story of the doings of a young British soldier in Gallipoli and his subsequent experiences as a prisoner of war with the Turks. It is told by Private David Melling, 1/8th Battalion Lancashire Fusiliers. He was a lad when he enlisted, his eyesight was destroyed by a bullet, he was captured on the battlefield by the Turks, and was the first British prisoner of war to be released from Constantinople. The narrator, when seen, was an inmate of the Blinded Soldiers' and Sailors' Hostel, Regent's Park, N.W., the wonderful institution which Mr. C. Arthur Pearson founded and controls with so much success in the interests of those whose affliction he understands so well.

I enlisted in the Lancashire Fusiliers in November 1914, when I was only seventeen years old, and in June 1915 I went to Gallipoli, where we landed in the night-time. A big ship had been run aground there—the *River Clyde*—and pontoon bridges had been made at the side of her, connecting with the shore. We left our transport and got into little steam trawlers, which were out at the Dardanelles as minesweepers and so on, and these took us to the pontoon bridges. We hurried over them, under fire, and having got ashore we went straight into a bivouac rest-camp. We spent five days in the camp, then we went into the support line of trenches, which is the second line, and after a week or two we went on fatigue.

We were in a Turkish communication-trench, digging it wider, and we came across all sorts of queer things. We dug a dead Turk up, a chap without a head, and near him we dug up one of our short Lee-Enfield rifles. He had equipment on, and when we looked into his pouches we found that he had some of our ammunition, besides his own. We supposed from the look of things that he had been knocked over by a shell and buried in the rubbish. We were throwing the earth out and making the trench deeper when we came across the Turk's head. One chap got it on a shovel and fired it over the top of the parapet. You got used to digging bodies up—it was nothing to strike one with your pick or shovel.

All this experience was good for us, and got us used to fighting before we were actually in it, because there was firing going on all the time, and preparations were being made for charging the Turks with the bayonet.

Things began to get very warm early in August. At about five o'clock on the afternoon of the 6th, which was a Friday, there was a heavy bombardment and a big advance on the left of the Peninsula—that was Suvla Bay. According to the arrangements we were to charge on the Saturday morning, two hours after the bombardment began. The bombardment was to have started at five o'clock; but somehow the Turks got to know about it, and our attack was postponed till ten o'clock. At that hour we were ready for our job.

I shall never forget that Saturday morning at Achi Baba. I had my sight then, and could watch all that was going on. We were on the ledge of our trench, waiting to spring over and rush at the Turks.

Our officer was standing by us, looking at the watch on his wrist—and a terrible strain it must have been.

"Two minutes to go!" he said. And we waited.

"One minute to go!" said the officer next time he spoke.

Then, at ten o'clock, "Over!" he shouted. That's all I remember of what he said. He may have said more, but I can't tell. "Over!" was the order, and over we went.

We all cheered, and then we went helter-skelter for the Turks with the bayonet.

They were said to be two hundred and fifty yards away, but it was a lot more than that—at any rate it seemed so. And the ground we had to rush over was terrible—rough and with a lot of vines about that twined round your feet and tripped you up. Some of our chaps were knocked flat in this way, some fell of exhaustion, and lots were killed or wounded. The best part of our lot were knocked out before we ever got near the Turks.

But when we reached the trench that we were going for we found that there were not many of the Turks left. Our gunners had settled them, so that the trench was full of dead Turks, some of them with their heads blown completely off.

Our task was simple enough. We had to go for one particular trench that was straight in front of us.

I can't give any special particulars about what happened, because it was all a sort of blur, but I remember a few things clearly, and it's these that I am telling of.

The trench was up a hillside, and when I got to it I saw that part of it had been blown up. I rushed at the opening, and fell into the trench. I was alone. I don't know whether I was the first man in the trench or not: but I do know that there were none of our chaps there—only myself and dead bodies.

I scrambled to my feet, and the first thing I noticed near me was a Turkish officer, wounded and unarmed.

There we were, the two of us, the Turk looking at me and me looking at him. I had my bayonet, and I could have settled him or taken him prisoner; but British soldiers don't touch unarmed men, and I was too busy to take him—and a man who is by himself doesn't as a rule make prisoners.

I was looking to see which way to go to get to our other chaps, and the Turkish officer, noticing this, motioned down the trench to the left to show me where they had gone.

I began to clear off to them, but in my eagerness and excitement I did not notice a wire which ran across the top of the parapet. Before I knew what was happening my rifle got fast in the wire at the bayonet-standard—that is, where the bayonet fixes on to the muzzle.

Then an extraordinary thing took place. My rifle was tilted over and the bayonet stuck in the back of a Turk who was huddled up in the bottom of the trench. The first I saw of him was when my bayonet struck him. I looked to see if he was dead, but he never moved. I don't know whether I killed him or not, but if he wasn't dead he was a good actor.

I had been about two minutes—it may have been longer—in getting my rifle clear of the wire, and all that time, for it seemed long, I was alone. When I pulled myself together and went on again in the trench I came face to face with a Turk who was coming from the opposite direction. He seemed to be mad, and made a lunge at me with his bayonet; but it was broken and no good to him. He saw that and turned to run away. As he did so I bayoneted him in the back, and he fell. I could have shot him, but my magazine was empty, for I had been firing a lot.

I passed the Turk and then I found our chaps. It seemed a good distance from where I got into the trench to where I found them—I know I had to go round one or two bends.

When we got together again—and it was a joy to be back with my chums—we were ordered to line the trench. I don't know who gave the order, but it wasn't an officer.

I was the end man of the line, and we were firing hard when a bullet came, and all I knew was that I could not see and that I was lying on the floor of the trench, with one of our chaps bandaging me—I don't know who it was.

I was left there while they went on firing.

I don't know how long I was lying there; but I was terribly thirsty, and drank two bottles of water—my own and one I took from a dead man near me. I could not see him, but I felt by groping about his equipment that he was a British chap.

There were not enough of our men to hold the trench, and they were forced to retire and leave me.

The Turks came up in the trench, and I heard them shouting something like "*Garrah! Garrah!*" though it may have been "*Allah! Allah!*"

They were fearfully excited, and I thought it was all up with me then. I never gave myself any hope.

The Turks were running about the trench, looking for our chaps. They ran over me, no doubt thinking I was dead. I was lying on my side, with my hands covering my head, holding the bandages to stop the blood from coming out. I had to do that, because it was only a field-dressing.

I knew then that I had lost my eyes.

I felt as if all the bones in my body were broken with the Turks running over me and stepping on me.

After some time had passed the Turks settled down a bit, not being so excited, and then they began to search the trench and examine the bodies and men in it. Seeing that I was not dead, they propped me up and began searching my pockets. They were talking away, but, of course, I could not understand them. They were not rough just then, but they were afterwards, when I was being led out. They took my pay-book and photographs and everything I had.

I stood up, and then the Turks took me to a communication-trench about ten yards away.

As I was passing them in the firing-line they hit out at me with their hands, trying boxing competitions on me. They dared not have done this if a Turkish officer had been about.

Two more fusiliers were being led away along with me. They had both been bayoneted, they told me, after they were captured.

I was taken to a place where there were Turkish doctors. One of them gave me a cup of tea. He could speak English, and he asked me how I was. I told him I was pretty bad. I was given a piece of dry bread, but I could not eat it, because my teeth were closed.

It was here that I met a New Zealander or an Australian, a gunner, who had been in the charge. He had no right to be in it, but you could not keep the Anzacs out of the scraps. He said that he and a pal were passing through the place when they saw what was going on. Each of them got hold of a rifle and bayonet and rushed into the charge. The pal was killed and the other man was taken prisoner.

From the doctors' place I was taken to a sort of dugout, which had some kind of grass in it that felt like heather. The two bayoneted chaps had been taken there as well, and I was very glad to have their company.

I was left in the dugout all night, with the other two fusiliers alongside of me. In the morning we were put into oxen carts, four wounded men in each. They were rough things without springs, and were slowly dragged over rough tracks—you could not call them roads—so that it was fair torture to us, bumping all the while.

At last we were stopped at a place and changed into another oxen cart, and taken farther on. We stopped again, and were given a drink out of a bucket—they must have thought we were horses. I suppose they must have been giving a mule a drink, and then it struck them that they might give us a turn. But bucket or no bucket it was a fine drink.

After that I went into a field hospital, and for the first time since I had been wounded I had my eyes properly attended to.

A Turkish doctor who could speak a little English said "Eyes!" then a word that sounded like "yolk." I suppose he meant that my eyes were gone; but I knew that before he did.

After I had been attended to I was put into a field hospital and fed three times a day. First of all we had a ration of bread, which had to last all day, and a drink of tea; about the middle of the day we were given some soup, which the chaps called "bill-posters' paste." It was awful stuff, and the chaps who were badly wounded in the body could not do with it, so they used to tipple their lot into my basin and I would get through it, as well as through my own. I could not eat bread or anything else, because my jaws were affected and my face was badly swollen—it is partly swollen still, but I could just manage to suck the "bill-posters' paste" through my teeth.

It was not until now that I really understood what had happened to me. A bullet had struck me on the left side of the forehead and gone clean through both eyes, just missing the brain, and out at the right side—a wonderful escape from instant death, as our own doctors told me afterwards.

We were given cigarettes in the field hospital—a packet of twenty on every one of the five days we were there; and those cigarettes were a real treat.

At the end of the five days we had another dose of oxen carts, and were jolted in them to the seashore, where we were put into a steamer. They told us in the field hospital that we were bound for Constantinople, and I was rather glad I was going there. I did not want to stop any longer under the everlasting shell fire.

When we went on board we got a loaf of bread and a drink of tea and a drink of water, and that was all we had for the three days we were in the ship. She was full, the place where I was put being crowded with Englishmen, though there was a Turk on a seat above me. I was lying on the floor under it.

It was a great relief to get to the end of the voyage and go ashore. I was taken off the boat, and as we went down the gangway chaps were handing out nice new pieces of bread, hot, and cups of tea. I was lucky, because I had my cup filled twice.

I was taken into a big hall—it seemed to be a sort of drill-hall—and was given another drink of tea and piece of bread. Then we were taken in open carriages, drawn by two horses, to different hospitals. I well remember that my carriage had rubber tyres—and that was very nice indeed after travelling in the oxen carts.

I was carried on a stretcher into a hospital near the quayside, and here I was turned into a sort of Turk, for I was served with a pair of Turkish trousers big enough to fit six of us. They tied round the waist and ankles. I had a shirt also given to me, a sort of big gown which was tied round the waist. We looked like Julius Caesar in them.

The Turks dressed my eyes and put me into a bed, and I was glad to get in, because I had been thrown about for ten days since I was wounded.

I was in this hospital for about three weeks, treated by Turkish ladies who were acting as nurses. A lady who was there was said to be an Egyptian princess, the late Khedive of Egypt's sister, and she could speak English. She asked me my age, parents' names, occupation and address at home, and said that next day she would write to my mother, to tell her how I was getting on; but when next day came I told her that a chap in my regiment had written home for me. She then told me a bit of joyful news, and that was that I was going to be sent home.

There was a German Bible-reader in the hospital. We called him Charlie, and I will say for him that he was like a brother to us. There are good and bad in every race, and this was one of the good Germans. He brought two Bibles in for chaps to read who could see.

At the end of the three weeks an order came for all prisoners to go into barracks, and I was taken off in a carriage. This time I suppose I looked a real Turk, for I had a *fez*, though I had my baggy trousers hidden by my khaki trousers, which I had put over them, the Turkish doctor having told me to do this to keep me warm. I scored there, because I don't think that the Turks meant me to walk off with the baggy breeches. But I kept them on all right, and I have them at home now, as a memento.

In these barracks we slept on a long platform, on a sort of thick matting, which was very verminous. At first we were fed pretty well, and then not so well, because the Turkish food is not fit for Englishmen, and they have only two meals a day. They gave us rice and meat, but only a very little piece of meat. The rice was cooked in olive oil, and it seemed good when we were hungry, though we did not care for it. We used to get a ration of bread every afternoon about four o'clock. When that time came our chaps, who were in good spirits, singing and whistling, used to kick up a row and shout, "*Hich, Hich!*" which was supposed to be Turkish, and meant hurry up with the bread.

It was the *sultan's* birthday while we were in barracks, but they did not give us anything extra on that account. The Turkish Christmas was celebrated in August, too, but we never heard anything about it.

The American Ambassador came and visited us and gave us forty *piastres* each, equal to six and eightpence. The ambassador used to come round to see that we were well treated, and we were always glad to see him. Through his efforts I got released, and was then sent into the American Hospital in Constantinople. I was there about a week, after which I was put in charge of two American sailors and sent to Dedeagatch, in Bulgaria, the place that has been bombarded lately. We stayed in a place called the Hotel London, supposed to be the best hotel in the town; but the sailors said it was nothing but an old shack.

We were paying for our food and so on, as the ambassador had supplied us with money for our fares and keep, and the two sailors looked after me all the time.

After two or three days' rest a train journey of a day took us to another town called Drama, which is in Greece; from there we went to Salonica, where I was handed over first to the American Consul and then to the British Consul, who passed me on to the military authorities. The British commander-in-chief asked me some questions about officers who were prisoners of war, and so on, and I told him what I could.

For a fortnight after that I was in a hospital ship in the bay, the *Grantully Castle*, happy and well looked after; then we went to Lemnos and on to Alexandria, where I had another spell in hospital—four days. Then it was really a case of homeward bound, for I was put on board the *Ghurka* on November 7, and we sailed for Southampton. On board the *Ghurka* we had concerts and a good time until the 19th, when we reached Southampton. I went to St. Mark's Military Hospital, Chelsea, then came to this wonderful place, St. Dunstan's Hostel, which Mr. C. Arthur Pearson founded, and where I am very happy and learning poultry farming.

Turkish prisoners marching down a gully in Gallipoli

CHAPTER 36

How the "Formidable" was Lost

Just after the New Year, 1915, had broken the British battleship For-midable, successor of the famous ship with which the name of the gallant Rodney is so closely associated, was lost while steering westward in the Channel. In the official announcement it was stated that the cause of her loss was either mine or torpedo, but it was not known which. Later, however, it was stated in the House of Lords that she had been twice torpedoed. The Formidable was a pre-Dreadnought of 15,000 tons and 15,000 horse-power. In herself she was not a serious loss; but she carried a crew of between 700 and 800 men, and of these only 201 were saved. Once more the unconquerable spirit of British seamen was shown, as will be seen from this story of the only survivor of his watch—William Edward Francis, who was a stoker in the lost battleship.

I had what I take to be a narrow escape of being lost when the three cruisers were torpedoed in the North Sea.

I had been called up from the Royal Naval Reserve and drafted to the *Cressy*, which, with her sister ships the *Hogue* and *Aboukir*, was lost; but almost at the last moment I was transferred, with a chum, to another ship.

I was spared to take a part in the victory of Heligoland Bight; then afterwards, from a port-hole of my own ship, the *Formidable*, I saw her sister, the *Bulwark*, blown up, with the loss of nearly every man on board. We were moored close to the *Bulwark* at the time, and it was a terrible sight to see her go like that. The Germans, however, had nothing to do with the loss of the *Bulwark*, which was destroyed by one of those mysterious accidents that are bound to happen in war.

Then, on Christmas Day, we had an amusing experience. A German airman came and had a look at things, including ourselves, and he hovered over us, but bolted without even dropping a bomb. No doubt he went back and spun a wonderful yarn of the way in which he had thrown us into a panic, when, as a matter of fact, we only laughed at him.

On the last day of the year 1914 the *Formidable* was one of the units of a Channel squadron.

She was an old ship, as warships go, but there was a lot of life left in her, especially when bad weather had to be met, and she showed that in the Channel on New Year's morn, for we had run into tremendous seas and a heavy gale of wind was blowing. On the last day of the Old Year the *Formidable*, like the rest of the British ships, was taking green water on board and she was properly washed. But that was a mere nothing—the British navy is used to it, and not to hiding in a canal.

That was the way the Old Year went out and the New Year came in—carrying on. It was a stormy ending to a stormy year. Night fell, but there was moonlight, and there was nothing to be heard except the roaring of the wind and the thudding of the seas as the brave old *Formidable* crashed into them and drove through them, going west.

Go where you will, in any part of the world, you'll find that Englishmen don't let the Old Year die without some sort of feeling and regret, and so it happened that those of us who were not on watch sat in our messes and talked about our homes and those we had left behind us, and of the big things that had taken place in the dying year. The Old Year had truly seen some stormy times, and it was going out in a living gale.

At about twenty minutes past two in the morning I went into the stokehole. The ship was, of course, rolling and pitching and there were plenty of big heaves, but almost as soon as I had got below I felt a heave which I knew could not be caused by any ordinary roll. This heave was immediately followed by a distinct tremble over the whole ship, a shivering which lasted for about ten seconds.

A stoker who had been in one of the bunker-holds ran out and said that water was coming in, and this fact was at once reported to the bridge. It was clear that something very serious had happened, but what it was there was not any means of knowing just then.

Captain Loxley, who was commanding the *Formidable*, was on the bridge—his little dog was with him—and as soon as he realised what had taken place he did everything he could to try and save his ship and her company. He issued orders calmly and deliberately, and shouted,

"Steady, men, steady! There's life in the old ship yet!"

The water-tight bulkhead doors were closed, and a signal was flashed to the other ships of the squadron that the *Formidable* had been struck; but, as every one knows by this time, orders were given by the Admiralty after the loss of the three cruisers that when a ship has been torpedoed other ships are not to stand by to give assistance. There was reason to believe that the *Formidable* had been torpedoed, and accordingly the remaining ships were warned to keep off, and they were soon lost to view in the wild night.

After being struck the *Formidable* became practically motionless, and very soon steam gave out and she was little more than a huge rolling mass on the heaving waters.

At this stage I visited the engine-room and found that the dynamos were just giving out, which meant that the ship would be plunged into darkness, and so add to the difficulty and danger of the situation. But there was nothing like panic on board. Commander Ballard had told everybody to keep cool, and had said that the first thing to do was to get the boats out.

All hands mustered on deck and efforts were at once made to launch the large boats, but owing to the failure of the steam these attempts failed. The ship had been struck on the starboard side, forward, and by three o'clock she was listing heavily and settling by the bows; and it was hard to keep a place on deck.

It was very soon after this that a submarine was discovered near the ship, and I need not say how grieved and furious we were when it was realised that it was impossible to train a single gun on the craft.

After tremendous and extraordinary efforts two boats were lowered and they pulled away into the darkness, crowded.

In the meantime all the tables, chairs and things that would float had been thrown overboard, so that the men who found themselves in the water should have a chance of clutching at something that would help them to keep up, and in addition to this there were the inflated collars which have been provided for the crews of warships since the war began.

Meanwhile the submarine had vanished, but very soon another shock was felt, this time on the port side of the *Formidable*, so it seemed as if the craft had gone round to make matters even.

"There goes another at us!" some of the men shouted, as an explosion tore the decks and killed a number of the survivors.

"The cowards!" I heard one of my pals growl; "aren't they satisfied at finishing us with one shot?"

It was a natural enough thing to say, but war is war—and British warships are not a canal fleet; they keep the seas and take their chances, and don't slink in hiding.

The lights of a small vessel had been noticed about six hundred yards away, and careful inspection left little doubt that she was a fishing-smack. She did not move and did not make any answer to the appeals for help. Afterwards she slipped away and disappeared, and I'm pretty certain that she covered the movements of the submarine.

Things, however, were not by any means all bad. Four or five miles away more lights were visible, and these came nearer at about four o'clock, when we found that they belonged to a light cruiser.

When the cruiser drew near, Captain Loxley, thinking only of his duty, and wishful that no other ship should share the fate of his own, signalled to her to keep away, saying that the battleship had been struck and that the cruiser might be struck also; but the cruiser swept around the *Formidable* in wide circles, nobly handled, and showed every sign of being ready to lend assistance.

The effect of the second explosion was to restore the battleship to something like an even keel; but having been torpedoed on each side she naturally sank lower and lower in the water, and it was soon clear that she would founder. Indeed, the first explosion was so terrible that there was little doubt that the ship was doomed, especially in such a sea as was then running. It was perishingly cold, with snow and sleet, and, to make matters worse, a good many of the ship's company were only slightly clad.

Of course there was not the least intention of abandoning the ship until it was perfectly clear that she could not keep afloat, and every effort was made to save her. There was hope that she might be kept going until the day broke, and that then it might be possible to get her into a Channel port; but she had been too badly damaged for such a hope to be realised and she listed terribly.

As the *Formidable* had been struck on each side water was rushing in very rapidly, through huge gaps, but the ship listed more and more. A fine attempt was made to train the big guns on the beam, and as these represent a very heavy weight, no doubt some good effect would have been brought about, but again there was not the necessary power available, and the effort had to be given up.

Listing more heavily as the moments passed, the battleship at last was almost lying on her side and there was no hope of saving her.

Shortly before this had happened, and when it was known that nothing more could be done, the survivors mustered on the quarter-deck, and it was very strange to see how coolly they accepted the situation—such is discipline and the usage of war, and such is the result of the splendid example which was set for us by our captain and the officers.

The captain remained on the bridge, smoking a cigarette, and some of the men smoked too, while others broke into song.

We had our life-saving collars on, and there we were, waiting for the moment to come when the ship would make her last plunge.

It was at this time that the chaplain, with his hands behind his back, walked up and down the deck, encouraging the men and comforting them—and all the time the most tremendous efforts were being made to launch the boats. This was a task that was both difficult and dangerous, and of four boats that were got out one, a barge, capsized and several men were thrown out and drowned. I might say here that another barge managed to get away with about seventy men, who were picked up by the cruiser, while a pinnace, with a good number of men, reached Lyme Regis, but that was not till more than twenty hours had passed and a score of men had perished through exposure. The fourth boat, a launch, with about seventy men, was knocked about for nearly twelve hours, then they were rescued off Berry Head by the Brixham trawler *Providence* and taken into Brixham.

But I am getting on a bit too fast—I must return to the quarter-deck of the sinking battleship.

There was near me a little fellow who, a few days before, when the *Formidable* had sailed, had said goodbye to his mother.

I have six children of my own, and my heart went out to the lad, so I took him by the hand and told him to carry out my instructions.

There was a log of wood floating near, and thinking that this was a favourable opportunity to try and save the youngster, I told him to jump and swim.

The plucky little chap obeyed, but in that heavy sea and the bitter cold he missed his chance, and shortly afterwards he was swept away. It was very pitiful, but there was nothing for it but to take a heavy risk that night.

I saw that there was not long to wait now until the very end came, and so I said to a chum of mine, who was standing near me, "Shall we jump now?"

"I think I'll wait," he said.

I looked around, I saw that there was nothing to be gained by waiting, and so I said, "I'm going. Goodbye," for by this time it was every man for himself.

"Goodbye, Bill," said my chum, and there was a grip of the hand. Then I dived into the heavy icy sea and made a struggle for it.

The water was bitterly cold, and in a very curious way I suffered intense pain, because the inflated collar prevented me from dipping my head to the breakers and they caught me full on.

Very soon after I reached the water I looked back and saw the *Formidable* disappearing. She had made a good fight for it, and had kept afloat for a considerable time after being struck by the first torpedo.

When the battleship had vanished the sea was covered with men who were struggling for their lives; but soon the number was lessened, because in that bitter weather only the very strongest could live. One by one men disappeared, numbed and unconscious, while others, like myself, managed to keep afloat and alive.

I was encouraged by the thought that there was a chance of salvation through the cruiser, and I kept on swimming towards her as hard as I could.

For one long dreadful hour I was in that icy sea, battling all the time, until I got up to the cruiser and managed to make them hear my shouts.

Lines were thrown overboard in the hope that survivors like myself could catch hold of them, and I managed to seize one of these and to hang on to it with the energy of despair until I was drawn up near enough to be gripped by some of the cruiser's people—and once they got a grip of us they didn't let go.

I was hauled up on to the cruiser's deck, and a good many of my companions were also rescued by her, so that with the survivors she carried to port and the men who were rescued by the trawler, and in other ways, a round two hundred of the crew of the *Formidable* were saved. The rest perished.

There is no doubt that the loss of life would have been far greater if it had not been for the skill and bravery of some Brixham fishermen. There happened to be in the Channel that night, not far from the spot where the battleship sank, a little Brixham smack called the *Provident*, manned by her skipper, William Pillar, and three hands.[1] She was under storm canvas, and was doing her best to seek shelter when

---

1. The mate of the *Provident* was lost, in another vessel, about a year later, in a heavy Channel gale.

the battleship's cutter was seen. The cutter was riding to a sea anchor and was in great peril, while the survivors who were in the little vessel were suffering terribly through exposure.

No sooner did the smack see the cutter than an effort was made to save the men; but in such a sea and at night it was the hardest thing imaginable to undertake a rescue, and it was not until more than two hours had passed and the smack had been handled as only a smacksman can handle such a graft, that a line was made fast between the cutter and the smack and the men were got on board, after a long struggle. They were all transferred to the *Provident* by about one o'clock in the afternoon of New Year's Day, and they were landed at Brixham, where they were most generously treated, and clothes and drink and food were given to them. At other places on the coast of the Channel other survivors were landed, and very soon we were able to leave for our homes for a little spell of rest.

It is well to remember the very fine life-saving work that was done by fishermen when the *Formidable* was lost, just as it was done by fishermen in the North Sea when the three cruisers were torpedoed. In their life-saving work at the loss of the *Formidable*, deep-sea fishermen added one more to the many splendid things they have done for the navy since the war began.

One result of the failure of the steam was that the wireless could not be worked, so that not much could be done with the sending out of calls; but there was the Morse to fall back on, and so into the night the lamp signals were flashed, warning the other ships of what had happened and telling them to keep clear. They had to obey, having no option in the matter, and it must have been hard for them to leave the old ship to her fate, though I daresay they were comforted by the knowledge that her company were sure to meet their end like good Englishmen.

The Morse signals were understood by the other warships, but it seems that there were one or two other fishing vessels about which would most surely have given help if they had realised what had happened and had understood the nature of the signals. The *Provident* was packed, having only a very small cabin and her hold and fish-room, but once on board of her the survivors were safe, though as far as room and comfort went, we who were saved by the cruiser were a good deal better off.

I do not want to dwell on the finish of the battleship, and the terrible hour or so I spent in the icy cold of the Channel seas in the very heart of winter. The disaster was so sudden and tremendous that it had a numbing effect on you, and many a poor fellow died through exposure, either in the water or in the boats, which were constantly swept by the freezing seas, so that there was little difference between being in the boats and in the water.

Captain Loxley went down with his ship, you might almost say as a matter of course, his first and last thought being for the safety of his people. Many of the officers went with him, and as for those who were saved, they were all, except one or two who had been ordered to the boats to take charge of them, rescued from the seas into which they had plunged or had been thrown to take their chance just like the men.

CHAPTER 37

A Trooper's Tale

It has been said that in this war cavalry have ceased to exist. As mounted men their opportunities have undoubtedly been very limited; but in other ways they have done much to maintain their ancient reputation. In the earlier days of the fierce attempt of the Germans to break through the Allied Armies and get to Calais the teller of this tale—Trooper Notley, of the 5th Dragoon Guards—was engaged and was finally wounded and invalided home.

There are a good many men who, like myself, were at Mons, the Marne and the Aisne, and then went into the Fight for the Coast, and I think they would all tell the same story—that that tremendous battle was fifty times worse than the Aisne.

The Aisne was very bad; but even there, though the Germans fought desperately to prevent themselves from being driven back and turned away from Paris, their efforts were not to be compared with the determination they showed in their attacks upon the troops who barred their way to Calais.

The Germans were mad in their resolve to fight their way through to Paris; but they were madder to break through and get to the coast, so that they could get within sight of hated England. They tried all they knew; even as I talk they are trying as hard as ever, but I'm as sure that they won't succeed as I am that tomorrow will come.

People have heard and read a lot about the fighting at Ypres and Messines, and it is of this part of the battle that I am going to talk, because it was at these places that the 5th Dragoon Guards shared in a great deal of furious fighting.

We had had a long innings at the Aisne, then our brigade moved on to the Ypres region, which we reached after being fourteen days in the saddle. We made a short break at Amiens, where it was thought that we might have to help the French; but before long reinforcements arrived for them and we went on our road to the north, approaching Ypres as the advanced guard of a brigade.

It had been hard going on the march, and there was plenty of excitement with it, even before we got into the real fight for the coast. There were prowling *Uhlans* everywhere, and nothing would have pleased us better than to get at them in a thundering charge; but they didn't give us the chance, and kept in scattered bodies. But at one point quite a little surprise had been prepared for us by about three hundred *Uhlans*.

We were marching along when we discovered that these *Uhlans* had taken up a position commanding a road, and they had planted a Maxim, so that they could give us a warm welcome. They soon discovered that we were not going to be caught napping. Instead of keeping to the road we were promptly ordered to leave it and to take to a field running alongside. We made for the *Uhlans* as fast as we could go, but they did not stop to finish the welcome; they vanished, and I was unable to see the end of them; but it seems that they were completely surrounded and gathered in by some of our infantry.

This was the sort of small action that was constantly happening, but it was a trifle compared with the real big fighting around Ypres. The cannonade was terrific, and the everlasting firing made it seem as though nothing existed on earth but the thundering of big guns and the screeching and bursting of shells all around.

In and around Ypres, the Allies had pushed far into the enemy's line, and the Germans were concentrating all their men and metal to crumple us up. They strained every nerve and made the most dreadful sacrifices to carry out the *Kaiser's* command to break through; but though they hurled themselves to certain death, in thousands, they were driven back.

Messines, a village quite near to Ypres, came within the zone of this furious attack, and it was at Messines that most of the brigade, including my own squadron, was posted.

When we got to the village, which we reached by way of the fields—rough going, but safer than the roads—my squadron was ordered to hold the place by the main road, and another squadron went about nine hundred yards up the road and spent the night in digging trenches, which were occupied by the whole regiment on the following morning.

As we moved into the trenches we were under incessant fire, and we were fired on all the time we were in them.

For twelve days and twelve nights we held fast to our trenches, against the onslaughts of forces that were certainly five times as great as our own—and, in spite of their countless losses, the proportion of the Germans was never less than that.

We seemed to have nothing but shell fire and night attacks, and to get anything like decent rest under such conditions was impossible.

There was a curious sameness in this life in the trenches. We had no chance, as we had at the Aisne, of digging ourselves in, because the lie of the land was against us. At the Aisne our positions were very strong and we could afford to smile at the efforts of the Germans to dig us out; but it was a very different matter in country which is as flat as a floor. There was nothing impregnable in our little artificial gullies, and in this absence of help from Nature we had to keep our wits about us to escape the shrapnel and to prevent the nightly visits of our German neighbours.

We were a mixed lot at Messines. Our line consisted of the Connaught Rangers, the Somersets, Bengal Lancers and some Ghurkas—a mere handful compared with the masses of Germans that were flung against us, with an enormous number of guns.

Day after day this fighting went on, the German attacks getting fiercer every day. Nightfall was the time when they would make particularly stubborn attempts to drive us out. They would leave their own trenches and advance two or three hundred yards at a time, then throw themselves flat on the ground before beginning the next stage. We had them under observation all the time, but did not let a sound reach them; in fact, we lured them on by seeming not to be there.

On they came, till they were something like fifty yards away, then we got the order for rapid fire, and let drive into the ranks that it was not possible to miss. In this manner great numbers of Germans were destroyed; we punished them terribly, for our rapid fire was certain destruction for their front ranks.

It is not always clear to people, I find, that trenches may be constructed according to the needs of the moment, at all sorts of odd corners and angles. The idea seemed to be that the Germans dug themselves in along a perfectly straight line, while we dug ourselves in along a parallel line a few hundred yards away. In our position by Messines the trenches were splayed out, so to speak, some of them making an angle of ninety degrees or so with each other. We were so

British cavalry at the Front

entrenched that we were inviting the Germans to step into a hollow square, or rather to form the fourth side of it, which with their heaps of dead and wounded they occasionally did. Of course the positions varied from hour to hour, both in guarding against attempts to enfilade us and in avoiding cross-fire between units of our own forces.

One night a supreme effort was made by the Germans. The Indians had relieved us that very morning, and one troop of our men had got into a barn and cut loopholes in the walls, while another troop had taken up a position at a barricade made up of old wagons and sacks of earth.

At about three o'clock in the morning we suddenly heard the sound of a bugle, and presently the Germans set up a hullabaloo and fairly hurled themselves at our trenches. They came in such strong numbers that the Indians, who had been dealing out death half the night, were overweighted by the enemy, who got round their flank and attacked them in the rear.

A Maxim gun section of the 11th Hussars was hurried down, and from the window of one of the buildings it blazed away at the Germans and covered the retirement of the Indians. The way in which the Maxims have been handled in the war has been a revelation to a lot of people. These handy weapons have been got into upstairs and downstairs rooms and even into the tops of trees, and they have caused terrific havoc in the Germans' solid ranks.

That night affair was desperate; but it seemed as if nothing could stop the mad onrush of the Germans, and at last there was nothing for it but to give way, and so we received orders to evacuate the barn.

Near this particular point the road forks, and a couple of men were left to fire up the right-hand road and two to fire up the road on the left, and for the time being we were effectually covered.

It was at this stage that there arose the chance for a Territorial regiment to come into action for the first time. The Territorials to win this great distinction were the London Scottish.

The Scottish had been ordered up to relieve the pressure, and they came on quickly and in gallant style and took up a position at one end of the barn, while the Highland Light Infantry, the brave old 71st, took up a position at the other, and between them the two carried the barn with a bayonet charge and killed, captured or drove away the Germans.

The Scottish had their baptism of blood in proper good style, with a very strange preparation in the shape of a cunning German trick.

Not far from the Scottish was a windmill which had had three of its sails blown away or destroyed, leaving only the fourth sail, and that looked as if it had been cut clean in half. It was noticed that this crippled sail was working about in the most astonishing fashion, and those who saw it were puzzled to account for the movements; but it was soon discovered that there was a German spy hidden in the mill, and that he was moving the sail to indicate the position of the Scottish, and so bring the German gun-fire to bear on them. When the dodge had been discovered and the signaller settled the Scottish got their own back.

By this time I was blazing away from a barricade in an old covered yard, and there was a straggling fire going on all around; but it was clear that we should want reinforcements if we were to hold our own and save Messines.

At last we heard shouts, and I cannot tell you what it meant to us when we knew that the shouts came from our own fellows, and that three battalions of infantry had hurried up and got into action and given the Germans more than they could comfortably carry.

It was at this moment of the saving of Messines that I was struck by a shrapnel bullet and had to leave the fighting-line and come home, with the fight for the coast going on. I had been in it right from the start and had got used to the awful business, even to the "coal-boxes," which the Germans were everlastingly firing. They made a particular target of the church, and for nine days bombarded it before they set the building on fire.

One of the strangest things about a shell is that you never know what it is going to do, and some of the "coal-boxes" acted like freaks.

During this bombardment of the church I watched one of the shells come, and expected that it would do something smashing, for it hit the building full in the middle of one of the main walls. I looked for the wall to be shattered, but the shell never shifted a brick or a bit of mortar; it simply burst in on itself, so to speak, and did no damage to anything except itself, and in the end the Germans got a fire going by sending a much smaller shell, something like a fifteen-pounder.

In a general way of speaking, however, these "coal-boxes" did some terrible mischief when they really exploded, and no living thing within their reach had a chance of escaping. Horses, guns, men, wagons, everything that came within the area of explosions was shattered or wiped out. Often enough men who were killed by the explosions were found in the holes, so that the shell which had destroyed them had also scooped out their grave.

There were all sorts of side issues to the actual fighting. We billeted in every kind of building, some of them very strange; but I think the strangest of all was a cow-house. This does not sound promising; but that cow-house was one of the finest places I ever slept in.

The farm itself was beautiful, and everything about it was on the latest and best scale, so that the cowhouse was lighted by electricity, and the fittings were in keeping with the illumination. I had a very comfortable stretch there, and it would not have been possible for us to be better looked after. The proprietor had had notice of our coming and had made every preparation for us, and we were only too grateful for the many good things he freely gave away. We had the same sort of kindness shown to us by the French wherever we came into contact with them.

It may seem somewhat odd that a cavalryman in talking of the war should dwell so much on the trench work and the shell-fire; but in this war a great deal of the work of the cavalry has been dismounted, and practically the same as the infantry, and there has not been the chance that every cavalryman longs for to get to close grips with the enemy's mounted forces.

We had heard so much about the *Uhlans* that we expected to have some stirring times with them; but these big encounters did not come off, and one great thing we learned about the *Uhlans* was their skill in avoiding us. We saw them everywhere, but in scattered bodies, and they never gave us a chance of getting at them in the mass. Whenever we formed up in anything like force they melted away; but one fine day we had better luck—we came across them when they were in fair numbers, and before they could perform their vanishing trick we had got at them. At the end we found that we had punished them pretty heavily, for we broke up seven hundred lances which we had captured from them.

CHAPTER 38

A Diarist Under Fire

There is a peculiar interest in any record of experiences which is made while they are being undergone. Imperfect and incomplete though they may be, yet they are of special value because of their reliability. This is particularly the case with some of the diaries which have been kept while the writers were on active service; and extracts from such a one form this story. The author is Private Charles Hills, 2nd Battalion Australian Infantry. His share in the operations he describes was necessarily brief, for he was dangerously wounded, and was partially blinded and invalided to England, prior to returning to Australia. Just before leaving England he was examined by a Medical Board, and it was then found that he was quite blind.

Lemnos, May 3rd, 1915. We arrived at Lemnos on the evening of the 1st of May. The place itself is, so far as we can see, just a small island, amongst a lot of other islands, and is evidently a meeting-place for a heterogeneous collection of shipping—cruisers, colliers and cattle-boats. Trading, trawling and touting seem to be the several achievements of this mass. We are lying just inside . . . the entrance of the harbour. All night the searchlights play across. Quite a little storm was caused by a small torpedo-boat "arresting" a collier with two shots from her biggest gun. Effective argument it proved. It seems she had not got her sailing papers in order. The defect was remedied.

It pleases the boys to see the neatness and quickness with which the English tars handle their craft, after the slipshod methods of Chinamen and *lascars*.

This is just a small island of, roughly speaking, 45,000 inhabitants, solely Greeks. The most outrageous street I ever struck—5*d*. for a copy of a London daily halfpenny. The least thing seems to be five *piastres*.

May 4th. Turned terribly cold last night. Sent us all below to fetch our overcoats. Some of the wounded are telling us terrible tales of maltreatment by Turks of prisoners they take. Evidently we are up against a lot of barbarians. We heard from the front two days ago that the Australians' heavy losses were entirely due to the fact that they charged full speed for a mile and were not content with that, but they must needs go and chase the Turks for five miles. Here they found the position untenable and had to retreat. During this retreat the Turks poured an enfilading fire into them and caused such heavy losses. The Tommy Terriers got just as far and without the enormous loss of life. Some of our fellows who left us at Abbasia suffered amongst the rest: one was killed and several injured more or less. No doubt their example should be to our profit.

May 5th. We have set sail at last, and every one has gone mad. Of course our destination is unknown. Ammunition is being served out, and extra guards set for torpedo-boats and any hostile craft. The weather is bitterly cold—a vast change from New South Wales. At present steering S.S.W., 6 p.m.

8 a.m., May 6th. Our move proved to be a very short one, and ended abruptly at about 10 p.m. As soon as we arrived we could hear distinctly the rolling of the guns, and sometimes see the flash of the shells bursting. When morning came we were better able to see where we had got to. The first thing I noticed was the cold. It was "some." The next was the number of boats. Besides our own we counted seventy-six, warships included. On looking round we seemed to be in the Dardanelles itself, but a visit to the map disproved this theory. It seems to me as though we are in the Gulf of Saros, and the narrow spit of land forming the left bank of the Dardanelles was on our right front. Over this, it seemed that the reports were from the guns of warships lying in the Dardanelles itself, bombarding the forts and answering the Turkish artillery in the hills.

We can plainly see the movements of the troops on the hills in front of us with the naked eye, although the distance must be some miles. The air is very clear....

The warships look positively wicked as they glide through the water. There are quite a number of them here. One came up quite close to us this morning. We could see the paint of the guns, no doubt used to disguise them and bewilder any aircraft that may be hovering about over them....

Australians landing under fire.

The war is amongst us in real earnest. Today we have been treated to what must be one of the most striking sights to imagine. Upwards of a dozen warships have been bombarding the coast-line. It seems as though we were just outside the range of the enemy's guns, and through it being such a bright day we are able to see everything, and to watch the marking of the naval gunners and the effect of their shots. Over fifty transports are above the line of fire, and we are to land under the guns of the battleships. Things are just beginning to get exciting. Long rows of lights are visible. I can only conclude that that is the enemy's rifle-fire.

May 7th. Well, we have arrived and landed, and contrary to expectations we have marched straight into the trenches. The Turks gave us a great reception, and shelled even the boats we were landing in.

11 p.m., May 8th. We are now drafted to our respective battalions. Have spent our first day in the trenches. There was quite a gathering of the clans when we joined up, and many old mates were overjoyed to see their friends unhurt. Since morning we have been treated to a consistent dispute of artillery and perpetually shelled with shrapnel and lyddite. The shrapnel is an awfully destructive projectile.

The Turks seem to be filling up their shells with any old rubbish—screws, nails, and even old bolts came in a shell. The worst of it is the occasional sniper in the surrounding bush. He has several scores to his credit. We have one good shot looking for him, and if he only gets a look at him he'll have to close his account quickly. The battalion has been very severely handled, and has lost, roughly speaking, about half its strength. Officers have suffered far heavier in proportion to their men, a brigadier, colonel, two majors and sundry smaller fry have been put out of mess.

I can go no further, as my head is fairly splitting with the noise of shrapnel, lyddite, and the continual lying down doggo in a dugout.

3 p.m., Sunday. Unfortunately Turks don't observe the Sabbath, and today has been as busy as any other day. To add to my splitting headache last night, I had scarcely any sleep at all for the third night in succession—and the first night in the trenches, with one hour out of three on the look-out. The consequence is a man feels thoroughly washed out. The Turks made one rush against us last night at about 2 a.m., and our boys had all to stand up with fully loaded rifles and bayonets fixed. After a few sharp rounds of rapid fire, however, they thought better of it, and retired and sniped the rest of the night.

The strain of your first watch was more intense than I thought anything could be, and had me fairly mazed for a time. However, I improved and finished up fairly well. This morning, after breakfast, Captain Linklater came along and detailed me for observation work at the right hand of Lewis. Armed with a periscope, I stationed myself at one of the observation-places, and became a target for all the snipers in the Turkish army, I thought. The place was well sandbagged and quite bullet-proof from front and flank, and so I enjoyed a thorough survey of the surrounding country and benefited much thereby....

8 a.m., May 10th. This morning we have another job in digging a small circular pit ten feet in diameter, to accommodate about four men.... The lieutenant in charge says it is for a guard-room. ,..

Barring a little more confidence and a little more dirt personally the position is unchanged. I am certainly not as nervous as I was at the beginning, although I have not been in a charge yet.

We've had two Indian Mountain Batteries join us, and a great acquisition they are, too. Muledrawn, they negotiate these hills as easily as the others do the open roads, and they are more accustomed to warfare than the Australian boys are. The Turks won't reply to them at all....

4 p.m., May 11th. Our position is unchanged, as far as I can make out.... Our much-promised "rest" consisted of navvying a roadway for the artillery, to get one of their big guns up a hill in position....

The weather has been terrible—a real English October day; squally thundershowers and as cold as a March wind, added to which I caught a severe chill last night, and you will see that I am not as happy as I could be. I have no doubt there are some worse off than I, but this is a chronicle of my experiences. Despite the fact that I am wearing heavy khaki flannel tunic, and worsted sweater, and flannel shirt, and another heavy overcoat, I am continually in a shiver. I am anxiously awaiting further symptoms to decide whether it is my old friend pneumonia turned up again. The food (iron rations), corned beef and biscuits and tea, and sometimes a little jam, is not conducive to mirth-producing. In the event of it being pneumonia I suppose it is hospital for me. Several have gone back already with it....

The exploding bullets are largely being used, and ill consequence the wounds are much more serious. One of our poor chaps got shot through with one of them, which must have exploded as it reached him. Fifteen pieces of lead were found in his head. Quite dead, of course.

2 p.m., May 12th. We have spent a quiet morning, after a rotten night. Sent out at 5 p.m. to dig and shape a trench for an artillery pit. We started off all right and presently it began to rain—quite an easy rain, but so wet and cold. We had no blankets with us, and at 10 p.m. there came a halt for sandbags to be fetched. On applying to the artillery officer in charge he considered they were in too dangerous a position to be fetched just then, so we camped in the rain, with no protection other than our overcoats. We waited and waited. No bags came along, and so we slept until four....

This morning we got orders to lie close, as the battery and battleships were going to do a bit of shelling in conjunction. My cold is not changing much, and the cold of last night would not tend to improve matters at all....

We heard a great cheering on the landing-stage this morning. Two battalions of Tommies and the 3rd Brigade, 6000 or so, all told, reinforcing our boys. Probably we shall get more sleep now. I have not washed since last Thursday, six days now not shaven. Some of them have not washed for a fortnight. If you get down to the beach you are under shot and shell the same as anywhere else, so you have a dry rub.

May 13th. Today we are back in the trenches in a different space. The lieutenant-colonel had us out and inspected us in full equipment. He complimented us on our fine showing, and also told us that the 2nd Brigade had distinguished itself down the coast for this sortie. The news came from him that Sydney had had high holiday over the display of their men. One town, Armidale, the home of Colonel Braund, had collected £365 10s. 6d. for the benefit of the battalion when we arrived at a decent permanent camp. Saw many of the old boys to-day, and looking well at that.

May 14th. One of our corporals had a remarkable escape from a shrapnel this morning. He and another man were sitting outside the orderly-room awaiting the result of a conference, and they both saw the shell coming. Private Beech moved out of the way, and the corporal turned over and got out of the way just in the nick of time. The shell touched his pants and tore them—another few inches and he would have been blown to pieces....

May 15th. Quite a quiet night and comparatively still. Had an encouraging sight. About a mile or so away we could see our warships shelling flying troops—and a large body of them, too. Mr. Lowe, our

P.C., informed us that it was the main body of the Turks retreating before the allied French, English, and Australian troops. We could see them with the naked eye from one of our shelter-trenches on the hills.

The warships' gunnery was marvellously accurate, and shell after shell fell in the ranks of the enemy. There is a large estimated loss amongst the Turks. . . .

One of the Turkish officers from a neighbouring fort having disagreed with some German superiors, was to have been shot at dawn. In the night he escaped and gave himself up to the Australians here. . . .

The view here is magnificent, but to be appreciated one has to risk one's neck and get up at four o'clock, when things are quiet and only a few snipers about. . . .

May 16th. The facts and results of the Light Horsemen's charge came out this morning. It seems that somewhere over one hundred went out against the machinegun on our left front. It seems ridiculous to send out a hundred men on a charge against an enemy well entrenched. Anyway, they got the gun, and lost seventeen killed and sixty or so wounded and missing. It was a victory, as a general result, but costly.

Today our platoon commander, Lieutenant Lowe, arrived with the telegraphic compliments showered on us by our enthusiastic population. They could not have cheered so hard if they had been as dry as we were.

Water is so scarce that we are allowed only one pint every twenty-four hours. Out of that we have to wash, shave, and provide the means of assuaging a bully-beef thirst. The consequence is I have had about one wash in about two fingers of water since I landed, just ten days ago. . . .

Our sniping friends have suffered severely, one man, a kangaroo shooter, catching four, three of them in half an hour. They fetch him along the line now when they happen to spot one.

The tin-tuff is getting monotonous, and I have broken a tooth on those infernal biscuits. Apart from that we have not had much to complain about.

The weather is getting hot in the day and not quite so cool at night, and ever so much more comfortable.

May 18th. Snakes have made their appearance, though they are small and nervous compared with the Australian specimen. Water is horrible, but, thank God, the weather is cooler, except just at midday, and does not entail a great thirst. Our rations make up for that. Boiled bacon has been added to the menu and is somewhat salt, and that, added to the dryness of our biscuit, and your ration of one pint per day, is —— small. In the tucker respect we are much better off than our opponents, who seem to be ill fed, ill clad, and, as usual, ill paid. . . . The drawback is washing. . . .

May 19th. Official reports to hand announce that Gallipoli is in ruins, owing to a very severe bombardment from the guns of *Lizzie* and a few of her ilk. There is absolutely no room for argument about *Lizzie* being effective. She is a whole army and navy in herself. At the outbreak of hostilities here the authorities were much troubled by the enemy having an armoured train armed with heavy guns, and of course extremely mobile. After it had done much damage *Lizzie* got her eye on it, and three shots put paid to its account. Their gunnery is little short of marvellous. The boys here are astounded because she puts her shells right over the strip of land we are on, and drops them on some unsuspecting vessel in the Narrows, seven or eight miles away. To get the line of fire and sight it is necessary to use aircraft. We have the great Samson himself here, squinting in the air for us, and are splendidly served in this respect. The Turks gave him a great reception last night, and every piece of gunnery was turned in his direction. Fortunately he was unhurt, being miles off range.

I drew my first issue of tobacco and cigarettes today—two packets of cigarettes and 2oz. of tobacco and a box of *fifteen* matches! Very welcome to a smoker, and I have no doubt they will secure many blessings in the future. . . .

May 20th. Contrary to expectation the Turks came again, and in large lumps, too. They gave us a perfect fusillade at tea-time last night—rifles, machine-guns, and artillery kept it up till dark. Then we being in the second line of defence (or supports), went to bed. About twelve o'clock Wednesday they started again, accompanied by bombs and machine-guns and rifles. They fairly lighted the night up, and as for row—Bedlam let loose was not in it.

The bombs gave us a bad moment or two. They did not kill anyone, but threw up such clouds of dust that we were literally blinded; and then the main attack started at about 2 a.m. on the right and developed all along the row of trenches. A lull occurred till about 3 a.m.

A British Soldier writing in his dugout. The heap of stones and two crosses in the top right-hand corner mark the graves of comrades.

We stood to arms, and then it really began.

First they chanted their war-cry and called on *Allah* and blew on a little tin trumpet. It sounded terribly weird at that time of the morning—it was pitch dark. We could only stand at our loopholes and strain our eyes to peer into nothingness. Firing continued in a desultory manner. All of a sudden their front wing was in the first line of trenches, which were about eighty yards in front of ours.

Half blinded by the dust and choked by the gas, the boys stuck to it like Britons, and sometimes staved the Turks off. Three Turks did manage to get in B Company's line, but they did not manage to get out again. By this time we had got our bearings, and then the boys settled down to steady firing. Never heard such a noise. I was strained to the utmost pitch of excitement. Times again they managed to get up to the earthworks, but failed to get into the line.

The German officers hooted them on and beat them with their swords; but after the terrible hail of shot one could not be surprised at their jibbing. Two or three officers were shot, with their hard black helmets, proving beyond doubt their nationality. . . .

Last night was a mixture of prayers and curses. Some of the boys yell for Turks to come on—they had some "back at work" shot for them.

The action was continued all day. Casualties were few, owing to excellent cover. . . .

5 a.m., May 21st. All night long we were waiting for them to come again, but the lesson had been too severe. All day yesterday they sniped and got a few, amongst them our special shot. . . . I have got the knack of keeping awake all night.

They have landed some 6-inch howitzers from the naval boats, and these are manned by marines. Firing lyddite, and manned by experts, they gave the Turks the time of their lives. The Turkish artillery is outclassed by them. Their big guns on the forts by the shore have a moving platform and consequently were hard to find; however, the boats got wind of where they were, and they started to shell our fellows last night at dusk. The tars saw their flash and fired three shells. Have heard nothing of them since, so suppose they hit something. . . .

Last night passed away uneventfully. Just a little rain of bullets now and then. Also the enemy fired a new kind of shell, believed to be melinite, which stifles a man to death and does not hit one at all. Nice respectable death, after the manner of some deaths!

A rain set in early this morning and brought attendant miseries with it, mud and dampness and general cussedness of every one concerned.

The beggars had the cheek to come over yesterday and demand that we surrendered. After such a pommelling as we gave them two days ago this is colossal. I think they just wanted to spy out a bit more of the defences.

Sunday, May 23rd. There is a furious bombardment going on out in the harbour. The warships are all standing in close and tackling the last of the main Turkish forts and strongholds in the Dardanelles. . . .

Quite a minor excitement was caused by the arrival of some submarines, supposed to be the pair that slipped by Gibraltar some days ago. The fact that first drew our attention to them was the small or mosquito craft which were running all round in circles, and the bigger vessels were all on the move. Nothing was heard as to whether they were captured or sighted again. I suppose the idea was to keep a good look out and also to provide a much more difficult mark than if they were standing still.

I had a night's sleep last night, the first undisturbed since we landed sixteen days ago. I feel splendid this morning, Sunday—not much like our usual one, though. I absolutely pine for St. John's, Wagga Wagga, for their singing and for one hour of Canon Joe Pike. Tommy Thornber is with me in this respect. The most profitable hours of my life were undoubtedly spent there. . . .

The Turks around us are very quiet today. It is Sunday, so they ought to be.

Empire Day, May 24th. Peculiar thing—the long-expected armistice arrived today, instead of yesterday. . . . I, being of fair size, was one of the assorted few who were to form the burial party. We set out at 8 a.m., and started carting the Turks to their own lines and handing them over to their friends. To attempt to describe the condition of the bodies, some of them having lain out in the sun for twelve or fourteen days, some of them since they landed a month ago, would be futile. . . .

A line of flags was drawn equidistant from both lines, and each party of men kept between their line and the centre line of flags. As this line of flags was made up by one Turk and one Australian alternatively, we had a good view of live Turks. In point of physique they are not our superiors, as I imagined, but of a stock top-heavy—all-chest-and-no-legs sort of build; dark almost to blackness, with such a variety of casts of feature that they cannot be said to possess a distinctive one.

The officers are undoubtedly German—that is, the principal; and a scowling, evil-looking lot they are, though some of them attempted to ingratiate themselves with our boys by offering cigarettes and so on. The body-carting finished about one o'clock, and such work as exchanging . . . equipment has been going on.

May 25th. The submarine that was reported three days ago got in her work on the *Triumph* this morning at about 12.30, and she sank in seven minutes. The loss has thrown quite a gloom over the trenches here in camp. Our boys could see the survivors struggling in the water and saw the old ship sink, and could not raise a hand to help them in their trouble. As a loss to the Navy it was not a big one, as she was one of the older class of vessel, and from what I can gather we did not lose many of the crew. . . .

I snatched about an hour's sleep this morning, or I should have seen the disaster to the *Triumph*. . . .

May 26th. The number of men lost was only fifteen in the sinking of the warship yesterday. . . . Our socks are stuck to our feet, and the blend of the smell of our socks, chloride of lime, and dead Turks is a subject for a connoisseur. . . .

May 27th. Today we have had our welcome spell. Never before did men stretch out to enjoy sleep in such circumstances. Our resting trenches are about half a mile away from the firing-line, and the only danger is from spent bullets, whizzing by too high to hit the trenches, and just beginning to drop as they get to us. After the first line that is easy.

CHAPTER 39

A Stretcher-Bearer at Loos

Continuing the Allied advance in France, the British forces on September 25th, 1915, captured the western outskirts of Hulloch and the village of Loos, and secured an advantage near Hooge. At the same time the French took Souchez and the rest of the region known as the "Labyrinth," and broke through the German line in Champagne. The fighting at this period was exceptionally severe, and was acknowledged by the bestowal of many honours, amongst them the award of the Distinguished Conduct Medal to Private Harold Edwards, 1st Battalion South Staffordshire Regiment, whose story this is. In the official description of the award to Private Edwards, "for conspicuous bravery and devotion to duty," it was stated that "he gave a fine exhibition of the highest courage and disregard of personal danger."

It was at a place called Hulloch that we battled it out—but it was Loos, all the same. All my fighting and what I saw of it was done in the Loos district. Our division was at Fromelles, Aubers, Givenchy and Festubert, and a lot of minor events, and I came through these engagements very luckily. Our first battle, however, was Neuve Chapelle, though we did not do any actual fighting there. We were in reserve; but from what I learned later this was worse than the fighting-line, because we seemed to get all the shell fire. It was not till the battle of Loos came along that I was unlucky and got "clicked."

I wanted to be a soldier, and the very day we declared war on Germany I enlisted in the South Staffordshire Regiment, the old 38th. I was trained hard for a few months; but that was easy work, because I had been employed in a Staffordshire forge. Then, before the Christmas of 1914 I was sent to France, and got a spell of trench Work until March, when, on the 10th, the British captured Neuve Chapelle.

It is not easy to say what stands out most clearly in my mind of those early operations, because what I chiefly remember is Loos; but I know that we were terribly troubled in the trenches and round about them by rats. These horrible things swarmed, and they went for anything that was going. They were huge, fierce brutes, and I know of more than one case of a sentry on a lonely post who in the night-time got a bad scare because he thought the Germans were on him, when as a matter of fact it was nothing worse than an enormous rat which was out foraging and made a jump at his face.

More than six months passed between the Battle of Neuve Chapelle and the Battle of Loos. Of course an ordinary soldier doesn't know much of what is happening, and he doesn't pretend to—he has his own business to mind; but we knew for several days ahead that something was coming off, judging by the amount of stuff that went up. What do I mean by stuff? Well, the shells, principally. They were preparing the way, and were smashing up the whole of the countryside. It was really terrible to see what havoc was done by the German shells at Vermelles—streets were blown to bits, churches and houses were just made into rubbish heaps, and as for men, especially Germans, they didn't count. It isn't easy to make anybody understand what happened; but perhaps the easiest way is to imagine your own house and street and the country near it turned from a smiling, prosperous place into a heap of dreary and desolate ruins.

In that Battle of Loos we were thrown up against all the latest German warfare, including gas. There was poison-gas and smoke-gas, terrible artillery, awful rifle-fire, and; of course the rifle and bayonet.

We were in reserve trenches on September 24th, and on the night of that same day we went up to the firing-line.

It was a miserable night, with drizzling rain all the time. We started at ten o'clock, creeping and crawling through a long communication trench. We did not finish this advance job till two o'clock next morning, and then we sat in the trench and waited for the dawn to break. It was a solemn business, squatting there in the cold drizzle, talking in low tones, and wondering which of us would go down.

It was a lovely morn that broke, and glad we were to see it. Then, at about a quarter past five, the band began to play. And what a time it was, to be sure! It was a terrible bombardment, with the whole countryside shaking and shivering with the crashing of the guns, and your head felt like bursting with the din.

We had to stand this horrible racket for some time. I don't know

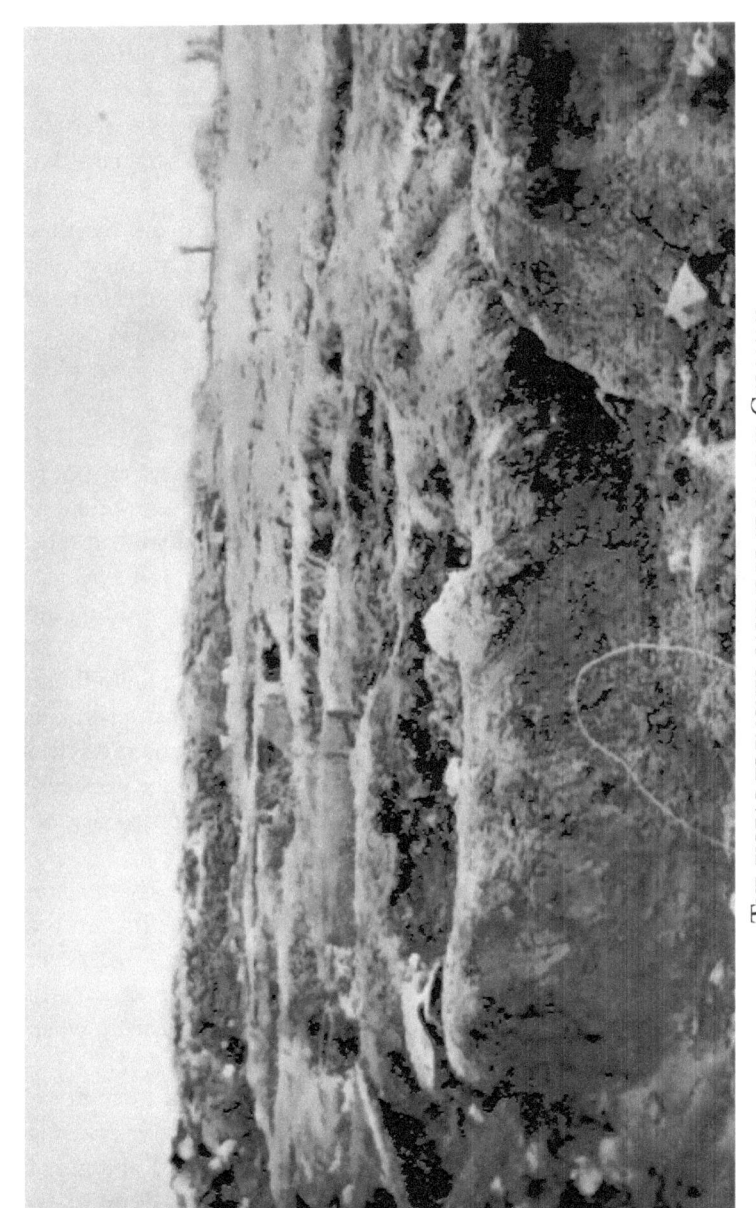

The zigzag trenches captured from the Germans

how long, but it seemed a fair stretch; then the word came to mount the parapet of the trench. It was a high parapet, and ladders were needed to get over it. There were plenty of ladders to each parapet, and as the order was one man to a ladder, no time was lost in getting out of the trench and on to the open ground over which the advance was made to the German trenches.

As soon as the men who were making the attack got over the parapet, the stretcher-bearers went after them with the stretchers. My chum with my stretcher was Private Pymm.

The men of our battalion had their smoke-helmets on, and they looked like devils. And that was a proper thing to look, for they went straight into a hellish fire—no other word will describe the storm of shells and bullets that met them. It seemed impossible for any one to live in it, yet our men went forward, and being a stretcher-bearer I had a wonderful view of them.

As soon as we got over the parapet the men began to fall, and we began to bandage them up. What we had to deal with were mostly "blighty" wounds, as we called them—just one through the thigh, or a flesh wound. We did the best we could for them; and we had soon tackled a few. Then we went on and tackled a few more. We had dropped our stretcher and were hurrying about, each of us doing the best he could.

I had got about ten yards ahead of Pymm, when I heard him shout; but there was such a terrible commotion that I could not make out what he said. We were at that time on the open ground, and it was bad to hear the cries of the poor fellows who were shouting for stretcher-bearers. I was that busy I forgot about Pymm, and supposed that he, like myself, was dressing and bandaging.

People at home in England, with things going on pretty much as usual in spite of the war, don't realise what cries for help from the wounded mean; but they are very terrible and pitiful, and I shall never forget them. But there is one fine thing about it—you never think of yourself, and the idea of danger doesn't bother you, especially when you're in the thick of it.

At this time the attack on the German trenches was very fierce, and there was a tremendous fire which seemed to sweep everything and everywhere. There did not seem to be a chance of escaping, and sure enough I got caught. I was hit, and I felt it; but I did not know how I was wounded, and I didn't care about it—I was too full of what was happening. And the wounded were crying for help; so I carried on.

I let myself gaze at the sights in front of me. I don't suppose that I gazed for more than a few seconds; but a lot took place in that short space of time, especially where I was.

I was not more than forty or fifty yards away from some barbed wire entanglements in front of me. These had not been properly cleared away, so it meant that our chaps had to rush them as best they could on their way to the German trenches. The wire-cutters dashed up and cut away at the stuff, and the other chaps rushed on with the bayonet. This seemed to me to go on for just a few seconds; but I may be wrong. At any rate, even in that short time, a terrible lot of chaps went down. I did not notice what the wire-cutters really did; but they must have used their wire-cutters well. At any rate, our chaps got through and made the Germans run.

Well, I watched all this for a bit, then I heard the cries again, and all I thought about then was to try and do something for the poor chaps who were wounded and were so much worse off than I was.

One of our men had gone down, and I hurried up to him and dressed and bandaged him as best I could. He ought to have gone to the dressing-station, but instead of that he rejoined his regiment and kept in the fighting-line for four days more; then, as he wasn't fit to do any active duty, he was sent away. I learned afterwards that this was Company-Sergeant-Major L. Ford, of my battalion, who has got the D.C.M.[1]

While I was busy on this job, several men offered to help me and to attend to my own wound; but I told them that I could manage all right, and wasn't in need of doctoring.

I was in full view of the Germans, but I didn't bother my head about that. I saw, lying in the open, a soldier who was wounded and wanted help, and I started off for him. I walked—I don't remember that I dodged or ducked much, because I wasn't caring. I remember that one of my officers shouted to me to hurry up and get out of it and seek some sort of cover. I shouted back that I was all right and that I didn't mind it. The funny thing is, that officers were so anxious about

---

1. This award was gazetted at the same time as the announcement of the D.C.M. for Private Edwards. It was "For conspicuous gallantry from September 25th to 29th, near Hulloch. Although severely wounded on the head in the early part of the operations, Company-Sergeant-Major Ford continued to advance and give encouragement to his men until he fell. His example and devotion to duty were of the highest possible value to all ranks. He had already been recommended for his gallant conduct at Festubert."

their men, and never seemed to give a thought to themselves.

I never reached the wounded man, for as I was staggering across the open towards him—I was beginning to feel the effects of my wound—I felt a sharp pain somewhere, and I gradually sank down to the ground and lay there. I did not know at the time what sort of a wound it was, or where; but I knew that it was a bullet, and that I had got a second good 'un which had nearly put me to sleep.

A black cloud seemed to come over me and I went into sweet slumber. I must have slept a long time, for when I awoke I could see only a few soldiers knocking about; but I could hear them still fighting it out. I can't tell what exactly took place behind the mine which was called Tower Bridge or at the quarries, because I was wounded before I reached the German line. What I am talking about relates to the things that happened on the open ground around me when I was wounded, and what I saw in my own neighbourhood at other times. You can't do more than that.

I had a few hours' sleep; then two soldiers came along and I awoke. I asked them to stick me up on my props and give me a lift; but they were wounded, too. However, they did the best they could, and put me up, and I staggered about six yards. Then I fell again, and I remember no more until I heard a fellow shouting, "Here's Edwards, sergeant!" Then somebody said, "Yes—and poor Pymm's lower down here." They were our own stretcher-bearers.

Then, for the first time, I knew that Pymm had fallen. He had gone down, mortally wounded, when I heard him shout. When I learned this it was well on into the afternoon, eight or ten hours after the fight began; and all that time I had had nothing to drink.

There were plenty of the trench ladders lying about, and one of these was got, and I was put on it by my chums and carried to a trench at the back, to the medical officer. Water was either not obtainable or they would not give it to me—I dare say that was it, because later I had empyema—so the medical officer gave me an acid drop; and I made the best of it.

When I reached the trench it started to rain, and I got soaked, for the soil was chalk stuff and the water could not get through. So I had to lie in the water for some hours, and it was not until next morning that I got to the first-aid dressing-station. I was two days more before I got down to the Canadian Hospital, where, afterwards, the medical officer, Captain Parnis, who had been kindness itself to me, told me that I had been recommended for the D.C.M.

By this time I knew that I had been shot through the lungs, and that the wound was dangerous. It was a very narrow squeak; but a miss is as good as a mile, though in my case it meant a long spell in hospital. But everything that it was possible to do for us was done, and outside people also are very kind; they write to you and come and see you, and they send you things—sometimes tracts, which you don't want. My picture was given in the papers and kind things were written about me, and the idea got about that I was a mere youngster. I dare say that was the reason why some children sent me a Christmas-box—thinking, perhaps, that I was their own age. They sent me half a dozen cigars—real cigars; a little wooden horse, and a "platter" dog, as we call that sort of crockery in Staffordshire, filled with chocolates. I valued the children's gift all the more because I *am* young—just out of my teens; I was in them when I enlisted—so I have a lot in my favour, and hope soon to be quite well again.

Here's a letter from one of the officers of my regiment—he wrote to my dad, too—saying how proud they are because I've got the D.C.M.

Well, I do feel proud, too, naturally; but it came as a great surprise to me, for never did I think of such a thing; and when people speak to me about it, I simply say, "I only did my duty, as others have done."

CHAPTER 40

A Fusilier in France

The following story of a baptism of fire and subsequent experiences at Loos and in France is told by Private Fred. Knott, who, soon after the war broke out, left civil life at the call of duty and enlisted in the Royal Fusiliers. Like so many present-day soldiers Private Knott kept a record, under fire, of many of his experiences, until he was wounded and invalided home. From this selection we become more intimately acquainted with the life of our men not only in the trenches but also, which is equally interesting, with their doings when they are resting and able to share in the foreign life around them. We have had abundant proof during the war of the considerable powers of observation and description which so many of our fighting men possess.

A year's hard training had got us more or less used to marching; yet when we got to Béthune we were nearly all done up, for we had been on the road three days. We eagerly sought our billets, which in my own case happened to be an attic in an empty house. Our "cookers" followed us, so that next morning we had a good breakfast; then we raided the pump at the back of the house, hurried through a wash and sallied into the street, where we saw a sight that will not be forgotten.

There was an almost continuous procession of ambulances, full of wounded men from the Loos front; and an endless stream of men of all regiments were walking down the street to the dressing-station. The British soldier has a happy knack of looking at the bright side of a gloomy picture, and even now amusement was caused by the spectacle of one or two Scotsmen wearing Prussian Guards' helmets and walking along quite unconcerned about their wounds, most of which were in the arm.

In the afternoon we left our billet for the trenches. At the first halt a party of 200 German prisoners passed us. I have never seen such a collection of dejected, worn-out individuals. One man, who was apparently a non-commissioned officer, leaned on the arm of one of the guards for support, and his face was the picture of despair and misery.

Knowing what this war means to France especially, and what the French have had to endure from Germany for over forty years, it was very interesting to notice the attitude of quite little French children towards the captives. These boys and girls, standing on the pavement, insulted and spat upon the Germans, who, however, took little notice of them.

On the road we passed some of our own Tommies, coming from the trenches, and rejoicing in their relief. They wanted to cheer us, and shouted, "Hurry up, chaps; there's plenty left for you to do up there." They were quite right, as we soon discovered.

From Béthune we marched to the town of Vermelles, where we had our first glimpse of the havoc caused by the enemy's artillery fire. The whole place was a mass of ruins, very few houses remaining intact. What had been a town had been smashed by German guns to a vast mass of rubbish. It was a melancholy sight, yet it strengthened the determination to do our best to overcome the tyrants who had brought about such widespread misery and ruin. To make the sight all the more impressive, we distinctly heard the booming of the guns as we marched along.

Another sight which filled us with silent reverence was a graveyard on one side of the road—graveyards, big and little, have sprung up in all sorts of unexpected places on and near the battlefields. There were many simple wooden crosses marking the graves of British soldiers who had fallen earlier in the war. The sight of these resting-places took the mind back to those terrible days when our men fought so magnificently against almost hopeless odds, and solemn thoughts came, almost unbidden, to many of us as we went on marching towards the trenches to get our baptism of fire.

Outside the town another halt was made to let some cavalry pass. We had to wait at least a quarter of an hour for this—and a fine sight it was to watch the passing of these mounted men, for the nature of this war has made it quite a rare thing to see considerable bodies of cavalry.

After leaving the main road and taking one or two cross-cuttings we found ourselves in a wild, desolate field, covered with fairly large shrubs and weeds. It was one of the most miserable and depressing fields imaginable, and to crown its wretchedness rain was falling heavily and steadily and the ground was sodden.

The ammunition mules were in the rear, and we were served out with 130 rounds each. This looked like real business, and when it was over we extended in artillery formation, and cautiously advanced along the field. Everything now was done as if we were actually in the presence of the enemy, and there was a singular thrill and excitement amongst us and a constant wonder of "What next?"

We had moved a considerable distance, when we reached a reserve trench. We were ordered to enter it, for obviously it would have been fatal to go any farther by daylight.

In this trench we were concealed until it was dark. We were in great discomfort owing to the rain, and we were almost knee-deep in mud. We were not sorry when, as evening fell, we got out of the trench and again advanced in artillery formation; but only for a few yards.

The order was now given to lie down, for the enemy flares were going up one after the other, and it seemed as if at any moment our presence would be made known and a heavy fire directed on us.

The long marching and exposure to the bad weather had had their effect upon us. We were sodden, and in addition to the weight of our clothing and equipment and ammunition we had the weight of the rain and the mud, so you can easily understand that as we lay flat on the ground we dropped off into a heavy sleep.

I don't know how long we slept—I don't think it was long—but we were galvanised into wakefulness in a second, for a shell had burst not more than twenty yards in front of us with a terrific report, and a shower of earth fell on us.

That was the beginning of my baptism of fire, and it was the most startling awakening I ever had. It was a stern warning, too, and we quickly retired to another reserve trench a short distance away and jumped pell-mell into it. There were some good goers that night, in spite of heavy ground and heavier equipment; but we soon recovered our composure when we were in the trench, and laughed and made the best of it.

From this reserve trench we entered the main communication trench, and here we had one of those mysterious and unnerving experiences which have been so often known in this tremendous war. Progress at the best was slow and difficult, but it was made far worse because of the repeated issue of the order, "Retire!"

For some time we kept going "about turn," up and down the trench, though when word was passed down the line all our officers denied having made use of the term, and they urged us forward.

This strange matter gave us something to talk about for a long time, and the general feeling was that it was the work of a German spy, though the mysterious agent was never discovered.

We were now getting really into the thick of things, and two companies of the battalion made their way into the firing-line, while my own company went into reserve; and there we had our first touch of gas, though luckily without any serious loss of life. When the gas attack had passed we tried to snatch some sleep, but this was impossible, as we were quickly detailed for various duties, such as ration-carrying and supplying the first line with ammunition. I found myself at the latter task, and started out to find a regiment which was holding the front line on the right.

And now I had one of those awful experiences which have so often fallen to soldiers in this war—one of the things which, little in themselves, mean so much to the individual, especially to one who has not got accustomed to such warfare as this.

After making my way through countless trenches, some of which were empty and absolutely reeked of gas, I found myself in a narrow ditch—it could not be called a trench—which was literally filled with dead bodies. Snipers' bullets were whizzing all around me, and often I had to take cover by lying alongside a dead comrade. Each side of the ditch was strewn with bodies, the wounds on which were too ghastly to be described. Thoroughly sickened at the sight, I had to press on, treading on poor fellows' bodies all the time. It was truly horrible, but the ammunition had to be got there, and this was the only way to get along.

At last I reached the regiment I wanted, and found that it was keeping up rapid rifle fire. Leaving the ammunition with an officer, I started on my homeward journey, which I thankfully accomplished, but with great difficulty. I was very much impressed by the flares as I went along, and I do not exaggerate at all when I say that they were distinctly reminiscent of a firework display.

Reaching my own lines, I found that I was not wanted for any more fatigues, so I thankfully crept into a dugout at the rear and fell fast asleep.

Early next morning we attacked the enemy, and I got my proper baptism of fire. Two of our companies had gone into action and had

Street names for trenches

lost rather heavily, and my company was ordered to reinforce.

I was amongst the men who were chosen to reinforce, and leaving the reserve trench we passed into the fire trench and so over the top, amid a shower of bullets.

The Germans were hidden in a coal-mine near the famous "Tower Bridge," and it seemed hopeless to try and dislodge them; but the British had determined to have a try, and so we advanced, dropping now and again for cover. Here again the ground was strewn with bodies, and often it was necessary to use one of them as a covering screen.

It became necessary for some of us, myself amongst them, to withdraw to the original fire trench, and there we remained for two days. On the second day a lull in the fighting occurred, though there was a sharp watch on both sides and rounds were exchanged. A strange thing happened at this stage of the fighting. One of our N.C.O.s, going through a deserted fire-bay, found a man in khaki who was behaving in a very mysterious way. The N.C.O. grew suspicious, and with the help of two privates he marched the man before the colonel. The man said he was a Welsh Fusilier, but one of our men who had previously served in the Welsh Fusiliers soon showed that the statement was utterly false.

The man was searched, and then the amazing discovery was made that he had no fewer than a dozen identification-discs of different regiments.

Further questionings showed beyond all doubt that he was a very bold and cunning spy, and he was shot with very little ceremony.

Another day passed, and at night we were relieved. When we marched back through Vermelles we were utterly exhausted, and I dare say we looked pitiful objects, for we were thickly covered with clay and were minus the best part of our equipment; but we were proud, all the same, and I think the pride was justified, for it must be remembered that many of the men who took part in the very heavy fighting at Loos were soldiers who, like myself, had only just had their baptism of fire. They had at any rate done their best to uphold the tradition of British courage and endurance.

Trench life forms such an immense feature of the war that it will be interesting, I dare say, to give a little detailed account of it, just to show how closely resembling animal and savage conditions are those which have to be endured, and which, as a rule, are borne cheerfully and in a thorough make-the-best-of-it spirit.

We had been ordered to go to the trenches, this time on a new front. The line was situated on a canal bank, and we took up our position at night, carefully picking our way, helped by the lights of the flares.

At the end of our journey we found a series of dugouts at the side of the water, and I and my chum quickly claimed one of them. This dugout just conveniently held two men, though space was very limited. The prospect was not promising, but two heads were better than one, especially on active service, and soon we had rigged up the "mac." sheet and the overcoats and made a cosy bed, and we made ourselves comfortable. We were the better able to do this because the night was mild and the firing confined to an occasional shell—a mere nothing as a disturber of harmony. The next order was a cup of *café au lait*, and I don't think people at home realise what a joy it is to set to work on such a little treat as this.

My chum carried a small, compact spirit-lamp, and with this and a tin mug we soon had a glorious steaming drink ready. We dwelt on it as much and as long as we could, then settled down to sleep, making ourselves snug by covering the doorway of the dugout with a piece of old sacking. This was not an easy matter, for the enemy had become aggressive, and a heavy bombardment started. It was bad enough to make us open our doorway and look out, and we soon saw that the shells were finding their mark in the canal in front of us, sending the water up in great sprays. This we could easily make out by means of the brilliant flares. Now and again a shell missed fire, and we just saw it as it plumped into the water.

Higher up in the officers' dugout a gramophone was playing, and amid the sound of bursting shells we heard snatches of songs that carried our minds back to England and home. Later the shelling ceased, and once more we tried to sleep. This time a new trouble arose, in the shape of huge rats crawling over us. By means of candle-light we started destroying them with a bayonet; but this was a difficult task, for the rats often enough were swifter than the jabs at them. There were plenty of squeals in the dug-out, and these and our own cries mingled with the shrieks that came from rats outside, both in front and rear of the trenches, which were fighting pitched battles. This uncanny and unpleasant hunt in the dug-out ended in time, and we managed to gain a little rest. I am reminded that in one lot of trenches which we occupied in another part of the line a tree-trunk had fallen across the fire-bay, and at night a continual procession of rats could be seen crossing it, in spite of repeated slashes at them with bayonets.

Next day we had an opportunity of scanning the surrounding district. Farther along we could see the damaged steeple of a church, once a handsome building, now in ruins, for it had proved a good target for the German guns. On the opposite side of the canal several fine trees had been struck down, leaving blanks in a stately avenue. I gazed at the canal itself and wondered how many brave fellows' bodies had found their last resting-place there, for it was the scene of a big advance earlier in the year. But my reflections were cut short by military duties, and I was detailed for various tasks, such as rifle-cleaning, fetching rations, etc., while my companion made a fire to cook the breakfast. We now settled down to a more or less regular routine, and waited our turn to strike an offensive blow at the enemy at the first opportunity.

It is usual after a spell in the trenches for a regiment to retire to a village in rear of the firing-line for a rest, and I was always glad of this change, because it afforded many a strange sight to me, an average British soldier. We reached our village at about four o'clock in the afternoon, and each platoon found itself billeted in a barn at one of the farms which abounded in that particular locality. Here the town-bred man had the chance to study foreign rural life, a little hobby which helped him for the time to forget the trenches and their inevitable discomforts and dangers.

After a time we easily adapted ourselves to the rough straw beds that were provided for us, and we very soon found that we must not object if we had a ferret or two in a cage quite close to the bed. As a matter of fact we were soon on good terms with the fierce little creatures, which have proved splendid friends to the soldiers in the trenches in hunting and killing the swarming rats.

When we went out on voyages of discovery we found that the typical village contained one or two *estaminets*—they are rarely called *cafés* in the rural parts of France—and possibly one or two little shops—*épiceries*—which sell a variety of things appealing to a soldier's simple tastes. At certain hours the British Tommy is allowed in the estaminets, where such drinks as beer and red and white wines and the customary *café au lait* are obtainable cheaply. It is found from experience that these places rarely have change for paper money, which at times is rather awkward, especially when combined with a vague knowledge of the language; and the usual reply is "No money"—truly a poor consolation to a thirsty soldier. In time, however, we became known to the keeper of the estaminet, and when money became circulated the difficulty was remedied. A brief stay in a village was enough to make the villagers friendly, and little kindnesses on both sides became a common practice.

A characteristic of every place was the lack of facilities to obtain extra meals, though at certain *estaminets* a good repast of fried eggs and chips, with an occasional dish of stewed rabbit, was procurable.

This is merely a glimpse of the peaceful and gladly welcomed break in the life of the soldier who is on active service. It makes you all the more fit for the trenches and that night sentry duty to which you are so often roused in your dugout by the corporal shouting, "Next relief!"

CHAPTER 41

The Daily Round

By way of contrast with the diary which was kept in Gallipoli by an Australian soldier, and is given earlier, and as an admirable companion to that work, there is this diary of a young officer, kept by him while serving on the Western Front. The diary is of the small, leather-bound pocket variety, and it was kept by means of the little pocket-pencil accompanying it, in small, yet clear and coherent writing, despite shell fire, bombs and other warlike elements. The extracts are made exactly as they were entered from day to day, and they form a deeply interesting record of what is "the daily round, the common task" of a very large number of junior officers who have undergone precisely the same experiences with unfailing cheerfulness and courage. The writer after serving in an Officers' Training Corps, was posted to a Service battalion of a famous old Line regiment.

Dec. 13th, 1915. Marched to ———, seven miles. Water in places up to the knees. No billets for B Co. on arrival.

Dec. 14th. Marched to ———, three miles.

Dec. 15th. Marched up to trenches, ———, eight miles. Awful condition. Big craters in front, and three saps in our line.

Dec. 16th. Narrowest escape of self yet recorded. Shell burst in trench and killed man one and a half yards away and blew your humble into the mud, together with another CO. and others. Two other men wounded. Felt a bit shaky for some time.

Dec. 17th. Relieved for forty-eight hours and marched to ———, four miles. Good billets. Delicious shave and wash, and two glorious nights in my valise.

Dec. 18th. Pass into ——, to see H.[1] No luck—on leave. He returned ten minutes after I left for ——.

Dec. 19th. H. ran over to see me, and we had two full hours' "jawing," and *café au lait*. Left for same trenches at 12.30. Had a warm reception with artillery, and owing to some "show" in the vicinity had to stand-to for hours. Raining hard and mud knee-deep—miserable, and thought and thought of the happy home, and wondered and wondered! Went out on patrol with one man at five next morning, but had to return post-haste, as three of the enemy were on similar job and washed our intentions out.

Dec. 20th. Shelling all day, both sides. Few men hit.

Dec. 21st. At stand-to, 6 a.m. Much shelling. Very uncomfortable. At 7.30 an enemy mine went up—a fearsome thing. The sensations were these—

1. A horrible rocking of the trench.
2. A tremendous dull roar.
3. A huge column of earth rising higher and higher into the sky.

Then came the falling matter, we lying in the bottom of the trench, while everything imaginable fell around—earth—huge clods—sandbags and timber. One big piece of wood landed with a thud a foot from my head and spattered me with mud. Escape No. 2 since I joined. Fortunately the mine was lifted just beyond our saps, and presumably in the same place as the crater. No one was seriously hurt—only two slightly knocked about. Of course an attack was expected, but none came, and we stood-to till 8.30. Had an awful time from mine explosion till we were relieved at 2.30 p.m. Marvellous how we all escaped. I thought my number was up every minute, and my nerves were not of the best and I was feeling a bit rocky.

While relief was being carried on we had an awful time: all kinds of shells, big and small, landing everywhere. Very fortunate to get out with no casualties. Incoming regiment had a few. At 11.15 p.m. I returned to trenches in order to go out again on patrol. Was out for thirty minutes, took survey and returned safely, covered with mud and pretty wet. Returned to —— Farm, where my platoon is billeted. It is a small fortress, built up with sandbags from a big ruined brewery. Last night while asleep, about 3.30 a.m., a big shell burst just outside my cellar door, and again I thought my number was up. Earth, etc., was shot into my abode, and the doorway blocked up, not to mention bricks; but I was left intact.

Dec. 22nd. Shelling this ruined village —— all the morning, and the trips to. the men at meal-times were very risky, the latter being in another keep 150 yards up the road. One had to dash for it every time. Shelling remained hot, so had to remain at the mess till after tea, 4.30 p.m.

Gas attack from our trenches at 9 p.m. Quiet for ten minutes, then fearful shindy. Stood-to in our redoubt, but had to get to cellars when shelling started—and *such* shelling: the worst I've ever experienced. They came in dozens. Then we began, and the noise was hellish. They fell all around us and some hit the shattered walls, making a hail of bricks.

I felt a peculiar tightening round the heart when one of the big variety buried itself under the cellar wall I was in and failed to go off. It fairly seemed to lift the floor, and the sickening thud was as bad as the fearful racking explosions. It was nothing short of miraculous that our cellar got off scot-free.

All this time we could see through our loop-hole the explosions of the shells on the trenches, 300 yards to the front, and by their light and the light of the German searchlights and fires we could see the huge clouds of gas on their death-dealing errand.

The Germans put huge fires on their parapets to lift the gas over their heads.

It was an unforgettable scene, with their and our own star-lights making night into day. It was indescribable pandemonium.

The shelling died down after a couple of hours, and we stood down and tried to sleep; but it started again at 12.45 a.m. for an hour, and again at 4.45 a.m.; and this practically meant stand-to all night.

One of the worst nights I've spent out here—in fact, the worst.

About 2 a.m. I got word that ——, one of our B Co. officers, was killed while waiting to go out on patrol to ascertain the effects of gas on enemy. He was a fine chap, and most popular, and even now it is difficult to believe he is really gone. Another lucky escape for us (B Co.) that we were not occupying the trenches. They were blown out of all recognition and the casualties were awful, the lines being strewn with dead and wounded and buried men.

---

1. H. is the writer's elder brother, a motor dispatch-rider, who has been at the front since the war began, and has done some fine, hard work.

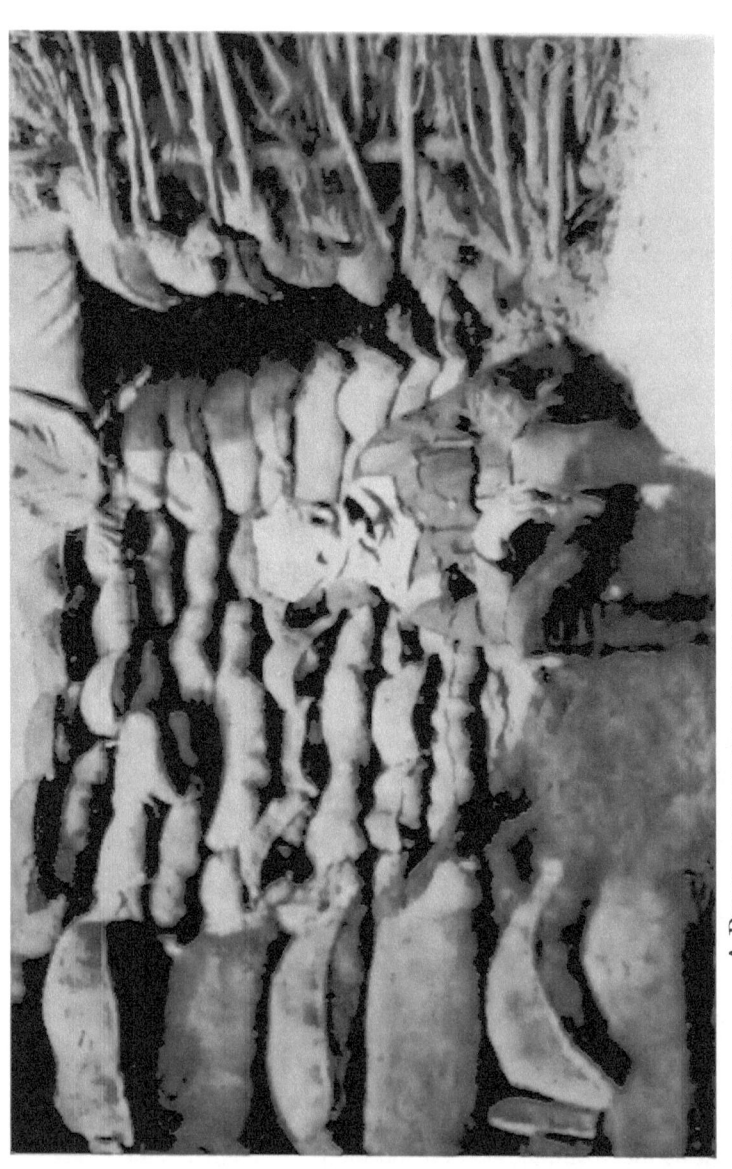

A British subaltern in the trench, wearing his gas-helmet

The trench occupied the previous night by my platoon is absolutely gone, and only six men are left in the platoon holding it at the time of the "show."

Dec. 23rd. Shelling continued all the morning—most uncomfortable, and we had many narrow escapes, walls round us being blown to h—; but still our cellar got off. We were relieved at 12.30, and, things being quieter, we got off down the road at top speed.

What joy to see actually motor buses waiting for us three miles back, which took us by way of —— to ——, a small village where our few days' rest and incidentally Christmas, will be spent. The change will be much appreciated by yours truly. I have just had my first wash and shave for four days, and feel cleaner than ever before in my life; and in a clean change and new suit I wouldn't call the king my aunt!

A delicious surprise was the sight of H. on the road, waiting for me as our convoy of buses neared ——. We had a good chat, and I hope to see him tomorrow again.

Dec. 24th. Morning with platoon, cleaning up, etc. Afternoon obtained pass to go and see H. Had a glorious Christmas Eve, far beyond expectations. Good tea, theatre, dinner, and two hours' solo. Fine evening. Came back on the carrier at 10.30.

Dec. 25th. Christmas Day in France.

Up at 6.30 and marched bathing party into ——. Left them and looked up H. In bed; got him up and had breakfast with him and a walk round, and marched my party back here —— by 10.30. Wrote two letters and found five waiting for me—long-delayed ones. This was a fine Christmas gift.

11 a.m. Went over to men's sports till 12.30 lunch. Helped to pay out from 2.30 p.m. till four. Tea and chat till dinner; chicken and plum pudding. *Very good.* Talked till 10.30 and then to bed. Very quiet evening, during which my thoughts were for the most part with the dear old folks at home....

NEXT CHRISTMAS???

Dec. 26th. Quiet day. Morning, church parade and men cleaned up. Afternoon, other officers out, so I was O.C. for the time being. Spent two hours censoring eighty letters! Quiet evening. Dinner and chat; bed 10 p.m.

Heavy bombardment going on in distance.

Dec. 27th. Morning, getting ready to move.

Moved at 2 p.m. Raining.

Got into trenches at 4.30 p.m. In reserve, 1500 yards from enemy—and a nice change for B Co.

At night I went on patrol with a man to find a way across country to A Co., who were holding a line to our right front. Awful going, but got there. Came back by road through —— village and Danger Corner. Out two and a half hours.

Slept as well as I could on a narrow board till 7.30 next morning.

Dec. 28th. Quiet day. Went out at night with CO. Got lost, and were out three hours. Good joke.

Dec. 29th. Quiet day. Went out in the morning on voyage of discovery round old trenches. Went in to the left shoulder in mud and water. Another good joke!

Dec. 30th. Quiet day. A few shells on the right; but we were left alone. At 5 p.m. I went out with a party of seventy, carrying all kinds of things to the front line. Out till 8 p.m. Quiet night.

Dec. 31st. A wet day. The road behind was shelled heavily all day, but fortunately it was quiet while we were being relieved after dusk. Had the real Bank Holiday feeling on getting to reserve line billets two miles away, and enjoyed a splendid night in my valise. Had one drop of whisky at 9.30 p.m. to drink the health of the New Year; but sleep was by far the most important thing, so to bed at 10 p.m., to dream of home and the dear old past.

Woke during the night to hear the guns in the back garden booming in the New Year, and shaking and rattling walls and windows. Dreams shattered!

Jan. 1st, 1916. What luck for the New Year?

How fervent is the hope for a glimpse of the *end* before many of the new months have gone.

In the morning looked round the men and inspected several things, followed by a little revolver practice. Had a sleep, or tried to, after lunch; but attempt was futile, owing to thoughts.

Went out with party of fifty at 5 p.m. to the trenches, repairing roads, filling up shell-holes, etc. Returned at 9 p.m., and to bed.

Sunday, Jan. 2nd. Church parade in top floor of rickety old barn at 11 a.m., followed by an impromptu Communion Service, during which my thoughts wandered. . . . These services always touch me more than anything else I know of, and unbidden thoughts rise and fill me with longings and yearnings that are inclined to be unpatriotic, as well as bringing the familiar lump to the throat which every one experiences out here at times, and a queer feeling round the heart.

Afternoon, went to —— in company with other officers in motor lorry, to attend lecture on telescopic sights and sniping. Returned at 6 p.m., and joyfully found I had just missed a working party to the trenches.

Tucked myself in my valise at 9.30.

Jan. 3rd. Platoons cleaning up. Inspected rifles, etc. Had my first lesson in riding. Felt rather insecure at first, but found the "bump" after an uncomfortable 100 yards jogging about, to the great delight and amusement of my men; at which I joined in. Had a small gallop before finish, and stuck on.

Afternoon, writing letters and reading, and out with working party to the trenches at 4.30 p.m., mending shell-holes in roads, etc. Returned at 9 p.m., and to bed.

Jan. 4th. Relieved and went to —— for a four days' rest, at 11.30 a.m. Spent afternoon in reconnoitring old trenches in neighbourhood, to see necessary repairs required, stores, etc. Quiet evening. Splendid billet—bedroom to myself, feather bed and sheets, washstand; very lucky for once. First bed since leaving Boseghem four weeks ago. Good mess-room, fire and two armchairs. House kept by two middle-aged women, very kind, do anything; also little niece, aged eight, who speaks English well. She and I are good friends.

Jan. 5th. Out with working party to repair trenches from 9.30 a.m. till 1.30 p.m. Lunch and letter-writing. Went up to —— later to execute several shopping commissions. Had splendid crop (first since ——) after patiently waiting *one hour.* Oh! these French hairdressers! One snip of the scissors every five minutes; one requires the patience of Job.

Went to pictures; pretty fair; and had dinner at the Lion d'Or. It seemed very quiet and deserted compared to my last visit, when the M.C.s were there. Back at 9 p.m., and to bed between the sheets.

Jan. 6th. Out with working party, as per yesterday, from 10 a.m. to 1.30 p.m. Lunch 2 p.m. Inspection of B Co. by CO. Me in command of company! Two-thirty, paid out to the men. Awful long job.

Jan. 7th. Morning, 10 a.m. to 1.30 p.m., out with working party. H. called for few minutes, 2 p.m. Lecture on arms and care of rifles, etc., 4 p.m. Met H. at Lion d'Or in B. at 4.45 (splendid being able to do this). Tea, long chat and theatre at six o'clock. Panto., *Aladdin*. Really tip-top, although men were disguised as girls. Plenty of fun and laughter. Sent in an application today for post as observer in R.F.C. Have great hopes. Life consists mainly of latter nowadays.

Jan. 8th. Working party repairing trenches 9.30 to 1.30. Lovely morning. Two p.m., lecture in field on use of rifle—old as the hills (lecture); but I suppose they must work on the motto, "*Anything to keep the time employed.*"

Sunday, Jan. 9th. Marched to trenches (same place as Dec. 15). Beautiful day and everything quiet—not a day for war at all. On nearing the line the noise of guns and bursting shells broke on our ears, increasing in sound as we drew nearer, until we got as per usual in amongst them.

Had to go in single file at intervals up the infernal road. No one hit.

Got in the same old corner, and found to our relief the trenches had been built up again passably well after the bombardment of the night of Dec. 22.

Jan. 10th and 11th. Contrary to expectations had two quiet days—of course, the usual few shells, but no great quantity. My platoon occupied the trench on left of company, instead of, as last time, close up on the right, 1000 yards from enemy.

Relieved at 8 p.m. on 11th, and we came back to the old keep (—— Farm). Everything very quiet all night, and enjoyed a good sleep on a stretcher in one of the cellars, despite the attentions of rats in plenty.

Jan. 12th. Quiet walk up to Headquarters for breakfast and back. Enemy began shelling roadway close by, and everything else within reach, at 11.20; still going on at time of writing, 12.45. When shall I be able to go up for lunch?

Got there intact.

Jan. 13th. Quiet day. Went back to front line at 7 p.m. for a further forty-eight hours. Quiet night.

Jan. 14th. Found in the morning that in addition to the usual bombs, grenades and shells we had a trench mortar opposite us, which kept lobbing big black objects over all day, burying men and knocking our trenches to pieces. There was not much else they could use on us now; but we gave them back two for every one we received, and at 2 p.m. we commenced a big "strafe" with rifle-grenades, bombs and mortars. It was good to see them bursting, and altogether we expended over 800 (!) in an hour.

We got all manner of things back, from a bullet to a 6-inch. The latter were falling 100 yards from the rear of our breastworks, and we could actually see them falling the last fifty feet or so.

All quiet by 4 p.m. Quiet night—far different to our expectations.

Jan. 15th. Each side shelling all day unceasingly, with the usual quota of bombs. We were relieved at 7.30 p.m., and came back in safety to ——, after six more days of *LIFE?*

Very weary, and thankful for quiet and my valise.

Sunday, Jan. 16th. Marched to a small village—seven miles, and found we had comfortable billets, and a mattress for the writer. Moving again to ——, nine miles from here, tomorrow. *HURRAH!* We are (or should be) "out" for sixteen days.

Jan. 17th. Marched to —— on the famous cobblestones of France the whole way. Poor feet! On arriving was delighted to find I had a cosy room with feather bed and a good mess 200 yards down the road. Spent the evening trying to get level with correspondence. Hope we shall stay here all the time. Shall spend most of my spare moments writing—one of my chief pleasures when out, especially now I've got a respectable pen!

Jan. 18th. Slack day. Enjoyed the luxury of a "mess" and a fire. Spent a lot of time writing.

Jan. 19th. My second birthday in the army. . . .

Today's events, musketry and rifle drill, and shooting on a temporary range in afternoon. Lovely day—like spring.

Jan. 20th to 28th. Detailed for course of bombing instruction; and between these dates I learn much concerning these nefarious love-tokens.

Jan. 28th to Feb. 14th. Our period of "Rest." (Time spent out of the trenches is so miscalled in the army!) It was extended for reasons known only to those in lofty positions, and we spent the time in performing all the evolutions of an infantry battalion in training, drill, manoeuvres, etc. Of course, all this is very necessary after the sometimes enforced inactivity of the trenches, and helps to pull out the kinks; but it gets rather monotonous, and when we heard that we were off to the line again everyone was glad.

Feb. 15th. Said goodbye to our friends of the village and headed once more for the Land of Thrills. It took us three days, doing it in easy stages.

Feb. 18th. Found ourselves in cellars in a much-ruined village just behind the line, *viz.* ———. There were exciting events last night, before our arrival, a few enemy mines having gone "up," and as soon as we arrived we had to begin fatiguing, connecting up the craters with the front line.

(At this point the diary abruptly finishes; but the writer was kept busy from day to day in the routine manner, doing his turn in each line, with the usual "hate" progressing, but nothing of great importance happening. Long exposure to the severe weather sent him into hospital, thence home, invalided. The very day after he reported "nothing of great importance happening" many of his comrades fell in a gallant and desperate assault on the Hohenzollern Redoubt.)

Chapter 42

Saving the Soldier

Leaving his great work in Labrador and Newfoundland, so that he might visit the front as a member of the Harvard Surgical Unit, Dr. Wilfred T. Grenfell spent three months in France as an army surgeon, and during a short stay in London related some of his experiences and indicated the marvellous advance that has been made in over-coming disease and saving our soldiers' lives. Not long ago in public, Field-Marshal Lord Grenfell said that when he and Dr. Grenfell went into large communities people did not say to Dr. Grenfell "Are you a cousin of Lord Grenfell?" They said to him (Lord Grenfell) "Are you a cousin of Dr. Wilfred Grenfell?" And he was very proud indeed to be able to say yes. Dr. Grenfell's two cousins, the twin brothers who were both captains in the 9th (Queen's Royal) Lancers, were killed in action, one of them, Capt. F. O. Grenfell, being the first of the recipients of the Victoria Cross granted for the present war. Two other cousins, the brothers Capt. the Hon. Julian Grenfell and Sec.-Lt. the Hon. G.W. Grenfell, sons of Lord Desborough, have also fallen in the war.

I am on my way from France to Labrador, and I am really sorry to be out of khaki, though I never was in it before.

While I was in the thick of my work on the other side of the Atlantic I was invited to join the Harvard Surgical Unit at the front. I found it possible to do so, because I knew that in my temporary absence my work in Labrador and Newfoundland would be faithfully carried on by my friends and devoted helpers. So I came over and was attached to the Harvard Unit with the rank of major, and the experiences I have gained as an army surgeon will remain amongst the greatest and proudest of my life.

I have had the opportunity of seeing what the British Army is doing in many ways in this terrible war. I have been at many places, including the base at Boulogne, and many great battle-centres, such as Ypres, Béthune and Armentières. And I have been in the trenches, so that I have had full chances of seeing what is really going on. It is hard, almost impossible, to find words in which to express admiration of the courage, endurance and humanity of the British troops in this terrible conflict.

All my life has been a roving one, ever since I took my degree as a doctor exactly thirty years ago. When I really began life I decided to look for some field of work where I could be useful. I went into the London Hospital, and very soon became intensely interested in the Royal National Mission to Deep Sea Fishermen. In those days the fishing vessels were all sail, and when a man was seriously injured he had to be transferred to some vessel that was carrying fish to Billingsgate, and then he was taken to the London Hospital. This state of things on the North Sea brought home to one the possibility of Christian men preaching the gospel of love and help; and men went out and largely brought about that wonderful revolution which we see today amongst North Sea fishermen.

I cannot help feeling that in the trenches, right along the line where the surgical men are working, there is just the same problem to deal with as we encountered in those early days of mission effort in the trawling fleets. Very great difficulties had to be overcome in performing operations in tiny mission hospital smacks on the open sea far from land; just as unusual obstacles have to be surmounted in treating wounded righting men at the front today. The problem in the North Sea was to heal men's bodies, as well as to help them to take a higher view of life; and it seems to me that the problem at the front is just the same.

In dealing with the body there have been preventive developments which are little short of marvellous. The history of war is not the history of wounds, as a rule it has been the history of disease; and speaking as an unbiased person I think that in this connection we are doing a perfectly magnificent work.

First of all, the troubles of the trench fighting have been the gas *bacillus*, which is an animal *bacillus*, and the tetanus *bacillus*. Both began operations in this war with terrible results, but now they have scarcely any effect.

It must be remembered that the soil in France and Flanders, where so much of the fighting has taken place, is highly cultivated, and is therefore splendid breeding-ground for these deadly *bacilli*. So much is this the case with tetanus that in the early stages of the war bits of uniform which have been driven into the body, however slightly, were infinitely more dangerous than serious wounds caused by clean shrapnel, for the cloth, by contact with the soil, had become infected with the *bacillus*. I have seen men with pieces of shrapnel left in their wounds and doing well, but a piece of uniform, sodden with the rich soil, was a very different thing.

But so wonderful has been the advance in the method of treating tetanus that today, if taken in time, such a thing as a fatal result is extremely improbable. Every soldier is so quickly and skilfully treated that danger practically does not exist.

The very terrible gas *bacillus* caused another very common disease, for the gas produced a kind of gangrene; yet now there is very little mortality indeed from this cause.

In the beginning, too, any number of men were lost from typhoid fever, but now typhoid is getting so rare that if a case occurs anywhere on the front it is known the same night at the French General Headquarters. That remark applies to the whole of our armies, and so rigid is the control which is kept over these matters that, on the day following the report, a searching local inquiry is held as to the cause of the disease.

At the front I saw men who came from all parts of the country where I have been working for the past twenty-five years—Canadians, Americans, and so on. And in passing just let me say that in connection with this war we are misjudging America because of the attitude which the president has taken. I have stayed with Mr. Wilson and with Mr. Roosevelt, and I know that the spirit of America is with us. It is because the whole spirit of the American people is with us that thirty-three doctors and thirty-six nurses—most of them giving up splendid practices—went out from America to the front, as the Harvard Unit, to help us. Just so the Chicago Unit, and many more Americans fighting in the ranks.

I have seen at the front men of all ages and of every rank in life—veterans who were a long way over the army age, and immature youths of sixteen or seventeen. The spirit of loyalty and the determination to do their bit made them go. Often enough a boyish patient would smile when I looked at the chart and asked him how old he really was. "Oh, that's my army age," he would say, and go on smiling.

I was right round the trenches two weeks ago, and as that was early in March and the winter has been exceptionally bad, the conditions were intolerable. There is no anxiety, because everybody is sure that the line is strong; but the wet, mud and exposure make you think that the men will get pneumonia and bronchitis; yet what mostly happens is trench-foot. I have seen a lot of that in Labrador, where we call it frost-bite. It is not, however, the same, though it appears to be. I have travelled many times in Labrador in winter, when the thermometer has been twenty and thirty degrees below zero, and I have never had frost-bite except once in my life. That was when I was driving my dog-team over the ice. The ice broke and my dogs went into the sea. They shared a floe with me throughout an awful night, and my life was saved at the sacrifice of theirs. I have told that story in detail elsewhere, so I need not tell it now.

I saw 150 men from a Highland regiment with frost-bite, but that was quite exceptional, and was due to the phenomenal weather and the impossibility of relieving the men when their relief was due, because they were fighting continuously for over forty-eight hours.

There is another direction in which immense strides have been made, and that is with respect to vermin. At one time, at the beginning of the war, there were as many as 4000 men who had scabies, or itch, and were out of action for the time being; but you hardly see such a case now, because of the wonderful measures which are taken to keep the troops perfectly clean and fit.

Close behind the trenches immense vats have been placed to serve as baths for the men, and the happiest fellows I saw were those who were rolling and splashing in these hot baths, while their uniforms and clothing were being thoroughly cleansed in super-heated steam-chests and finished off with heavy hot irons.

Just as we got into one of these cleaning depots a Jack Johnson burst very near us, but nobody took the slightest notice of it, so accustomed does one become to the happenings of war. Five or six men were in each hot bath, and something like 2000 baths a day are given. The men become thoroughly clean personally, and their clothing also is perfectly freed from vermin and filth, and the troops look as happy as possible.

I was greatly struck by the coolness and courage of all who worked in these laundries, women as well as men, and I could not help thinking that if I stood one week of it I should be entitled to the D.S.O. Endless thousands of uniforms, socks and articles of underclothing are constantly dealt with in the manner I have described, and many of the workers are under artillery fire all the time.

In the treatment of bad wounds, too, there has been a very great advance, and for such cases as broken femurs such an ingenious device has been hit upon that you might well say that instead of putting a man into bed you put the bed on to the man. The R.A.M.C. is really doing its very best, and I shall go back to America feeling perfectly satisfied that the British soldier is getting all the attention that I could wish to have myself.

When the war began the surgeons did not know where to put the wounded, because of the varying fortunes of the fighting. Even Boulogne, Calais and Havre were not certain of safety, so that attending to the wounded and accommodating them was a precarious thing; but the temporary hospitals have been gradually replaced by stationary hospitals, the mobile makeshift has been succeeded by the permanent institution, and so splendid and complete are our resources now that in one day the enormous total of 100,000 casualties could be dealt with by the R.A.M.C.

Casualty clearing-stations, field ambulances, advanced dressing-posts and fixed hospitals are about as perfect as they can be made; and so admirable are the arrangements that I saw one man who had been shot through the abdomen and was in hospital in less than an hour from the time he was wounded—which is almost quicker than you would do it in London.

A great many of the less seriously sick and wounded do not have to go to the base at all; at times one rest-camp was sending 80 *per cent*, straight back to the line, entirely new men; and, as they say in America, it would "tickle you to death" to see how these things are done.

If you count up the men who have been wounded and invalided from all causes you will find that there are still twice as many sick people as there are wounded; and the strange thing is that as there are more wounds there is less sickness, because directly a "push" comes the men don't think nearly as much about sickness as when there is nothing doing.

If you take 1000 persons in ordinary civil life you will find that there will always be 3.3 sick per 1000; but at the front the rate is not quite half as many—only 1.8 per 1000 men. It is a very strange thing, but I have met with a number of men who were always more or less sick in civil life, yet who got quite well again at the front. The trenches are the place for a change of air!

I am sure that after this war a very great many men will never go

BACK TO PRIMEVAL LIFE. AT THE END OF A TRENCH, SHOWING A FIRE WHICH COOKS AND GIVES WARMTH.

back to the civil life they were in before. They must have more life in the open air; and there can be no finer field for them than that glorious Canada which I know so well, with its boundless possibilities of harvests and material development.

One is impressed at the front with the apparent valuelessness of human life, and deeply impressed by the lavishness with which that life has been laid down by all ranks for king and country. This remark applies to every rank of life without exception, to the highest of the aristocracy as well as to the humblest private. And very remarkable, too, is the zeal and willingness to serve in quite subordinate positions of men who have had every advantage in life, particularly the University type.

I remember at one place, when we were sitting in the mess, a sergeant brought in a paper, which he handed to the colonel to read. It was a most elaborate scientific treatise on the body vermin that so greatly trouble our troops, and it was beautifully illustrated. In addition to that the paper showed the willing endurance of personal suffering for practical purposes that I for one should not have cared to undergo, for the sergeant had made himself thoroughly well acquainted with the effects of the visitation of the pests he described.

I was so much impressed by the performance that I said to the colonel, "Who is your sergeant?" and he replied, "Oh, he's the Professor of Entomology in the University of ——!"

As I talk my mind takes me back to Labrador and its ice-bound coast, and I recall that when working through the ice-fields in our little mission ship, the *Strathcona*, or travelling in lonely regions with my dog-teams, I saw so many evidences of the eagerness of men out there to do their bit in this tremendous war. Almost to a man, when they heard that we were fighting, they wanted to come over. But at first in Labrador we got very little news, and when news did come it was not credited. "Oh," said the men, "don't you believe it. They've always got some scare on. They're going to put the price of fish up!" Fish, you know, is the greatest of all material things out in that vast and lonely land.

But what happened when they knew that it was not a scare, but real war, and a fight for liberty and justice? Why, 1500 men of Labrador and Newfoundland went into the navy alone, and these brave and splendid fellows crowded into the army too. A thousand of them were in Gallipoli. And wherever they were they found their hard experience of the utmost worth. Our trappers soon learn the knack of getting a seal with the gun, though the seal only just pops his head through an ice-hole and the tiny target is the hardest of all things to see. But the trapper gets him—he seldom misses; and whenever a German puts his head out—well, he gets it too.

I have been in Labrador twenty-five years, and I am proud of the way in which my friends out there have done their duty at the front.

My own view of life is that one has to do one's duty in any place where one happens to be; and I know from what I have seen that our splendid fellows at the front have the same outlook. There are many, many soldiers out there who, with practically nothing to look forward to when the war is over, are sustained by one great thing, and that is the knowledge that they are doing their best.

I have mentioned Canada as a great place for receiving men who will be set free when the war is over. I have just seen the statement that Canada has gone prohibition from end to end, and that pleases me very much. I have spent thirty years amongst deep-sea fishermen and sailors as a medical missionary and a master mariner, and I have shared many dangers with them in the North Sea, out on the Labrador coast and elsewhere, but I have seen more sorrow and misery in the homes of our seafaring men through drink than I ever found in even small craft at sea.

All these things that I have spoken of come under the heading of practical religion and real Christianity, and rightly so. I do not believe in the Christian religion being negative; it is essential that you make it positive.

ALSO FROM LEONAUR
AVAILABLE IN SOFTCOVER OR HARDCOVER WITH DUST JACKET

DOING OUR 'BIT' *by Ian Hay*—Two Classic Accounts of the Men of Kitchener's 'New Army' During the Great War including *The First 100,000* & *All In It*.

AN EYE IN THE STORM by *Arthur Ruhl*—An American War Correspondent's Experiences of the First World War from the Western Front to Gallipoli and Beyond.

STAND & FALL by *Joe Cassells*—A Soldier's Recollections of the 'Contemptible Little Army' and the Retreat from Mons to the Marne, 1914.

RIFLEMAN MACGILL'S WAR by *Patrick MacGill*—A Soldier of the London Irish During the Great War in Europe including *The Amateur Army, The Red Horizon & The Great Push*.

WITH THE GUNS by *C. A. Rose & Hugh Dalton*—Two First Hand Accounts of British Gunners at War in Europe During World War 1- Three Years in France with the Guns and With the British Guns in Italy.

EAGLES OVER THE TRENCHES by *James R. McConnell & William B. Perry*—Two First Hand Accounts of the American Escadrille at War in the Air During World War 1-Flying For France: With the American Escadrille at Verdun and Our Pilots in the Air.

THE BUSH WAR DOCTOR by *Robert V. Dolbey*—The Experiences of a British Army Doctor During the East African Campaign of the First World War.

THE 9TH—THE KING'S (LIVERPOOL REGIMENT) IN THE GREAT WAR 1914 - 1918 by *Enos H. G. Roberts*—Like many large cities, Liverpool raised a number of battalions in the Great War. Notable among them were the Pals, the Liverpool Irish and Scottish, but this book concerns the wartime history of the 9th Battalion – The Kings.

THE GAMBARDIER by *Mark Severn*—The experiences of a battery of Heavy artillery on the Western Front during the First World War.

FROM MESSINES TO THIRD YPRES by *Thomas Floyd*—A personal account of the First World War on the Western front by a 2/5th Lancashire Fusilier.

THE IRISH GUARDS IN THE GREAT WAR - VOLUME 1 by *Rudyard Kipling*—Edited and Compiled from Their Diaries and Papers Volume 1 The First Battalion.

THE IRISH GUARDS IN THE GREAT WAR - VOLUME 2 by *Rudyard Kipling*—Edited and Compiled from Their Diaries and Papers Volume 2 The Second Battalion.

AVAILABLE ONLINE AT **www.leonaur.com**
AND FROM ALL GOOD BOOK STORES

ALSO FROM LEONAUR
AVAILABLE IN SOFTCOVER OR HARDCOVER WITH DUST JACKET

THE ART OF WAR by Antoine Henri Jomini—Strategy & Tactics From the Age of Horse & Musket.

THE ART OF WAR by Sun Tzu and Pierre G. T. Beauregard—*The Art of War* by Sun Tzu and *Principles and Maxims of the Art of War* by Pierre G.T. Beauregard.

THE MILITARY RELIGIOUS ORDERS OF THE MIDDLE AGES by F. C. Woodhouse—The Knights Templar, Hospitaller and Others.

THE BENGAL NATIVE ARMY by F. G. Cardew—An Invaluable Reference Resource.

ARTILLERY THROUGH THE AGES—by Albert Manucy—A History of the DEvelopment and Use of Cannons, Mortars, Rockets & Projectiles from Earliest Times to the Nineteenth Century.

THE SWORD OF THE CROWN by Eric W. Sheppard—A History of the British Army to 1914.

THE 7TH (QUEEN'S OWN) HUSSARS: Volume 3—1818-1914 by C. R. B. Barrett—On Campaign During the Canadian Rebellion, the Indian Mutiny, the Sudan, Matabeleland, Mashonaland and the Boer War Volume 3: 1818-1914.

THE CAMPAIGN OF WATERLOO by Antoine Henri Jomini—A Political & Military History from the French perspective.

RIFLE & DRILL by S. Bertram Browne—The Enfield Rifle Musket, 1853 and the Drill of the British Soldier of the Mid-Victorian Period *A Companion to the New Rifle Musket* and *A Practical Guide to Squad and Setting-up Dtill.*

NAPOLEON'S MEN AND METHODS by Alexander L. Kielland—The Rise and Fall of the Emperor and His Men Who Fought by His Side.

THE WOMAN IN BATTLE by Loreta Janeta Velazquez—Soldier, Spy and Secret Service Agent for the Confederancy During the American Civil War.

THE BATTLE OF ORISKANY 1777 by Ellis H. Roberts—The Conflict for the Mowhawk Valley During the American War of Independenc.

PERSONAL RECOLLECTIONS OF JOAN OF ARC by Mark Twain.

CAESAR'S ARMY by Harry Pratt Judson—The Evolution, Composition, Tactics, Equipment & Battles of the Roman Army.

FREDERICK THE GREAT & THE SEVEN YEARS' WAR by F. W. Longman.

AVAILABLE ONLINE AT **www.leonaur.com**
AND FROM ALL GOOD BOOK STORES

www.ingramcontent.com/pod-product-compliance
Lightning Source LLC
Chambersburg PA
CBHW021956160426
43197CB00007B/152